I0755047

J. Bien, lith. Photo. by Childs.

JACKSON MINE

GEOLOGICAL SURVEY OF MICHIGAN.

UPPER PENINSULA

1869-1873

ACCOMPANIED BY AN

ATLAS OF MAPS.

VOL. I.

PART I. IRON-BEARING ROCKS (ECONOMIC). *T. B. Brooks.*
PART II. COPPER-BEARING ROCKS. *Raphael Pumpelly.*
PART III. PALÆOZOIC ROCKS. *Dr. C. Rominger.*

PUBLISHED BY AUTHORITY OF THE LEGISLATURE
OF MICHIGAN.

UNDER THE DIRECTION OF THE

BOARD OF GEOLOGICAL SURVEY.

NEW YORK
JULIUS BIEN
1873.

PART I.

IRON-BEARING ROCKS
(ECONOMIC).

BY

T. B. BROOKS.

MEMORANDUM.—It has been deemed advisable that the Appendices, referred to in this Part, should be issued separately as Vol. II.

ATLAS PLATES

REFERRED TO IN PART I.

---

1. Map of the Upper Peninsula.*
2. Map of the Central Portion of the Upper Peninsula.
3. Map of the Marquette Iron Region.
4. Map of the Menominee Iron Region.
5. Map of Iron Mines at Negaunee.
6. Map of Republic Mountain and vicinity.
7. Map of the Champion Mine.
8. Map of the Washington and Edwards Mines.
9. Map of the Lake Superior and Barnum Mines.
10. Map of the New York Mine.
11. Magneto-geologic Chart of Republic Mountain.
12. Statistical Tables of the Iron Ore Trade and Iron Mines of the Upper Peninsula.
13. Statistical Tables of Furnaces consuming Lake Superior Ores, with composition and character of the Ores.

---

* This map refers also to Parts II. and III.

LIST OF ILLUSTRATIONS.

VIEWS.

PLATES.

FIGURES.

FIGURES—Continued.

TABLE OF CONTENTS.

APPENDICES. (VOL. II.)

Governor J. J. BAGLEY, Hon. W. J. BAXTER, Hon. DANL. B. BRIGGS, } *Board of Geological Survey of the State of Michigan.*

GENTLEMEN,

Herewith I transmit a Report, with maps and illustrations, containing in part the results of my economic survey of the Iron Regions of the Upper Peninsula, made in accordance with a plan approved by your predecessors, under the chairmanship of ex-Governor H. P. Baldwin. I have labored diligently to produce "as complete a manual as possible of information relating to the finding, extracting, transporting, and smelting of the iron ores of the Lake Superior Region;" a book that should possess interest and value to the practical man and capitalist interested in our mines, which have for several years produced nearly one-fourth the ore raised in the United States.

Absence in Europe, on account of ill-health, prevents my giving the book that supervision, in passing through the press, which is essential to accuracy and finish in a work of this kind, especially when, as in this case, the author is not accustomed to bookmaking. Your publisher, Mr. Julius Bien, has promised to perform this duty, which is a guarantee that it will be well done.

I hope that the iron trade of the West will find in this a useful, although incomplete, manual, and that the people of Michigan will approve of the manner in which I have expended the money entrusted to me.

Very respectfully and obediently yours,

T. B. BROOKS.

London, May 1st, 1873.

INTRODUCTION.

It is customary to preface Geological Reports with a history of the surveys on which they are based; in this case, however, it will be impossible to give more than a brief sketch, without omitting some part of the report itself, the limits of the book, for the publication of which funds were provided, having already been considerably exceeded.

The first survey of the State by Dr. Houghton, which was discontinued on account of his death by drowning in Lake Superior in 1845, is noticed in the first chapter in connection with the discovery of iron ore. The present survey was inaugurated by act of the Legislature in 1869, which appropriated $8,000 per year for the work, one-half of which went to the Upper Peninsula. This amount was again divided equally between the Iron and Copper Regions, which gave $2,000 per year for each to cover all expenses, including salaries, supplies, instruments, travelling, etc. To the $8,000 aggregate for four years from this source, the Geological Board added $1,000 for chemical work, making $9,000 in all received by me from the State for the survey of the Iron Region. In addition to this sum I have expended about $2,000 of my own means, and have not received any compensation for my services.

This small sum would have been inadequate to have accomplished anything worthy of the importance of the work undertaken, had not several corporations and individuals generously come to my relief; indeed on this source of help I counted largely in undertaking the work, and made it an express condition in the arrangement that I should be permitted to avail myself of all the assistance of this kind I could obtain, and also that during the progress of the work I should be free to continue the practice of a profession from which I was sure to obtain further facts bearing on the objects of the survey.

The companies which have contributed valuable data in their

possession, or have instituted special surveys at my suggestions, with the view of furthering the object of the survey, are :—The Marquette, Houghton & Ontonagon Railway, The Portage Lake & Lake Superior Ship Canal Co., The Republic, Washington, Lake Superior, Champion, New York, Spurr Mountain, Iron Cliff, Cannon and Magnetic Iron Companies. E. Breitung bore a part of the expense of making Map No. V., and John Fritz, A. Pardee, and Daniel J. Morrell, of Pennsylvania, S. P. Ely, of Marquette, and A. B. Meeker, of Chicago, contributed generously to the chemical fund, the results of the analyses being given in Chapter X.

The law of 1869 established a Board of Survey, consisting of H. P. Baldwin, Governor; W. J. Baxter, President of the Board of Education, O. Hosford, Superintendent of Public Instruction, with power to select the Geologists, disburse the money appropriated, and perform other necessary duties. Prof. A. Winchell was made Director, who approved the plan for the survey of the Iron Region which I submitted to him, and which is contained in the following letter:

LETTER OF INSTRUCTIONS,

Referred to in Agreement with T. B. BROOKS, *dated Negaunee, Mich., June 5th*, 1869.

" *To Major* T. B. BROOKS, *Assistant of the Geological Survey of Michigan.*

" SIR:—You are hereby authorized and requested to make a Survey of the Marquette Iron District, and to draw up a report on the same, substantially in accordance with the following suggestions:

" 1. By the Marquette Iron District is meant the region embracing all the deposits of iron ore extending from the shore of Lake Superior on the east, through Townships 46, 47, and 48 north, as far as Range 31 west, inclusive, being the region which for the present finds its outlet by railroads through Marquette and Escanaba.

" Your report on this district would appropriately furnish—

" 2. A historical sketch of discovery in the Iron Region of Lake Superior.

" 3. A physiographical sketch of the Marquette Iron District; general topography, hydrography, timber, soil, climate, etc.

" 4. The general geological structure of the district (not entering into details, nor theoretical discussions); identification of iron range stratification; outline description of the rocks; general description of the ores of iron occurring in the district.

" 5. The mines in general; their distribution and grouping.

" 6. Special notices of the mines and mining locations of the District; local structural geology, topography, mineralogical specialties of the ores.

"7. Discovery of ores; geological principles applicable; the use of instruments.

"8. The working of Iron Mines; methods in use here and elsewhere in analogous regions; advantages of each; machinery.

"9. The manufacture of iron and steel; special adaptations of the different varieties of ore in the District; the use of charcoal and mineral coal; resources of charcoal in Michigan; manufacture of charcoal; fluxes; location of furnaces; construction and operation of furnaces.

"10. Transportation of iron ores, and of iron; market; prices.

"11. Commercial statistics of iron ores, and of iron.

"In the discussion of the above topics, it is intended that you make such reference to other iron regions as may be necessary to thorough treatment and illustration of the general subject.

"It is not intended to lay down any stringent rules for your procedure, but only to furnish a general conception of the ground to be worked over. It is desired to produce as complete a manual as possible of information relating to the finding, extracting, transporting, and smelting of the iron ores of the Lake Superior Region, and it is believed that your own experience and the suggestions which may occur to you in the progress of the work will render it proper to deviate from the letter of the foregoing programme, according to the dictates of your own judgment. Specimens are to be collected according to the requirements and provisions of the law of 1869.

"In the prosecution of your field work, it is obvious that you cannot with the money at your disposal enter into detailed and complete examinations of individual properties, but it will promote the interests of the general work, if proprietors can be induced to defray the expenses of such detailed surveys beyond the limits to which you may be able officially to prosecute them; and it is evident that the interests of proprietors, no less than those of the State, will be promoted by committing such detailed surveys to your direction.

"The report, with the requisite maps, plans, and other illustrations, is to be ready for publication by the 31st day of December, 1870.

"(Signed) A. WINCHELL,
"Director Geological Survey,
"Ann Arbor, Mich."

On the completion of this survey of the Marquette Region, the Board decided to extend the work over the Menominee Region as well as further West before publishing, thus embracing all the known iron-fields of the Upper Peninsula. Professor Winchell having resigned in 1871, this part of the work was done under the direction of the Board.

Prof. R. Pumpelly has been engaged, with interruptions, in the Copper Region during the same period I have been at work in the Iron (see his Report, Part II.), and in the spring of 1871 Dr. C. Rominger commenced work on the Palæozoic rocks; his Report on the Silurian rocks of the Upper Peninsula is contained in Part III. of this volume.

The sum appropriated ($20,000) for publishing 2,000 copies of the three reports, with Atlas of maps, enabled the Board to contract for no more than a 500 octavo-page volume, which at the time was deemed sufficient space. I have been generously allowed more than one-half this space, but find that it was not sufficient to contain the material which I had accumulated, and which it seemed to me could be advantageously embodied in the proposed report. It was for some time a question with me, whether I should attempt to consider all the points named in the above scheme (giving each its relative space), which plan would have excluded a large amount of valuable material, or whether I should only attempt to treat each subject in order, as fully as my material would admit and its importance seemed to demand, without attempting at this time to cover the whole ground.

I choose the latter plan, and have in consequence been obliged to entirely omit all consideration of the important subjects of the location, construction and operation of furnaces; of fuels, fluxes, and ore mixtures; of the resources and manufacture of charcoal in Michigan,* as well as the consideration of the question of steel manufacture. The question of the transportation of ore and iron, of markets and prices, was also forced out for want of space. A proper treatment of these subjects would fill a volume.

I trust those gentlemen, who have favored me with lengthy and carefully prepared replies to my numerous inquiries on these excluded subjects, will feel that no injustice has been done them in withholding their papers, until they can be properly presented.

---

* The subject of the resources of Michigan in Charcoal and the location of charcoal furnaces both on the Upper and Lower Peninsulas has been carefully worked up and illustrated by Timber Maps, but there is unfortunately no means provided for their publication.

The following named gentlemen are well acquainted with their respective localities on the Lower Peninsula, and are prepared to give information regarding the timber, etc., which is in many instances unsurpassed:

JOSEPH DAME, North Port.
E. E. BENEDICT, Manistee.
E. B. MILLS, Mayville.
GEO. N. SMITH, Bear river.
W. H. C. MITCHELL, East Traverse bay.
LEROY WARREN, Pentwater.
J. S. DIXON, Charlevoix.
O. W. HART, Torch lake.
A. G. BUTLER, Frankfort.
JAMES LEE, Bingham.
W. H. HURLBURT, South Haven.
DENNIS T. DOWNING, Little Traverse.
DELOS L. FILER, Ludington.
WILLIAM H. FREY, West Olive.

It may be questioned, whether with the purely practical object I have had in view in preparing this report, and the limited space, that so large a place should be given to the subject of Lithology, so ably treated by Mr. Julien, in App. A, Vol. II. The reasons which led to this were my own inability to properly treat this subject, its great relative importance in the study of rocks devoid of fossils, but above all I had collected and catalogued during seven years a more complete suite of specimens from the Azoic of the Upper Peninsula, than had before been got together, which collection I believed worthy the study and paper referred to, and which I saw no better way of utilizing to the public, than as has been done It is open to question whether Mr. Julien's paper should not have been published through some scientific channel, rather than in an industrial report, where it will stand nearly alone as a contribution to science.

Grouping Iron Deposits.—It has been found convenient in this report to disregard such political divisions as counties and towns in designating localities, and to employ instead, either the precise and simple method of U. S. linear surveyors, which can be readily understood by an inspection of Maps II., III. and IV. of Atlas; or, by the use of what may be termed the mineral or industrial geography of the Upper Peninsula, by which it is conveniently divided into regions, districts, groups, etc., which, although not sharply defined, may be considered at present to have the following boundaries: The *Marquette Iron Region* (see Map III., Table XIII., and Chap. IV.) embraces all the developed iron mines of the Upper Peninsula, the ores of which now find their outlets via Marquette, L'Anse and Escanaba by the Marquette, Houghton and Ontonagon and Chicago and Northwestern railroads. This again is subdivided into the (1) Negaunee, (2) Michigamme, (3) Escanaba, and (4) L'Anse districts. These divisions may be conveniently carried still further by a subdivision of the Negaunee District into the Cascade Range, Negaunee Hematite Mines, Ishpeming Group, New England and Saginaw Range; and of the Michigamme District into the Washington, Champion, Spurr and Magnetic Ranges, and Republic Mountain Basin. The S. C. Smith is the only worked mine in the Escanaba District, and no ore has yet been shipped from the L'Anse District or Range. The *Menominee Iron Region* (see Map IV. and Chap. IV.), which as yet has sent no ore to market, is divided into (1) The North Belt in south part of T. 42, (2) The South Belt in Ts. 39 and 40, and (3) The Paint River District. The *Lake Gogebic and Montreal River Region or Range* (Chap. VI.) is so little known that it may be questionable whether it should have a place in this economic grouping; it embraces the country between Lake Gogebic and the west boundary of Michigan, and is 100 miles west of the Marquette Region.

It but remains for me to express my obligations and gratitude to the many gentlemen who have contributed in various ways to the objects of this survey, to officially acknowledge their services and to thank them cordially for myself and on behalf of the Board for what they have done.

To S. P. Ely, of Marquette, the survey is more deeply indebted than to any other person; indeed, I would not have undertaken the work except from assurance of his support, which has been constant and generous from the beginning. To Messrs. H. B. and F. L. Tuttle, of Cleveland, Ohio, I am indebted for a considerable amount of the material embodied on Statistical Tables XII. and XIII. of Atlas, much of which I believe it would have been impossible for me to have procured, except through them; App. J, Vol. II., contains a letter from H. B. Tuttle, who has always, with great promptness and care, answered my various inquiries. To Major Fayette Brown, Cleveland, the survey is indebted for a most valuable paper on the amount of air required by charcoal furnaces and the mode of applying it, based on his experience with the Jackson Co.'s furnaces at Fayette, the almost unparalleled success of which gives his statements great value. S. L. Smith, on the part of the Marquette, Houghton & Ontonagon railroad, placed all the results of that company's explorations, made under my direction, at the disposal of the survey. J. J. Hagerman, Milwaukee, furnished a statement regarding the working of Lake Superior and Iron Ridge, Wisconsin, ores with anthracite and coke, and the successful use of the metal in making rails. John L. Agnew has furnished drawings of the new charcoal furnace, superintended by him at Escanaba, 50 feet high and 12 feet bosh, the largest, so far as I know, in the world. M. R. Hunt, Depere, Wis., has given full details of a remarkable long and successful blast of the First National Iron Co.'s furnaces.

The Historical chapter has been made far more complete and reliable than would otherwise have been possible through the contribution of facts and documents by Messrs. William and John Burt, Messrs. Everett, White, Harlow, Hewitt, and Ely, of Marquette; also by Messrs. Jacob Houghton and Charles T. Harvey. This chapter was rewritten by Charles D. Lawton.

I am indebted to so many persons for the facts embodied in the chapter on Mining, that I can only mention W. E. Dickinson, J. C. Morse, William Sedgwick, A. Kidder, Peter Pascoe, George and Eugene St. Clair, and D. H. Merritt, of Marquette county, and Prof. R. Akerman, of Stockholm, Sweden.

C. H. V. Cavis, S. H. Selden, and George P. Cummings, civil engineers, have greatly aided in the work by their personal efforts in procuring information which is embodied in the maps. The valuable explorations of C. E. and Frank Brotherton, and of A. M. Brotherton, deceased, made for the C. & N. W. and M. H. & O. roads, has been to a large extent placed at my disposal by the officers of these companies.

The nature of the valuable scientific aid given to this work by Alexis A. Julien, Prof. R. Pumpelly, Dr. T. S. Hunt, Prof. George J. Brush, Dr. H. Credner, and Charles E. Wright, are explained in the text of chapters III., V., VI., and in Appendices A, B, and C, Vol. II.

Edwin Harrison, of St. Louis, has given me full and detailed statements regarding the working of his Irondale furnace, which has one of the best records ever made by a charcoal furnace. Robert Wood has prepared most of the manuscript for the press, and, with Mr. Bien, will take care of the publication and indexing.

The survey is indebted to the University of Michigan, Ann Arbor, for the use of rooms without charge, and for the same courtesy (most cordially extended) to the School of Mines, Columbia College, New York, on which institution the survey had no claim.

The Marquette, Houghton & Ontonagon, Chicago & Northwestern, Michigan Central, the Great Western, and Grand Trunk railways have in every instance, when requested, granted passes to persons connected with the survey.

To the gentlemen and companies above named, as well as to Messrs. J. N. Armstrong, American Iron & Steel Association, S. C. Baldwin, William H. Barnum, J. B. Britton, C. M. Boss, J. R. Case, Mr. Childs, Girard Iron Company, C. H. Hall, A. Heberlein, Alexander L. Holley, E. C. Hungerford, Prof. Hayden, Gilbert D.

Johnson, F. B. Jenny, Prof. J. P. Leslie, J. S. Lane, A. W. Maitland, David Morgan, Capt. H. Merry, F. W. Noble, Charles H. Pease, New York Mine, J. R. Orthey, Freiburg Royal School of Mines, James M. Safford, Samuel Thomas, J. M. Wilkinson, H. N. Walker, Walter Williams, Capt. R. D. Weston (deceased), Washington Mine, Dr. White, and Charles R. Westbrook, who have in various ways promoted my work, I am under great obligations. Without their aid this report could not have been prepared. I have forwarded to the Board of Survey a full list of their names and addresses, with the request to furnish each with a copy of this Report and accompanying Atlas.

CHAPTER I.

HISTORICAL SKETCH OF DISCOVERY AND DEVELOPMENT.*

NOTE.—Statistical Tables XII. and XIII. of Atlas contain many facts relevant to this subject, which could not well be incorporated in the text.

MINERAL explorations along the south shore of Lake Superior began at a very early period, and the existence of copper was made known to the world as long ago as 1636, by La Garde, in a book published in Paris. During the subsequent portion of the 17th century frequent mention is made in the "Relations" of the Jesuit Fathers of the finding of this metal.

These Relations† extend from 1632 to 1672, and are made up of the reports or simple narratives of these humble but zealous missionaries, scattered as they were all over the region of the great Lakes, then controlled by the French Government, and are necessarily of inestimable value to the historian and archæologist; and also contain much that is highly interesting to the geologist, as indicating the early discoveries of minerals and the knowledge of their localities and uses, possessed by the natives. In illustration of the allusions to copper found in these reports, we quote simply from one, Claude Allouez, who seems to have been a man of intelligence, as well as one of the most persevering and deserving of these early missionaries. He first visited Lake Superior in 1666, and makes mention of a large mass of copper to be seen near the shore of the lake, with its top rising above the water, giving an opportunity for those who passed that way to cut pieces from it. The writer says, this "rock" has disappeared, having become buried, as he opines, beneath the sands, through the action of the waves. He also states that pieces of copper weighing from 10 to 20 lbs. are frequently found among the savages, who esteem them

* C. D. Lawton, Esq., rendered much assistance in the preparation of this chapter.

† These valuable documents have been republished by the Canadian Government.

as domestic gods, and hold them in superstitious awe, preserving them, in some instances, time out of mind, among their most precious articles.

In 1672, a map was published in Paris of this region, which was made by these early Jesuits, and on which is represented 1,600 miles of coast and many islands, with what may be considered remarkable accuracy.*

In 1689, Baron La Houtan, in a book relating to travels in Canada, mentions that "upon Lake Superior we find copper mines, the metal of which is fine and plentiful; there being not a seventh part base from the ore."

In 1721, P. De Charlevoix described the native copper deposits, and the superstitions which the Indians had in regard to them, in considerable detail. The occurrence of native copper being so frequent, the wonder of the early voyageurs was naturally excited, being increased also by vague rumors (gathered from the savages) of the existence of gold, silver, and diamonds.

In 1765, Captain Jonathan Carver visited Lake Superior, and in his account dwelt so largely on the abundance of native copper, that a copper company was formed in England in 1771, which actually began mining operations on the Ontonagon river, under the direction of Mr. Alexander Henry, who seems to have been a better historian than miner; for he gives a detailed account of the winding-up of his operations in 1772 and concludes, as the result of his unsuccessful experiment in mining, that the country must be cultivated and peopled before the copper can be profitably mined.

In 1819, Mr. H. R. Schoolcraft accompanied as mineralogist and geologist a government exploring expedition along the south shore of Lake Superior, having for its object the investigation of the copper mines.

In 1823 another government expedition, under charge of Major Long, passed along the north shore of the Lake, having come from the northwest; and mention is made of their having observed copper boulders in the region of the headwaters of the Mississippi.

Steps had been taken with a view to an exploration of this region

---

* A fac-simile of this map, and much other interesting matter relating to the early history of the copper region, may be found in Foster and Whitney's Report, Exec. Doc., 1850, Part I.

during the Presidency of John Adams, but nothing was ever effected. The work of systematic, scientific exploration of the Upper Peninsula of Michigan was first undertaken by Dr. Douglas Houghton, the earliest State Geologist. Dr. Houghton had commenced his examination of this region in 1831, and in his first annual report to the Legislature in 1841 presented the results of his labors up to that period in so able a manner, that the attention of the world became directed to the Northern Peninsula with greatly increased interest. In 1840, Dr. Houghton wrote to the Hon. A. S. Porter, under date December 26th, regarding the mineral wealth of the south shore of Lake Superior: "Ores of zinc, iron and manganese occur in the vicinity of the shore, but I doubt whether either of these, unless it be zinc and iron, is in sufficient abundance to prove of much importance. Ores of copper are much more abundant than either of those before mentioned, and a sufficient examination of them has been made to satisfy me that they may be made to yield an abundant supply of the metal."

In his Geological Report of 1841 Dr. Houghton says: "Although hematite ore is abundantly disseminated through all the rocks of the metamorphic group, it does not appear in sufficient quantity at any one point that has been examined to be of practical importance:" At this date Dr. Houghton had traversed the south shore of Lake Superior five times, in a small-boat or canoe, on geological investigations. It is therefore probable that up to 1841 no Indian traditions worthy of credence, in regard to large deposits of iron ore, had come to his knowledge. As there are, so far as known, no considerable outcrops of iron ore, which come nearer than seven miles to the shore of the Lake, it is plain that investigations, based on observations taken along the shore only, could have determined no more than its probable existence, which is plainly indicated in the extracts given. Dr. Houghton was not aware of the existence of iron ore in quantity, until the return of Mr. Burt's party of surveyors to Detroit in the fall of 1844, his examinations in the interior of the country having been confined to the Copper Region. Attention at that early period was entirely directed to searching for ores of more value than iron, and it is worthy of remark, that the Jackson and Cleveland Iron Companies, which were the first two organized, were formed to mine copper, silver, and gold.

The remarkably rapid development of the mineral resources of the Upper Peninsula is largely due, among other causes, to the fact that the United States Linear Surveyors were required to combine geological and topographical observations with their surveys. The use of Burt's solar compass, which permits of rapid and precise observations of local variations (so important in the economic survey of a primitive iron region), served greatly to enhance the value of the results, by making known the position of rocks containing magnetic ore.

The honesty, skill and enthusiasm with which the field-work was executed resulted in the collection of a large amount of geological data, which at the completion of the survey would have left little to be done save the final report, in which the master-mind should classify, group, and harmonize the facts, and thereby develop nature's law from the mass of material collected. Dr. Houghton's untimely death by drowning in Lake Superior, while in the midst of his labors, prevented him from performing the crowning work. Any one familiar with the geology of the Upper Peninsula, who will peruse the manuscript notes * left by Dr. Houghton, will be convinced that his views regarding the geology of the older rocks were far in advance of his time, and such only as geologists years afterward arrived at, and those which are but now, thirty years after he recorded them, universally accepted (see Appendix E, Vol. II.). A brief statement of the origin of a work from which such important results have accrued will be given. In 1843 the financial troubles of the State of Michigan arising out of the "Five Million Loan," as it was called, were of such a character as to cause the Legislature to withhold the annual appropriation for the Geological Survey, which then had been for several years in successful operation under the direction of Dr. Houghton. Thoroughly interested in his scientific work, and believing that the best interests of the State and the cause of science demanded the continuance of the survey, Dr. Houghton asked from the General Government the aid which his own State felt unable to grant, and succeeded in obtaining, in the appropriation for the Public Surveys of

* These manuscript notes are now in the University Library at Ann Arbor, having been presented to that Institution by Dr. Houghton's widow. Dr. Houghton, it will be remembered, was at the time of his death a Professor in the University of Michigan as well as State Geologist.

IVES' MAP, SHOWING IRON HILLS, 1844.

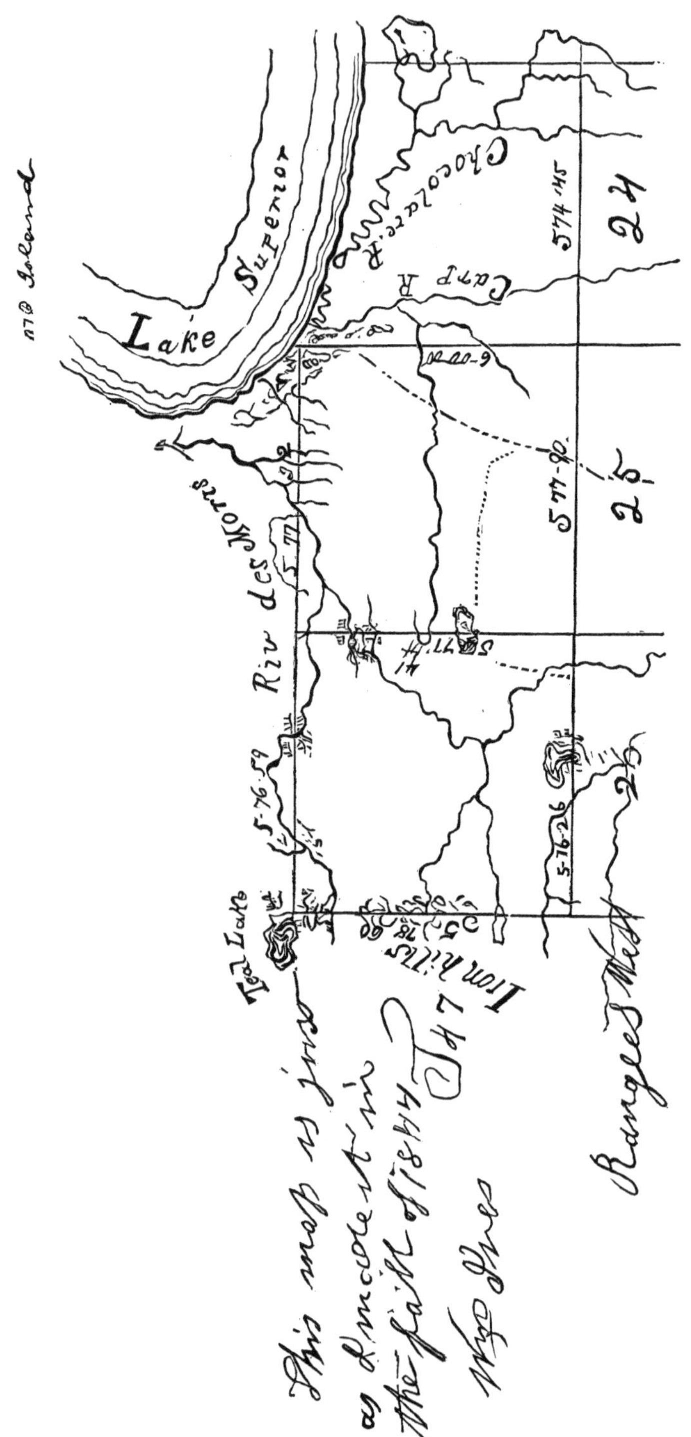

the Upper Peninsula of Michigan, an additional allowance per mile to cover the cost of the geological work. In order to expedite the work and insure the best scientific results from the adoption of his plan, Dr. Houghton himself took the contract from the Government for completing the surveys on the Upper Peninsula, which had been previously begun in 1840 under the direction of the Hon. William A. Burt, United States Deputy Surveyor. In the spring of 1844 Dr. Houghton commenced operations under his contract, the field-work being in charge of Mr. Burt, who received in compensation therefor the allowance granted by the Government. It is proper to add that Mr. Burt entered with deep interest into Dr. Houghton's plans and had, during his survey in the Lower Peninsula, collected for him many specimens and important geological information not required by his instructions.

In 1844 Mr. Burt, with a party consisting of William Ives, compassman, Jacob Houghton, barometer man, H. Mellen, R. S. Mellen, James King, and two Indians named John Taylor and Bonney * was engaged in establishing Township lines and making geological observations, as previously described.

On the 19th September, while running the east line of Town. 47 north, Range 27 west (the great iron Township), they observed by means of the solar compass remarkable variations in the direction of the needle, amounting to 87° from the normal. (See Appendix D, Vol. II.) Ascribing this phenomenon to iron ore, they sought for and found it in the ledges or outcrops at several points. Specimens † were collected and named by Mr. Burt and Dr. Houghton (See Appendix D, Vol. II.), and were described by them in their official returns; the fact of the great variation and large amount of ore being also especially commented upon. (See Appendix and official notes in Land Office, Washington, Lansing and Marquette.) A map made by Mr. Ives at the time, a fac-simile of which is given in Pl. I., has written along this line the words "Iron Hills." As the Jackson range is not magnetic at this locality, and does not outcrop on the line in question, it is not probable it was seen, but instead one or more of the ranges of flag or soft hematite ore further south.

---

* Bonney's real name was Michael Doner; himself and Taylor are now dead.

† Mr. R. S. Mellen has still in his possession a piece of the ore found that day, which he brought away with him.

In the month of June following, Dr. Houghton and Mr. Burt, with their party, were engaged in subdividing the Township above mentioned (Town. 47 north, Range 26 west), when the former made a personal examination in reference to iron ore, especially at the corners of Sections 29, 30, 31, 32 (see Appendix D, Vol. II.), now known as the Cascade mines, and remarked to Jacob Houghton and others, who were members of the party, that it would some day be very valuable and the basis of an active industry.

It thus appears that the U. S. surveyors, in the fall of 1844, officially established the fact, that iron ore in considerable quantities existed in the Upper Peninsula of Michigan. It is also undoubtedly true, that Indians had previously observed the ore and were acquainted with locations of it, without, however, being able to identify it.

The Jackson Co.—The manner in which this, the earliest developed, and one of the most important of the iron properties on Lake Superior, was discovered (although the enterprise was not mainly undertaken with a view of finding iron), is reliably set forth in the following letter, written by P. M. Everett, now of Marquette, to Captain G. D. Johnson, now of the Lake Superior mine. The letter is dated at Jackson, Mich., Nov. 10th, 1845, and is as follows :—

"I left here on the 23d of July last and was gone until the 24th of October. . . . . I had considerable difficulty in getting any one to join me in the enterprise, but I at last succeeded in forming a company of thirteen. I was appointed treasurer and agent to explore and make locations, for which last purpose we had secured seven permits from the Secretary of War. I took four men with me from Jackson and hired a guide at the Sault, where I bought a boat and coasted up the lake to Copper Harbor, which is over 300 miles from Sault Ste. Marie. . . . . We made several locations, one of which we called iron at the time. It is a mountain of solid iron ore, 150 feet high. The ore looks as bright as a bar of iron just broken. Since coming home we have had some of it smelted, and find that it produces iron and something resembling gold—some say it is gold and copper. Our location is one mile square, and we shall send a company of men up in the Spring to begin operations ; our company is called the 'Jackson Mining Co.'"

The actual discovery of the Jackson location was made by S. T.

Carr and E. S. Rockwell, members of Everett's party, who were guided to the locality by an Indian chief, named Manjekijik.*

The superstition of the savage not allowing him to approach the spot, Mr. Carr continued the search alone, resulting in the discovery of the outcrop, which he describes as indicated in Mr. Everett's letter. Previous to the discovery he was led to suppose from the Indians' description, that he would find silver, lead, copper or some other metal more precious than iron, as it was represented and found to be "bright and shiny."

July 23d, 1845, articles of association of the Jackson Iron Company were executed at Jackson, Mich., and by these articles Abram V. Berry was appointed the first *President*, Frederick W. Kirtland, *Secretary*, Philo M. Everett, *Treasurer*, and George W. Carr and William A. Ernst, *Trustees*.

Mr. Berry gives the following account of the early history of his company, in a letter dated at Jackson, Mich., Oct. 21st, 1870:—

"In the summer of 1845, an association was formed in this city, then a village, for the purpose of exploring the mineral region on the south shore of Lake Superior. The company consisted of P. M. Everett, James Ganson, S. T. Carr, G. W. Carr, F. W. Carr, E. W. Rockwell, F. W. Kirtland, W. H. Munroe, A. W. Ernst, F. Farrand, of Jackson, and S. A. Hastings, of Detroit (John Watkins, of Detroit, was interested with Hastings). Eleven individuals of the association procured permits from the War Department to locate one square mile each of mineral land on the south shore of Lake Superior. John Western, of Jackson, was then added to the

---

* In reward for the service of the Indian on this occasion, the officers of the Jackson Company subsequently gave him a written stipulation, of which the following is a copy:—

"RIVER DU MORT, LAKE SUPERIOR,
May 30, 1846.

This may certify that, in consideration of the services rendered by Manjekijik, a Chippeway Indian, in hunting ores of Location No. 593 of the Jackson Mining Company, that he is entitled to twelve undivided twenty one-hundredths part of the interest of said mining company in said location No. 593.

A. V. BERRY, *Superintendent.*
F. W. KIRTLAND, *Secratary.*"

This agreement on the part of the company was never fulfilled, and Manjekijik finally died in poverty; his relatives, now living in Marquette, are in the same miserable condition, without ever having received, as is averred by those who are cognizant of the facts, any compensation for the services mentioned.

company, making thirteen in all. In the fall of 1845 a company of explorers, consisting of S. T. Carr, P. M. Everett, W. H. Munroe, and E. S. Rockwell, visited Lake Superior, when what is now known as the Jackson location was secured by the permit granted to James Ganson, in the unsurveyed district, the section lines not having been run. The location was described by metes and bounds, commencing at a certain large pine-tree, the position of which was fixed by its course and distance from the corner of Teal lake. When the land was surveyed it was bought at $2.50 per acre. * * *

"In the spring of 1846, another expedition was fitted out, consisting of F. W. Kirtland, E. S. Rockwell, W. H. Munroe and myself, members of the company and several other adventurers; the object being to make further examinations of the iron and to use the remaining permits, by entering other mineral land. * * * * * I found our location much beyond what I had anticipated. After spending twelve days in the woods, exploring the surrounding country, including what was afterwards known as the Cleveland location and building what we called a house, we returned to the mouth of the Carp with 300 pounds of ore on our backs. We then divided; one party was left to keep possession of the location, another went farther up the Lake to use the remaining permits, while I returned to the Sault with the ore. It was my intention at this time to use another permit on the Cleveland location, but on arriving at the Sault I met Dr. Cassels, of Cleveland, agent of a Cleveland company, and having arranged with him that his company should pay a portion of the expense of keeping possession, making roads, etc., I discovered to him the whereabouts of the Cleveland location. He took my canoe, visited the location, and secured it by a permit. On arriving at Jackson we endeavored on two occasions to smelt the ore which I had brought down, in our common cupola furnaces, but failed entirely. In August of the same year, Mr. Olds, of Cucush Prairie, who owned a forge (in which he was making iron from bog ore), then undergoing repairs, succeeded in making a fine bar of iron from our ore in a blacksmith's fire, the first iron ever made from Lake Superior ore. In the winter of 1846–47 we began to get up at Jackson a bellows and other machinery for constructing a forge on the "Carp;" and in the summer of 1847 a company of men commenced building the same, and continued until March, 1848, when a freshet carried away the dam. * *

"—The association was then (1848) merged into an incorporated company, and by some means the pioneers in the enterprise are now all out."

In a book* on the mineral region of Lake Superior, with map by Jacob Houghton, Jr. and T. W. Bristol, published in 1846, only one iron company is mentioned—The Jackson. The description of the company's property is as follows:

Permit No. 593—somewhere in T. 46, N.-R. 27 or 28 W., while on Section 1 of T. 47, R. 27, Permit No. 158 is marked, which was granted to D. Hamilton, of Watervliet, New York. Section 3, same Township, embracing the New York mine, is covered by Permit No. 160, granted to T. Williams, of Newburg, N. Y. Section 10, same Township, embracing parts of the Cleveland and Lake Superior mines, was covered by Permit No. 177, granted to T. Ricket, of Copper Harbor.

In 1846 Fairchild Farrand explored the Jackson location and mined some ore. The company, under the superintendency of Wm. McNair, began, in 1847, the construction of a forge on the Carp river, three miles east of the mine, the first iron being made Feb. 10th, 1848, by forgeman, now Judge, A. N. Barney. Work was stopped in a few days by a freshet which carried away the dam. Mr. Everett came up in the summer of 1848, had the dam repaired and resumed the manufacture of blooms. The first iron made was sold to E. B. Ward, who employed it in the construction of the steamboat "Ocean." This forge was afterwards carried on under leases by B. F. Eaton, and later by the Clinton Iron Co., subsequently by Peter White and lastly by J. P. Pendill; it made but little iron and no money. The quality varied from the highest (as shown by the experiments of Major Wade, of the U. S. army) to indifferent, the trouble being a lack of uniformity in the blooms. The power was supplied by the Carp river, a dam 18 feet high having been constructed across the stream for this purpose. There were upon either side of the stone arch, and arranged opposite each other, four fires, from each of which a lump was taken every six hours, which was placed under the hammer and forged into blooms

* This little volume, (afterwards revised by Mr. Houghton,) thus early issued, contains much interesting and valuable matter relating to the early discoveries and mining operations of Lake Superior, especially regarding the copper region.

four inches square and two feet in length; the daily product being about three tons, requiring two teams of six horses each to convey them over the intervening ten miles of horrible road to Marquette. These teams, when so fortunate as not to break down, on returning brought back supplies for the men and animals. The same difficulties attended the procuring of the supply of ore and charcoal. The power was also found to be insufficient, owing to a scant supply of water occurring at certain seasons of the year. These difficulties were too numerous and serious for the maintenance of the existence of the concern, and resulted in its abandonment in 1856.

On the 6th of June, 1848, a meeting was called to act on the question of the acceptance of an act of incorporation passed at the preceding session of the Legislature, and it was decided to incorporate the company under the act referred to. The organization was completed under the title of the Jackson Mining Co., of Jackson, Michigan—Fairchild Farrand, *President*, W. A. Ernst, *Secretary*, George Foot, *Treasurer*, F. W. Carr, F. W. Kirtland, Lewis Bascom, and John Western, *Directors*. The capital stock of the company, as also that of the New England Mining Co., organized at this time, was fixed at $300,000, in shares of $100 each; the purpose of each being the mining of copper as well as iron. April 2d, 1849, an amendment to the charter of the Jackson Mining Co., of Jackson, was obtained, when the title was changed to its present form—**Jackson Iron Co.** The first officers under this organization were Ezra Jones, *President*, Wm. A. Ernst, *Secretary*, John Watson, *Treasurer*, S. H. Kimball, James A. Dyer, and James Day, *Directors*.

In 1850, Mr. A. L. Crawford, proprietor of the iron works at Newcastle, Pa., took with him from Lake Superior about five tons of the Jackson ore, and there worked it up. Part of the ore having been made into blooms and rolled into bar-iron, was used for special purposes, and part used for lining in the puddling furnaces. The iron was found to be excellent. About the same time, General Curtis, of Sharon, Pa., proprietor of extensive iron-works at that place, came to Lake Superior to inspect the Jackson and Cleveland locations; his object being to secure an interest, with a view to a future supply of ore for his works, of a better quality than he then possessed. Failing to make an arrangement for the Cleveland, he bought up sufficient stock in the Jackson Co. to give him a controlling interest in the management of its affairs; so that for some years the location was known as "Sharon."

It is proper to remark that General Curtis believed, as did also John Western before him, that, as soon as practicable, the best policy for Lake Superior iron mines to follow would be to sell their ore to the furnaces of Ohio, Pennsylvania, and elsewhere; and in 1852 about 70 tons of the company's ore were taken to Sharon, Pa., and there made into pig-iron in the "old Clay Furnace." There were frequent changes of officers and directors in the Jackson Co. up to 1860, and the history of the company was one of disappointment and financial embarrassment. Between 1860 and 1862 the gentlemen who now compose the Board of Directors came into office, and in 1862 the first dividend was made. The great demand for iron occasioned by the war caused the iron interests of Lake Superior, for the first time, to assume a very successful aspect. The first regular shipments of ore from the Jackson mine were made in 1856, which amounted to about 5,000 tons. Up to this time the different forges in the district had consumed about 25,000 tons of ore. (See Table, Pl. XII. of Atlas.) The Jackson mine, earliest discovered, and first opened and tested, became widely known from the outset, and has ever continued to remain the leading mine in the district. The important village of Negaunee, within whose corporate limits the Jackson mine is situated, dates its origin with the commencement of the company's o erations. As the Chicago and Northwestern and the Marquette, Houghton and Ontonagon railroads form a junction in Negaunee, facilities are thus afforded for shipments over either road—that is, by the way of Escanaba or Marquette. The "openings," or pits, are irregular and numerous, and extend from the west edge of the village of Negaunee west for three-quarters of a mile. The greater portion of the product finds its outlet through a tunnel, which enters the mines from the north side of the hill and is of sufficient size to admit railroad cars and small locomotive engines. From the main tunnel radiate several branches, which extend to, or are being extended to, the different stopes and shafts. The main shafts are supplied with ample steam-power for pumping and hoisting purposes. For details of workings, geological structure, etc., see accompanying maps, tables, and text.

The New England Mining Co. was, like the Jackson, *incorporated* by a special act of the Michigan Legislature passed in 1848. The purpose for which the organization was effected is stated as being the mining and smelting and manufacturing of ores and minerals in the State of Michigan, the language stating the company's objects being identical with that of the Jackson Company; the capital stock was placed at 300,000. It does not appear that anything noticeable was accomplished by this company, thus early organized. The charter came in 1855 into the possession of Capt. E. B. Ward, by whom it is now held.

The Marquette Iron Co.—In the summer of 1848, Mr. Edward Clark, of Worcester, Mass., was sent to Lake Superior by Boston parties, to look for copper, but at the Sault he fell in with Robert J. Graveraet, who induced him to stop at the Carp river and see the iron mines. The Jackson Company's forge was at work and had made a little iron. Clark, on his return to Worcester, carried with him a bloom and some ore from the Jackson Iron mountain, which, on being drawn into wire at a factory, proved excellent. Clark at once proceeded to form an association for the purpose of building a forge on the far-off shore of Lake Superior, assisted by Graveraet, who also appeared in Worcester at this time (having travelled from Marquette to Saginaw on snow-shoes); he succeeded in organizing a company, March 4th, 1849, consisting of E. B. Clark, W. A. Fisher, A. R. Harlow, of Worcester, Mass., and R. J. Graveraet, of Mackinaw; Clark and Graveraet putting in against the capital of the others leases of iron lands of which they claimed to have possession. These iron lands constitute what subsequently became known as the Lake Superior and Cleveland mines, and over which a long controversy arose as to which party should possess the land, and which was finally decided by the Interior Department at Washington in favor of what was known as the Cleveland Company. Mr. Harlow constructed and purchased the necessary machinery to the value of $8,000, and in the spring of 1849 shipped it to Marquette, starting himself with his family on the 11th of June, and arriving in Marquette on the 6th of July thereafter. Graveraet had reached there on the 17th of May previous, taking with him a small party of men, among whom was Peter White, then a lad, but subsequently largely identified with numerous interests in the Iron

Region, and now President of the First National Bank of Marquette. The forge was completed, making the first bloom in just one year from the date of Mr. Harlow's arrival.

The Marquette Iron Co.'s works started with 10 fires, and used Cleveland and Lake Superior ores, mostly the former, making blooms exclusively, which were sold in Pittsburg at prices ranging from $35 to $50. The works were in operation somewhat irregularly until 1853, when the Marquette Company was merged into the Cleveland Company, under the auspices of which the forge continued in operation for a few months longer, and was finally destroyed by fire in 1854. Like all bloomeries started in Marquette County, it was from the first, financially, a failure. The cost of the plant was great, transportation difficult and expensive, and the price of iron during the entire period disproportionately low. There was no dock at Marquette, no canal at the Sault, scarcely a road in the country, no shop for repairs, no skilled labor but what was, together with all supplies, imported "from below," and no regular communication. During the summer of 1849 only three sailing vessels and five propellers arrived at Marquette. The stock of the Marquette Company was bought up by the Cleveland Company, and its property passed to the ownership of the latter.

In 1852 John Downey, Samuel Barney and others began the construction of a forge on the "Little Carp," but after having built some houses, constructed a wheel, etc., permanently abandoned the enterprise.

In 1849 and 1850 a *whetstone quarry* was opened in a bed of novaculite, near the outlet of Teal lake, and Messrs. Smith and Pratt established a factory, for the purpose of sawing these blocks, at the mouth of a small stream near the Marquette landing, and carried on a "thrifty business."

The Iron Mountain Railroad.—The question of transporting the rich ores of Marquette county to the coal of Ohio and Pennsylvania, being one that came to be seriously considered, it naturally suggested the necessity of *a railroad* from the mines (those near the present villages of Negaunee and Ishpeming) to Marquette bay. In 1851 Messrs. Heman B. Ely and John Burt strongly advocated the enterprise, and in the following year Mr. Ely caused a survey to be made; at that period the entire population of Marquette county was less than 150 persons. There being no general railroad law in the State at that time, the construction of the railroad was undertaken by Mr. Ely, assisted by his brothers George H. and Samuel P. Ely, of Rochester, New York, as an individual enterprise, he having previously made a contract with the Jackson and Cleveland Iron Mining Companies and Mr. John Burt, as the representative of other companies, for the transportation of their ores. This contract the two first-named iron companies subsequently attempted to break, and sought to defeat the railroad by constructing a plank-road in opposition to it, thus instituting a serious and embarrassing controversy, which continued until 1855, when all matter of dispute then pending between the Railroad Company, under charge of Mr. Ely, and the Plank-road Company, under charge of Mr. S. H. Kimball, were submitted to arbitration and settled to the satisfaction of both parties—Messrs. C. T. Harvey and Austin Burt being arbitrators. Immediately after the passage of the General Railroad Law of this State in 1855, the Messrs. Ely incorporated the railroad under the title of the Iron Mountain Railroad, and John Burt was first President. A year later the company was strengthened by the addition of Jos. S. Fay, Edwin Parsons, Lewis H. Morgan, and other capitalists; and in 1857 the road was completed and put in operation. Mr. H. B. Ely, to whose foresight and energy the origin and success of the enterprise was largely due, and to whom the interests of Lake Superior became otherwise greatly indebted, died in Marquette, in 1856, before the work upon which he had labored so intently was completed.

The death of his brother, and his own connection with the road, was the occasion of bringing to Marquette Mr. S. P. Ely, who is now more largely identified with the business management of many of the leading enterprises in the Iron Region than any person resident on "Lake Superior." The Iron Mountain Railroad became subsequently a part of the Bay de Noquette and Marquette Railroad, this becoming afterwards, by consolidation, the Marquette and Ontonagon Road, and still later, by further consolidation, a part of the through line of the Marquette, Houghton, and Ontonagon Railroad. The plank-road to which reference is here made was built by the Jackson and Cleveland Companies jointly, but was never used as a plank-road; longitudinal sleepers were laid down and covered with strap-rail, on which horse cars were run. The road was used for two seasons, and cost $120,000, which amount was practically sunk. The cost of transportation was nominally one dollar per ton; each team would make the round trip in a day, bringing four tons of ore. It is proper to add that the rates of transportation fixed by these H. B. Ely contracts, although afterward deemed by the iron companies much too liberal, were lower than any at which ore has ever been carried over the road; the present rates being more than double those agreed upon with Mr. Ely.

Among the most important enterprises early connected with the development of the Lake Superior iron interests was the construction of the **Sault Ste. Marie Ship Canal.** In the St. Mary's river or strait, connecting the waters of Lakes Superior and Huron, occurs, nearly opposite the village of Sault Ste. Marie, a rapid of about one mile in length, and about seventeen feet fall, forming a complete barrier to the communication between the lakes. Some years previous to the construction of the canal this barrier had been overcome partially, by the construction and use of a portage flat-bar railroad, over which all articles of commerce between the lower lakes and Lake Superior were transported and reshipped in both directions. The important and growing interests of Lake Superior demanded more easy and effective means of commercial communication with the lower lakes. The matter being brought before the National Legislature, Congress granted to the State of Michigan, by Act approved Aug. 26th, 1852, 750,000 acres of land for the purpose of aiding in the construction and completion of a ship canal around the falls of Ste. Marie. On the 5th of February following, the State of Michigan, by an Act of its Legislature, accepted the grant of land above mentioned; and to further the objects thereof, authorized the Governor of the State to appoint Commissioners to let the contract for the construction of the canal, and to enter the lands authorized under the grant.

The Commissioners appointed under this legislative act entered into contract with Joseph P. Fairbanks, Erastus Corning and others for building the canal within two years from date thereof; the consideration being the U. S. Government grant of lands. This contract was soon after duly assigned to the Ste. Marie's Falls Ship Canal Co., which company had been organized in the city of New York on the 14th of May, 1853, under an Act of the Legislature of the State of New York, passed April 12th, immediately preceding. At the organization of the company, the following persons were chosen officers and directors of the company: Erastus Corning, *President*, J. W. Brooks, *Vice-President*, J. V. L. Pruyn, *Treasurer* and *Secretary*. *Directors:* Erastus Corning, J. W. Brooks, J. V. L. Pruyn, Jos. P. Fairbanks, John M. Forbes, John F. Seymour, and James F. Joy.

Subsequent to the passage of the grant by Congress, but previous to the acceptance thereof by the State of Michigan, Mr. Charles T. Harvey was authorized by Messrs. Fairbanks and Corning to cause a survey to be made, which he proceeded to do during the month of November, 1852, having secured the services of an experienced engineer from the Erie Canal, Mr. L. L. N. Davis. After the organization of the company, Mr. Harvey was appointed its general agent, and the supervision of the construction placed under his control.

Early in the season of 1853 Mr. Harvey, with 400 men, proceeded to the Sault, and on the 4th of June broke ground for the canal. The remoteness of the locality, and many other unfavorable circumstances, rendered the construction of a work of such magnitude exceedingly difficult, and necessitated at every step of the operations unusual care and energy in the management as well as heavy pecuniary expenditures. Mr. Harvey remained in control of the construction for one year, when he was relieved and placed in charge of the finance, and also appointed agent for the State to select lands under the grant in the Upper Peninsula. Mr. Harvey selected about 200,000 acres of land, 39,000 of which were taken in Marquette county, and were subsequently sold for $500,000 cash, to the Iron Cliff Co. Among the copper land selected was the quarter section on which the Calumet and Hecla Company's mine is situated, and which was sold by the canal company for $60,000, now worth, on the basis of late sales of stock, $13,000,000. The 750,000 acres granted by the General Government were entered by the company as follows: on the Upper Peninsula, 262,283 acres of iron, copper, and timber land, and 487,717 acres of pine land in the Lower Peninsula. A land agency was established at Detroit for the purpose of locating the lands obtained through the grant.

During the summer of 1854 the difficulties necessarily attendant upon building the canal were very much enhanced by disease among the workmen; some 200 of whom died of the cholera, and among them was Mr. Ward, who had charge of the construction. Mr. Harvey was again placed in charge of the work, which, owing to the panic among the workmen, had become nearly suspended; but by the exercise of much skill and energy he succeeded in reorganizing the force, and pushing the work vigorously forward to final completion. On the 19th of April, 1855, the water was let into the canal, and in the following June the work was opened for public use, under the superintendency of Mr. John Burt.

The total cost of the construction of the canal, which includes also the expense attendant upon the selection of lands, as contained in the report of the company under date of January 1st, 1858, was $999,802.46.

The State of New York, by act passed April 15th, 1858, granted a charter incorporating the "**St. Mary's Canal Mineral Land Co.**" Under this act of incorporation, a company was duly organized, and to it was transferred the canal company's lands of the Upper Peninsula. It was soon found that the canal failed to meet the growing wants of the commerce of Lake Superior, owing to the variation in the general level of the Lake Superior becoming somewhat lower than when the canal was completed, thus making a variable difference in the depth of the canal of from one to one and one-half feet; and also that the General Government, by successive appropriations, has caused the channels through Lake George and the St. Clair Flats to be so widened and deepened, that vessels of far heavier tonnage than was originally anticipated could be employed. The Michigan State Legislature adopted a resolution in the session of 1869, offering to cede the canal to the U. S. Government; although Congress has not as yet formally accepted the offer made by the State, nevertheless, under its system of internal improvement, the General Government is now engaged in the enlargement of the canal. The width of the canal is to be increased to 300 feet, and its depth to 16 feet, the locks are to be double, 80 feet in width and 450 feet long. The amount of the government appropriations under which this improvement is being effected is in the aggregate $800,000; and the work, when completed, will be fully adequate to the wants of commerce.

The report of superintendent Guy H. Carleton shows the following to be some of the principal exports and imports through the canal during 1871 and 1872:

	1871.	1872.
Flour, bbls	25,146	42,141
Pork, bbls	8,887	10,306
Beef, bbls	3,054	4,161
Bacon, lbs	163,763	242,475
Lards, lbs	283,141	213,394
Butter, lbs	519,545	559,137
Cheese, lbs	187,340	200,994
Tallow, lbs	104,354	106,170
Soap, boxes	21,799	18,205
Apples, bbls	18,359	20,025
Sugar, lbs	4,062,087	5,454,559
Tea, chests	3,864	7,980
Coffee, bags	5,228	7,815
Salt, bbls	36,199	42,690
Tobacco, lbs	258,179	321,836
Nails, kegs	29,843	34,984
Dried Fruit, lbs	115,366	73,230
Vegetables, bush	27,619	35,263
Lime, bbls	2,338	6,067
Window Glass, boxes	25,226	7,492
Cattle, head	2,639	3,608
Horses and Mules	435	528
Hogs, head	1,625	1,567
Brick, M	1,225	9,067
Furniture, pieces	13,616	44,768
Machinery, tons	1,595	10,593
Engines	18	28
Boilers	17	34
Liquor, bbls	4,366	7,082
Malt, lbs	653,140	1,545,875
Coarse Grain, bush	283,503	444,875
Mdse., tons	23,245	38,215

The following are some of the principal exports from Lake Superior for 1871–72 :—

	1871.	1872.
Mass Copper, tons	1,091	1,709
Ingot Copper, tons	7,666	8,547
Stamped Work Copper, tons	5,705	4,365
Iron Ore, tons	327,461	383,105
Pig Iron, tons	23,304	29,341
Fish, half bbls	26,041	14,529
Wheat, bush	1,376,705	567,134
Tallow, lbs	59,225	64,567
Flour, bbls	179,093	94,270
Barley, bush	25,320	898

	1871.	1872.
Silver Ore	464	306
Stone, building, tons	5,528	5,213
Potatoes, bush	.....	636
Copper, manufactured, tons	.....	395
Quartz, tons	.....	591
Wool, tons	.....	30

In 1853 the **Lake Superior Iron Company,** one of the three oldest companies in the district, was formed; articles of association were filed March 13th, capital stock $300,000, in 12,000 shares of $25 each. The capital stock was subsequently increased to $500,000, which has all been returned to the stockholders in dividends. The incorporators were Heman B. Ely and Anson Gorton, of Marquette, Mich.; Samuel P. Ely, George H. Ely, and Alvah Strong, of Rochester, New York. The company commenced operations in 1857 on 120 acres of land in Sections 9 and 10, T. 47, R. 27, which was purchased of John Burt, being a part of the Briggs and Graveraet claim spoken of above under the Cleveland Company. Subsequent purchases enlarged the company's estate to 2,000 acres, its present dimensions. The company's principal openings are upon the land originally purchased. The first shipment of ore (4,658 tons) was made in 1858; since which the increase has been so great that its shipments now exceed those of any mine in the district, as will be seen by reference to the tables. This company have recently constructed, in Marquette, the Grace Furnace, which went into blast in December, 1872, using anthracite coal in the manufacture of pig-iron. The furnace is located on the shore of the bay, within the limits of the city, and is the first anthracite furnace built on Lake Superior. A map of the Lake Superior and Barnum mines accompanies this report.

The Eureka Iron Company was organized October 29th, 1853, with a capital stock of $500,000 in 20,000 shares. The corporators were Eber B. Ward, Harmon De Graffe, Silas M. Kendrick, M. Tracy Howe, P. Thurber, Elijah Wilson, Thomas W. Lockwood, and Francis Choate, with office in Detroit. The organization was effected with a view of mining ore and of manufacturing charcoal pig-iron from Lake Superior ores; preparations were made to build a furnace in Marquette county, but the location was finally changed and the furnace erected where now stands the flourishing city of Wyandotte, becoming the nucleus of the extensive iron works which have since grown up in that locality. The Eureka Company was also the first iron enterprise in which Captain E. B. Ward, subsequently so widely known as a successful iron master, became engaged. The company was formed by Philip Thurber, and a quarter section of land purchased near Marquette of Mr. A. R. Harlow, on which a few hundred tons of ore were mined; but it becoming evident that the ore did not exist in quantity, the work was abandoned. This land was subsequently sold back to Mr. Harlow for his shares of the company's stock, and is now known as Harlow's Mill.

The Cleveland Iron Mining Company filed articles of association March 29th, 1853; capital stock, $500,000, in 20,000 shares. The corporators were John Outhwaite, Morgan L. Hewitt, S. Chamberlain, Samuel L. Mather, Isaac L. Hewitt, Henry F. Brayton, and E. M. Clark, with office in Cleveland, Ohio. The early history of this celebrated mine, one of the oldest and most important in the district, is referred to in connection with that of the Jackson Co.

Dr. J. Lang Cassels, of Cleveland, to whom reference is made in Mr. Berry's letter, visited Lake Superior in 1846, and took, as he expresses it, "squatter's possession" of a square mile for the Dead River Silver and Copper Mining Co. of Cleveland; the property here spoken of includes the mines of the present Cleveland Co. The Jackson Co. had previously taken possession of their lands, and Dr. Cassels obtained guidance thereto from an Indian, there being no white men in the region; the doctor went up from and returned to the Sault in a bark canoe. During the succeeding year, Cassels having left the country, the location was taken possession of by Messrs. Samuel Moody, John Mann and Dr. Edward Rogers. The two former claiming what became the Cleveland mine, and the latter what is known as the Lake Superior. When the Marquette Forge Co. was organized in Worcester, as previously described, Clark had authority from Mann and Moody to lease their location, and Graveraet had similar power from Rogers.

In this manner leases of these lands were put into the organization against $20,000 cash capital, to be paid by Messrs. Harlow and

Fisher. Both the Cleveland Co. and Graveraet, representing Messrs. Moody and Mann, claimed priority of right to the land under a "pre-emptor's mining act." These conflicting claims went before the Department at Washington, where a decision was rendered, which gave the right of purchase to the Cleveland Co. The entries which the Cleveland Co. made did not cover the Lake Superior location, Graveraet still claiming it, in behalf of the Marquette Co., on the ground of the Rogers pre-emption. Previously Isaiah Briggs had been on the land, but, leaving it, Rogers had taken possession. Rogers lost his interest, however, by not being present at the Government sale of lands in November, 1850, and establishing his claim, having been detained by a storm on the lake while endeavoring to proceed to the Sault (where the land office was located) for that purpose. The location was purchased by John Burt, on the basis of the Briggs claim, he having agreed to lease an undivided one-half interest to Graveraet, who was also present in behalf of the Rogers claim. This lease to Graveraet was assigned by him to the Marquette Co., passed with the company's other assets into the possession of the Cleveland Co., and was finally sold for $30,000 to the Lake Superior Iron Co., that company having previously purchased the Briggs title.

The Cleveland association, although formed in 1849, did not do any business in Lake Superior until 1853; at that date the Cleveland and Marquette companies became finally merged by the former company purchasing (including 64 acres of land on which the forge was located) the assets of the latter, and the present Cleveland Iron Co. was formed. The Cleveland Co. continued to run the forge for about two years, until it was burned down. The company mined in 1854, 4,000 tons of ore, which was made into blooms at the different forges in the vicinity. In 1855 they shipped 1,449 tons of ore to the furnaces "below," thus preceding the Jackson Co. one year, and becoming the first to send out of the region any considerable amount of ore. The Jackson Co. had sent a few tons to the World's Fair in New York in 1853, and in 1852 some had been sent to Sharon, as before mentioned. The Cleveland Co. has also an ore dock at Marquette, entirely similar to the docks of the M. H. & O. R. R. Co., of which full descriptions and illustration are given.

On Nov. 8th, 1853, the **Collins Iron Co.** filed articles of association, with a capital stock of $500,000 in 20,000 shares. The corporators were Edward K. Collins, of New York, Solon Farnsworth, Edwin H. Thomson, Robert J. Graveraet, and Charles A. Trowbridge, with office in Detroit.

The company built a forge in 1854, and began to make blooms late in the fall of 1855; Robert J. Graveraet, Supt., and C. A. Trowbridge, Managing Director. E. K. Collins largely interested himself with a view of obtaining a superior quality of iron for the shafts of his ocean steamers. In 1858, about the time the Pioneer Furnace was completed, Mr. S. R. Gay, who had been engaged on that work, leased the Collins Forge and put up a cupola there in which he made some pig-iron. The company immediately thereafter constructed a blast-furnace under the direction of Mr. Gay. This furnace was completed and put in operation December 13th, 1858, with a single stack; all the necessary power being afforded by the Dead river, upon which the furnace is located.

On August 28th, 1854, **the Peninsula Iron Co.** filed articles of association, with a capital stock of $500,000 in 20,000 shares. The corporators were Wm. A. Burt, Austin Burt, Wells Burt, John Burt, Heman B. Ely, Samuel P. Ely, and Geo. H. Ely; the two latter of Rochester, N. Y., the others of Michigan. Office of the company, Marquette, Mich. The company originally owned 800 acres of iron lands, which it sold in 1862 to the Lake Superior Iron Co., and determined on building a blast-furnace at Hamtramck, Detroit, Mich., which furnace was completed in February, 1863, and is still in successful operation. The company also operated a sawmill for a few years, which they built on the Carp river, a short distance from Marquette.

Oct. 11th, 1854, the articles of association of the **Chicago and Lake Superior Iron Mining and Manufacturing Co.** were filed. Capital stock, $500,000, in 20,000 shares. The corporators were B. S. Morris, Isaac Shelby, Jr., Geo. Staley, Henry Frink, and Samuel S. Baker, all of Chicago, Ill.; and Solomon T. Carr and Fairchild Farrand, of Jackson, Mich. No permanent mining work was ever done by this company.

The Clinton Iron Co. Organized by forgemen from Clinton Co.,

New York, Jan. 20th, 1855.. Capital stock, $25,000. *Corporators,* Azel Lathrop, Jr., H. Butler, Chas. Parish, and Daniel Brittol.

The object for which the organization was effected was to lease and operate the Jackson Forge. The company being composed of workmen, who at the time were employed in that concern and were locally styled the "Mudchunk." The market price of blooms being much below the cost of their manufacture, they were enabled to operate the forge but a brief period, and having become hopelessly involved in indebtedness, the company permanently suspended.

The Forest Iron Co. filed articles of association, September 22d, 1855, with a capital stock of $25,000 in 1,000 shares. The corporators were Matthew McConnell, Wm. G. Butler, Wm. G. McComber, M. L. Hewitt, and J. G. Butler. This company was organized for the purpose of putting up a bloom forge on Dead river, and the location became known as Forestville. McConnell, Butler and McComber commenced operations at this point as early as 1852 on their own private account, but becoming financially embarrassed, they sought relief by organizing a company as above indicated, who continued the manufacture of what was called half blooms, the production of which cost them from $180 to $200 a ton. These selling in Pittsburg for $35 to $40, on six months' time, it naturally resulted in the ruin of the company.

To the original projectors of the **Pioneer Iron Co.** belongs the credit of having established the first blast-furnace on Lake Superior; previous to that all the iron manufactured had been made in bloomeries. Mr. C. T. Harvey was the mover of the scheme, and the originator and manager of the company. He induced capitalists (chiefly in New York) to embark in the enterprise, Mr. E. C. Hungerford of Chester, Conn., being chosen Secretary and Resident Treasurer. Although the business was unknown to a single man on Lake Superior, the most sanguine views prevailed from the outset, and a two-stack furnace was constructed near the Jackson mine.

The late S. R. Gay and L. D. Harvey, now Superintendent of the Northern Furnace, were the builders; the work being commenced June, 1857, and completed so as to make the first iron in February of the next year.

Much of the material, including two millions of brick, was brought from Detroit and had to be hauled 13 miles from Marquette by teams; the engines were made at the West Point Foundry. The original stock was $125,000, in 5,000 shares; the articles were filed July 20th, 1857, the corporators being Moses A. Hoppock, Wm. Pearsall and Chas. T. Harvey. Most of the parties interested in the concern were totally ignorant of iron-making and as an instance illustrating the fact, it is related that one of the directors, during the period of construction, inquired when the furnace would be completed so that it might be sent up to Lake Superior; he supposing it was being made in Detroit. These unfavorable circumstances, combined with the financial depression of 1857, at which time the company were obliged to sell their iron for $22, while the cost of its production was $24 per ton, gave no return save anxiety and disappointment.

In the spring of 1860, the furnace was leased for four years to Mr. I. B. B. Case, he agreeing to deliver the pig-iron on board the vessels at Marquette for $17.50 per ton, and paying all the expenses of its manufacture; the company furnishing the timber, standing, for the charcoal, and giving him the advantage of a contract with the Jackson Company for the ore, the royalty for which ($1.00 per ton of iron) he paid. This price proved to be less than the iron could be made for. The furnace was burnt down August 9th, 1864; number two stack was at once rebuilt and put in operation in January following, by Mr. Case.

In 1865, Dr. J. C. McKenzie, then President of the Pioneer Iron Company, entered into negotiations with the Iron Cliff Company, which subsequently resulted, largely through the instrumentality of Major T. B. Brooks, Vice-President of the latter company, in an arrangement (ratified by the stockholders of both companies, March 10th, 1866) by which the Iron Cliff Company came into possession of the furnace, on consideration that it pay to its former proprietors one-third of the profits of the business. Soon after the two companies became practically one, through the purchase of the stock of the Pioneer by the Iron Cliff Company.

The Detroit Iron Mining Company filed articles 15th August, 1857. Capital, $500,000, in 20,000 shares at $25 each, with office in Detroit. Corporators were Patrick Tregent, Guy Foot, Joseph

P. Whittemore, John H. Harmon, John W. Strong, Oville B. Dibble, Nelson P. Stewart, Andrew T. McReynolds, Thornton T. Brodhead, Henry T. Stringham, Henry J. Buckley, Joseph L. Langley, of Detroit, and Edwin H. Thomson, of Flint. The company having ascertained, as they believed, that their lands did not contain sufficient ore for mining purposes, sold them to Mr. J. P. Pendill, and upon them is now built a portion of the village of Negaunee. The McComber mine, which lies at a short distance south of that village, is on this land.

The Excelsior Iron Company filed articles October 6th, 1857. Capital stock, $100,000; 4,000 shares, at $25 each. Corporators were: C. T. Harvey, Sarah V. E. Harvey, E. C. Hungerford, George P. Cummings, and Joseph Harvey, all of Marquette. This company did little but organize. It originated with Mr. C. T. Harvey, and some of the land which it owned has since proved to be valuable mining property, as it embraces the Barnum mine, now owned by the Iron Cliff Company; upon it is also situated a portion of the village of Ishpeming.

The Lake Superior Foundry Company filed articles of association July 14th, 1858. Capital stock (paid in), $10,000; 400 shares, at $25 each. *Corporators:* John Thorn, Isaac Maynard, Thomas Maynard, Nathan E. Platt, of Utica, N. Y., and Charles T. Harvey, of Marquette, Mich. This establishment, which was started in 1858, is now running on a much enlarged scale, under the name of the **Iron Bay Foundry,** D. H. Merritt, proprietor. The location is near the bay, within the city of Marquette.

The Grand Island Iron Company filed articles May 3d, 1859. Capital, $400,000; 16,000 shares, at $25 each; paid in, $110,000. *Corporators:* Thomas Sparks, Henry W. Andrews, William Lippincott, John L. Newbold, John D. Taylor, John R. Wilmer, Samuel Pleasants, William M. Baird, Samuel J. Christian, L. de la Cuesta, William A. Rhodes, Charles Lennig, James C. Fisher, Samuel T. Fisher, Lewis Seal, Coleman Fisher, Henry Maule, William Gaul, J. T. Linnard, Howard Spencer, Caleb Jones, Charles W. Carrigan, of Philadelphia, and Devere Burr, of Washington, D. C., with office in Philadelphia. The property belonging to this company, consisting of 3,000 acres of land, situated on Grand Island harbor, in Munising Township, was sold in 1867 to the Schoolcraft Iron Company, and their operations were confined to some minor improvements in the way of wharves, etc.

The Northern Iron Company filed articles May 16th, 1859. Capital stock, $125,000, in 5,000 shares of $25 each. *Corporators:* John C. Tucker, Moses A. Hoppock, of N. Y., and Charles T. Harvey, of Marquette, with office in Marquette. This company was formed through the efforts of C. T. Harvey, and constructed a blast-furnace at the mouth of the Chocolate river, 5 miles south of Marquette, with a view of making pig-iron with bituminous coal, being the first enterprise of this kind inaugurated in this region. After making about 1,000 tons of iron, the furnace was changed into and run as a charcoal furnace up to June, 1867; since which time it has not been working, and it is now being changed back into a bituminous coal furnace. This is the first charcoal furnace on the Upper Peninsula that has been permanently blown out.

1863.—The great financial prostration of 1857, combined with numerous causes which readily suggest themselves, naturally embarrassed and, in instances, extinguished the new and struggling enterprises of Lake Superior to the extent, that comparatively little was done in the manufacture of iron or the mining of ore up to the opening of 1863. During this interval of time no companies of importance filed articles of association in this region. Very early in the war, however, the greatly increased demand for iron which it occasioned, began to be felt over the country and finally extended its influence to Lake Superior, causing the revival of the languishing enterprises already started and the organization of many new ones. The abundance of ore, together with its surpassing richness in iron and freedom from deleterious substances, the facility with which it could be mined and the greatly improved means of transportation, were becoming generally known, and the strength and exceeding tenacity of the iron manufactured therefrom universally acknowledged. Thus altogether there was opened to the Marquette region an outlook of prosperity, which it had not heretofore experienced, enabling its mining and iron manufacturing companies to assume a basis of more successful operation, and confidently to push forward their improvements.

The articles of association of the **Teal Lake Co.** were filed on the 7th of June, 1863, with a capital stock of $500,000, in 20,000 shares, and an amount paid in of $100,000. The corporators were George A. Fellows, John W. Wheelwright and Charles L. Wright, of New York, with office in New York. Beyond some explorations this company never did any work on Lake Superior, confining its operations chiefly to stock speculations, it being the only iron mining company organized in this region, whose stock was sold at the Brokers' Board in New York.

The articles of association of the **Morgan Iron Co.** were filed on the 1st of July, 1863, with a capital stock of $50,000, in 2,000 shares, and $26,000 paid in. Corporators were Joseph S. Fay, of Boston, Lewis H. Morgan, of New York, Harriet H. Ely, Samuel P. Ely, Ellen S. White and Cornelius Donkersley, of Marquette, with office in Marquette. The capital stock was subsequently increased to $250,000, in 10,000 shares fully paid. The company own 20,000 acres of timber land. In 1863 they constructed the Morgan Furnace, eight miles west of Marquette on the M. H. and O. R. R., and the location has since become known as "Morgan." The furnace was put up under the supervision of Mr. C. Donkersley and has been successful. It went into blast Nov. 27th, 1863, making that year 337 tons of iron, and was the first furnace company in the region to pay a dividend to its stockholders. The extreme high price of iron, created by the war, enabled the company to realize, during the first ten months of the operation of the furnace, a dividend of 100 per cent. over and above the total outlay in its construction. Having exhausted the fuel in the vicinity, the company constructed charcoal kilns upon their lands at a distance of nine miles north from the furnace, and provided for the transportation of the coal by building a wooden railway thereto. The kilns and railway were made in 1869, and most of the coal now used is prepared at these kilns.

In 1867 the Morgan Company built the **Champion Furnace**, which went into blast Dec. 4th of that year. This furnace is located at what is now Champion village, on the line of the M. H. and O. R. R., 31 miles west from Marquette. The ore used is mainly magnetic from the Champion mine, and the record of the furnace is one of gratifying success.

The articles of association of the **Marquette Iron Co.** were filed April 9th, 1864, with a capital of $500,000, in 20,000 shares of $25 each. *Corporators:* George Worthington, Truman P. Handy, Samuel L. Mather, N. B. Hurlbut, Richard C. Parsons, G. D. McMillen, John Outhwaite, of Cleveland, Ohio, and Charles I. Walker, of Detroit, Mich. This company was organized for the purpose of mining iron ore and owns 400 acres of land, lying contiguous to, and south of, the Cleveland mines, 240 acres of which was originally held by the latter company. Its stock is held by stockholders of the Cleveland Company. The year of its organization it shipped 3,922 tons of ore, and has been somewhat regularly in operation since that period.

The Magnetic Iron Co. was organized in 1864; the articles of the company were filed May the 6th of that year, with a capital stock of $500,000 in 20,000 shares. *Corporators:* John C. McKenzie, Alex. Campbell, of Marquette, and Edwin Parsons, of New York. Office in Marquette, but now in Philadelphia, Pa. The property owned by this company consists of 520 acres of land on Section 20, T. 47, R. 30. A shaft 60 feet in depth has been sunk, and other explorations made to test the ore-deposit and the company expect to take out ore, as soon as a branch road is built to the mine.

The Chippewa mining property comprises Section 22, T. 47, R. 30, W., owned by J. S. Waterman, of Philadelphia, and S. S. Burt, of Marquette; considerable exploring has been done on the property and some fair ore found, but no mining done. This property lies on the east side of Michigamme river and opposite the Magnetic and Cannon properties.

The Phœnix Iron Co. filed its articles of association June 7th, 1864. Capital, $500,000, in 20,000 shares, of which $20,000 was paid in. The Corporators were Wm. C. Duncan, Henry J. Buckley and Simon Mandlebaum, of Detroit, with office in Detroit. No mining or manufacturing was ever done in the Marquette Region by this company.

Washington Iron Company filed its articles of association July 30th, 1864. Capital stock, $500,000, in 20,000 shares, at $25 per share; amount paid in, $100,000. The Corporators were Edward Breitung, I. B. B. Case and Samuel P. Ely, of Marquette, Joseph S. Fay, of Boston, and Edwin Parsons, of New York.

This company made its first shipments of ore (4,782 tons) in 1865, and has since been in active operation. The land owned by the company comprises 1,000 acres in the northeast part of T. 47, R. 29, which was purchased of Silas C. Smith, J. J. St. Clair, J. C. McKenzie, and Alexander Campbell, who derived their title from the United States Government. The mine is on the M. H. and O. railroad, at a distance by rail from Marquette of 27 miles. All the company's surplus earnings have been expended in making extensive improvements, of which an adit or tunnel, now over 1,100 feet long, constitutes the chief. Their plans and expenditures have been on an extensive scale, and contemplate operations for a long period to come. The details of the mine, shafts, adit and underground workings, together with the geological structure, are fully shown by the map of the Washington mine, accompanying this report.

The Bancroft Iron Co. filed its articles of association September 12th, 1864; capital stock being $250,000 in 10,000 shares, of which $100,000 was paid in. The Corporators were Wm. E. Dodge, of New York, Samuel L. Mather, John Outhwaite and Wm. L. Cutter, of Cleveland, Peter White and Samuel P. Ely, of Marquette, and Henry L. Fisher and L. S. McKnight, of Detroit, with office in Marquette.

The location of this company is the same as that of the Forest Iron Co., heretofore described; the property of the latter having been purchased by Mr. S. R. Gay, in 1860, he erected on the water-power employed by the old forge a blast-furnace, this being the second furnace he had built on Dead river, the one at Collinsville having been constructed by him the winter before.

Mr. Gay * having died in 1863, his furnace at Forestville passed to the ownership of the Bancroft Iron Co., who have since continued

* It is a fact worthy of note, in connection with the services rendered by Mr. Gay, that he was the first among the iron men who visited Lake Superior to recognize the value of the hematite ores; while engaged in the construction of the Pioneer Furnace, he observed that the Jackson Co. were wasting their soft hematite in large quantities, they supposing it to be worthless. He at once called their attention to its value.

to operate it. The furnace is worked by Mr. L. Huillier on contract, the company paying him a certain price per ton for the iron delivered on the dock in Marquette.

The articles of **The Iron Cliff Co.** were filed September 15th, 1864, with a capital stock of $1,000,000, in 40,000 shares at $25 each. *Corporators:* William B. Ogden and John W. Foster, of Chicago, and Samuel J. Tilden, of New York. Office at Negaunee, Mich. This company in 1864 purchased of the St. Mary's Ship Canal and Mineral Land Co. the 38,000 acres of land which that company owned in Marquette county. Subsequently, as heretofore mentioned, the Iron Cliff Co. came into possession of the Pioneer Co.'s property, thus increasing its estate to over 40,000 acres. The company soon began the construction of a furnace near the Foster mine, which has never been completed. They own and are working the *Barnum* and the *Foster mines*, the latter of which was opened in the spring of 1865. The product is a soft hematite, which forms a good mixture with hard ores. This mine is situated on Secs. 22 and 23, T. 47, R. 27. The first shipment of ore therefrom was made in 1866, and the mine has since been continually worked.

The **Barnum mine** is situated on Sec. 9, T. 47, R. 27, connecting with the Lake Superior Co.'s principal opening. The first shipments of ore were made during 1868, the ore being specular and of excellent quality. The C. and N. W. R. R. has a branch running into the mine, over which shipments are made. The mine is supplied with pumping and hoisting machinery. The map of the Lake Superior mine, which will be found in the accompanying Atlas, embraces the Barnum mine.

On that portion of the estate purchased of the Excelsior Company, in addition to the Barnum, a deposit of specular ore has been found near the corner of Secs. 5, 6, 7, and 8, T. 47, R. 27, which promises well; a branch railroad has been surveyed to it. Besides those already mentioned the company have several other openings. One on Sec. 15, adjoining the Pittsburgh and Lake Angeline Co., opened during the past season, which gives a fine showing of hematite ore. The Cliff-Parsons, also opened during the past season, adjoins the *Old Parsons*, on Sec. 21, T. 47, R. 27.

Another opening is near the quarter-post between Secs. 17 and 18, T. 47, R. 26, from which ore was shipped during the season. A second opening is being made on this same line, at a point farther north, near the section corner. These openings belong to the Negaunee Hematite Group. In addition to their own mines the company are working the Pioneer opening of the Jackson mine on a lease. Near the Foster mine the company have in operation a saw-mill, to which is attached shingle and lath mills.

In 1864 the *Ogden* and *Tilden* mines, situated on Secs. 13, 23, and 24, T. 47, R. 27, were extensively opened, and the branch road, which also extends to the Foster, built to them. The ores, however, proved of too low a percentage to sell in the then existing market, and the work was abandoned. The purchasers of the Iron Cliff estate also controlled the Chicago and Northwestern Railroad, and a short time previous to the purchase effected a consolidation with the Peninsula Road of Michigan, with a view to the future development of iron deposits on this extensive property, and the control of the railroad facilities for transporting the product of these and other mines to Lake Michigan.

The Iron Mountain Mining Co. filed its articles of association Nov. 1, 1864, paid in $100,000. *Corporators :* Geo. E. Hall, of Cleveland, O., Richard Hays, Henry A. Laughlin, and Irwin B. Laughlin, of Pittsburgh, and Gilbert D. Johnson, of Ishpeming. The company own 320 acres of land, being the S. ½ of Sec. 14, T. 47, R. 27. The first shipments of ore were made in 1865, a branch of the C. and N. W. R. R. extending into the mine. All work at this mine has been discontinued, owing to the leanness and refractory nature of the ore, its yield being less than 50 per cent. of iron in the furnace. This mine has been recently leased to Messrs. Clark and Colwell, under whose auspices work will be resumed in the spring of 1873, with the view of finding hematite.

The Michigan Iron Co. filed its articles of association Dec. 30th, 1864. Capital stock, $500,000, in 20,000 shares of $25 each. *Corporators:* Henry J. Colwell, Andrew G. Clark and Samuel P. Ely, of Marquette, with office there.

This company own a large amount of woodlands, two furnaces and considerable other manufacturing property. The Michigan

4

furnace was built by them in 1866, went into blast June, 1867, and has since been in constant operation; it is on the M. H. and O. R. R., 23 miles west of Marquette, and is surrounded by the village of Clarksburgh.

The remaining furnace owned by this company, known as the Greenwood, went into blast in June, 1865, and was purchased by the Michigan Co., together with about 8,000 acres of land of the M. and O. Rd., in 1868. Greenwood is 27 miles from Marquette, on the line of the M. H. and O. R. R., and the furnace has continued in blast since the time of its purchase by the present owners.

In 1864 **The Peninsula Railroad,** from its junction with the Marquette and Ontonagon Railroad at Negaunee to Escanaba (a distance of 62 miles), was completed and put in operation. The project which has resulted in opening this important outlet to the great iron mines was first definitely broached in 1855. In that year meetings were held at Ontonagon, Marquette, and all important points to Milwaukee, with a view to the united action of the people along the route, in the endeavor to obtain governmental aid in the construction of the railroad. These meetings were chiefly initiated by Mr. C. T. Harvey and H. B. Ely. Mr. Harvey, John Burt and others, immediately proceeded to Washington and were instrumental in obtaining from Congress the passage of an act, June, 1856, which donated a large amount of land in aid of railroad enterprises.

Among the projects for which provision was thus made in this grant were the building of a railroad from Marquette to Little Bay de Noquette, and also from thence to Menominee, as well as for the extension of a road from Fond du Lac to this latter point. In 1859, the Chicago, St. Paul and Fond du Lac Railroad Co. (which company had received from Wisconsin the congressional grant), through the agents of its bond-holders, organized under the name of the Chicago and Northwestern Railway Company, and in 1861, under a law of the State of Wisconsin, proceeded to locate a line by the way of Fort Howard to the Menominee river. In 1862 the State of Wisconsin conferred upon the C. and N. W. R. R. Co. all the franchises and rights heretofore granted to the several companies of which it had become the successor; and in the same year the road was extended to Green bay, a distance of 242 miles from Chicago.

The Iron Mountain road was completed and became consolidated with the Bay de Noquette railroad in 1858. The location of the Marquette and State line grant was changed by act of Congress in 1860, so as to extend from Menominee northward along the shore of Green Bay, and thence to Negaunee; and in 1863 the Marquette and State line grant, with the remainder of the Bay de Noquette grant (being coincident with it from Negaunee to Escanaba) having been suffered to lapse, were, by agreement between the grantees, conferred by the State upon the Peninsula Railroad Co., of Michigan. Surveys were made in 1862 (the enterprise being set on foot by C. T. Harvey, who subsequently transferred it to S. J. Tilden, of New York), and work began in the summer of 1863, and in December of the following year the road was opened to the public. During the preceding October, however, the Peninsula road had consolidated with the Chicago and Northwestern, and the line from Marquette to Menominee became known as the Peninsula division of the C. and N. W. R. R. The lands owned by the Peninsula division embrace in the aggregate 1,200,000 acres.

An extensive ore dock was constructed at Escanaba, upwards of 1,300 feet in length, 32 feet in height, and 37 feet in width, capable of receiving in the pockets 20,000 tons of ore at a time, and of shuting it thence into the holds of vessels. This dock was built at an expense of about $200,000. Communication to this excellent and accessible harbor being thus opened, and such ample facilities afforded for the transmission and shipment, large and increasing amounts of ore have since been carried yearly over this route.

Corning Iron Co. filed articles of association March 23d, 1865. Capital stock, $200,000—8,000 shares of $25. *Corporators:* G. C. Davidson, S. Churchill and Chas. T. Harvey, with office in Marquette. This company did nothing worthy of note.

The New York Iron Mining Co. Incorporated April 8th, 1865. Capital stock, $250,000, in 10,000 shares of $25 each. *Corporators:* Samuel J. Tilden, J. P. Sinnett and J. Rankin, of New York.

The mining operations of this company are conducted in the southeast ¼ of southeast ¼, Sect. 3, T. 47, R. 27, being 16 miles west from Marquette and adjoining the Cleveland. The mine is worked under a lease from Mr. A. R. Harlow and the stock is all held by Mr. S. J. Tilden and Messrs. W. L. and F. W. Wetmore. Operations were commenced in the mine in 1864, during which year 8,000 tons of ore were shipped. The statement of its yearly product and other details will be found by reference to the tables in this work; the workings and geological structure are shown by a map. This company is identical with the New York and Boston Iron Mining Co., and also with the New York iron mine, incorporated March 31st, 1865; it soon after changed to the New York Iron Mining Co., as above described.

The Pittsburgh and Lake Angeline Iron Co. was incorporated Nov. 11th, 1865. Capital stock, $500,000, in 20,000 shares of $25 each. James Laughlin, *President*, T. Dwight Eels, *Secretary* and *Treasurer*. The company own 1,376 acres of land, situated in T. 47 and 48, R. 27 and 28, of the former Town., and R. 31 of the latter. They also hold a lease of about 300 acres, on which is located the Edwards mine. The company's mines consist of the Lake Angeline and Edwards; the *Lake Angeline* mine is situated on the south shore of Lake Angeline and on the line of the M. H. and O. and C. and N. W. R. Rs., 17 miles from Marquette and 66 miles from Escanaba, and produces both specular and hematite ore, the latter of first quality.

The **Edwards mine** lying contiguous to the Washington, is also on the line of the M. H. and O. R. R., distant from Marquette 28 miles, and produces only magnetic ore. Work was commenced in 1865, the first shipments being made in the following year. The mining is all conducted underground, the ore being raised to the surface through shafts and is the only mine in the Iron Region which has been exclusively worked in this way. The results of this company's operations are shown in the accompanying tables and the mine workings by maps and illustrations.

The Schoolcraft Iron Co. filed articles of association April 8th, 1866. Capital stock, $500,000, in 20,000 shares of $25 each. Paid in, $250,000; the remaining 10,000 shares being held by the company. *Corporators:* Hiram A. Burt, Peter White and H. R. Mather, of Marquette; office at Marquette, Michigan.

A furnace was constructed by this company at Munising, Schoolcraft county, on Grand Island bay, which went into blast in June, 1868, and was blown out in about six months thereafter. The furnace continued "in and out" of blast somewhat irregularly, until the company went into bankruptcy. In 1871 the furnace and other property, including 40,000 acres of hard wood land, which had belonged to them, passed into the hands of Peter White, Esq., by whom it was transferred to the Munising Iron Co., an organization effected for the purpose of owning and operating this estate, which is now being successfully done. Mr. Peter White, of Marquette, is managing director.

The Marquette and Pacific Rolling-Mill Co. filed its articles of association Oct. 1st, 1866. Capital stock, $500,000, in 20,000 shares of $25 each. The corporators were John Burt, Samuel P. Ely, Wm. Burt, Edward Breitung, Timothy T. Hurley, Cornelius Donkersley, W. L. Wetmore, Peter White and Alvin C. Burt, of Marquette. Office in Marquette, Mich.

The company has constructed at Marquette a bituminous blast-furnace, with rolling-mill connected therewith. The works are located near the lake shore, at a short distance south from the city, went into operation in the summer of 1871, and are connected with the M. H. and O. R. R. by a branch track. Upon their land at Negaunee, the company have opened a mine of manganiferous hematite ore, to which a side track has been extended, connecting it with both railroads; from this mine the company's furnace at Marquette is in part supplied. This rolling mill is the first erected on Lake Superior, and the furnace the first which has continually used bituminous coal. H. A. Burt is superintendent.

The *Fayette Furnace* was constructed and put in operation in December, 1867, the enterprise originating with Major Fayette Brown, general agent of **The Jackson Iron Co.** It is located at "Snail Shell Harbor," in Big Bay de Noquette, 20 miles east of Escanaba, and about it has grown up the beautiful village of Fayette. It is owned by the Jackson Iron Co., with general office in Cleveland, Ohio. The company own 16,000 acres of land, excellently well timbered with hard wood, and generally adapted to agricultural purposes, the soil being of limestone formation. From the ledges of limestone, which exist in the immediate neighborhood, material for the necessary flux is obtained, as well as for the manufacture of all the lime used by the company. They possess a full complement of charcoal kilns, and a large portion of the necessary wood is purchased, the company preferring to save their own timber as long as possible. This wood is delivered by the parties of whom it is bought at the furnace, or along the line of the company's railroad, of which they have constructed for this purpose six miles, laid with T-rail, and operated with two small locomotive engines, it being the only furnace on the Upper Peninsula that operates a locomotive railway for the exclusive purpose of transporting fuel. The company have also a saw-mill, machine-shop, etc. The furnace, as originally started, consisted of a single stack, which is shown in the accompanying illustration. A second one was subsequently erected, and both stacks have since been in operation with results more favorable, than any other charcoal furnaces using Lake Superior ore. The extraordinary favorable working of these furnaces will be fully realized from the following statements, furnished from the company's reports: During the 73 days immediately preceding April 13th, 1872, there were made in the No. 1 stack an average of $27\frac{6}{10}$ tons per day, using 94 bushels of charcoal and 125 lbs. of limestone per ton, the ore being from the Jackson mine and yielding from $62\frac{1}{2}$ to $64\frac{1}{2}$ %. On August 4th following, the same stack again went into blast, making, during the first quarter, a period of 91 days, 2,258 tons of iron, an average of 27^{8} tons per day, using by measure 92 bushels of charcoal per ton. No. 2 was also in blast during a portion of the same period with corresponding results. On December 14th No. 2 stack had produced, during the previous four weeks, an average of $26\frac{39}{100}$ tons per day, and on January 18th, 1873, had produced, during the previous five weeks, an average of $29\frac{34}{100}$ tons per day; the charge used during this time was $26\frac{1}{2}$ (called 30) bushels of charcoal, 1,000 lbs. of ore ($\frac{1}{3}$ soft and $\frac{2}{3}$ hard specular Jackson), 35 lbs. of limestone and 10 lbs. of clay.

These results require no comment relative to the efficiency of the management. The coal is of the best quality, kept dry under shelter, as is also the ore, which is crushed finer than is customary. The stacks are each 42 feet high inside and 9 feet 6 inches bosh;

4 feet 8 inches, and 5 feet 8 inches diameter, 3 feet below the top, and 4 feet and 5 feet at the top respectively. The hearths are 4 feet diameter battering from the bottom; the tuyeres, three in number, with 3½ inch nozzle, are placed 40 inches above the bottom of the hearth. Two blowing engines are used, the cylinders respectively 36 and 48 inches in length, with diameter of 50 and 44 inches. The engines make from 24 to 28 revolutions per minute, and both of them are only run when the two stacks are in operation. The temperature of the hot blast averages in one about 600° and in the other 750°. Originally No. 2 stack had a five-foot cone, but did not make as much iron, nor as cheaply, as the other, until the cone was reduced in height to 4 feet 4 inches, since which time it has worked equally well with the other. The total product of these furnaces during 1871 and '72 was 19,117 tons, which were used as follows:

For	Bessemer Steel..............	17,465 tons.
"	Malleable Iron	88 "
"	Wheels.....................	787 "
"	Foundry, etc................	400 "
"	Forge purposes..............	377 "

Genl. Agt., Major Fayette Brown, Cleveland, Ohio. Local Agt., C. L. Rhodes, Fayette, Mich. Founder, Jos. Harris, Fayette, Mich.

The Deer Lake Iron Company.—Articles of association were filed July 9th, 1868. Capital, $75,000—3,000 shares at $25 each. *Corporators:* George P. Cummings, of Marquette, Edward C. Hungerford, of Chester, Conn., Gardner Green, Caleb B. Rogers, Moses Pierce, Samuel B. Case, Theodore T. McCurdy, John E. Ward, James Lloyd Greene, James C. Colby (Ex'r), Daniel T. Gulliver, William R. Potter and Enoch F. Chapman, of Norwich, Conn.; Giles Blague, Jr., New York, Geo. Smith, New York, G. F. Ward, E. R. Ward, Old Saybrook, Conn., and James H. Mainwaring, of Montville, Conn., with office at Marquette, Mich.

This company organized for the purpose of smelting iron ore, and immediately constructed a furnace, which went into operation in Sept., 1868. This furnace, the smallest in the district, is located at Deer lake on the Carp river, two miles north from the village of Ishpeming on the M. H. and O. R. R., with which place it is connected by a tram railway. The stack is 33 feet high and 7 feet 8 inches bosh, thus making it perhaps the smallest furnace which has been built in the United States during the past 7 years. Another peculiarity of this furnace is the comparatively enormous size of its hot-blast oven, to which is doubtless due in part the favorable results, which, considering its small size and peculiar management, the furnace has accomplished. The oven, on the Pleyer plan, contains 45 tons of metal, which is 50 per cent. more than that contained in the ovens of our largest charcoal furnaces; having twice the capacity of the Deer lake stack. The furnace is driven by water, employing an 18-inch turbine wheel under 35 feet head, thus leaving all the gas available for heating the blast, which is brought to an extremely high temperature. It runs but six days in the week, "banking up" Saturday night and starting again on Sunday night. Notwithstanding an arrangement necessarily disadvantageous to the greatest production, the furnace has averaged during several consecutive weeks 11 tons of pig-iron per day, using 110 bushels of charcoal to the ton, one-half of which is made from pine slabs,—the ore used being hard ore from the New York mine, averaging 66 per cent. The origin of this enterprise is due to Mr. E. C. Hungerford, who also determined its unusual size and the peculiar policy under which the furnace has been managed. Near the present one the company are now building a new iron shell furnace, 9 feet bosh.

The Cannon Iron Company.—Articles filed July, 1869. Capital, $500,000; 20,000 shares, $25 each. *Corporators:* Bernard A. Hoppes and Wm. H. Berry, of Philadelphia, and Samuel S. Burt, of Marquette, with office in Philadelphia. This company organized for the purpose of mining iron ore, but beyond making explorations on their lands with this view, nothing has as yet been done.

Bay Furnace Company.—Articles filed July 19th, 1869. Capital stock, $150,000; 6,000 shares at $25 each. *Corporators:* William Shea, of Munising, Mich., George Wagner, Jay C. Morse, Frank B. Spear and James Pickands, of Marquette, John Outhwaite, of Cleveland, and John P. Outhwaite, of Ishpeming, Mich., with office in Marquette.

This concern organized for the purpose of smelting iron ore, and immediately proceeded to the construction of a blast-furnace for that purpose. This furnace was completed and went into operation on the 6th of March, 1870. It is located at Onota, in Schoolcraft county, on Grand Island bay, 40 miles from Marquette. But one stack was originally constructed; a second one, however, has since been erected and put in readiness for the blast. The ore used is from the Cleveland and McComber mines, received by the way of Marquette. This company own about 20,000 acres of land, mostly hard wood timber, from which the fuel for the furnace is obtained.

The Whetstone Iron Company.—Organized Aug. 20th, 1869. Capital stock, $150,000, in 6,000 shares of $25 each. Office at Marquette. This company have not commenced operations. Corporators were William Burts, Samuel Peck, A. A. Cole, Thomas O. Hampton, Clark Stratton, A. S. Harvey and A. G. Benedict.

Champion Iron Company.—Organized August 23d, 1869, with a capital stock of $500,000, in 20,000 shares of $25 each. *Corporators:* Joseph S. Fay, of Boston, Edwin Parsons, of New York, Thomas C. Foster, of Cambridge, Mass., and Samuel P. Ely and Peter White, of Marquette. The company own about 1,600 acres of land, but their mining operations are conducted on that portion of their land comprising the south half of Sec. 31, T. 48, R. 29, being 32 miles by railroad from Marquette. The ore is principally magnetic, though a large amount of slate ore is obtained. The Champion mine is upon the south outcrop of the magnetic ore basin, which underlies Lake Michigamme, and near the village of Champion, about half a mile distant from the furnace of that name. The company are now working chiefly underground, as is fully shown in Map VII. of Atlas, where the geological structure and all other important details will also be found.

The Lake Superior Foundry Company filed their articles of association Sept. 2d, 1869, with a capital stock of $50,000—2,000 shares at $25 each. *Corporators:* Daniel H. Merritt, Lotan E. Osborn, Henry J. Colwell, William L. Wetmore, Jay C. Morse, Alfred Kidder, James Pickands and Thomas Fitzgerald, of Marquette, Mich.; Gilbert D. Johnson, Seymour Johnson, Harvey Diamond and Robert Nelson, of Ishpeming. The works (located at

Ishpeming) are quite extensive and adapted to general and particular foundry and machine work. (See Iron Bay Foundry, p. 33.)

Silas C. Smith Iron Company.—Articles of association filed Jan., 1870. Capital, $500,000, in 20,000 shares at $25 each. *Corporators:* Silas C. Smith, of Ashtabula, O., Oliver F. Forsyth and Wm. H. Lyons, of Flint, Mich., with office at Ashtabula, O.

The property of this company consists of 703 acres of land in Sections 18, 20, and 28, T. 45, R. 25, upon which have been made numerous openings, showing soft hematite ore in quantity, the main one being near the E. ¼ post of Sect. 18. A tunnel is being driven into the deposit, of sufficient size for the admission of railway cars from a branch road five miles in length, which connects with the Chicago and Northwestern railroad. The ore at present is loaded into the cars from temporary docks, provided with pockets for that purpose. The principal stockholders are Silas C. Smith, the discoverer, General James Pierce, of Sharpsville, Pa., and Henry Fassett, of Ashtabula, O. The shipments of ore and other details will be seen by reference to the mining tables.

The Pittsburgh and Lake Superior Iron Co. filed articles of association June 28th, 1870. Capital stock, $500,000, in 20,000 shares of $25 each. *Corporators:* James McAuley, C. T. Spang, C. G. Hussy, Thos. M. Howe and James M. Cooper, of Pittsburgh; Sherman J. Bacon, of New York, Joseph G. Hussy, of Cleveland and W. M. Sinclair, of Philadelphia; with office at Pittsburgh, Pa. The company own 2,691 acres of land in Towns. 47 and 48, Ranges 25 and 26, their title to which was derived direct from the United States Government. Work was commenced on their property near the Cascade mines in Sept., 1872, houses, etc., were erected, a railroad side track built and a pit opened on Sec. 32, which is called the Hussy mine, and from which about 2,000 tons have been shipped.

The Republic Iron Co. was organized Oct. 20th, 1870. Capital stock, $500,000, in 20,000 shares. Office in Marquette. *Corporators:* E. Breitung, S. P. Ely and Ed. Parsons. This company own 1,328 acres of land, being in part in Sections 6, 7, and 18, T. 46, R. 29, comprising what was formerly known as Smith mountain, which is unquestionably one of the largest deposits of pure specular and magnetic ore on the Upper Peninsula, if not in the United States. The great extent and value of this deposit was observed and commented on by the early United States surveyors, when engaged in running the township lines in that locality in 1846. The property was explored and selected by Silas C. Smith, of Marquette, and entered in the name of Dr. James St. Clair, in 1854 and 1855. A branch from the M. H. and O. R. R. has been constructed to the mine, over which the shipments of ore are now being made. See Tables, Plts. XII. and XIII. of Atlas. A complete map of this property, based upon careful surveys, exhibiting the topography, geological structure, magnetism and other important details, will be found in the Atlas accompanying this work, together with full descriptions.

The Cascade Iron Co. is an association of Pittsburgh men, owning 3,120 acres of land in Sections 19, 20, 29, 30, 31, and 25, T. 47, Ranges 26 and 27. These lands were entered by Waterman Palmer and purchased by the present company in 1869. An examination of the iron deposits in this locality was made by Dr. Douglas Houghton, in 1845, while engaged in running the interior section lines. (See Appendix D., Vol. II.)

The company's mines are provided with side tracks, connecting with a branch road of six miles in length to the C. and N. W. R. R. Mining operations commenced in 1871, and the openings (including the leased mines) are seven in number. There are other improvements, such as a saw-mill run by water, a store, sufficient number of dwellings, barns, repair-shop, etc. The expenditure which these improvements (including the branch railroad and side tracks) have necessitated has been very large, and future operations are contemplated upon a scale of considerable magnitude. (See Statistical Tables.)

The Cascade Company, under another organization, to wit, **The Escanaba Iron Co.**, are constructing a blast-furnace at Escanaba, to consist of two stacks, one of which will go into operation in January, 1873; the height of stack, 56 feet; diameter of bosh, 12 feet. The entire structure is built in the most complete and substantial manner, and when finished, will probably not be surpassed, if equalled, in capacity, durability, or beauty, by any similar furnace in the United States. The principal owners are Joseph Kirkpatrick, William Bagaley, James Lyon, William Smith, Samuel Riddle and Samuel Hartman; Joseph Kirkpatrick, *President*, James Lyon, *Treasurer*, and John L. Agnew, *General Superintendent*.

The Emma Mine, one of the Cascade openings, is on the E. ½ of E. ½ of N. E. ¼, Sec. 31, and is being worked under a lease from the Cascade Company by an association of Pittsburgh gentlemen, who are represented at the mine by Mr. James E. Clark. They commenced shipping ore in 1872.

The Bagaley Mine, likewise one of the Cascade openings, is also worked under a lease from the Cascade Company, by Messrs. Wilcox & Bagaley, and its total product is about 6,000 tons.

The Gribben Iron Co., having a capital stock of $500,000, in 20,000 shares of $25 each, was organized 1872. The mining property comprises a lease on the S. E. ¼, Sec. 28, T. 47, R. 26, being on the Cascade range. Mining and exploring operations during the season have resulted in taking out considerable ore, some of which has been shipped for testing. The company have built a side track, which connects with the Cascade branch of the C. and N. W. R. R. Officers of the company are: W. C. McComber, *President*, C. H. Hopkins, *Secretary*, and James Mathews, *Treasurer;* all of Negaunee, Mich.

The Carr Iron Co. was also organized in the summer of 1872, with a capital stock of $250,000. Its real estate comprises forty acres of land, situated on Sec. 33, T. 47, R. 26, being also in the Cascade range. The officers are Amos Root, *President*, Jackson, Mich.; E.W. Barber, *Secretary*, Jackson, Mich.; and W. H. Maynard, *Managing Director*, Marquette.

Negaunee Hematite Mines. A large number of new companies have recently been organized for the purpose of mining hematite ore in the vicinity of Negaunee. These new locations, which have been and are in process of being developed, are situated in Sections 6, 7, 8, and 18, T. 47, R. 26, and comprise what are known as the McComber, Grand Central, Rolling Mill, Himrod, Ada, Negaunee, Calhoun and Spurr, Green Bay, Allen, the Iron Cliff "Sec. 18," and other mines. The McComber mine, opened by William C. Mc-

Comber in 1870, is worked on a lease from J. P. Pendill, of Negaunee, at a royalty of fifty cents per ton for ore. The mine has been worked for the past three seasons, and in the spring of 1872 the lease was sold to parties interested in the Cleveland mine, who in July organized a company. The Rolling Mill mine, heretofore spoken of, is worked in part under a lease from A. L. Crawford. The company, however, own the greater portion of the land.

All these workings, except Sec. 18 and the McComber, are worked on leases from Edward Breitung, at 75 cents per ton royalty, he having leased from the owners, Messrs. Harvey and Reynolds, at 50 cents per ton royalty. Some of these pits have been worked during the past season, and nearly all of them are prepared for active operations during the coming year. Railroad side tracks are either completed, or in process of construction, to the several mines ; dwellings and other improvements have been made, or are contemplated at each, and several of the locations bid fair to be the scene of active mining operations. The product is for the most part a soft hematite, containing usually from one to five per cent. of manganese, which renders the ore more easily worked in the furnace and is probably beneficial to the iron. The yield of metallic iron of the best of these ores is 50 per cent. and upwards, the average, however, is below that. See Map No. V. and Table Pl. XII. of Atlas.

Among the promising iron properties upon which work has been commenced during the present season, and from which large shipments may be reasonably anticipated, are the Michigamme and Spurr Mountain mines, at both of which work has actively commenced ; side tracks are being constructed at both places, connecting with the M. H. and O. R. R. The mines are situated upon the same magnetic range and are about two miles apart.

The property of the **Spurr Mountain Co.** (which company was organized in September last) comprises 160 acres of land, and the point at which mining operations have been commenced is at what is known as Spurr mountain. The preliminary work has uncovered the south side of a very large mass of magnetic ore of a great degree of purity ; rising at the highest point to a height of 60 feet above the surface of the ground at the base of the hill. This remarkable outcrop of ore is situated (as will be seen by reference to the accompanying map) 900 feet east and 700 feet north from the west and south boundaries respectively of the company's property. It was first discovered to the public in 1868. The examinations which have been made, established beyond any reasonable doubt the presence of the ore in a very large quantity and of a uniform purity and quality. The natural facilities afforded at Spurr mountain for commencing mining operations are excellent, and with the exception of Republic mountain there is, so far as known, no other locality in Marquette county where occurs so large an exposure of pure ore, rising at so great an elevation above the general level and at which there is apparently so little preliminary work necessary.

This range has been explored to a considerable extent in either direction; westerly, across the east half of Sec. 23, owned by the M. H. and O. R. R. Co., the examinations show the presence of the ore, but to how great an extent the deposit exists future workings alone can determine; easterly, as is elsewhere more fully related, the range has been traced along the north side of Lake Michigamme for several miles. The officers of the Spurr Mountain Co. are: H. N. Walker, Esq., of Detroit, *Prest.;* Col. Freeman Norvell, *Supt.* and *Sec.* The distances from the mine to the ports of L'Anse and Marquette are respectively, by rail, about 24 and 39 miles.

The Michigamme Co. was organized in the winter of 1870–71, the organization being effected mainly by persons already largely identified with Lake Superior iron interests. The land owned by the company comprises 1,400 acres, situated on the north side of Lake Michigamme. Preliminary work was begun in the spring of 1872, and prosecuted during the summer. The point selected for the commencement of mining operations is near the shore of the lake, and upon each side of the line between Sections 19 and 20, the developments resulting from this work thus far being of the most promising character. Improvements, not previously indicated, consist of a large, substantial steam saw-mill, with other machinery attached thereto, an office, dwellings, etc. At a short distance south and west from this location the company have laid out a village plat, to be called "Michigamme," and which promises to be built up with considerable rapidity. The distance to L'Anse is about 26 miles, and to Marquette 37, by rail. The officers of the company are: William H. Barnum, of Lime Rock, Conn., *Prest.;* James Rood, of Chicago, *Sec.* and *Treas.;* and Jacob Houghton, *Supt.*

The Keystone Iron Co. also organized in the fall of 1872, with capital stock of $500,000, in 20,000 shares of $25 each. The property comprises the southeast 1/4 of southwest 1/4, Sec. 32, T. 48, R. 29, distant from Marquette, by rail, 29 miles, from Escanaba 77, and from L'Anse 35. The company are at work preparing for mining the ensuing season. A. P. Swineford, Marquette, *General Agent.*

A number of mining enterprises, comprising **The Albion, Saginaw, Lake Superior Company's new openings, The New England, Winthrop, Shenango, and Parsons,** in Secs. 19, 20, 21, 16, T. 47, R. 27, are situated east and west, parallel and contiguous ranges of specular and hematite ore, are all connected by branches with the M. H. and O. R. R., and soon to be with the C. and N. W. Road.

The Albion mine, opened in 1871 by the brothers St. Clair, who hold the property comprising the northeast 1/4 of the northwest 1/4, Sec. 19, on a lease from Messrs. E. Breitung and S. L. Smith, at a royalty of 75c. per ton; up to the present time but a small amount of ore has been mined. The opening is immediately west of the Saginaw mine and on the same ore belt.

The Saginaw Mine, situated on the northwest 1/4 of the northeast 1/4 of Sec. 19, T. 47, R. 27, was opened in 1872, and during the same season shipped (via M. H. and O. R. R.) 19,000 tons of specular ore. The mine was worked on a lease by Messrs. Maas, Lonstorf and Mitchell, of Negaunee, on a royalty of 50c. per ton for the ore. During the fall of 1872 the lessees sold out to parties representing the Cleveland Rolling Mill Co. for $300,000, and immediately thereafter the Saginaw Mining Co. was organized with a capital stock of $500,000 in 20,000 shares. A. B. Stone, of Cleveland, *Prest.*, and A. G. Stone, of Cleveland, *Sec.* and *Treas.* A side track has been surveyed, to connect with the Chicago and N. W. Railroad, and the grading finished to the Winthrop mine. The land on which the Saginaw mine is located was purchased of the State of Michigan, with four other contiguous "40's" situated about the centre of same section, seven years ago, by Messrs. Heater, Elison and Conrad; the latter having made the selections.

Between the Saginaw and New England mines, on Sec. 20, the Lake Superior Iron Co. have a very promising opening, from which a considerable shipment of specular slate ore was made in 1872.

The New England Mine, on same range, is situated on the east ½, northeast ¼, Sec. 20, T. 47, Range 27. The shipments from this mine commenced in 1866, and up to the present time about 60,000 tons of ore have been mined and shipped via Marquette. The property is mainly owned by Captain E. B. Ward, of Detroit, and the mining operations are conducted by H. G. Williams under a contract. The principal part of the product is a hematite ore. A very narrow bed of excellent specular slate ore was worked several years, but not proving sufficiently profitable, work was discontinued. The ore is chiefly consumed at the extensive works controlled by Capt. Ward at Chicago, Milwaukee, and Wyandotte.

Adjoining the New England is the **Winthrop Mine**, situated in the southwest ¼, Sec. 21, T. 47, R. 47, owned by A. B. Meeker and A. G. Clark, of Chicago, and H. J. Colwell, of Marquette, and opened in 1870 by Messrs. Richardson and Wood, who work the mine on contract. Up to the close of 1872 about 25,000 tons of ore have been shipped, and the indications are favorable for increased shipments during the coming year. The product is a hematite ore, one of the richest of the class in the district. A. B. Meeker, of Chicago, is *Prest.*, A. G. Clark, *Sec.* and *Treas.*, and H. G. Colwell, Clarksburgh, *Gen'l Agt.*

The Shenango Iron Co. was organized in September, 1872, with a capital stock of $500,000, in 20,000 shares of $25 each. The land worked by the company comprises the north-west ¼ of south-east ¼ of Sec. 21, T. 47, R. 27, and adjoins the Winthrop, the deposit being a continuation of that mine.

The officers are C. Donkersley, of Appleton, Wis., *Prest.*, and H. D. Smith, *Sec.* and *Treas.*; in addition to these, E. Decker, Charles Reis and George L. Hutchinson, constitute the Board of Directors. A small amount of ore was shipped during the fall of 1872, and the company are erecting machinery, including the sinking of a shaft 60 feet in depth, with the view of doing considerable mining the coming season. The land is leased of the Williams Iron Co., who in turn lease of the Pittsburgh and Lake Angeline Co., who are the owners of land. The ore is mined by Messrs. Hurd and Orthey, part owners, on contract.

The Boston Mine, situated on the southwest ¼ of the northeast ¼ of Sec. 28, was organized in 1872, and a lease of the property above described secured by Messrs. Day, Anderson and others, with a view of mining operations. The lease of these parties is the same as that of the Shenango.

The Parsons, or **"Old Parsons,"** mine is located between the New England and the Lake Superior Companies' opening on Section 16, northeast of the Winthrop. Several thousand tons of specular slate ore were shipped from each of these mines, but work has been discontinued.

The Kloman Iron Co. was organized in December, 1872, with a capital stock of $500,000, in 20,000 shares. The corporators were Andrew Kloman, William Coleman, Thomas M. Carnegie, Jacob Houghton and T. B. Brooks. The company own 437 acres of land adjoining and northwest of the Republican mountain, being in part in Sec. 6, T. 46, R. 29, on the west side of the Michigamme river. The company have commenced mining on the continuation of the Republic mountain deposit and are building a short railroad to connect the mine with the Republic branch.

The Howell Hoppock Iron Mining Co. filed articles of association January 13th, 1873. *Corporators:* Lewis J. Day, Wm. R. Bourne, Wm. Rice, James S. Ward and Frank Austin. Office in Ishpeming, Mich. Organized to mine on the northwest ¼ of northeast ¼ of Sec. 28, T. 47, R. 27. Capital stock, $500,000, in 20,000 shares.

The Watson Iron Co. filed articles of association January 16th, 1873, with capital stock fixed at $500,000, in 20,000 shares of $25 each. *Corporators:* C. J. Hussey, E. T. Daro, Thomas M. Howe, M. K. Moorhead, George F. McLeane, W. J. Moorhead, Charles F. Spang, John W. Chalfant, Campbell B. Herron and James W.

5

Brown, all of Pittsburgh, Pa., and James W. Watson, of Marquette county, Mich. The property of this company comprises the northwest ¼ of Sec. 32, T. 47, R. 26 and which constitutes $325,000 of the capital stock. This ¼ section is a part of the estate of the Pittsburgh and Lake Superior Iron Co. and is on the Cascade range. Operations were commenced in September last by this latter company, of which mention has already been made under the Hussey mine.

In the **Menominee Iron Region** two companies, called respectively the Breen and Ingalls Iron Mining Companies, have been organized and are engaged in explorations, and in addition to the operations inaugurated by these companies, explorations are being made by private parties. The completion of the Peninsula railroad from Escanaba to Menominee, affording better promises for transportation, will stimulate operations of this character, which have heretofore been deferred from want of railroad communications.

The Breen Mining Co. owns 120 acres of land in Sec. 22, T. 39, R. 28, distant from Escanaba by proposed road 35 miles, from Menominee 55 miles and from Deer river 28 miles. The ore is chiefly flag, with some hematite. The property is being explored by Capt. E. B. Ward, J. J. Hagerman and J. W. Vandyke, who have an option of leasing or purchasing the mine. The officers are E. S. Ingalls, *Pres.*, T. B. Breen, *Sec.*, S. P. Saxton, *Treas.*, Thomas Breen, Bently Breen, and S. P. Saxton, *Directors*—all of Menominee, Mich.

The Ingalls Mining Co.'s property constituted 240 acres of land situated in Sections 8 and 9, T. 39, R. 29. The distance from Escanaba by proposed road is 44 miles and from Menominee 64 miles. The officers are E. S. Ingalls, *Pres.*, C. L. Ingalls, *Sec.*, and F. S. Mullburg, *Treas.*

An effort has been made to manufacture pig-iron by using *peat as a fuel*, but has not as yet proved in the requisite degree successful. **A peat furnace** was constructed at Ishpeming and went into operation early in the year 1872, but very soon went out of blast; subsequently it started again and made about 200 tons of iron and again stopped, it being the intention to alter and enlarge the stack, the better, it is thought, to adapt it to the peculiarities of the fuel. The peat is prepared from a bed of the material which exists in proximity to the furnace.

The Ericson Manufacturing Co. was organized in April, 1872, to conduct general manufacturing operations, with a nominal capital of $150,000. *Corporators:* Peter E. Ericson, John Carlson, A. J. Burt and Wm. Burt.

The company are operating a foundry and machine-shop, which they have built on Whetstone brook, within the city of Marquette. The machinery is driven by water-power.

Mr. Jno. Burt commenced, in September, 1872, the construction of a charcoal furnace, on the lake shore, at the mouth of the Carp river; south of Marquette. The stack is being built of stone, with a nine-foot bosh, and the whole is to be completed and put in operation in the spring of 1873. It is intended to supply the fuel from points along the lake shore, transporting it to the furnace in boats in the same manner that the wood for the Burt furnaces in Detroit is obtained, of which latter furnaces the one being built at the Carp will be a duplicate, and will be the first built on the Upper Peninsula based on this plan of obtaining fuel.

Very recently **The Carp River Iron Co.** has been organized, and own the furnace and about 500 acres of land at that point, including the water-power on the Carp, etc. The business office will be in Marquette.

SANDSTONES.

The Lake Superior sandstones are very carefully described by Dr. Rominger in his accompanying report, commencing with page 80, and the results of his observations, as therein described, are of great practical and scientific interest. There are two organized companies now engaged in quarrying and marketing sandstone within the limits of the city of Marquette, the locations being contiguous.

The Marquette Brown Stone Co. was organized in August, 1872, with a capital stock of $500,000, in 20,000 shares. The corporators were Peter White, Wm. Burt, F. P. Wetmore, S. P. Ely,

Sidney Adams, J. H. Jacobs, H. R. Mather and Alfred Green. In addition to quarrying stone, the company's franchises include the mining and smelting of ore, etc. Office in Marquette, Mich.

This company's property was previously known as the Wolf Quarry, located on the farm formerly owned by J. P. Pendill, and has been worked for some time past, the stone being principally used in Chicago. It is of a uniform dark-brown color, free from pebbles and clay holes. It apparently exists in great quantity, and is readily quarried and transferred to vessels. Mr. Peter White is constructing in Marquette a fine business block with a variety of stone from this quarry, which is variegated and striped with different colors, giving to the building a unique and pleasing appearance.

The articles of association of **The Burt Free Stone Co.** were filed Oct. 3d, 1872. Capital stock $500,000, in 20,000 shares of $25 each. The corporators were John Burt, William Burt, Hiram A. Burt, A. Judson Burt and Wm. A. Burt. Office in Marquette.

This company have opened a quarry of sandstone adjoining the one described above and the deposit is similar, the stone being lighter colored.

Both companies are prepared to furnish stone in large quantities. For full description of the sandstone found in these quarries, see Dr. Rominger's report, pages 90 and 91.

In addition to the above, **The Lake Superior Stone Co.** has been more recently formed with the amount of capital stock and number of shares as the preceding. The company own and hold in lease about 296 acres of land, situated on the west side of Keweenaw bay and on the north side of Portage Entry. The stone outcrops horizontally in a bluff, which rises from the water of the bay and is thus readily accessible for removal from the bed to vessels.

It is intended to begin operations in the spring. The corporators are H. H. Stafford, V. B. Cochran, W. S. Dalliba, E. J. Mapes and A. Kidder. Office, Marquette, Mich. See Dr. Rominger's report, page 95.

The fine new Court-House at Milwaukee is built with sandstone obtained from Bass island, near Bayfield, on Lake Superior, at which point stones have been quarried for several years.

The quarry described by Dr. Rominger, page 89 of his report, is now owned by Messrs. Winty and Mossinger, of Chicago, and Thomas Craig, of Marquette.

ROOFING SLATE.

There are three companies which were organized for the purpose of quarrying and selling roofing slate; but one of them, however, has actually commenced operations and is now at work on explorations.

The Huron Bay Iron and Slate Co. filed articles of association January 19th, 1872. Capital stock, $500,000, in 20,000 shares. The corporators were Peter White, W. L. Wetmore, F. P. Wetmore, J. C. Morse, James Pickands, A. R. Harlow, M. H. Maynard, D. H. Ball, Wm. Burt, D. H. Merritt, Sidney Adams and H. R. Mather. Office, Marquette, Michigan. The company own 2,000 acres of land in T. 51, R. 31.

The Huron Bay Slate and Iron Co. was organized subsequently, with same capital stock and number of shares. The corporators are W. L. Wetmore, Peter White, M. H. Maynard, Wm. Burt, Thomas Brown, J. J. Williams, S. L. Smith, Alex. McDonald, John H. Knight, W. C. Wheeler, H. R. Mather, Jas. D. Reid, F. P. Wetmore and R. C. Wetmore. Office in Marquette. The company own 1,100 acres of land in T. 51, R. 31, and have commenced work near Slate river, about four miles south of Huron bay, on the northeast quarter of section 33 in the above town. The slate apparently exists in very large quantities.

The Stafford Slate Co., an association comprising H. H. Stafford, V. B. Cochran, E. J. Mapes, A. Kidder, J. M. Wilkinson, Wm. Burt A. J. Burt and W. S. Dalliba, own 1,900 acres in T. 51, R. 31. The operations of this company thus far consist in having cut out a road from L'Anse to their property on Section 27, in the above town, a distance of 15 miles.

The color of the slate found in T. 51, R. 31, is somewhat varied, the green, purple and gray are found on Sections 14, 15, and 16. South of this are found large deposits of black slate, extending several miles east and west, with an apparent thickness of several hundred feet, the cleavage planes dipping to the south.

SAW-MILLS.

The following saw-mills are now in operation, all of which, with the exception of the ones at Whitefish Point, at Onota and Fayette (the two former of which are in Schoolcraft county and the latter in Delta), are in Marquette county:

Name of Firm.	Location.
Decker and Steele....	Eagle Mills.
Edward Fraser...............	Cherry Creek.
George Wagner..............	Laughing Whitefish Pt.
A. R. Harlow................	Little Presque Isle.
H. A. Stone...........	Bancroft.
Jackson Iron Co..............	Negaunee.
Iron Cliffs Co................	"
Mr. Jackson..................	Palmer Falls (Cascade).
Hartman and Connelly........	Little Lake.
Cleveland Iron Co............	Ishpeming.
Lake Superior Iron Co........	"
Deer Lake Iron Co...........	Deer Lake.
Michigan Iron Co	Clarksburg.
Michigamme Iron Co	Michigamme.
Edward Breitung.............	Republic Mt.
C. T. Harvey................	Chocolate.
Bay Iron Co.................	Onota.

These mills produced in the aggregate, during the year 1872 (besides shingles, laths and a small amount of hard wood), thirteen and a half million feet of pine lumber, all of which, excepting the product of the three mills above designated, was, or will be, consumed in Marquette county. The total product during the coming year, if the winter is favorable, will be much greater, as most of these companies are preparing to get in a larger amount of logs. The Michigamme mill, which has a nominal capacity of 4,000,000 feet, has but recently started, and thus did not contribute to the total product of 1872.

COMPLETION OF THE RAILWAY SYSTEM.

Marquette, Houghton and Ontonagon R. R.

Among the most important events affecting the interests of this portion of our State, which transpired during the year 1872, was the extension of the C. and N. W. R. R. from Menominee to Escanaba, the consolidation of Marquette and Ontonagon Railroad with the Houghton and Ontonagon, and the completion of the line to L'Anse, thus making complete railroad communication from the head of Keweenaw bay to Chicago, a distance of 462 miles.

The development of the mineral resources of a country are so intimately blended with the improvement of its facilities for transportation, as to render it essential in considering the progress of the former, to give due credit to the latter. Iron ores having a low value per ton must be reached by rail or water before their value can be realized ; differing in this particular from the ores of the precious metals, which will bear wagon or even pack-mule transportation. Especially is this true with reference to an isolated region like the Upper Peninsula, which is as yet a comparative wilderness, possessing but a small population, a rigorous climate, few thoroughfares and with a surface so rough and rocky in portions of its territory, as to render their construction a matter of much difficulty. It naturally follows, that the addition of two so important avenues of communication to the railroad facilities of the Peninsula becomes in a pre-eminent degree a matter of congratulation and importance. The history of the enterprise, which has thus resulted in the connection of the bays of Marquette and Keweenaw, is in brief as follows:

As has been previously related in speaking of the Peninsula road, the United States granted to the State of Michigan, by an act passed on the 3d of June, 1856, every alternate section of land for six sections in width, designated in odd numbers, to aid in constructing a railroad from Little Bay de Noquette to Marquette and thence to Ontonagon, and from the two last places to the Wisconsin State line. The State, by an act passed Feb. 14th, 1857, conferred this grant upon the Little Bay de Noquette and Ontonagon Railway

Co., and two other railroad corporations, all of which lines were required to be completed within ten years, a condition with which neither of the companies complied.

In 1863 the State conferred the forfeited franchises and grant previously given to the Marquette and Ontonagon *Railway* Co., upon the Marquette and Ontonagon *Railroad* Co., under certain conditions. Congress in 1864 extended the grant five years, in the subsequent year added four sections per mile thereto, and in 1868 fixed the time for a full compliance with the conditions of the grant until Dec. 31st, 1872. During the period of its existence, the company built twenty miles of main line of railroad, commencing near the Lake Superior mine at the terminus of what was formerly the Bay de Noquette road, and extending to a point on the south side of Lake Michigamme.

In 1870 the State decided that the company, by reason of its failure to complete any extension of their lines, had forfeited the greater portion of the grant. On the 24th of Jan., 1871, the Legislature confirmed the action taken by the State Board of Control during the month of April previous, which conferred the forfeited or unearned lands upon the Houghton and Ontonagon Railroad Company, a new organization, incorporated Jan. 15th, 1870, and of which the following Michigan men were among the principal stockholders: H. N. Walker, *President*, S. L. Smith, Chas. H. Palmer, Geo. Jerome and S. F. Seager. The conditions of the act of Congress required the completion of thirty miles of road before the close of the year 1872, which fortunately this company have succeeded in accomplishing. Jacob Houghton was chosen Chief Engineer; and having located the line from Champion to L'Anse during the winter, the construction was begun in the spring of 1871 at the L'Anse terminus, and on the 16th of Dec., 1872, the first train passed over the entire line to Marquette, sixty-four miles; the whole having been placed under one management by the consolidation of the two companies effected during the previous summer. The completion of the road to L'Anse, exclusive of innumerable other advantages, opens to market the products of several iron mines, among the most promising of the region.

In anticipation of future shipments of ore from L'Anse, the company have constructed at this terminus of the road an extensive dock, a full representation of which from careful drawings is herewith presented.* They have also built, at this point, in a very substantial manner, a round-house, turn-table, machine-shop, etc.

The charter of the company and the grant of lands provide for the extension of the road to Ontonagon, and it is but reasonable to assume that the energy, which has characterized the prosecution of the enterprise thus far under its present efficient management, will result in the accomplishment of the work before the expiration of the time fixed by law. The length of the main line is 62 miles, of branches 20 miles and of sidings 18 miles, making 100 miles of road now constructed and in operation.

The dimensions and capacity of the company's railroad dock at Marquette, a representation of which is given in the accompanying view, are as follows:—Total length, 1,222½ feet; working length, 720 feet; height above water, 38 feet, and width of top, 53 feet, on which are four tracks for cars. Whole number of pockets, situated on both sides, 136, of which 120 have a capacity of 55 tons each, and 16 (steamboat-pockets) of 100 tons each. From both sides 8 vessels can be loading at the same time, and 6,000 tons have been loaded in a single day. Three vessels arrived on Saturday, after 8 o'clock in the evening, and were loaded and gone early Sunday morning. Vessels with a capacity of 476 tons may be loaded in one hour and fifteen minutes; vessels of 683 tons, in one hour and thirty-five minutes; the average time is three hours. The average capacity of vessels is about 650 tons, ranging from 400 for the smallest to 1,100 for the largest. Total amount of ore shipped over the dock from May 12th, 1872, to the following Nov. 25th, 301,210 tons, of which 75,000 tons were taken by steam, and 225,000 by sail-vessels; the estimated capacity of the dock, with a sufficient number of vessels to receive the ore, is 500,000 tons.

The working capacity is indicated by the amount of rolling stock, which at the opening of navigation, 1873, will consist of 1,600 ore-cars, 50 box and platform-cars, 7 passenger and baggage-cars and 28 locomotives. The present officers are: H. N. Walker, of Detroit, *President*, S. P. Ely, Marquette, *Vice-President*, Moses Taylor, New York, *Treasurer*, Freeman Norvell, Detroit, *Secretary*, Jacob Houghton, Michigamme, *Chief Engineer*.

Directors: H. N. Walker, Detroit, C. H. Palmer, Pontiac, S.

---

* Appendix F., Vol. II.

P. Ely, Marquette, John Steward, New York, Alexander Agassiz, Boston, S. L. Smith, Lansing, George Jerome, Detroit, Moses Taylor, New York, C. Francis Adams, Jr., Boston.

By the Peninsula division of the **Chicago and Northwestern Railway** the distance from Escanaba to Lake Angeline is $67\frac{30}{100}$ miles, and the branches completed and in course of construction, $37\frac{90}{100}$ miles; sidings, $15\frac{90}{100}$ miles; making a total length of track between these points of $121\frac{10}{100}$ miles.

The total amount of track between Escanaba and Menominee is $65\frac{70}{100}$ miles, of which $2\frac{30}{100}$ are side-track, making a total amount of track between Menominee and Lake Angeline, inclusive of sidings and lurches, $186\frac{80}{100}$ miles.

Estimated amount of rolling stock, which will be necessary and available for the business of 1873, between Escanaba and Negaunee:

Number of locomotives	33
" ore-cars (750 of them 6-wheeled)	3,000
" other cars	100

For the estimated business between Escanaba and Menominee:

Number of locomotives	6
" cars (exclusive of ore-cars)	100

S. C. Baldwin, *Div. Supt.*
Marvin Hughitt, *Gen. Supt.* } C. & N. W. R. R.

Statistics showing past production, with present condition and capacity of the mines and furnaces of the Upper Peninsula, might properly follow this historical sketch, thus bringing it to date and supplying facts, which could not well have been incorporated into the text. It was thought better, however, to arrange such information in tabular form, which has been done on Plates XII. and XIII. of Atlas, to which attention is here again called.

The Marquette Mining Journal, of Marquette, Mich., publishes an interesting yearly exhibit of the product and condition of the mines and furnaces.

In Appendix G, Vol. II., will be found statistics of population for the whole Upper Peninsula, from the United States Census for 1870.

CHAPTER II.

GEOLOGICAL SKETCH OF THE UPPER PENINSULA.

(*Where to Explore.*)

1. GEOGRAPHICAL DISTRIBUTION OF THE ROCK SYSTEMS.

IN prospecting for valuable minerals the intelligent explorer should constantly observe several kinds of phenomena. If his search degenerates into a simple blind hunt for ore, he would deserve the success of a hunter who went into a gameless region, or who hunted for game whose habits he did not understand. The following general geological facts and laws will possess value to the explorer in enabling him to wisely select his field of labor and in prosecuting his work.

As all the *sandstone* suitable for building, which has yet been found in the Lake Superior region, belongs to a system of rocks named by geologists Lower Silurian, and all the workable deposits of *iron ore* have been found in another system called the Huronian, while all the *copper* and workable *silver*, in a third system appears known as the Copper-Bearing Rocks; and as no workable deposits of useful minerals have yet been found in the fourth and oldest system, the Laurentian or granitic rocks, it follows, that it is of the utmost importance to the explorer that he be acquainted with the boundaries of these several fields and not waste his energies on unproductive ground. I do not mean to assert that iron ore will not be found in the Silurian sandstones, for in St. Lawrence County, N. Y., and in the Maramec district, Missouri, valuable deposits of ore exist in rocks of this age. Large deposits of iron ore also occur in the Laurentian (granite) rocks of Canada and Northern New York, and again, the iron ores of Thunder bay are contained in rocks which the Canadian geologists declare to be the equivalents of our Copper series; but at this date it is a fact, that no workable deposits of iron ore have been found in the Upper Peninsula in rocks of these systems, and an explorer or miner would not be considered wise, who should search for iron outside the Huronian limits. It is not only important that he be acquainted with the boundaries of the four great rock systems, but also with their leading characteristics. We will therefore first sketch in some detail the geographical distribution of these systems, as developed on the south shore of Lake Superior, beginning with the youngest and uppermost. The reader should have before him the map of the Upper Peninsula Pl. I. of the Atlas. The boundaries marked are not always exact, but embody the best information available and are not far wrong.

I. *Lower Silurian.*—The Lower Silurian system, the youngest or lowest division of the Palæozoic rocks represented on the Upper Peninsula, is made up of various sandstones and limestones which are fully described in Dr. Rominger's Report, Part III. The entire Peninsula, east of the meridian of Marquette, is underlaid by Silurian rocks and the "Copper range" is flanked by a Silurian flat on the south side, which separates it from the iron series, until the two, together with the South copper range, come together west of Lake Gogebic.

About two-thirds of the whole area of the Upper Peninsula, or 9,982 square miles, is underlaid by this system.

II. *The Copper-bearing Rocks*, corresponding with the upper copper-bearing rocks of the Canadian geologists, occupy a narrow belt on the northwestern edge of the Upper Peninsula. These rocks have less superficial extent than either of the other formations, underlying only about 1,186 square miles, or, say 7 per cent. of the whole surface. For descriptions of them see Prof. Pumpelly's Report, Part II.

III. *The Iron-bearing Rocks*, corresponding, it is assumed, with the Huronian system of Canada, consist of a series of extensively folded beds of diorite, quartzite, chloritic schists, clay and mica slates, and graphitic shales, among which are intercalated extensive beds of several varieties of iron ore. The same rocks occur on the east and north shores of Lake Superior, where they also contain iron. The Huronian area represented on the map equals about 1,992 square miles, or nearly one-eighth of the whole area of the Upper Peninsula.

IV. *The Granitic Rocks*, which so far have produced no useful minerals, and which are believed to be the equivalents of the Laurentian of Canada, are represented as underlaying about 1,839 square miles, equal to 12 per cent. of the total area.

As our examinations in the southwestern part adjoining the Wisconsin line have not been thorough, there is considerable uncertainty regarding some of the lines dividing the Huronian and Laurentian rocks, and a portion of this region, equal to about 668 square miles, or 4 per cent. of the whole area, is left blank on the map.

While, as has been stated, it is not proven that iron ore may not exist in the other great systems in workable quantities, there is every reason to believe, that by far the greater part, if not all the workable deposits, are contained in the Huronian area above described. It must not, however, by any means be understood, that all of this area is iron-bearing. The several iron districts, which have been more or less explored, will be described in another place; they will be found to cover not more than about one-fifth part of the Huronian area, or, say one-fortieth of the whole area of the Upper Peninsula, and on less than one-half of this area have the ores been proven to have commercial value.

Recapitulation.

I.	Lower Silurian area, about............	9,982	square miles.
II.	Copper-bearing area, about..........	1,186	"
III.	Huronian or Iron-bearing area, about..	1,992	"
IV.	Laurentian area, about	1,839	"
	Unknown area, about.................	668	"
	Total area of Upper Peninsula, exclusive of islands, about.....	15,667	"

In a complete and systematically arranged geological sketch the lithology of the four systems would properly belong here, but what is written on this subject necessarily pertains almost entirely to the Huronian, the whole matter will therefore be considered in Chapter III., following, and in Appendices A, B and C, Vol. II.

II.—TOPOGRAPHY.

It is of importance to the prospecter to carefully observe the topography or form of the surface, for it is well known that useful minerals generally occur in corresponding topographical positions over considerable areas ; again, the topography is the very best key to the nature of the underlying rocks, if these be concealed by earth, as is often the case. As the human physiognomy indicates the fundamental characteristics of the man, so the earth's physiognomy suggests the forces and materials lying beneath. It is safe to assert that within certain limits an experienced topographical geologist can, from a correct topographical map, judge of the nature of the rock underlying the surface represented; and conversely, from a geological map, he can predict the general form of the surface. In the same way, an experienced explorer does not hesitate to express an opinion as to whether he is on the "mineral range," from the form of the ground. We will now sketch in some detail the characteristic topography of the four great systems.

I. *Silurian.*—The prevailing surface characteristic of the Silurian region is a nearly level plain, underlaid by horizontal sandstones and limestones, often swampy and sometimes, where fire has destroyed the timber, a desert. The tame, flat, sandy and swampy country along the line of the Chicago and Northwestern Railroad, between Escanaba and Negaunee, is underlaid by Silurian rocks, but is far below the average in the value of its timber. Where rivers or water-courses have cut into these rocks, or waves wasted them, perpendicular bluffs are presented, which afford an excellent opportunity to explore and study the formation. The famous "Pictured Rocks" are bluffs of this character, from 50 to 200 feet high. From the top of these bluffs the country is flat, proving that they are the results of the action of water cutting its way into a horizontal plane, and are not, so to speak, built up and completed hills like those of the older rocks.

There is one apparent exception to this general flatness of the Silurian topography. Many of the highest hills and mountains in the Menominee iron region are capped with horizontal sandstone and limestone, which is never found in the valleys; the base, however, embracing the great mass of these elevations is always an old rock, and in the iron fields always Huronian. There is no doubt but that the sandstone once filled the valleys, extending in an unbroken bed of irregular thickness across the whole of the Menominee region, covering the older rocks, just as it now covers them further east. Since its formation it has here been mostly eroded, but still caps the elevations as described. If it were all gone, the hills, made as they are, largely of highly inclined beds of quartzite, marble and ferruginous rocks, would remain, but with somewhat diminished heights.

Should the eastern part of the Upper Peninsula be elevated at any future time, so as to bring the underlying azoic rocks above the lake level, the Silurian rocks may there also become so eroded as to only cap the Huronian hills, as they now do in the region described. That the older rocks extend eastward under the Silurian, is, I suppose, a geological necessity, and is, I think, directly proven by the existence of local magnetic attractions in this Silurian area, which are undoubtedly due to the existence of beds of iron ore in the underlying Huronian. The explorer in the Menominee region finds these beds of sandstone much in his way, covering, as they do, in some instances, the ores.

Small lakes of clear water, with sandy bottoms but no outlets, are a characteristic feature of the Silurian area. The U. S. Survey maps represent about one-half of the whole surface of these rocks, which underlie the central and eastern portion of the Upper Peninsula, as swamp ; the solid rock has often been found within a few feet of the surface in the swamp region. The western Silurian area being the prolongation of the Keweenaw Bay valley west, and embracing in part the Sturgeon, Ontonagon, Presquisle and Black rivers, has fewer lakes, much less swamp, and is more broken, than the eastern part already described.

Soft woods, including pine, are more prevalent on the Silurian rocks than on the older series ; but on the other hand, some of the finest bodies of sugar-maple and beech found on the Upper Peninsula, are on these rocks. Beech has not, so far as I know, been found growing on the older rocks ; whether this be due to climatic or soil influence has not been determined.*

The water divide, or height of land, of the central and east part of the Peninsula, is much nearer Lake Superior than Lake Michigan. It is an irregular line, approximately parallel with the shore of the lake, having an elevation where it crosses the Peninsula railroad of about 650 feet. See Map, Pl. I.

II. *Copper-bearing Rocks.*—There is probably no more striking

* A timber map has been prepared, but could not be published for want of means.

topographical feature in Michigan, than the "Mineral" or Copper range, including Keweenaw Peninsula, of which it is the backbone. Ranges would better express the fact, for west of the Ontonagon river there are three; the Main or central Range which extends from Keweenaw Point far into Wisconsin, being flanked on the north by the Porcupine mountain range and on the south by the South copper range, each separated from the other by broad Silurian flats. The general trend of the three ranges is north, 60° east, and south 60° west, but they are not quite straight, as may be seen on the map. The ridge is broad, generally more than three miles, and the crest quite even, but is cut down to lake level at Portage lake, and further west is deeply eroded by the Fire steel, Flint steel, Ontonagon and other rivers. The surface of the ridge or plateau is from 500 to 600 feet high in the vicinity of Portage lake, and rises to a height of 884 feet at Mount Houghton, near Keweenaw Point. Between the Ontonagon river and Lake Gogebic the Central range attains, in isolated peaks, an elevation of 1,100 feet, and the Porcupine mountain range is over 900 feet high; the range is more broken towards the west, and in the vicinity of Rockland presents a series of oval mammillary hills with steep escarpments on the south side. This is also the character of the South copper range, between Lake Gogebic and Montreal river.

The iron range immediately south of the South copper range, and west of Gogebic, is lower, the hills having more gentle slopes; the range being in places obscured by low ground. As this is the only part of the Upper Peninsula, so far as I know, where the iron explorer may come in contact with copper rocks, it is important to observe the topographical differences above noted, especially as the copper traps in some places resemble the diorites or greenstones of the iron region. Lakes and swamps, so numerous in the iron and granite regions, are infrequent on the copper belt, as must follow from the form of the surface. The reason for the striking regularity in the leading topographical features of the copper range is to be found in the great uniformity in the strike and dip of the rocks, as is explained under Stratigraphy. The timber of the copper range is generally sugar-maple, is abundant and of excellent quality; very little pine or other soft wood occurs here.

III. *Iron-bearing Rocks.*—The topography of the Huronian rocks differs essentially from that of either the Silurian, or the copper series. It is almost everywhere hilly and often mountainous, forming peaks higher than any in the copper range ; but instead of a continuous range, or series of parallel ranges, it is rather a broad belt or irregular area of mountains, hills, swamps and lakes. It may be said, that the ruling topographical features, especially the mountains, have a general east and west trend, but there are numerous exceptions to this law; for example, the Michigamme river, from the lake to Republic mountain, runs northwest to southeast; and Michigamme lake itself has a north-south arm, nearly as long as the main lake, which runs east-west. The ridges west of Paint river, in T. 42, R. 33, run north-south, conforming with the bedding of the rocks.

Probably one of the most persistent ridges in the Marquette region is formed by the "lower quartzite," which outcrops on the shore of Lake Superior just south of Marquette, and rising rapidly from the lake it forms Mt. Mesnard on Sec. 34, T. 48, R. 25 ; from this peak it extends westerly, crossing the railroad at the Morgan furnace, then by way of the old Jackson Forge and along north side of Teal lake to south side of Deer lake, it holds its westerly course for a total aggregate distance of over 15 miles. The Chocolate and Morgan flux quarries and the Teal lake whetstone quarry are in this range. More persistent and conspicuous, and nearly as long, is the Greenstone ridge, which skirts the north side of the Michigamme and the Three lakes extending from the Bijiki river to the west end of the First lake, a distance of eleven miles :—points on this range are three hundred feet above Michigamme lake, which is 950 feet above Lake Superior. Summit mountain, one mile easterly from the Foster Mine, is one of the prominent landmarks of the region, looking as it does from an elevation of about 1,300 feet over the flat granite and Silurian region to the south. It forms one of a chain of hills which extend from the south end of Lake Fairbanks westerly for about 10 miles, but which form in no sense a ridge.

The mountains, or hill ranges, above described are exceptional in their regularity and continuity. Broken chains of irregular hills and short ridges of various sizes, separated by lakes and swamps, is the prevailing character; the highest hills are seldom over 300 feet above the low grounds at their base and about 1,300 feet above Lake Superior. Outcrops of rock, forming often perpendicular ledges of moderate height, are more numerous in the iron-bearing

6

rocks, than in either of the systems described, except in the westerly part of the copper range. Although the relief of the surface is considerably modified by drift, it is generally plain that the strike, dip, and texture of the underlying rock has determined the general outline or contour; we should therefore expect that the great variation in these rocks, hereafter to be described, would produce this varied topography.

The topography of the Marquette region is very like the iron region of southern New York and northern New Jersey, except in its smaller elevations; a profile running north and south through the Jackson Mine, Marquette, would closely resemble a profile running northwest and southeast through the Sterling Mine, New York, platted say to half the scale.

Passing to the Menominee iron region, we find greater simplicity in the geological structure and a correspondingly less varied surface. Obeying the influences of the great rock beds beneath, the elevations there have a tolerably uniform east-west trend and consequent parallelism. The south iron range, of which the Breen Mine is the east end so far as known, can be traced through a greater part of its course by a ridge, often bold, which crosses Town. 39, R. 29, and T. 40, R. 30, for a distance of over 15 miles, the bearing being west-northwest. The north iron range, about 12 miles from the other in the south part of Town. 42, Ranges 28, 29 and 30, is in places a prominent topographical feature. The capping of horizontal sandstones, which has already been mentioned as characterizing the Menominee hills, gives a somewhat more even character to the crest lines, and in places produces a strikingly different profile.

The Gogebic and Montreal river range, above referred to, is better marked by its running parallel with and lying south of the South copper range, than by any essential character of its own.

IV. *Laurentian.*—The surface of the granite country south of the Marquette region, at the same time the most extensive and best known, is not unlike that of the iron-bearing rocks on a much smaller scale. There are no mountains, the hills are lower, being usually mere knobs, seldom exceeding 50 feet in height; the ridges shorter and swamps more numerous. A coarse pitting of the surface, or promiscuous sprinkling of little hills, and low, short ridges may convey the idea. Sometimes the knobs range themselves in lines constituting low ridges, with jagged crest line ; these ridges, when near the Huronian rocks, are usually parallel with them ; if they have any prevailing direction, it is east and west.

Perpendicular walls of granitic gneiss 15 to 40 feet in height sometimes face the ridges for several hundred feet in length, constituting the most regular topographical feature within the Laurentian area.

Small beaver meadows are common here as in the other rocks, and sometimes a succession of dams, one above the other, forms a long narrow meadow, which produces considerable quantities of wild hay.

This region was once heavily timbered, largely with pine, which has been prostrated by a hurricane, and since burned over several times. The soil, naturally light, has burned up and so washed away, as to expose the white-gray, pink and dark-green rocks in every direction, affording an unsurpassed opportunity to study this series; the boulders are very numerous and often of great size. The light colors of the rock, scarcity of vegetation and an abundance o. standing trunks of dead trees give the landscape a peculiar aspect ; but a second growth of poplar and wild cherry is rapidly changing this dismal character.

The fallen timber, swamps, steep bluffs and ledges, and numerous boulders, make travelling through the Laurentian area difficult and laborious in the highest degree. Florida swamps have denser vegetation and are much larger ; sea-coast marshes often have more mud ; the highlands of the Hudson present more formidable elevations, but, all in all, the writer believes it requires more physical exertion to travel 5 miles per day (all a man can accomplish with a pack) through Lake Superior granite windfall, than in any other region east of the Mississippi. The trees were prostrated by northwesterly winds, judging by the direction in which they lie ; persons have travelled in a southeasterly direction on the trunks of fallen trees (mostly pine) for over a mile without once touching the ground.

III.—STRATIGRAPHY.

Scarcely second to the two classes of phenomena already mentioned is the observance of the rock masses, or strata, as to their direction or strike, and inclination or dip; the order of their superposition and thickness; but more important than either is to ascertain between what rocks the mineral sought for occurs. Useful minerals which occur in beds, like the iron ores of Lake Superior, will usually be overlaid and underlayed by rocks, having different characters and which maintain those characters for considerable distances. Next to finding the ore itself, it is desirable to find the hanging or footwall rock. Whoever identifies the upper quartzite in the Marquette region, or the upper marble in the Menominee region, has a sure key to the discovery of any ore that may exist in the vicinity.

With few exceptions, all the rocks in the region we are describing are stratified—that is, arranged in more or less regular beds or layers, which are sometimes horizontal, but usually highly inclined. This stratification or *bedding* is generally indicated by a difference in color of the several layers, oftentimes by a difference in the material itself, but occasionally the only difference is in the texture or size and arrangement of the minerals, making up the rock. Thus, rocks made of quartz, sand and pebbles, may vary from a fine sandstone to a coarse conglomerate. In general, a *striped rock*, whether the stripes be broad or narrow, plain or obscure, on fresh fracture or weathered surface, is a stratified rock. Usually rocks split easier on the bedding planes, than in any other direction; but the converse is true in the case of most clay slates and in some other rocks, which split more easily on their *joints* and *cleavage* planes, the direction of which seldom coincides with the bedding and is often at right angles with it. If a rock splits most easily along its striping, it is always safe to assume, the true bedding planes have been found. Such planes are supposed to have had their origin in the original deposition of the mud and sand, of which most rocks are made. Similar marks can be seen in excavations in sand and clay, which may be regarded as unconsolidated rocks. The cleavage and joint planes above indicated, which are always more regular in strike and dip, than the others, are supposed to have originated from pressure, subsequent to the formation of the rock.

The term plane, as used in describing bedding, must not be understood to signify a straight-line surface; on the contrary, they are usually curved planes, sometimes folding and doubling on each other, so as to produce a very intricate structure. Not only do these plicatures take place on the small scale, as shown in hand specimens, but precisely similar folds exist in masses of rock, which may be hundreds of feet thick. The resulting curved strata take the name of troughs or basins, if the convexity is downward, the general term *synclinal* structure being applied to this form. Connecting the synclinal troughs and basins are *anticlinal* domes and saddles. The whole may be described as rolling or wave-like forms. Sometimes the power which produced the *folds* seemed greater than the rocks could bear, and cracks or breaks, and *faults* or throws, are the result, though these are not numerous in the Lake Superior region. Cracks so produced and filled with material, other than that constituting the adjacent rocks, are called *dykes;* or if the material be crystalline and metalliferous, *veins.* As iron ore in workable quantities does not occur in this form in this region, vein phenomena will not be considered here.

An examination of the four great rock systems will illustrate and prove the above remarks on stratification.

I. Beginning, as before, with the uppermost or youngest, which is at the same time the softest and lightest rock, the *Silurian* brown and gray sandstones and limestones, so well exposed on the south shore of Lake Superior, we have a perfect illustration of the regular and horizontal bedding, without folds, faults, or dykes. An inspection of the Marquette quarry, or any of the numerous natural exposures, will convince any one that these rocks are but consolidated sandbanks.

II. *The Copper-bearing Rocks.*—Some beds of this series are sandstones nearly or quite identical with the Silurian in appearance, but the great mass is made up of different varieties of copper trap, which are often amygdaloidal; interstratified are beds of a peculiar conglomerate. The stratification of these rocks, considered in large masses, is nearly as regular as the sandstones, and differs only in the fact that the layers are inclined, dipping northwest and north toward Lake Superior at a varying angle, which seems to be greatest on the south side of the range, and is there often vertical. It is least at Keweenaw Point, where it is as low as 23°.

III. *The Iron-bearing* or *Huronian Rocks* are immediately beneath, and are exposed to the south of the copper rocks. This series are, on the average, heavier and harder, than either of the others and folded to a far greater degree. The prevailing rock is a greenstone or diorite, in which, like the copper traps, the bedding is usually obscure ; but the intercalated schists and slates which usually bear strong marks of stratification, make it usually not difficult to determine the dip of the beds at any point. This dip varies both in amount and direction, but is generally at a high angle, and is more apt to be to the north or south than in any other direction.

IV. Descending to the oldest or bottom rocks of the Lake Superior country, the granites and associated beds (*Laurentian*), we find the bedding indications still more obscure and often entirely wanting. Here there is, if possible, more irregularity in strike and dip, than in the Huronian.

IV.—BOULDERS (FLOAT ORE).

Fragments of iron ore which have been detached from the parent ledge and are found loose on the surface, or in the drift beneath, possess great interest to the explorer, and are among his most important helps and guides. The same remarks are applicable, but to a less extent, to boulders of other rocks. As a rule, in the iron region of Lake Superior, it is safe to assume, that when boulders of a particular variety of rock are abundant on the surface, a ledge of the same will be found in place very near—if not immediately under the boulders, then up hill from them, or perhaps a little to the north or east ; the more angular or sharp-cornered the boulders, the nearer we would expect to find the ledge.

In the Menominee region it may almost be said, that this rule is invariable, as there seems to have been less movement of the drift material here than farther to the north.

In the Michigamme district a large amount of float ore is found some distance south of the iron range, part of the fragments being very large and containing at least 100 tons of ore. Sections 19, 29, and 30 of T. 48, R. 30, and Sections 25, 36, and 35 of T. 48, R. 31, contain many such boulders, which were probably derived from the Michigamme range. Considerable digging has been done at several of the larger boulders, which has failed to find the ore in place, and the magnetic attractions are of a character which indicate detached boulders and not a continuous ledge. For mode of distinguishing boulders of magnetic ore, see chapter on use of the magnetic needle.

These Michigamme ore boulders are all found south of the iron range which produced them, and but few at a greater distance than two and one-half miles, most of them being much nearer. This southerly and westerly direction of the drift is, so far as I know, universal in the iron region of the Upper Peninsula, and it is fully confirmed by the direction of the drift scratches in the solid rock, which vary from north to east, averaging about northeast and southwest.

Therefore, if iron boulders be found in considerable abundance, the explorer may assume, especially if they are angular, that he has iron underneath the surface ; if rounded or abraded, the ledge may be to the north or east. If the boulders be magnetic, the place of the ledge should be found, with comparative ease, by means of the needle ; but if specular, it may be an expensive and difficult work. Soft hematite, from its nature, can never occur in the form of boulders, as it would weather into a reddish soil. Iron boulders are often met with in digging test-pits and shafts ; in such instances, if near the ledge, I have generally found the ore in place very near ; if considerably above it in the drift, the same rules would apply as to surface boulders.

Attention should be given to the character of boulders other than iron, which may be associated with it, or found where there is no iron. Occasional granite boulders occur everywhere in the Lake Superior iron region and have no economic significance. I have never seen an abundance of granite boulders, however, except over granitic rocks, and so far, these rocks have not produced workable deposits of iron.

Boulders of quartzite, diorite and slate usually accompany those of iron in the Marquette region, and marble boulders, as well as quartzite, are most significant in the Menominee region.

The above laws, regarding the occurrence of *iron boulders*, give the facts regarding their geographical distribution great importance in iron explorations. If, where there are iron boulders, we may confidently look for iron, then conversely, where there are none, we should not expect to find iron. I do not assert that every deposit of hard ore is marked by float or boulders, but, so far as the facts have come to my knowledge, this is the case in the region under consideration.

Except in one or two instances, which have not been verified, I have heard of no iron boulders in the so-called silver-lead region, which extends north from the Marquette iron region to Lake Superior, which would lead one tò believe, that merchantable hard ores will be found there. And except the L'Anse range in north part of T. 49, R. 33, this is true of the belt of country, west from the so-called silver-lead region. The region, without iron boulders, may be briefly described by saying, that it is bounded west and south by the line of the Peninsula division of the Chicago and Northwestern, and by the Marquette, Houghton, and Ontonagon railways. In other words, a person travelling by rail from Escanaba through Negaunee to L'Anse would have the region of iron boulders on the left, and the boulderless region on the right hand, or towards the lake.

Limiting their distribution still further, we may say, that iron boulders have only been found in quantity and quality, which would point toward economic importance in (1.) T. 45, R. 25, in the vicinity of the S. C. Smith mine, which is the most easterly locality in which they have been observed on the Upper Peninsula of Michigan; (2.) the Negaunee and Michigamme iron districts, extending in belts of irregular width from Negaunee west to the First lake in S. 17, T. 48, R. 31; (3.) the L'Anse iron range, in north part of T. 49, R. 33; (4.) south and southwest from Michigamme lake, embracing wholly or in part Towns. 44 to 47 north, and Ranges 39 to 32 west; (5.) the Menominee iron region, embracing wholly or in part Towns. 39 to 42 north, and from Range 28 west to the Menominee and Brulè rivers, but not west of Range 33; (6.) the Lake Gogebic and Montreal river iron belt, south of the South copper range.

Hunting for boulders is something like hunting game; when on the ground the best woodsman, the most active and observant will be the most successful, assuming, of course, that he knows at sight what he is looking for. (See chapter on Explorations.) I have found Indians good help in this kind of work, and believe that the incentive of a bonus in money for boulders or outcrops is often good policy. The best places in which to observe boulder phenomena is in the beds of rapid streams and under the roots of trees, the latter, probably, having been the most fruitful field. A windfall is as good as five thousand dollars' worth of test-pits to the section.

With boulder phenomena may be classed the reddish or *brownish earth*, which comes from the disintegration of iron ore rocks of a hematitic character, and *magnetic sand*, which is very generally distributed, and which comes from the disintegration of magnetic ore. Such material may, for our purposes, be regarded as made up of minute boulders and the same remarks will apply, except that I should not expect to find red earth far removed from the ferruginous rock which produced it. Minute quantities of magnetic sand can be found almost everywhere in this region.

CHAPTER III.

LITHOLOGY.* (*Mineral Composition and Classification of Rocks.*)

In the preceding sketch the terms sandstone, limestone, conglomerate, trap, diorite, granite, etc., occur. It is evident that no satisfactory and useful progress can be made in geological field-work, which includes prospecting, until one has learned to recognize and name the more common varieties of rock. For this purpose we have to give attention to their mineral composition, that is, we must ascertain of what simple mineral or minerals the rock in question is chiefly made up and to observe, whether such minerals are angular, presenting bright facets (crystalline), or whether they are rounded like sand and gravel (fragmental). Not only must the prospector be able to recognize at sight the mineral he is seeking, but in case it is not exposed, which often happens, then those rocks, which are known to indicate its presence or absence. Experienced prospectors will not spend much time in looking for iron among granite rocks, nor in the copper traps, nor yet in the region of horizontal sandstones and limestones.

The mineral composition of rocks, by which they are identified, described and named, constitutes the science of Lithology, one of the most abstruse departments of Geology. A high authority on this subject has remarked :—"In all attempts to define and classify rocks, it should be borne in mind that they are not definite lithological species, but admixtures of two or more mineralogical species, and can only be arbitrarily defined and limited." When rocks present recognizable crystalline minerals, the task of describing and naming is comparatively easy ; but when the constituent minerals are obscure, as is often the case in the rocks we are considering, the attempt to employ specific names, which shall define such vaguely compounded aggregates, will be exceedingly difficult.

---

* The stratigraphical order of the rocks here considered will be found in the succeeding chapter.

The difficulty may be illustrated by supposing, were an attempt made, to give such name to a common brick, as will designate its composition and structure. Bricks are made in general of sand and clay, but several varieties of sand, and as many of clay, are employed in different localities, which, being mixed in various proportions and differently burned, give rise to a wide variation in composition and appearance and could not be expressed by a single word or term. In the case of rocks we have, of course, no previous knowledge of the numerous ingredients employed in their composition, by which the difficulty is greatly increased. It may seem at first sight, as if chemical analysis should form a reliable basis for rock nomenclature, but this is not the case. Van Cotta asserts, that a rock containing 72 silica, 11 alumina, 2.8 oxide of iron, 1 lime, 1.2 magnesia, 1.2 potash, 2 soda and 0.4 water, may be either a granite or a gneiss, protogine, granulite, quartz-porphyry, felsite, petrosilex, pitch-stone, trachyte-porphyry, obsidian, or pearlstone; and by giving a little range in the percentages of some of the constituents, half a dozen other rock names could be added. Here we have eleven different rocks, having precisely the same chemical composition, but widely different in physical character.

It must be borne in mind, in studying this subject, that the solid crust of the globe is almost entirely made up of ten or eleven simple *chemical elements*, which variously combined, according to the laws of chemistry, produce the few *minerals* which in turn, mechanically mixed, constitute ordinary *rocks;* hence we should expect, that the average chemical composition of a series of rocks, wherever found and of whatever character, would nearly agree.

The materials of the first formed rocks, whatever their origin, have been worked over and over by rains and waves and chemical forces, distributed over sea-bottoms, consolidated and elevated, to pass again through the same process by just such means, as are now at work in producing similar results.

The reader who may not be familiar with the physical characters and composition of the minerals—quartz, feldspar, hornblende, chlorite, talc, argillite, mica and the oxides of iron and manganese, which make up the great bulk of the rocks herein described, is advised to refer to some elementary work on geology or mineralogy.

Extensive rock formations are now generally named after the locality, where they were first thoroughly studied, or are best exposed, and their minor beds and layers are often named according to their peculiar mineral composition, or with reference to their relative age, that is, order of superposition. The names Laurentian, Huronian and Silurian are geographical names of the first class. No attempt will here be made to describe the lithological character of either the Copper bearing traps, conglomerates and sandstones, nor the Silurian sandstones and limestones ; these will be fully treated by Prof. Pumpelly and Dr. Rominger, respectively. What has been and will hereafter be said of the geographical distribution and topographical and stratigraphical character of these rocks was considered necessary, to acquaint the prospector and explorer with those general principles of geology, which lie at the foundation of intelligent and successful work. Whoever would become thoroughly acquainted with these systems is referred to Parts II. and III. of this volume. A number of specimens from the Laurentian are described in Appendix A, Vol. II. (see descriptions 252 to 299) ; but they do not cover all the lithological families represented in that system.

In subdividing the Huronian or iron-bearing series, which we have particularly to study, the rocks have been grouped (1) *lithologically*, *i.e.*, according to their mineral composition, and (2) *stratigraphically*, *i.e.*, according to relative age. As this system was first described and named by the Canadian geologists, their names have been employed as far as possible in the body of this report; the identity in composition of many of our rocks with theirs, having been established by an examination of a large number of Marquette specimens by Dr. T. Sterry Hunt.

Alexis A. Julien, A.M., of the School of Mines, New York, has made careful studies, both in the field and laboratory, of a large number of specimens from the Lake Superior region, his results being in part given in Appendix A, Vol. II. As his paper was not obtained in time to modify this chapter and the geological descriptions which follow, in accordance with Mr. Julien's nomenclature and orthography, what follows may be regarded as an independent and popular presentation of this subject, which is scientifically and more fully treated in the Appendix, the practical needs of the explorer and miner being here chiefly considered.

The specimens examined by Mr. Julien are in part from the Marquette region ; the L'Anse, Menominee, and Gogebic districts are also well represented, thus embracing an area over 125 miles long and having an extreme width of 60 miles. The specimens described belong to a catalogued collection, numbering over 2,500 specimens, being probably the most complete suite of rocks from the Azoic of the Upper Peninsula yet collected. Those from the Montreal river and Gogebic district were collected by Prof. R. Pumpelly and myself, and are believed to be the first described from that region. Prof. Pumpelly took very full lithological notes in the field, but has not yet, so far as I know, made them public. Dr. H. Credner's publications are very full on the lithology of the Menominee region, he having spent two seasons in that field.

Appendix B, Vol. II., contains a list (named by Mr. Julien) of the specimens constituting the State collection, over thirty duplicate suites of which were collected and have been distributed among the incorporated colleges of Michigan and other leading institutions and cabinets, of this country and Europe.

Appendix C, Vol. II., contains a list of 76 specimens, number 1,001 to 1,076, determined by the microscope by Chas. E. Wright, under the direction of the Faculty of the School of Mines, Freiberg, Saxony. A suite of these rocks is at Freiberg and others in Michigan.

The several beds or layers of the Huronian system, as developed in the Marquette region, are numbered upwards from I. to XIX., always written in Roman numerals. These strata being particularly described as to thickness, geographical extent, etc., in following chapters, it need here only be said in general that I., II., III., IV. are composed of beds of silicious ferruginous schist, alternating with chloritic schists and diorites, the relations of which have not been fully made out; V. is a quartzite, sometimes containing marble and beds of argillite and novaculite; VI., VIII. and X. are silicious ferruginous schists; VII., IX. and XI. are dioritic rocks, varying much in character; XIII. is the bed which contains all the rich specular and magnetic ore, associated with mixed ore and magnesian schist; XIV. is a quartzite, often conglomeritic; XV. is argillite or clay slate; XVI. is uncertain, it contains some soft hematite; XVII. is anthophyllitic schist, containing iron and manganese; XVIII. is doubtful; XIX. is mica schist, containing staurolite, andalusite and garnets. This classification, it will be borne in mind, applies only to the Marquette region, the equivalency of the rocks of the Menominee and other regions not having been fully made out.

These beds appear to be metamorphosed sedimentary strata, having many folds or corrugations, thereby forming in the Marquette region an irregular trough or basin, which, commencing on the shore of Lake Superior, extends west more than forty miles. The upturned edges of these rocks are quite irregular in their trend and present numerous outcrops. While some of the beds present lithological characters so constant, that they can be identified wherever seen, others undergo great changes. Marble passes into quartzite, which in turn graduates into novaculite; diorites, almost porphyritic, are the equivalents of soft magnesian schists. In this fact is found the objection to designating beds by their lithological character, while to numbers or geographical names no such objection exists. The total thickness of the whole series in the Marquette region is least at Lake Superior, where only the lower beds exist, and greatest at Lake Michigamme, where the whole nineteen are apparently present, and may have an aggregate thickness of 5,000 feet.

Near the junction of the Huronian and Laurentian systems, in the Marquette region, are several varieties of gneissic rocks, composed in the main of crystalline feldspar, with glassy quartz and much chlorite. Intersecting these are beds of hornblendic schist, argillite and sometimes chloritic schist. These rocks are entirely beneath all of the iron beds, seem to contain no useful minerals or ores and are of uncertain age. No attempt is here made to describe or classify them.

The following description and classification has resulted from an examination of a large number of specimens of "ore and rock," collected with the view of embracing all varieties found in the iron-bearing series of the Marquette region, together with a study of the parent masses in the field, which latter is of great importance on account of the variations in composition of the same bed, to which attention has been directed.

The *specific gravity* of over five hundred specimens, weighing from 3,000 to 10,000 grains, was determined by a balance, which turned when loaded, by the addition of two grains. The magnetic properties were carefully examined and are given in part in the chapter on the magnetism of rocks. Most of the specimens examined were arranged into ten *lithological groups* (having no reference to age), which are designated in what follows by the first ten letters of the alphabet. When a specimen represented a very small and unimportant layer, it was thrown out as exceptional and not important to the object of this report.

It must be constantly borne in mind, that the divisions between these ten lithological groups or families are not sharply marked; one passes into the other by insensible gradations, thus producing many intermediate varieties, which it was difficult, if not impossible, to classify or describe. The first family, A, will include all valuable iron ores, the remaining nine (B to J) will include "rocks." But as iron ore, in large masses, has all the geological characters of the associated rocks, the popular general classification of minerals into "ores" and "rocks" will be disregarded except as above mentioned. Except in a few instances, where Mr. Julien's collection was incomplete, all minute lithological descriptions have been omitted, for such, frequent reference will be made to his paper; and for the reason that he had not access to maps and sections, which gave the stratigraphical distribution of the various rocks, this part has been made quite full in that respect.

In a few instances reference is made to the full suite of Marquette rocks, numbered 6,000 to 6,222, deposited by me in the cabinet of the University of Michigan, at Ann Arbor.

A. Iron Ores.

(Occurring in formations X., XII., XIII. and below V.)

Only such ores as are now employed in the manufacture of iron will be described under this head. They are in order of present supply, the (a) specular hematite or *red specular ore*, as this class is designated in the iron trade; (b) *the magnetic;* (c) the "mixed" or *second-class ore*, which may be either specular or magnetic; (d) the *soft hematite*, and (e) *the flag ores.* Another variety, the magnetic specular, might be added, which, as the name implies, is a mixture of the black and red oxides, which gives a purple streak. The local terms "hard," embracing both the magnetic and specular ores, and "soft," for the soft hematites, are convenient.

The commercial statistics, modes of mining, and composition will be considered under their proper heads,* attention being directed here chiefly to the mineralogical and physical character of each

---

* See Chapters IX. and X., Plate XIII. of Atlas, and Appendix J, Vol. II.

ore. Under Woodcraft and Surface Explorations, Chapter VII., are given some brief practical rules for distinguishing iron ores, for the benefit of those, who know little or nothing of rocks.

All the specular, magnetic, and mixed ores, and a part of the soft hematites, are found in one formation; bed XIII. of my arrangement, which has its most easterly exposure near the Jackson mine and extends irregularly and indefinitely westward, embracing all the mines now producing rich hard ore.

It may be said of these ores in general, that they are essentially oxides of iron, with a few per cent. of silica added, and generally contain minute quantities of sulphur and phosphorus, but no titanium. Alumina in quantity not exceeding two and one-half per cent., with one-fourth as much manganese, is sometimes found, together with alkalies, which seldom aggregate over one and one-half per cent. The soft hematites are in part hydrated sesquioxides, hence contain water and usually more silica, than the hard ores; traces of organic matter are sometimes found, and manganese is almost exclusively confined, to the soft ores. Many specimens of specular and magnetic ore have been analyzed, which gave ninety-eight per cent. of oxide of iron, the balance being nearly pure silica. For numerous analyses of all the ores, see Chapter X., Appendix J, Vol. II., and Plate XIII. of Atlas. Weathering has no appreciable effect on the hard ores, except to crumble and cover with soil the more granular varieties. The exposed surfaces of the compact ores (by far the most prevalent variety) are of almost as high lustre as fresh fractures, and are often highly polished, showing no weathered coating like almost all other rocks. In the "mixed ores" the jasper bands are sometimes slightly elevated on the weathered surface, due to their greater hardness.

a. Red Specular Ores.—Miners divide these into *slate* and *granular*. The former resembles closely in its structure the soft greenish chloritic schists, commonly associated with it. The slabs, into which the slate ore easily splits, are not uniform in thickness like roofing-slate, but taper always in one and often in three ways, producing elongated pieces often resembling in form a short, stout, two-edged sword-blade, with surfaces as bright as polished steel, but striated and uneven. See Specimens 46, 47, 48, State Collection, Appendix B, Vol. II., and 1,050 Appendix C, Vol. II. Thin edges of such slates can be pulverized into a bright scaly powder by the finger-nail, and occasionally the whole mass is too friable for economic handling. The magnet will generally lift one or two per cent. of the powdered ore, and occasionally one-fourth of the whole, in which case the streak is purple. These last, constituting magnetic slates, are more friable than the pure red specular slates, due in some way to the larger admixture of magnetite. See Specimen 49, State Collection, Appendix B, Vol. II.

The *granular* or massive specular ore shows no tendency to split in slabs, and is made up usually of minute crystalline grains, which are sometimes, however, so large that their octahedral form can be easily recognized without the aid of a lens; fine specimens of this variety occur at the Cleveland and New York Mines. Mineralogists apply the name *martite* to the red oxide of iron, when it has the crystalline form of the octahedron, which belongs to magnetic ore. See Specimens 2, 43, 44 and 45, State Collection, Appendix B, Vol. II. It is not improbable, that all of the granular specular ores under consideration may have once been magnetic and in some way have gained the two per cent. of oxygen necessary to change them from black to red oxides. See Dana's System of Mineralogy, 5th ed., p. 142.

The granular ore is generally firm in texture and never friable, like the granular magnetic. Some highly compacted varieties, which contain a little silica, are very hard, constituting the hardest rock to drill which the miner encounters. This variety is called the "fine-grained steely ore;" some specimens of it possess almost the highest specific gravity observed, 5.23, while the rich softer ores of the same class averaged about 4.85. See Spec. 45, State Collection, Appendix B, Vol. II.

From the examination of a considerable number of specimens of red ore, it was found that the magnet would usually lift an appreciable portion of the powder. In the case of one coarse-grained specimen of pure ore from the New York mine, one-third of the pulverized ore was removed by the magnet. Spec. 1060, App. C, Vol. II. The percentage of powder lifted by a magnet in twenty-one specimens, together with color of powder, is given in Table, App. H, Vol. II. Numerous specific-gravity determinations of this variety of ore will be found in App. B, Vol. II.

b. Magnetic Ore.—The description given above of the granular specular ore applies with equal force to this class, except that the latter is more of granular and often friable, has the magnetic property and gives a black or purple powder instead of red. Sometimes the rich magnetites crumble easily into grains, like some Lake Champlain ores, to which the term "shot ore" is applied; again, it is very hard, as in Pit No. 8 of the Washington mine. See Specs. 39, 40, 41 and 42, State Coll., App. B, Vol. II. The compact tabular form so frequent in the magnetic ores of New Jersey and Southern New York is not common in the best ores of the Marquette region, nor are the latter ores as highly magnetic as the former, or at least good loadstones are not so common; the ore from the Magnetic mine (see Spec. 17, State Coll.) has most of this tabular character.

Typical *slate* ores occur with the magnetites, but they are of the character already described, that is, mixtures of the two oxides, the magnet not removing over one-fourth of the powder, while it takes all in the case of the granular variety. The specific gravity of the granular magnetic ores, as will be seen in Appendix B, Vol. II., varied from 4.59 to 5.01, the average of many specimens being 4.81. Specs. 1,054 and 1,059 of Appendix C, Vol. II., are also varieties of this ore.

The following minerals and rocks are most commonly associated with hard ores: a soft grayish-green *chloritic schist*, which sometimes, owing to bad sorting, goes to market in sufficient quantity to perceptibly reduce the furnace yield. The magnesia it contains might tend to stiffen the slag, otherwise it can have no effect in the furnace further, than what is mentioned above. This rock is described under Group D. See Specs. 53, 54, and 55, State Coll., App. B, Vol. II.

Micaceous red oxide of iron often occurs in scales and bunches, particularly in proximity to jasper. It has been improperly called plumbago, but is in reality in no way related to it, being chemically pure oxide of iron, having the crystalline structure of mica. A soft whitish mineral, often called *magnesia*, and appearing not unlike flour, occurs occasionally in specular ore and frequently in "soft hematite." This substance is usually most abundant in the more jaspery varieties of specular ore; an examination by Prof. Brush determined it to be *kaolinite*, a hydrated silicate of alumina (clay) in minute crystalline scales. The presence of this clay in small quantity could not but help the working of the furnace, by forming a more fusible slag, but it would of course diminish the yield of iron, if in quantity.

The needle and velvety forms of the mineral *Göethite* (a hydrated oxide of iron) are not uncommon at the Jackson mine, and "*Grape ore*" (botryoidal limonite), sometimes finely colored with yellow ochre, is found at several of the mines, but always in soft hematite. Fine specimens of crystallized quartz are rare, and no form of lime has been observed, although analyses show minute quantities. Bunches of *iron pyrites* are occasionally found, especially in the magnetic mines. At the Champion mine a thin layer containing this mineral occurs next the hanging wall, but it is easily separated from the ore, and is not sent to market. Hornblende, so generally present in the magnetic mines of New York, New Jersey and Sweden, is rare in the Marquette mines, of XII. and XIII.

c. Second-class Ore.—By far the most abundant, and commercially objectionable ingredient in the Marquette ores of all kinds, is the so-called jasper, a reddish ferruginous quartz, which is invariably found associated with the best ores, usually in thin seams or lamina conforming to the bedding, but sometimes in a form approaching a breccia. In the hard ores this impurity can usually be readily distinguished, but in the soft hematites it is often only found by analyses. As this rock possesses considerable scientific as well as commercial interest (the better varieties constituting the second-class ores), I will attempt to describe and illustrate it somewhat minutely. It consists of jasper, varying from bright red to dull reddish-brown, with occasional seams of white quartz, and usually pure specular or magnetic ore of high lustre. These materials are arranged in alternating lamina, varying in thickness up to one inch. These lamina are often highly contorted, zigzagging, and turning sometimes in opposite directions within a few inches. The jasper bands are in places broken up into little rectangular fragments, which are slightly thrown out of place, as it were, by tiny faults; the ore fills the break, so that the whole mass has the appearance of a breccia. There can be little doubt, but that the true breccia at the east end of the Jackson mine has this origin, and it would be interesting to consider whether this idea might not be extended to other conglomerates in the Huronian series. The contorted laminated structure, with the striking contrast of colors, is beautiful, and affords fine miniature examples of the anticlinal and synclinal folding and faulting of large rock masses. Sometimes the lamina are very irregular and indistinct, and one or the other of the minerals greatly preponderates. When the jasper layers all thin out (as they usually do somewhere), the ore becomes first class. Some phases of this interesting rock, with descriptions, are given in Appendix K, Vol. II., Figures 19 to 29. See Specs. 36 and 37, State Coll., Appendix B, Vol. II.

The miners call this material "mixed ore;" and those varieties in which the jasper does not constitute over 20 per cent. of the whole, are sold as second-class ore, yielding about fifty per cent. in the furnace; for rail-heads and some other uses requiring a hard iron, the presence of silica in the ore is not objectionable. The quantity of "mixed ore" is greatly in excess of the pure ore, and it will some time undoubtedly have considerable commercial value. Its nature is such, as to admit of the ready mechanical separation of the pulverized ore from the jasper by jigging, a process now employed in separating ores in the Lake Champlain region. For fixing puddling furnaces, or for any branch of iron industry which may demand pulverized ore (as the Elerhausen process promised to), it is very probable that this method may advantageously be employed, and a cheap ore produced.

"Mixed ore" is seen in outcrops far oftener than the purer ores, the softer character of which has caused their erosion, whereby they had become covered with soil; but as the mixed ores are usually associated with the pure varieties, their outcrops possess great significance in prospecting. It is important in this connection not to confound the "flag ores," (e) to be described, which they sometimes closely resemble, with this variety. The quartz of the magnetic mixed ore is usually white, or lighter colored than the red mixed ore.

d. The *soft hematites* of the Marquette region differ entirely from the ores above described, and are closely related to the brown hematites of Eastern Pennsylvania and Connecticut. In color they are various shades of brown, red and yellow, earthy in form, and generally so slightly compacted, as to be easily mined with pick and shovel. They are invariably associated with, or rather occur in, a limonitic silicious schist, from which they seem to have been derived by decomposition and disintegration. These ores occur in two distinct formations, X. and XII., and probably in others, in irregular bunches or pockets, surrounded by the schist and passing by gradations, often abrupt, into it. Scattered through the ore, and conforming in their positions with the original bedding of the rock, are fragments of the schist. When the ore shows stratification, which it often does not, it also conforms with the bedding of the schist. The specific gravity of the soft hematite ore varied from 3.50 to 3.81, the average of five specimens being 3.59, and specimens of the schist varied from 2.80 to 3.38. Strictly this schist should be described under the next group of rocks, B, to which it belongs, but its assumed parentage of the hematite ore, here considered, has led to the digression. See Specs. of soft hematite 1,067, 1,077, 1,079, and of schist 1,040, 1,065, and 1,069, Appendix C, Vol. II.; also, Specs. 25 and 26, State Coll., App. B., Vol. II.

The following analyses of the schist and ore, from the Foster mine, by Dr. C. F. Chandler, will help to make their relations better understood:—

		Schist.	Ore.
Sesquioxide of iron		44.33	79.49
Alumina		2.14	1.19
Oxide of Manganese		.16	.25
Lime		.36	.27
Magnesia		.13	.33
Silica		47.10	9.28
Phosphoric Acid		0.13	0.19
Sulphuric Acid		0.17	0.17
Water		5.19	8.74
		99.71	99.91
Equivalent to	Iron	31.03	55.64
	Sulphur	.068	.068
	Phosphorus	.057	.083

It will be observed that the essential difference is in the amount of silica, of which the schist has over 47 per cent., while the ore has less than 10 per cent., and again the ore has 25 per cent. more metallic iron than the rock. The one would evidently be converted into the other, both as to its chemical and physical characters, by the abstraction of the greater part of its silica. It is not at all improbable, that this change may have been brought about by the alkaline waters of former thermal springs, such as are now producing similar results in other parts of the world. There seems to be very little sand or clay in this ore, and washing has not appeared to improve its quality, as is the case with the eastern ores which it resembles. If the fragments of silicious rock, which are scattered through it, are carefully picked out by the miner, an ore uniform in character is obtained. Except the ever-present silica, there are only two minerals, which it is necessary to mention as being generally associated with this variety of ore. 1st. The *white clay* (kaolinite), above described, which is far more abundant in this ore than the hard ores; bunches as large as a hen's egg being sometimes seen. There can be no doubt but that the kindly working of the furnace usually obtained by using the best quality of this ore, is due in part to this clay as well as to the porous character of the ore. (Calcining the ore would expel the water, of which it contains from 2 to 9 per cent., and should also cause it to reduce more easily in the furnace.) The second and most important mineral to be mentioned is the *oxide of manganese,* usually if not always in the form of Pyrolusite; minute quantities of this metal, always less than one per cent., are sometimes found in the hard ores, but from 1 to 4 per cent. is constantly present in several of the hematite deposits, which is so important an element in their value, as to almost warrant the subdivision of the soft hematites into two classes, the *manganiferous* and *non-manganiferous.*

The recently developed hematite mines near Negaunee, belonging to formation X., contain most manganese; others contain little or none. Scarcely enough of the ore has been worked to determine its place in the market; but there can be no doubt, that when equally rich in metallic iron, the manganese would give this ore the advantage, as a mixture for the furnace, over the non-manganiferous varieties. See Spec. 25, State Coll., App. B, Vol. II.

The hematite ores now in the market, as a class, vary greatly in richness, from an average of not exceeding 40 per cent. of metallic iron for some deposits, to at least 55 per cent. in the case of others. This difference is in part brought out in Chapter X.

Passing from the Marquette region to the undeveloped districts, we find on the L'Anse range, at the Taylor mine, a large deposit of hematite of excellent quality. At the Breen mine, on the south belt of the Menominee region, is also a good "show" of hematite. Promising indications of this ore were also found between Lake Gogebic and Montreal river; all of these localities and their ores will be described hereafter.

e. The last variety of merchantable ore, to be described in this report and designated *Flag*, has been in use so short a time, that but little can be said of its metallurgical character. It corresponds more nearly with the second-class ores (*c*), than with either variety described, differing from it more in structure than in composition. The ores embraced under this head are abundant and have received various local names, which will be found significant and convenient, as lean ores, iron slates, magnetic slates and silicious ores. They have also been called "lower ores," in reference to their subordinate geological position, being older than the rich ores of formation XIII., already described. Flag ores are in reality only varieties of the ferruginous schists, constituting Group B, next to be described, which are sufficiently rich in iron, to possess market value. The percentage of metallic iron in these ores and the associated schists varies from say 5 to nearly 60, those above 50 now constituting a merchantable ore. The remaining material is generally silica, always silicious, but sometimes contains more or less chlorite, manganese, argillite, mica, garnet, or hornblende added. This ore is always flaggy in structure, the layers being occasionally thin enough, to warrant the application of the term slate. All forms of the oxide of iron can be observed, a mixture of the black and red prevailing. The hydrated oxide, producing limonitic silicious schist, has been described above, as the rock from which the soft hematite ore seems to have been derived, and an analysis is there given, to which nothing need be added here.

Stratigraphically these rocks are older than the ores described under *a* and *b*, and constitute at least four beds, X., VIII., VI., and below V., separated by diorites, chloritic schists, quartzites and argillites. Like the mixed ores (*c*) they are banded, but the marking is seldom bright and often obscure, produced by the interlamination of a dull reddish or whitish quartz, with dull *silicious* instead of *pure* ore. There are exceptions to this rule, but they are not numerous in this region. As this is a point of much importance to iron prospectors, it may be asserted, that when white or red quartz (jasper) is found banded with an ore which can be scratched with the knife, it is in all probability the "mixed ore," which accompanies the pure ores of bed XIII.; but if the quartz be dull and not sharply defined in its layers, and particularly if the knife marks the ore layers like a pencil, instead of cutting them, then we probably have one of the flag-ore formations. It is difficult to say, whether the red or black oxides prevail in many flag ores ; hence whether particular varieties should be described as hematitic or magnetic.

All ores and ferruginous rocks become more magnetic as they are followed west in the Marquette region, the maximum amount of magnetite occurring in the Michigamme district. The ferruginous schists of the Republic Mountain series are among the most highly magnetic rocks in the whole region. At the Ogden mine, Section 13, T. 47, R. 27, the abrupt transition of the hematitic into the magnetic variety can be plainly observed, by following the *strike* of the beds less than 200 feet. This transition probably often occurs in the same bed, and, of course, might occur still oftener in crossing the formations, that is, in passing from one bed to another.

Several varieties of *flag ore* will now be described, showing a wide range in lithological character, which we should not be warranted in grouping together in a strictly scientific classification ; but our arrangement of rocks, as has been stated, is rather economic and for the use of practical men.

(1) A showy, granular, chloritic, specular ore was found in a small pocket-like mass at the north ¼ post of Sec. 26, T. 47, R. 26, at locality known as the Gillmore mine. A specimen having a specific gravity of 4.28 gave Dr. C. F. Chandler metallic iron 60.46, alumina 3.49, lime 0.60, magnesia 1.33, silica 7.05, sulphur 0.30, phosphoric acid 0.08, water and alkalies not determined 0.77.

A similar ore, but containing some magnetite and peculiar white glistening spots, which appear to be mica scales, is found at the Chippewa location, Sec. 22, T. 47, R. 30. A specimen of this gave Prof. A. B. Prescott metallic iron 53.17, and insoluble silicious matter 20.20. Neither of these varieties are flaggy. See Specs. 6,156 and 6,206, University of Michigan cabinet.

(2) A specular slate ore, holding reddish specks on freshly fractured surfaces, is found at the Cascade location, bedded with layers of jasper, having the local significant name of "Bird's-eye Slate." A specimen of this gave J. B. Britton metallic iron 59.65, insoluble silicious matter 12.24, alumina 0.88, lime 0.14, magnesia 0.08, oxide of manganese 0.02, water 1.08, with traces of sulphur and phosphorus. See Spec. 6,190, University of Michigan cabinet, and Spec. 6, State Coll., App. B, Vol. II.

(3) South of the Cascade range is a flag ore, beautifully banded with

red jasper and silicious iron ore, closely resembling some of the mixed ores of Bed XIII. above described, and interesting on this account.

(4) Northeast of the Cascade location, and near the centre of Sec. 29, T. 47, R. 26, is a granular slate ore showing on fresh fracture a peculiar fine reticulated appearance and indistinct octahedral forms. A specimen of this gave Mr. Britton 59.42 per cent. of metallic iron. See Spec. 6,191, University of Mich. cabinet. Since the foregoing was written, shipments of flag ore have been made from the Cascade mines (see Plate XII. of Atlas), and with it a considerable amount of a good quality of specular ore.

(5) At the Tilden mine, while the prevailing ore is a 40 per cent. ordinary red flag ore, there are seams or layers of bright steely ore, very hard and heavy, which yield, according to analyses made by Dr. Draper, 62 per cent. metallic iron. This ore possesses particular interest from its close resemblance to the Pilot Knob ore, Mo.

(6) While the most abundant ore at the Iron Mountain mine, Sec. 14, T. 47, R. 27, is much like the Tilden and Ogden ores already mentioned, there is a peculiar variety, containing manganese, which is also found on the hills south of Negaunee and on the lands of the Deer Lake Company, north of the New York mine. This ore is a very dark-colored silicious hematitic schist, containing on the average several per cent. of manganese, single specimens of which have proved to be nearly pure oxide of manganese. Some of this ore from Iron Mountain was tested in the furnace as a mixture, but was found to be silicious. The need of ferro-manganese in steel-making would make ores of this character a legitimate object of exploration. An experienced iron-master recently expressed the opinion that a 30 per cent. iron ore, with 12 to 20 per cent. of manganese, would soon have commercial value. It is possible that such a variety may exist in some of the beds under consideration. The soft or hematitic variety of this ore has already been mentioned.

(7) Passing from the Negaunee to the Michigamme district, we find two flag ores worth noticing. On the Magnetic Company's property, Sec. 20, T. 47, R. 30, is a large amount of a very compact, hard, heavy, highly magnetic ore, laminated with a greenish horn-blendic mineral, producing an unusual banded structure. A piece of one of the layers of ore gave Mr. Britton 56.78 metallic

iron, 19.44 insoluble silicious matter, less than one per cent. of alumina, lime and magnesia, and a trace of phosphorus. See Spec. 18, State Coll., App. B, Vol. II.; also Chapter X. Recent explorations have developed a workable deposit of this ore.

(8) Adjoining this property, to the southeast is Sec. 28, owned by the Cannon Iron Co., on the north side of which is a thin layer of micaceous specular ore, closely resembling that described above under A, but containing more silica. A specimen of this afforded Professor Prescott 55.12 metallic iron, 19.80 insoluble silicious matter, with traces of sulphur and phosphorus. This and the banded ore associated with it, has a closer resemblance to the slate and "mixed ore" of some of the old mines, than any place I have seen in the flag-ore series, to which it seems to me geologically to belong; its relation to the associated mica schist is interesting. See Group H below. The Chippewa ore, near the Cannon, has already been mentioned above in connection with the Gillmore.

The foregoing brief descriptions of several varieties of flag ore embrace all those, which have come under my notice in the Marquette region and give promise of having early commercial value.

As will be elsewhere (Chapter V.) more fully described, the hard ores found in the Menominee region up to October, 1872, are more nearly allied to flag ores than to either of the first-class ores of the Marquette region. Flag ores of a low grade have also been found in the L'Anse and Gogebic districts, as will be mentioned hereafter.

A very limited experience in working these ores, together with the little I have been able to learn from others, leads me to believe, that they require more limestone and coal and produce a harder metal, having comparatively little strength, but which is probably well adapted to making rail-heads. I think a large mixture of manganiferous hematite might help the working of a furnace consuming flag ore. Precisely the same remarks may be made of the second-class ores (*c*); indeed, these two classes are to all intents and purposes identical in their metallurgical character, and are only separated here because of their different geological occurrence. The second-class ores are, it will be remembered, simply inferior grades of the rich hard ores of XIII.

The flag ores have here received relatively far more attention, than their present commercial importance warrants, for the following reasons:—1st, Their quantity, so far as can now be judged, is greater by tenfold than the first-class hard ores, and for this reason they must, at some future time, constitute a large part of the total production of the region. 2d. Very serious disappointments and losses have occurred in the past, and are likely to be repeated in the future, from mistaking flag ore for first-class ore. This arises from the fact, that the better varieties of flag ore closely resemble the poorer varieties of the rich ore. So close is this resemblance, that the best judges of ore in the Marquette region have erred. It is doubtful, if the matter can be settled definitely, except by thorough explorations, aided by the well-known laws of the geological occurrence of the two ores, which will be more fully brought out in succeeding chapters.

It is not asserted that first-class hard ores may not be found associated with the flag ores, hence below and older than formation XIII. ; but it is a fact, that over one million dollars have been sunk in such search, and excepting the West End mine of the Cascade range (if that is an exception), no workable deposit of strictly high grade hard ore has been found in the flag-ore series.

B. Ferruginous, Silicious, and Jaspery Schists.

(Occurring in formations XII., X., VIII., VI., and below V.)

The best general idea of the character of the rocks embraced here can be conveyed by saying, that they are identical with the flag ores last described, except in containing less iron and usually more silicious matter. On geological grounds, as has been remarked, the flag ores should be embraced under this head and described as a subclass, rich in iron. It remains therefore for me to mention briefly, a few of the remaining varieties of this series, which are so poor in iron as to render it highly improbable that they will ever possess value as ores : I design to embrace in this group Mr. Julien's quartz schist, silicious schist, and jasper schist, Appendix A, Vol. II. For minute lithological descriptions of numerous varieties see Specs. 154 to 173, App. A, Vol. II.

At Republic Mountain are three highly magnetic beds of silicious, chloritic and hornblendic schists, numbers VI., VIII., and X. See Map No. VI. of Atlas. The peculiar striping—whitish, greenish, brownish, and yellowish—exhibited in the large outcrops suggested the name "rag-carpet schist." A specimen made up of numerous chippings of this rock gave 31 per cent. of metallic iron; this is believed to be above the average. Both the red and black oxides are present, and some of the layers hold an ore, which, if it could be separated, might yield 50 per cent.

South of the Washington mine these rocks contain the minimum amount of iron, a specimen of which gave Charles E. Wright less than 5 per cent. Garnets and anthophyllite, or mica, seem to replace the iron, producing a grayish and brownish schist, the mineralogical character of which is obscure. See Group I. The old Michigan mine ore, Section 18, T. 47, R. 28, seems to be a variety of this peculiar schist, but much more highly charged with metal, specimens of which, I should judge, would afford 30 to 40 per cent. of metallic iron.

Passing to the Negaunee district we find in the railroad cut at the northwest end of Lake Fairbanks a chloritic, magnetic, silicious schist of a brownish gray color, faintly banded and very hard; it is aphanitic in character, and shows no disposition to split on the planes of bedding. In the railroad cut near the centre of Section 8, one mile and a half southeast of Negaunee, is a soft variety of ferruginous rock, affording some good red chalk. The rock seems to be chloritic, layers of which are impregnated with red oxide of iron. A similar material was found in numerous test pits in the east part of Section 18, T. 47, R. 26. Recent explorations in this vicinity prove this rock to be associated with the Negaunee hematites, which are fully described in Chapter IV.*

One of the best characterized and abundant varieties of this group is the banded ferruginous jaspery schist, which constitutes in the Michigamme district the whole of formation XII., and is also abundant in parts of ore formation XIII. Such varieties of "mixed ore," as contain too little iron to give them commercial value (unfortunately the greater part), would be classed here. The full descriptions and illustrations already given of "mixed ore" under A, will make any further description unnecessary, for this is a similar rock with little or no iron. See Spec. 32, State Coll., App. B, Vol. II., and for several other varieties of this group see Specs. 1,026, 1,034, 1,061, and 1,064, Appendix C, Vol. II. The Felch mountain series contain a large amount of a similar rock.

---

* It is questionable whether this rock should be classed under D or G.

C. Diorites, Dioritic Schists and Related Rocks (*Greenstones*,)*

(constituting formations XI., IX., VII., and one or more beds below them.)

These obscurely bedded rocks, locally designated greenstones and sometimes traps, are co-extensive with the ferruginous rocks A and B, very abundant, outcropping throughout the Huronian region, and present much variety in appearance. They range in structure from very fine-grained or compact (almost aphanite) to coarsely granular and crystalline, being sometimes porphyritic in character. The color of the fresh fracture is from dull-light to dark or blackish green, the weathered surface being usually lighter and of a grayish green or brownish color, not unfrequently spotted or mottled, showing a dark-green, or black, lamellar mineral (hornblende), set in a whitish, and sometimes reddish, softer mineral (feldspar). The rock is exceedingly tough, powdering under blows of the hammer rather than break. It can be scratched by the knife, giving a light grayish-green powder, and is fused without difficulty before the blow-pipe. On the one hand, it graduates into a heavier, tougher, blacker variety, which is unquestionably hornblende rock, with some feldspar, well shown at the Greenwood Furnace quarry, on Sec. 15, T. 47, R. 28. See Specs. 1,018 and 1,020, App. C, Vol. II. On the other hand, it passes into a softer, lighter colored rock of lower specific gravity, which, while it has the same streak, weathers similar to the true diorite, is eminently schistose in character, splitting easily, and appearing more like chloritic schist than any other rock. The Pioneer Furnace quarry at Negaunee contains this schist and several transition varieties, some of which approach the granular massive rock. See Specs. 1,001, 1,005, 1,006, and 1,015, App. C, Vol. II. On the north side of Lake Michigamme, and west, varieties occur having a true slaty structure in appearance, although not splitting easily. See Spec. 1,028, App. C, Vol. II.

At several points dioritic schists, semi-amygdaloidal in character, were observed, and in one instance the rock had a strong resemblance to a conglomerate. See Spec. 1,024, App. C, Vol. II.; and

* See Dr. Houghton's Notes on Diorites, Appendix E, Vol. II.

Spec. 71, State Coll., App. B, Vol. II. It is of much practical importance to distinguish between the schist of this group and the true chloritic schist to be described under the next head, D, which is usually found associated with the pure ores of Bed XIII.*

At Republic mountain a dioritic schist graduates into black mica schist, and large garnets are there found in typical diorite. Iron pyrites are usually seen sprinkled through the rock, and epidote is sometimes observed. Dr. Hunt found chromium in two specimens. South of the Old Washington mine, in Bed XI., occurs a variety, which in places may almost be described as hornblendic schist; that in other parts of the same bed, near at hand, graduates into the above-described dioritic schist.

In the railroad cut at the foot of Moss Mt., west of Negaunee, is an exposure of soft dioritic schist, in which are imbedded rounded lumps of diorite, which, when broken, show a crystalline reddish feldspar. See Specs. 1,001 and 1,002, App. C, Vol. II. Spec. 77, App. B, Vol. II., is another beautiful and rare variety, in which the feldspar is red. On the south side of Sec. 9, T. 49, R. 33, is a heavy bed of coarse-grained friable diorite, which has in places disintegrated into sand. Mr. Julien regards this and the associated dioritic rocks of the L'Anse range as possessing such distinctive characteristic as to warrant him in describing them as a distinct variety. See Specs. 342 to 353, App. A, Vol. II. He also classes the well-known peculiar serpentine rock of Presque isle with the diorites. See Spec. 321, App. A, Vol. II, also App. E.

The magnet usually lifts less than one per cent. of a powdered diorite, but in one case it took nearly all, and the specimen attracted the needle. This piece was from the ridge south of the New England mine; it had the essential character of a compact, perhaps hornblendic diorite, but its magnetic property and very high specific gravity, 3.29, prove that it is exceptionally rich in iron. It will be shown below, that in addition to the magnetite, seventeen per cent. of metallic iron exists in some diorites in the form of combined protoxide, which does not attract the needle. The specific gravity of the typical rock varied from 2.84 to 2.96, the average of six specimens being 2.91. The hornblendic varieties ranged as high as 3.01, while the schistose variety fell as low as 2.70,

* See Julien's remarks under Chloritic schist, App. A, Vol. II.

averaging 2.82. A garnetiferous specimen, from Smith Mountain, gave 3.02, while a peculiar variety from north of Greenwood Furnace, which appeared to be feldspathic in character, gave but 2.71. Numerous additional specific gravity determinations are given in App. B, Vol. II. The precise character of the constituent minerals of this rock is obscure. Mr. Julien has minutely described numerous varieties in App. A, Vol. II., Specs. 302 to 353.

The following analysis of a specimen from bed XI. is from Foster & Whitney's Report, Part 2d, p. 92. The specimen was from Sect. 10, T. 47, R. 27, on south side of the Cleveland and Lake Superior ore deposits :—

		OXYGEN.
Silica	46.31	24.06
Alumina	11.14	5.21
Protoxide of iron	21.69	4.82
Lime	9.68	2.76
Soda	6.91	1.78
Water	4.44	
Magnesia	trace.	
	100.17	

From this it is deduced that the rock is a mixture of labradorite feldspar with hornblende or pyroxene. Regarding the presence of water, numerous analysis of similar rocks in Canada show the same result. See Geology of Canada, pages 469, 604, 605, and 612. Dr. Hunt expresses the opinion, that in the case of the Marquette diorites, the hornblendic mineral often becomes softened and hydrated, passing into a degenerate form more nearly allied to chlorite or delessite (in which water is an essential constituent), than to a true hornblende. This chloritic mineral is sometimes seen scattered through the body of the rock, and very often near the weathered surface.

The absence of *magnesia*, which is regarded as an essential ingredient of chlorite and delessite, and as very rarely absent from hornblende, as shown by the above analysis, deserves notice. Dr. Hunt remarks that the hornblendic element may very likely be the iron hornblende described by Dana, System of Mineralogy, 5th ed. p. 234, under the name grünerite. The unusually large amount of iron shown by Whitney's analysis and the high specific gravity observed would favor this view. The conversion of this non-magnesian diorite into a magnesian schist (chloritic or delessitic) would require the introduction of the magnesian element under some law of pseudomorphism, the possibility of which is proven by chemical geology.

Magnesia is not, however, absent from all varieties of the diorite. A chromiferous specimen from near the centre of Sec. 36, T. 48, R. 28, was found by Dr. Hunt to be rich in magnesia, containing more of this element than of lime; the specimen was not a typical one, but showed a tendency to pass into a steatitic rock, which might be expected to contain magnesia. Until, however, the presence of magnesia in the schists and its absence from the diorites is proven by more analyses, it is not worth while to conjecture in the matter, and I here digress only to record a few facts, bearing on an interesting and unsettled question in chemical geology. In the absence of any additional light, we adopt the hypothesis that the Marquette "greenstones" are diorites, composed essentially of a non-magnesian iron hornblende and some feldspar other than orthoclase.

It is of great importance that the prospector should have a good practical acquaintance with this rock, for it is everywhere associated with iron ores in the Upper Peninsula. He should be able to recognize it at sight, to distinguish its varieties, and especially he must not confound the Huronian diorite with a similar rock, found in the Laurentian, nor with Copper trap. More than one piece of land has been bought for iron on the Laurentian area, because "greenstone" was found on it.

The bedding of these rocks is generally obscure, and in the granular varieties entirely wanting. It is usually only after a full study of the rock in mass, and after its relations with the under and overlaying beds are fully made out, that one becomes convinced, whatever its origin, it presents in mass precisely the same phenomenon as regards stratification, as do the accompanying schists and quartzites.

I have nowhere seen the granular diorites show more unmistakable evidence of bedding than on the small knob southwest of Bear Lake, Republic Mountain, shown in Fig. 1, scale $\frac{1}{50}$th. The cross shading represents massive diorite, and the parallel shading a slaty silicious iron ore.

No reference is here made to the false stratification or joints, which are numerous and interesting, but which, unfortunately, for want of space, can receive no other attention here, than to warn the observer against mistaking *joint* planes for *bedding* planes, which is sometimes done, even by experienced observers.

This description, as has been stated, is intended to apply to the diorites of the iron-bearing or Huronian series, and more especially

Fig. 1.

Stratification of Diorite.

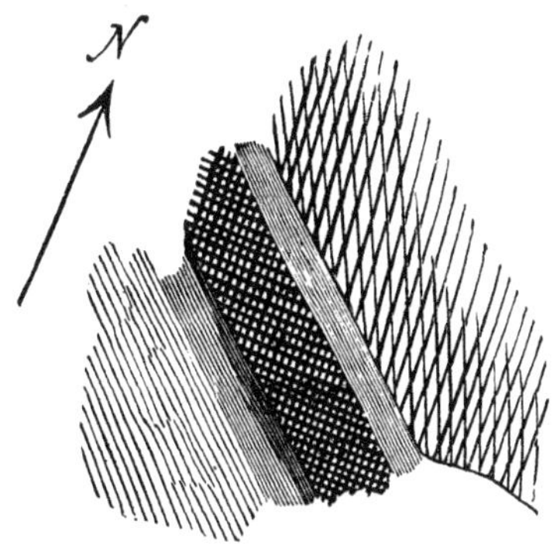

to the Marquette region; but a similar rock, as has been observed, occurs abundantly in dykes or veins, and probably in beds in the Laurentian rocks. A fine example of such a dyke can be seen penetrating a granitic gneiss, near the northeast corner of Sec. 7, T. 46, R. 29. At other points in the Laurentian area immense masses of a dioritic rock were observed, the stratigraphical relations of which to the gneiss and granites was not made out. The average specific gravity of the dyke diorite was 3.03. Mr. Julien describes some specimens of diorite from the Laurentian in App. A, Vol. II.

The following designated specimens, in addition to those already referred to, constitute a tolerably full collection of the more important varieties:—Granular diorites, 1,007, 1,008, 1,009, 1,010, 1,011, 1,012, 1,014, and 1,016; Dioritic schists, 1,001, 1,019, and 1,023 of App. C, Vol. II. The State Collection, App. B, Vol. II., also contains a large number of specimens of diorite of several varieties.

The distribution of this rock in the Huronian of the Upper Peninsula is interesting. It is far more abundant in the Marquette region and contiguous to the ore deposits, than elsewhere. The related rocks in the L'Anse region are abundant; but in the West iron district, and on its prolongation into Wisconsin, where it forms the Penokie range, diorites are rare. In the Menominee region they seem to be replaced to a great extent by chloritic schists and hornblendic schists, as described in Chapter V. Whether future explorations will prove that the best ores are always associated with the typical diorite, remains to be seen.

D. MAGNESIAN SCHISTS (*mostly chloritic*).

(See Mr. Julien's description, Specs. 179 to 188, App. A, Vol. II.)

Intercalated with the pure hard and mixed ores, at all the mines worked in formation XIII., are layers of a soft schistose rock, of some shade of grayish green, and often talcy in feeling. The Cleveland, Lake Superior and Champion mines are good localities for an examination of this rock. It is unquestionably a magnesian schist, varying from chloritic to talcose in character, and sometimes apparently containing a large percentage of argillite. In places, as at the Old Washington, its character is unmistakably talcose. Specimens obtained there held 4.2 per cent. of water, and had a specific gravity of 2.81, with light grayish-green color, and other characteristics of talcose schist. See Specs. 1,046, App. C, Vol. II. The corresponding schist at the Champion mine is also decidedly talcy. On the same magnetic range, but further west, at the Spurr Mountain, the equivalent schist is unmistakably chloritic. See Specs. 179 to 181, App. A, Vol. II. A rare variety of talc schist is represented by Spec. 74, App. B, Vol. II., obtained at the Grace furnace, Marquette.

In the Lake Superior and Barnum mines this rock is, in places, of a light green color, less soapy in feel, has a higher specific gravity and is of uncertain composition. See Spec. 55, State Coll., App. B, Vol. II. At this locality it has a marked cleavage structure, the planes of which trend east and west, and are nearly vertical, being distinct from its bedding, which latter is very obscure. Its structure bears a striking resemblance to that of the specular slate ores, noticed under A, even to the presence in both of minute octahedral crystals. Prof. Pumpelly has suggested, that one may be a pseudomorph after the other. In this connection it may be remarked, that no gradual transition of one into the other was observed, the division planes being in each instance sharply defined.

Specimen No, 1,043, App. C, Vol. II., from the Washington mine, is grayish, less schistose in structure than the last described variety, and gave up, when pulverized, one-third its bulk to the magnet. A similar massive variety from the same mine, which contained three per cent. of water, held black hard scales, which Prof. Brush decided had the character of ottrelite.

A reddish gray variety of this rock (see Spec. 6,164, University of Mich. Cabinet), holding grains of vitreous quartz, is from a heavy bed on the northeast side of the S. C. Smith soft hematite ore deposit, on Sections 17, 18, and 20, T. 45, R. 25.

South of the Edwards mine, at the Republic Mountain, and at other places in the ferruginous schists, occur bunches and thin irregular beds of a pure chlorite, often micaceous, which always contain garnets. See Spec. 6,097, University of Mich. Cabinet. This specimen shows, under the lens, minute elongated crystalline faces, closely resembling those seen in the diorite. Spec. 184, App. A, Vol. II., is garnetiferous. The "keal" or red chalk, found at several mines, is a variety of this schist impregnated with oxide of iron. See Spec. 6,183, University of Mich. Cabinet.

A very peculiar occurrence of this rock are the so-called "slate-dykes," which can be seen at the New England, Lake Superior and Jackson mines, but still better in the quartzite ridge, just north of the outlet of Teal lake. These dykes are often several feet in width, cut across the stratification, and are filled with a magnesian schist. If space permits, this subject will be more fully considered elsewhere. See Specs. 1,053, 1,068, App. C, Vol. II.

The Lower Quartzite bed V. often contains talc in bunches, small beds and disseminated, producing in places a talcy rock. The *novaculite* of that formation is due to the presence of talc and argillite. These rocks will, on account of their association, be more fully described in the Quartzite group.

It would be difficult for a skilled lithologist, and impossible for me, to draw the line between the chloritic schists here considered and the dioritic schists mentioned under Group C. So far I have chiefly noted occurrences of the magnesian schists, in formations XIII. and V., where they are not associated with true diorites. But at the Marquette quarries we find what may be called typical chloritic schists, bedded with granular diorites. See Specs. 182 and 183, App. A, Vol. II. At this locality the planes separating the two kinds of rock are well defined; at others, which have been designated, the transition is gradual.

Along the north border of the Laurentian area, which lies south of Lake Gogebic (see Map I.), are numerous exposures of a chloritic schist (see Specs. 187 and 188, App. A, Vol. II.), which in places becomes massive and granular, a form designated "greenstone" by the United States Linear Surveyors, and so marked on their maps. See Specs. of Diorite, 309 and 212, App. A, Vol. II.

The specimens of Laurentian Gneiss, 275 and 299, App. A, Vol. II., contain chlorite as an essential ingredient, proving this mineral to be as widely disseminated in the Laurentian as Huronian. An examination of Prof. Pumpelly's very exhaustive chapters on the lithology of the copper-bearing rocks, will show chlorite to be of frequent occurrence in that system; demonstrating it to be next to feldspar and quartz, one of the most universally diffused minerals in the Azoic of the Upper Peninsula.

E. QUARTZITE—*Conglomerates, Breccias, and Sandstones.*

(Principal development in Formations V. and XIV. See Mr. Julien's descriptions, 126 to 140, and also 358 and 359, App. A, Vol. II.)

After diorite and the ferruginous schists, no rock is more abundant in the Marquette region, and none more frequently found in outcrops, than the different varieties of this group. Two extensive beds exist—XIV. lies immediately over the ore formation, and V. near the base of the series. The last appears to be the most persistent and wide-spread member of the Huronian system. It can be traced from the shore of Lake Superior, near Chocolate river, westward for 40 miles, and possesses unusually economic interest from its affording the marble, used to a limited extent as furnace flux, and the whetstone rock (novaculite), which was at one time quarried for market. This quartzite has also recently been successfully employed as lining for Bessemer converters.

The Upper Quartzite (XIV.) is co-extensive with the ore formation XIII.; it is seen as the hanging wall of the most easterly point, at which rich hard ore is mined, and overlays the most westerly deposit yet explored. Between these is a third bed, seen in the railroad cut near the west end of Lake Fairbanks, the extent of which has not been made out. See Spec. 21, App. B, Vol. II.

At the west end of Lake Michigamme, near the centre of Sec. 25, T. 48, R. 31, is a large mass of quartzite, which appears to be a ledge, but if so, the bed is concealed to a greater extent than usual, for it has not been observed elsewhere. No. XVIII. is assigned for this quartzite, or for whatever rock may be found in the gap between Beds XVII. and XIX. The Cascade iron range is divided by a thin bed of quartzose rock, which varies from a quartzite to the coarsest conglomerate I have observed in the region, but which, like the two last-mentioned beds, seems to be local. At the Greenwood furnace is a heavy and persistent bed of quartzite, in which are intercalated layers of clay slate; its age has not been determined; it resembles the lower quartzite.

The extreme hardness of quartzite (the knife makes no impression on it, and it will readily scratch glass), and its general dissimilarity to the other members of the series, renders its recognition easy and much description unnecessary.

Vein quartz, occurring in bunches, seams and veins, in nearly all rocks, is not embraced in this description; nor are those slightly ferruginous quartz schists, already described in Group B, which a strictly scientific classification would place under this head. Quartzite is seldom white, often light-gray, or dark-gray and sometimes reddish or greenish. The effect of weathering does not penetrate the rock beyond a mere film, dulling the lustre and color of a fresh fracture rather, than changing it; but the latter effect is sometimes produced in the impure varieties. Broken pieces often show grains of glassy quartz; and the arenaceous character is sometimes so plain, as to leave no doubt in the mind, that the rock is a metamorphosed sandstone or conglomerate (see Fig. 2). Again, the whole mass is compact, having much the appearance of vein-quartz. In structure it is usually massive, and the bedding obscure; but in places, as at the northeast corner of Teal lake, it is banded, presenting a flaggy structure, like the ferruginous schists. The mean specific gravity of a large number of specimens was 2.69. See App. B, Vol. II.

The foregoing description applies in general to all the beds; but as it is often of importance to the explorer to distinguish the Upper bed on account of its relation to the ore formation, a few points of difference will be noted. As has been remarked, the Lower bed is often calcareous, turning in places into a true marble, as at the Morgan Furnace; and the same formation is often talcy in character, containing in certain localities bunches and beds of a talcy material and in other places beds of argillite. An intimate mixture of these minerals with the quartzose material produces novaculite, which was formerly quarried just east of Teal Lake outlet. See Spec. 13, State Coll., App. B., Vol. II. Red oxide of iron in grains and small bunches, is not infrequent in the Lower bed, as can be seen in northeast quarter of Sec. 22, T. 47, R. 26.

So far I have seen neither marble, talc, nor novaculite in the Upper Quartzite, and only once, at the Lake Superior Mine, have I seen argillite associated with it. As this exception has much interest, it will be fully considered in another place. The Lower Quartzite is seldom conglomeritic, the upper one often so, and in places on the Spurr Mountain range it is a true conglomerate, containing pebbles of white and glassy quartz and jasper. See Specs. 115 to 118, App. A, Vol. II. At Republic Mountain large fragments of ferruginous schist are seen in the base of the Upper bed. Southwest of the Old Washington mine it is a coarse conglomeritic rock, which is in places schistose or slaty. See Spec. 122, App. A, Vol. II.

The matrix of this variety (See also Spec. 6,085, University of Mich. Cabinet) is a soft, micaceous, slaty material, containing fine grains of specular ore and holding pebbles of white quartz. The Upper bed overlying the east end of the Jackson, and that over the New York mine, also hold pebbles. Mica scales and epidote were found in the same bed at the Republic Mountain, and in places it had almost the appearance of fine-grained granite.

As if to leave in our minds no shadow of doubt, as to the sedimentary origin of this rock, nature has, in addition to the conglomerate on the Spurr Mountain range, given us a variety of the Upper Quartzite, which can only be described as a fine-grained, friable, banded *sandstone*. See Specs. 358 and 359, App. A, Vol. II. The alternations of magnetic sand with quartz sand, producing the stripes, is very interesting in connection with the origin of these ores. It is doubtful if any true breccias (conglomerates with angular pebbles) occur associated with the rocks here described, if at all in the region. The brecciated rocks, a variety of "mixed ore" found in formation XIII., is believed to have had the origin ascribed under Group A.

Specimens of University of Mich. Cabinet, Nos. 6,193, 6,084, 6,180, 6,211, 6,219, and 6,122 are from these quartzite beds. Specs. 8 to 14, State Coll., App. B, Vol. II., are from the Lower bed, and Specs. 50, 51, and 52, same Coll., are from the Upper. The extensive beds of quartzite, which occur in the Menominee region, will be fully considered in Chapter V. This rock is also of frequent occurrence in the L'Anse range and toward the Montreal river, as will appear in following Chapters. A beautiful example of false stratification, or discordant parallelism, was observed in this last-named region, as is shown by Fig. 2, sketched near the south quarter post of Sec. 10, T. 47, R. 45. It was a true granular quartzite, but showed deposition marks almost as plainly as a fresh-cut sandbank.

Fig. 2.
False bedding (discordant parallelism) of Quartzite—Gogebic Region.

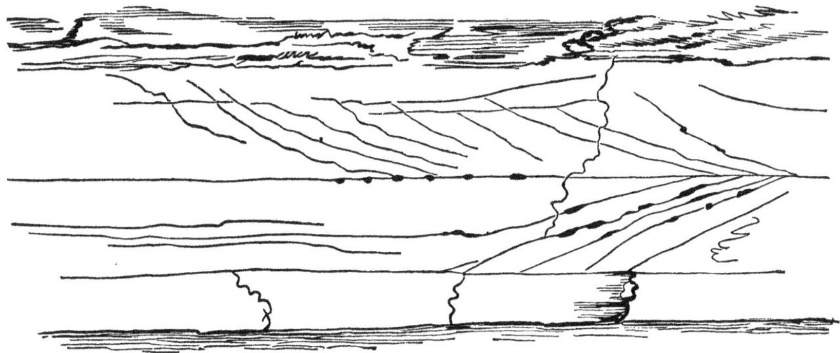

F. MARBLE (*Limestone and Dolomite*).

(See Mr. Julien's descriptions, 101 to 113, App. A, Vol. II.)

The association of this rock with the Lower Quartzite, or rather the transition of the latter into marble, has been mentioned. This transition is seldom complete, the marble being always more or less silicious. As is usual in such cases, the change is gradual, producing all varieties, from calcareous quartzite to silicious marble. The prevailing colors are light gray, salmon and reddish. The purest varieties often present a sparry structure, with large lamellar facets like orthoclase feldspar, with which it is often confounded, but from which it can readily be distinguished by its softness. Beds of argillite are invariably associated with the marble. See Fig. 19, App. E, Vol. II. Outcrops often present minute ribs or ridges of the more silicious layers, left by the weathering away of the purer marble.

The mean specific gravity of a large number of specimens averaged 2.82. See App. B, Vol. II. Pure marble has the same composition as pure limestone, of which it is simply a crystalline or highly altered form, that is, it is a carbonate of lime ;—if carbonate of magnesia is present in considerable quantity, as is often the case on the Upper Peninsula, the rock becomes a *dolomite*. Marble is readily distinguished from its effervescing with acids, when pulverized.

Marquette marble has been considerably used as a blast furnace flux, for which purpose it only answers passably well, on account of the silica so generally present ; silica, in the form of quartz, and jasper being always present in the *ores*, it is very desirable to have none in the *flux*, for it is to get rid of silica in the form of slag, that lime is used in the furnace. Large amounts of Kelly island limestone, which is quite pure, is now being imported. For building purposes, its hardness, variability in texture and the difficulty of securing large blocks, have so far prevented its use ; beautifully variegated small blocks can, however, be easily procured. Specs. 6,198, 6,199, 6,200, University of Michigan Cabinet, are from the Morgan Furnace quarry, and Specs. 106 to 113, State Col., App. B, Vol. II., from the Chocolate quarry, just south of Marquette, all belonging to formation V., represent the chief varieties of this rock.

No marble has been observed in the L'Anse district, nor between Lake Gogebic and Montreal river, but it is one of the most abundant rocks in the Menominee region, where it occurs in a much purer form than in Marquette, usually more dolomitic. See Chapter V. and Specs. 102 and 103, App. A, Vol. II. Marble of similar quality is also abundant in the vicinity of Fence and Michigamme rivers, in Towns 44 and 45, R. 31. See Spec. 105, App. A, Vol. II.

G. Argillite or Clay Slates and Related Rocks.*

(Constitutes bed XV., and occurs in bed V. and elsewhere.)

It was previously mentioned under Groups E and F, that beds of clay-slate were sometimes interstratified with layers of quartzite and marble. Fine examples of this, in the case of both rocks, can be seen respectively at the Greenwood and Morgan furnaces. In addition to these, at least two distinct beds of argillite have been made out; one immediately beneath the ferruginous schist of formation X., to be seen in outcrop on the south shore of Teal lake, near west end, and in the railroad cut about one mile east of Negaunee. See Spec. 20, App. B, Vol. II. Another and far more extensive bed is XV., which forms the stratum next above the Upper Quartzite; boulders of this bed, which had the appearance of being near the parent ledge, were found in the railroad cutting, near the pockets at the Washington mine. At the Champion this formation is exposed in the branch railroad, and it is found at numerous points on the north shore of Lake Michigamme.

The prevailing color of this rock is usually dark brown or blackish, but where associated with the marble it is sometimes reddish. It has a true slaty cleavage, distinct from the bedding, but seldom splits in sufficiently large or regular slates to warrant us in supposing it may in places produce roofing slates, although experienced persons express the belief, that good slates will yet be found in the Marquette region. Black carbonaceous matter is often present in this slate, a preponderance of which produces the rock which will be described hereafter under J. A variety at the Greenwood furnace contains a large amount of iron-pyrites; and the first stack built of it had to be taken down, from the decomposition of this mineral. The slate in the branch railroad cut, at Champion, shows a slight tendency to be micaceous and holds garnets. See Spec. 56, App. B, Vol. II. Silicious bands often exist

---

* Mr. Julien has in App. A, Vol. II., given the results of much study of these rocks, and has divided them into the true argillites and several other varieties possessing a different composition. See descriptions 189 to 225. As this difference cannot readily be made out by the unscientific, and as it is not important to the practical man, it will not here be attempted to separate these varieties.

in this rock, faintly marking its bedding at an angle with the cleavage, as can be seen in Spec. 20, App. B, Vol. II.

Overlaying the Lake Superior and Barnum ore deposits, hence occupying the place of the Upper Quartzite, is a greenish-gray schist, obscure in its composition, and somewhat like the magnesian schists D, but apparently of the same general character as this group. See Spec. 55, App. B, Vol. II. This rock may very properly be regarded as the connecting link between Groups D and G, which evidently graduate into each other, as did C and D. It is frequently stained reddish-brown along the seams and cracks, proving the presence of protoxide of iron, and shows in places beautiful dendritic delineations of manganese. This formation does not show the cleavage structure, so conspicuous in the schists of Group D, which are bedded with the pure ore at these mines. At the most westerly opening of the Lake Superior, thin beds of quartzite appear, indicating that the presence of argillite in this bed is probably only local. See Map No. IX.

An example of a magnesian schist (D) graduating into an argillaceous variety can be seen in the slate which overlies the specular ore of No. 1 pit, New England mine, which, by its high specific gravity (3.03), evidently contains considerable iron. Another ferruginous and probably chloritic variety occurs on N. W. ¼ Sec. 31, T. 47, R. 25, where explorations for iron have been made by the Morgan Iron Co.

The average specific gravity of a number of typical specimens of argillite was 2.75. See App. B, Vol. II. The rocks above described are illustrated by Specimens 1,039, 1,072, and 1,036, App. C, Vol. II.

Beyond the limits of the Marquette region, we find in the recently explored Huron Bay district, particularly in the south part of T. 51, R. 31, the finest clay slates so far discovered in Michigan. Several competent experts have examined this district, and pronounced the slates of the best quality for roofing and other purposes, and in immense quantity. See Spec. 81, App. B, Vol. II. Companies are now at work in this district, the organization of which is given at the end of Chap. I. For an account of the clay-slates in the Menominee region, see Dr. H. Credner's papers (Leipsic).

This rock also occurs west of Lake Gogebic, as will be mentioned hereafter.

H. MICA-SCHIST.

(Formation XIX. contains the principal development of this rock. See Mr. Julien's description, No. 301, App. A, Vol. II.)

There appears to be but one extensive stratum of this rock, the character of which is unmistakable, which is at the same time the youngest and one of the thickest beds of the whole Huronian series. This formation, which I have numbered XIX., forms the surface rock along the south shore of Michigamme lake, among its islands, along the outlet for several miles, and westward from the lake through the southern parts of T. 48, Ranges 31 and 32, as shown on Map III. The rock is sometimes so silicious as to be rather a micaceous quartzite, but usually its true character is very plain. It frequently contains seams and bunches of white quartz, occasionally seams of black hornblende, and often holds numerous imperfect crystals of a delicately pink-colored, coarsely fibrous mineral, which Prof. Brush decided was andalusite, and brownish, smaller, and more perfect crystals of staurolite.

Andalusite and staurolite have not been observed elsewhere in the Marquette region in rocks of any age. Imperfect small reddish garnets are sometimes abundant, but they were not observed at the same places as the first-named minerals, and seemed to be nearer the base of the formation. The mica, which usually holds but little quartz, is of a brownish color on fresh fracture, weathering more grayish; its scales show a constant tendency to bend themselves around the imbedded crystals, like the fibres of wood around a knot. The projecting rounded crystals give the weathered rock a warty look, having somewhat the appearance of a conglomerate, as can be seen on the most southerly islands in Lake Michigamme. The specific gravity of this porphyritic mica-schist varied from 2.81 to 2.89, the mean being 2.84. See Specs. 1,031, App. C, and 61, App. B, Vol. II.

Descending in the series, the next mica-schist to be noticed is entirely different from the above, in being black, and decidedly dioritic in its affinities. It occurs in the upper part of diorite bed XI. at Republic Mountain. The deposit is not extensive, and its relations with the diorite indicate that it is a local variety, apparently graduating into dioritic schist.*

* The local micaceous character of bed XV. has been noticed.

One other mica-schist, that associated with the Cannon ore on Sec. 28, T. 47, R. 30, deserves notice. This rock resembles XIX. only in the brownish color of its mica; it contains no crystals of other minerals, and is always quartzose, sometimes to the point of becoming a micaceous quartz-schist. The age of this rock has not been satisfactorily determined, but it is near the base of the series. The striking peculiarity of this variety is the fact, that in places the mica is replaced by micaceous specular iron ore, thereby becoming a specular schist, a rock very nearly related to the itaberite of some writers. The Cannon Iron Company's explorations, in which a fair specular slate ore has been found, are located in a highly ferruginous part of this bed. See Spec. 16, App. B, Vol. II. The relations of this rock with the lower quartzite of the North belt, Menominee Iron region, is fully discussed in another place.

I. ANTHOPHYLLITIC SCHIST.—(in bed XVII. and others.)

(See Mr. Julien's descriptions 174 to 178, App. A, Vol. II.)

Immediately below the great mica-schist bed, XIX., and probably separated from it by a stratum of quartzite, XVIII., is a well-defined stratum of a slightly magnetic rock, varying in color from brownish-black to dull slate on fresh fracture, and grayish to blackish in outcrop. It often shows manganese,* and always a fibrous, light-brown mineral, which Prof. Brush, from the examination of some imperfect specimens, decided to be anthophyllite,† a variety of hornblende, and suggested the name here employed for this group.

Numerous outcrops of the rock occur along the north shore of Michigamme lake, and a fine development at the mouth of the Bi-ji-ki river, as well as at the Champion furnace, where layers rich in manganese occur. A specimen afforded Dr. C. F. Chandler 25.2 per cent. of metallic iron, and 4.37 per cent. of metallic manganese. See Specs. 58 and 59, App. B, Vol. II., and 178 App. A, Vol. II.

Below the ore formation XIII., at the Spurr Mountain, are layers of schist of a similar character, a specimen of which afforded Mr. Britton 45.21 metallic iron, 1.78 metallic manganese, 26.36 silica.

---

* This variety resembles plumbago, and may contain carbon.

† Prof. Dana now regards anthopholite as a distinct mineral.

A moderate increase in the percentage of iron and manganese therein found (which may very likely take place in some part of the bed) might render this rock a workable ore, particularly as the associated mineral is an easily fusible hornblende instead of the silica so common in the other ores. Ores containing 12 to 20 per cent. of manganese need not be rich in iron, to give them merchantable value.

Underlying this formation (XVII.), or perhaps forming its base, is a rock, numbered XVI., which at Champion and on Sec. 26, T. 48, R. 31, shows a tendency to pass into a *limonitic schist*, and may very likely afford workable soft hematite ore in some part of its course. The propriety of giving this rock, about which so little is known, a distinct stratigraphical designation, may be questioned; but its ferruginous character, pointing toward the possibility of commercial value, led to this course.

South of the Washington mine, and therefore stratigraphically below the ore formation,—for the whole dips north,—there is an obscure schistose rock of a gray color, weathering brown, and containing very little iron, often garnets, but made up chiefly of a light brownish fibrous mineral, which is probably anthophyllite, but which in places resembles mica. These rocks are extensive, stretching from the Champion mine eastward to the old Michigan mine. They are generally slightly magnetic, and unquestionably occupy the place of the silicious ferruginous schists of Group B. The diorites associated with them are also peculiar, the two sometimes resembling each other. This obscure series is well illustrated by Specimens 6,086 to 6,099, University of Mich. Collection. See also Specs. 174 and 175, App. A, Vol. II., and 27, App. B, Vol. II. Their affinities are apparently with this group.

J. Carbonaceous Shale.

(See Mr. Julien's descriptions, 246 to 251, App. A, Vol. II.)

The presence of plumbago or graphite (a form of carbon) was noticed in the anthophyllitic schists, last described. Carbonaceous matter has also been observed in various clay-slates, as was noticed in describing the Argillite Group, and we could have placed this rock there as a variety of clay-slate, very rich in carbonaceous matter. It is of a bluish-black color, but burns white before the blow-pipe, marks paper like a piece of charcoal, is soft and brittle, slaty in structure, and is the lightest rock yet found, having a specific gravity of but 2.06.

This rock has been found in the Marquette region only at two localities: 1. The S. C. Smith mine, T. 45, R. 25, where it seems to bound the iron-ore formation on the northeast. See Spec. 6,163, University of Mich. Collection.

(2.) On the south side of Sec. 9, T. 49, R. 33, along Plumbago brook, as will be fully described in the account of the L'Anse Iron range, is a large deposit of carbonaceous shale, a specimen of which gave Prof. Brush—carbon, 20.86; earthy matter, 77.78; moisture, 1.37. Another sample from same locality gave Mr. Britton—moisture and carbonaceous matter, 22.51; oxide of iron, 4.37; earthy matter, 73.12. See Spec. 64, App. B. Vol. II. These analyses prove the material to have no commercial value, but possess scientific interest as proving the existence of a large amount of carbon in the Huronian rocks. The equivalency of these shales with the members of the Marquette series has not been established; they are undoubtedly Huronian, and are, I suppose, younger than the ore formation XIII.

CHAPTER IV.

GEOLOGY OF THE MARQUETTE IRON REGION.

1. MICHIGAMME DISTRICT.

IN describing the geological structure of the Marquette Iron series, I shall begin with the Michigamme district, because its structure is simplest, the iron ranges easily followed on account of their magnetism, and because my explorations and surveys have there been more thorough than in either of the other districts.

The **Champion mine**, 33 miles west of Marquette, is at one of the most extensive, regular and typical deposits of ore in the whole region (see Map No. VII.). The strike is a few degrees south of west, and dip north at an angle of 68°. The extent and nature of the workings at the date of the survey may be seen by reference to the map. Up to this time the mine has produced an aggregate of 225,000 tons of magnetic and slate ore of first quality. The general form of the ore mass is that of a huge irregular lens, or flattened cylinder-shaped mass, which thins out to the east and west to so narrow a width, as not to be workable. The easterly portion of the deposit is black, fine and coarse-grained magnetic ore; the westerly portion is specular slate ore, with a small admixture of magnetite. The local magnetic attractions are very strong and are fully considered in Chapter VIII. The position of the plane dividing the two varieties is approximately shown in the sketch of workings on Map No. VII. The whole mass here described is not, however, pure ore, as may be seen by inspecting plans of the first and second levels on the map. Minor irregular lens and pod-shaped masses of pure ore, "mixed ore" (banded ore and quartz), together with whitish and greenish magnesian schists, alternate like the muscles of an animal, forming, as a whole, a comparatively regular deposit. Overlying the ore on the north side is a hanging wall of gray quartzite, the thickness of which is considerable, but could not be accurately determined on account of the drift. Immediately south of the ore, if it may not be regarded as a part of the ore formation, is a banded jaspery or quartzose rock, containing some iron. Next south, and underlying the whole ore formation, as may be seen by an outcrop near the east end of the mine, is a bed of diorite ("greenstone"); this rock in places becomes schistose and chloritic in character. South of the diorite is a silicious schist and then a swamp. The arrangement of these beds may be seen in geological section A—A," on the map, where they are numbered in Roman numerals X. to XIV., the latter designating the quartzite.

Following the Champion range east one mile, we arrive at the **Keystone Company's mine,*** where but little work has been done, and the arrangement of the rocks in consequence not so easily made out. A small bed of magnetic ore was opened at this locality two years ago, and what is said to be a large deposit of specular ore has but just been discovered on the same place. Five hundred feet north are a number of outcrops, indicating the presence of a heavy bed of conglomeritic schist, which holds masses of quartzite, varying in size from pebbles to others two feet by one thick, and even larger. It also contains flattish fragments of various schists and slates. Further north it passes into a brownish schist, containing pebbles of quartzite. This rock is believed to correspond with the overlying quartzite of the Champion, and is marked XIV. on the map and sections. North of this, and exposed in the railroad cut, is a micaceous slate, containing garnets, marked XV., and represented by Specimen 56, State Collection, App. B, Vol. II.

North and west of this locality, about one-fifth of a mile, are a number of test-pits, in many of which is exposed a soft, brownish, ferruginous rock, which affords hand specimens of soft hematite ore. This rock is marked XVI., and is represented in the State Collection by Specimen 57, App. B, Vol. II. Immediately south of the Keystone workings is a specular schist or conglomerate, in which flattened pebbles, or very uneven lamina of quartz, are contained between thin layers of micaceous specular ore. This formation is believed to be the equivalent of XII. of the Champion mine section, and is so numbered on the map.

West and south are numerous extensive outcrops of a brownish banded magnetic schist, marked X. on Section C—C", Map VII.

---

* Late "Parsons Mine."

The arrangement and character of the rocks along the intermediate section, B—B,' will be sufficiently understood from the above descriptions and an inspection of the map. The other formations represented will be considered in another place.

At the **Spurr and Michigamme mines** we find rocks identical in their general character and sequence, although the order is reversed, this series being on the opposite side of the basin from the Champion. Projecting all the facts observed along the north shore of Michigamme Lake on one plane, which we will assume to pass north and south through the Spurr Mountain mine, the following Geological Section is easily made out:

Commencing at the most southerly and uppermost bed (the whole series dips to the south), we have, first, a comparatively soft, grayish and blackish flaggy rock, containing considerable iron, a little manganese and often made up largely of a hornblendic mineral, which occurs in needle-shaped crystals. Professor Brush calls this rock anthophyllitic schist. See Specimens 58 and 59, State Collection, App. B, Vol. II., and Chap. III.

This rock is numbered XVII. on geological section No. 9, map of the Marquette Iron region, which see. It is also well exposed at the mouth of the Bi-ji-ki river, in the railroad cut just east, at the Champion furnace, and at numerous projecting points along the north shore of the lake.

The next rock to the north, in descending order, (numbered XVI. on the map and section,) on account of its tendency to decomposition, has never been seen in outcrop; it is exposed by the explorations for ore, made on the north side of Sec. 26, T. 48, R. 31, and at the Champion; its character was indicated in describing the Champion series, and need not be repeated here. As will be seen, this rock has the same number in each section, and the two exposures are believed to belong to the same bed. It is not improbable that future investigations may prove it to be a variety of the ferruginous anthophyllitic schist XVII., already described, a point which was considered in Chapter III., Group I.

Next below is a dark-colored clay-slate, which also, on account of its softness, is seldom seen in outcrop. It is, however, exposed on the point in northeast part of Section 29, and at other places along the north shore of the lake. On the Spurr mountain, geological section No. 9, this formation is numbered XV., and is believed to underlay the swamp and creek immediately south of the mountain which finds easterly prolongation in Black bay. As will be seen by reference to the Champion sections, this rock is regarded as the equivalent of the micaceous clay-slate XV., there described.

North of this clay-slate, and immediately overlying the ore at both the Spurr and Michigamme mines, is a quartzose rock numbered XIV., which is in places a hard conglomerate, and again, especially when in contact with the ore, a fine whitish sandstone. See Specimen 52, State Collection, App. B, Vol. II., and Julien's descriptions, Specs. 358 and 359, App. A, Vol. II. This rock is unquestionably the equivalent of the upper quartzite XIV. of the Champion section, which, on the whole, it closely resembles in its lithological character. See also Group E, Chapter III.

The prevailing variety of ore of the mines on this range is a fine-grained, somewhat friable, rich, blackish magnetite. See Specimens 40 and 41, State Collection, App. B, Vol. II., and also Iron Ores, Chap. III. There is also at the Michigamme mine a hard, fine-grained, steely magnetic ore, in considerable quantity. Analyses of these ores will be found in Chapter X. The surface indications, magnetic attractions, explorations and mining operations but just commenced, point unmistakably to large deposits of high grade magnetic ore at both localities.

The **Spurr Mountain** is an east and west ridge, the summit of which is 118 feet above Lake Michigamme and 75 feet above the creek, which passes south of it. This ridge terminates abruptly to the west near the centre of the northwest ¼ of the southwest ¼ of Sec. 24, T. 48, R. 31, where there is a natural exposure of merchantable ore 40 feet thick horizontally, being the largest outcrop of pure magnetic ore I ever saw. Mining operations, just begun, have demonstrated the thickness to be still greater, and the deposit to extend at least several hundred feet east and west, with a probability, based on magnetic attractions, of its extending much farther. The bold face, small amount of earth covering, softness of the ore, its apparent freedom from rock, convenience of the railroad and accessibility, present facilities for mining and shipping, which could not well be surpassed. The magnetic observations made at this locality, where the attractions were remarkably strong, are given with illustrative diagrams in the special chapter devoted to that subject. It is easy by means of the dip compass, to follow this iron range two-thirds of the distance along the north side of Michigamme lake, and west-northwest from the Spurr to the First lake, an aggregate distance of over nine miles, as may be seen by the map of the Marquette Iron region, No. III. It must not by any means, however, be supposed, that here is a workable deposit of ore nine miles long; this has not been proven, but on the contrary, it has been proven that for a considerable portion of this distance the ore is not workable, having altogether too large an admixture of rock. Therefore, while it may be confidently asserted, that all of the rich hard ore which will be found in this vicinity, will be in or near the belt of magnetic attraction already described, it may be asserted with equal truth, that at least three-fourths of the whole length of this belt is barren ground, according to the present standard of merchantable ore. The law of the distribution of the rich "chimneys," "shoots," or "courses of ore," as they are designated in different mining regions, along a given iron range, has not been made out. The subject is more fully considered in Chapters VII. and IX.

Besides the deposits already described on this range, one other has to be mentioned, that on the east side of railroad Sec. 23, adjoining the Spurr on the west. The magnetic attractions here are remarkably strong, and explorations have revealed the existence of a small workable deposit of first-class magnetic ore. Whether this deposit connects with the Spurr or not, was not fully determined.

As has been remarked, both the granular and compact varieties of magnetic ore occur at the **Michigamme mine.** The explorations on this location, which were conducted by the writer, developed in a distance of 1,200 feet, east and west, seven places, where pure ore existed of a thickness of from seven to thirty-five feet, rendering it probable, that the ore deposit is continuous and workable for the whole of this distance. Mining operations, which have commenced at this location, confirm these results. Pure ore was found in place at two points on same range west, on Sec. 19 of the Michigamme Company's property, but not enough work was done to prove their extent. Eastward the ore can be traced by the magnetic needle into Michigamme lake, on the south side of Sec. 20.

There can be no doubt these deposits and the Champion belong to the same horizon, being the opposite croppings of the synclinal basin, which passes under Michigamme lake; although the Champion deposit has not been traced westward, nor the Michigamme range eastward, to points where they come directly opposite each other. Whether the specular slate ore found so abundantly at the Champion will be found on the north side of the lake, remains to be seen. I see no reason why it should not; the explorations, so far, have been based entirely on magnetic attractions, and would therefore not be likely to result in finding specular ore.

Underlying the pure ore here, as at the Champion, is a ferruginous quartzose rock, which has an immense development on the Spurr-Michigamme range, where it is a well-characterized reddish quartz schist (jasper), containing thin layers of pure specular ore; these layers being occasionally thick enough to afford hand specimens. See Specimen 33, State Collection, App. B, Vol. II. A similar rock is found, as will be seen hereafter, at the Republic mountain, where it has the same relative position and number, XII.

Underlying this iron series we find, as at the Champion, a diorite (greenstone), but which here has a much greater development, forming a conspicuous ridge which borders the Michigamme and Three Lakes valley on the north, and which has already been described under Topography in Chapter II.

This greenstone ridge is separated from the granite region to the north by a valley about half a mile wide, which is underlaid by various schists and quartzites, about which little is known. Two are marked X. and V. on the Spurr-mountain section No. 9.

The most easterly developed mines in the Michigamme district are the **Washington** and **Edwards**, represented by map No. VIII. The general structure, which we are now considering, can be easiest made out at the Edwards and "old mine," which are adjacent, and about three-fourths of a mile west of the Washington mine proper. The general character and order of the ore and accompanying rocks at this locality is so similar to that of the mines already described, that a careful inspection of the map and accompanying sections leaves but little to be said. The Upper Quartzite XIV. is fully exposed in outcrop, as well as in the railroad cut, just west of the mines, where it is a coarse conglomerate, often schistose, as is shown by Specimen No. 51, State Collection, App. B, Vol. II.

The same formation is a compact gray quartzite at the Edwards mine, and at other points in the vicinity.

The ore formation XIII. affords at this group of mines all the varieties, already designated as being found at the Champion, Spurr, and Michigamme mines. Like the Champion, here are intercalated beds of magnesian schist, the arrangement of which are shown on the sections of workings given on the map already referred to, as well as in the plan of the Edwards mine, by A. Kidder, Plate XIX., Chap. IX., where the subject of detailed structure is more fully considered. One of these schists, of a decided talcy character, is represented by Specimen 54 of State Collection, App. B, Vol. II.

The underlying ferruginous quartzose rock, XII , has a large development south of the Edwards mine, and to it probably belongs the "red ore" of the old Washington. Southwest of the latter mine are large exposures of the peculiar conglomeritic specular schist, mentioned as occurring on the Keystone property, east of the Champion.

The dioritic formation, XI., is represented by a large outcrop of a greenish schistose rock, apparently chloritic, which can be seen immediately south of the old mine. Below this formation are alternating schists and diorites of different varieties, which are sufficiently well shown on the map and sections. One of the most interesting varieties is represented by Specimen No. 27, State Collection, App. B, Vol. II., procured 500 feet south of Pit No. 9, Washington mine.

The Washington mine proper presents some of the most complicated structural problems, to be found in the Marquette region, and I will not here either attempt their solution, or even advance the hypothesis which I have formed. Suffice it to say that, in general, the mine is a monoclinal deposit, dipping away from the St. Clair mountain (which term I apply to the high ground to the south) to the north and under the great swamp. The minor rolls, the peculiar faulting at the East Hill, and the trap dykes, would, if fully considered, occupy a chapter.

I cannot, however, pass to another mine, without noticing the singular manner in which the mass of ore, known as Anderson's cut, or Pit No. 1, is terminated in its downward course, as shown by Figs. 3 and 4. It will have been observed, that the usual form of ore masses is *lenticular*, *i.e.*, they generally terminate by *wedging out* more or less gradually each way. This exceptional mass, as will be seen, is obliquely and abruptly cut off, the bottom rock be-

Fig. 3.—Looking East.

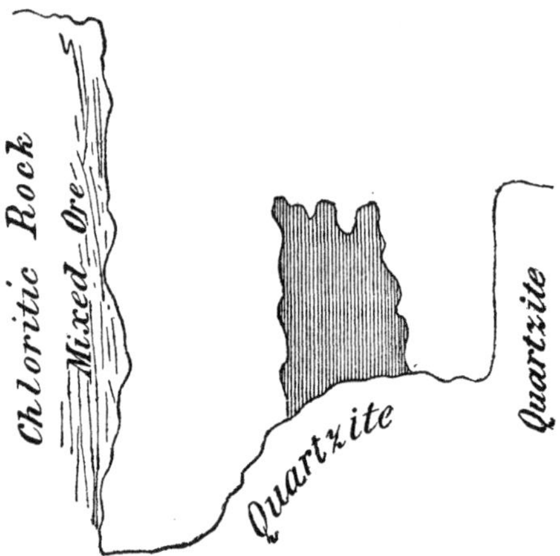

ing a quartzite of the same kind, that bounds the deposit on the north, and there is no evidence of faulting on the plane of this floor,

Fig. 4.—Looking East.

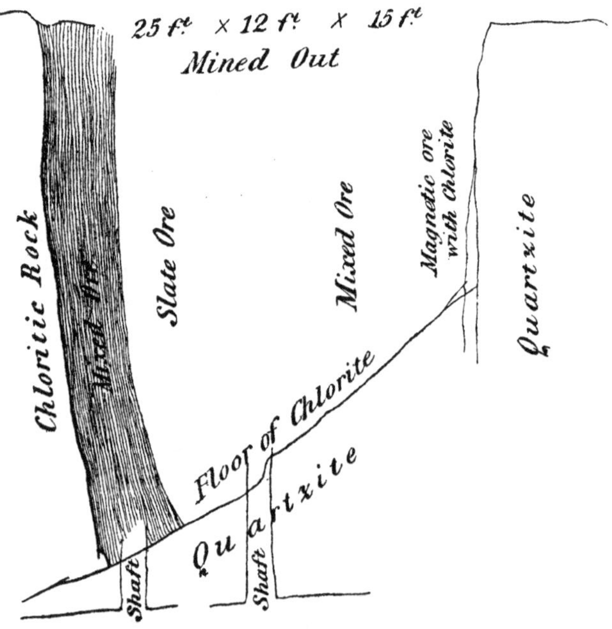

or along the quartzite wall. An hypothesis to account for this phenomena, based on a sedimentary origin for these rocks, will readily suggest itself and need not be stated.

The **Republic mountain** and its prolongation on the Kloman lot, is the only remaining ore deposit of the class under consideration, which remains to be described in the Michigamme district. See map No. VI. The **Magnetic mine** group, embracing the Cannon and Chippewa locations, belong to a different geological horizon, produce different ores, and will be considered hereafter.

The immense mass of pure specular ore, which was naturally exposed near the centre of the north ½ of the southeast ¼ of Sec. 7, T. 46, R. 29, could leave no reasonable doubt in the mind of the experienced observer, that this deposit of ore was one of the largest, if not *the* largest, in the Marquette region. This outcrop, the extent of which is shown on the map of the Republic mountain, being there marked "pure specular ore," is, so far as I know, the largest outcrop of any equally rich ore, ever found in the United States.

The elevation of the ore, 120 to 150 feet above Michigamme river, gives an unsurpassed opportunity for mining operations, which began in the spring of 1872, and confirm, as far as they extend, the "surface show." Several other small outcrops of pure ore occur in the iron belt, one of the largest of which is near the centre of the Kloman mine lot, in southwest fractional ¼ of Sec. 6, same Township.

The numerous outcrops of rock and ore at this mountain, the strong magnetism possessed by three of the beds, the remarkable uniformity in thickness of the several formations, and the bold topographical features presented, all of which were carefully surveyed and are faithfully represented and explained on the accompanying topographical, geological, and magnetic maps and charts (Plates VI. and XII. Atlas), leave but little more to be said in this place, regarding the general structure of the Republic mountain.

The lithological character of the rocks and ores will also be fully understood from the 14 specimens from this locality, which are embraced in the State Collection, App. B, Vol. II. The ten formations represented by colors on the map, as composing the Huronian series, will now be enumerated, commencing with the lowest, which reposes non-conformably on the Laurentian granites and gneisses.*

The lowest bed of the series will be numbered V., for reasons which will hereafter appear.

V. A quartzose rock, which is exposed at but a few points, and is best seen near 4,600 southwest and 6,200 southeast (see rectangular ordinates on map), from which locality Specimen 8, State Collection, App. B, Vol. II., was obtained.

VI. Is a magnetic, bright, banded, silicious and chloritic schist, containing considerable iron. See Specimen 15, State Collection, App. B, Vol. II., from near locality of Specimen 8. Very large exposures of this schist occur on the northeast side of the mountain, and southeast of Bear lake. The regular, various-colored stripes,

---

* This sketch (6,100 southeast and 4,700 southwest, Map VI.) represents outcrops of Huronian quartzites and schists dipping north-northwest, and the Laurentian gneisses, *a a*, dipping northeast, the latter being within 50 feet of the former. The actual contact is not seen, but the stratigraphical relations indicated, in connection with the wide difference in

Fig. 5.

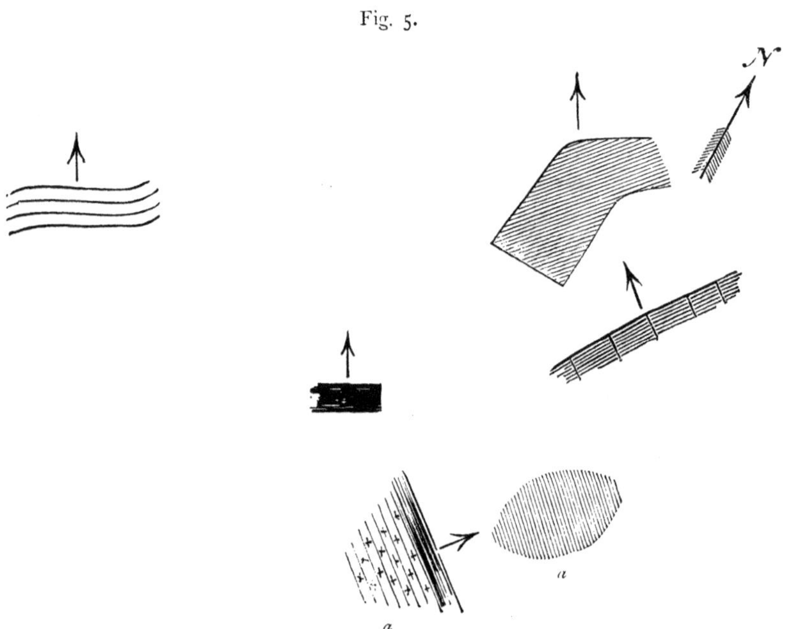

their lithological character, leaves no doubt in my mind of the non-conformability of the two systems, the Huronian being the youngest. This non-conformability can also be observed on the L'Anse Range. See page 156.

which this formation, as well as VIII. and X. displays, strongly suggests a rag carpet. The greenish layers are apparently chloritic, the whitish and grayish are quartz, and the brown and dark gray are silicious layers of the red and black oxides of iron. Some of these lamina are quite pure iron ore, and the whole mass may contain from 15 to 30 per cent. of metallic iron. The magnetic power displayed by these schists is remarkable, as will be seen by inspecting the charts and explanatory text already referred to.

VII. Is a diorite of the general character of those, so fully described by Mr. Julien in App. A, Vol. II., as will be seen by reference to Specimen No. 18, State Collection, App. B, Vol. II.

VIII. This magnetic silicious schist in its lithological character differs in no essential particular from No. VI., already described. See Specimen No. 19, State Collection, App. B, Vol. II. This formation is noticeably thin, not exceeding 40 or 50 feet, the other beds being from three to five times this thickness, as can be seen on the map.

IX. Is a Diorite similar to VII. See Specimen No. 22, State Collection, App. B, Vol. II.

X. A magnetic silicious schist similar to VIII. and VI., but containing in places more iron, as at 5,600 southeast and 2,500 southwest, from which locality Specimen 23, State Collection, was obtained. This, it will be observed, is a fair specimen of magnetic flag ore, containing probably 45 per cent. of metallic iron.

XI. This formation is made up of a coarse-grained diorite, in which a light grayish and reddish feldspar is a conspicuous ingredient, as may be seen on the Kloman lot, as well as at the knob southwest of Bear lake, from which Specimen No. 29, State Collection, App. B, Vol. II., was obtained.

A schistose variety, containing considerable black mica, occurs in the same formation, at 3,400 southwest and 5,300 southeast, where Specimen No. 30, State Collection, was obtained, although it does not truly represent the prevailing variety at this locality.

XII. This is a reddish quartz or jasper schist, containing thin lamina of specular ore, and very similar to the corresponding formation of the Spurr mountain series already described, as will be seen by an examination of Specimen 32, State Collection, App. B, Vol. II.

XIII. We have now reached the iron-ore formation, the principal outcrops in which have been enumerated. Four varieties of material chiefly make up this formation, which in the order of apparent quantity are as follows:

a. A banded rock made up of alternating layers of red quartz or jasper and specular ore, designated by the miners as "*mixed ore*," the richer varieties of which are now shipped as second-class ore. See Specimens 36 and 37, State Collection, App. B, Vol. II. The contorted and plicated lamina of this rock, brought out by the alternating bright red and steely bands, and which could be but poorly illustrated in Figs. 19 to 29, App. K. Vol. II., are very beautiful, being often contorted and plicated in a striking manner. See Iron Ores, Chapter III. It may be remarked in passing, that such contortions in the constituent lamina of rock formations generally indicate the presence of great folds in the whole formation, as is plainly the case at this locality.

On the southwest side of the basin, at points in the ore formation marked "specular conglomerate" on the map, occurs a true schistose conglomerate, in which pebbles, chiefly quartz, are bedded in a matrix of silicious ore. On the supposition that this rock may be a secondary form of the laminated or mixed ore, and from a desire not to multiply subdivisions in this connection, it will at present receive no further consideration.

b. Next to the mixed ore in quantity, so far as can be judged by what can be seen, is the pure *specular* ore. See Specimen 46, State Collection, App. B, Vol. II. The specific gravity of these specimens varied from 5.09 to 5.56, the average of four being 5.24, or greater than that of any other ore in the region, which should indicate a somewhat greater richness in metallic iron; whether furnace work will confirm this, remains to be seen.

c. The next in supposed order of quantity is a rich, black, *magnetic* ore, similar to the Spurr and Champion ores, but much coarser in its grain. See Specimen 39, State Collection, App. B, Vol. II.

d. Dividing the specular ore below, from the magnetic ore above, can be seen, in cut No. 1, Republic mine, a bed several feet in thickness of a *magnesian schist* similar to that previously mentioned, as being found in the Washington and Champion mines. See Specimen 53, State Collection, App. B, Vol. II.

XIV. The Upper Quartzite at Republic mountain is a gray massive rock, sometimes banded, and, near the contact with the iron, sometimes conglomeritic, containing large and small flattened fragments of flaggy ore. The prevailing variety is represented by Specimen No. 50, State Collection, App. B, Vol. II.

XV. Near the south point of Smith Bay is a considerable outcrop of what appears to be a dioritic schist, not unlike Specimen 31, State Coll., containing mica and garnets. It has some resemblance, as will be seen by the description, to the micaceous clay-slate of corresponding number of the Champion section, Specimen 56, App. B, Vol. II.

The horse-shoe form of the surface rocks, as indicated by outcrops, which is so conspicuous a feature on the map, taken in connection with the dip of the strata, as indicated by the arrows and geological section, leave no doubt whatever as to the structure of Republic mountain. It is evidently the south-east end of a synclinal trough with Smith's Bay in the centre, under which, at an unknown depth, all the rocks represented would be found and in the same order. The conjectural division plane, dividing the quartzite and ore (see section), may be regarded as hypothetical, only as to its position, which of course can finally be determined by boring.

It will be observed, that where the northeast side of the horseshoe crosses the river, there is an offset of about 250 feet to the right, and that where the southwest arm of the shoe should cross the river, but very little appearance of Huronian rocks can be discovered on the west side, the Laurentian rocks to a great extent taking their place. These facts can be best explained, by supposing a *fault* to follow the line of this portion of the river, the east being the down side. On this supposition the Huronian rocks on the west side would have been eroded to a much greater extent than on the east, leaving as a consequence the narrow and incompleted series, shown on a section through the Kloman mine.

The proximity of the Champion ore deposit to the Laurentian, it being only about 400 feet distant, while at the Keystone (three-fourths of a mile east) the distance is three or four times as far, leaving room for a greatly increased thickness of vertical brownish banded magnetic schist (see Map VII.), can be best explained, by supposing a *fault*, similar to that just described, but having a direction nearly at right angles ; that is, east by south.

These two instances are the best established cases of faults on a large scale, that have come under my notice, in the whole region.

Calling to mind the series of rocks, which have been described as occurring at the Spurr, Michigamme, Champion, Keystone, Edwards, Washington, and Republic mines, we are irresistibly led to the conclusion, that they are equivalents of each other, belong to the same series, and are of the same age. This hypothesis has already been introduced and carried through the descriptions by the corresponding numbers, which have been attached to equivalent formations in each section ; it will no longer be regarded as an hypothesis, but accepted as a demonstrated theory. The Republic mountain section, it will be seen, is most complete for the rocks immediately below the iron, and the Spurr mountain section for those above. The latter embraces one formation of great extent and interest, which was not described, viz. :—XIX., which is made to include the several varieties of mica schists, so extensively developed on the south shore and among the islands of Lake Michigamme. This schist is often very silicious, and, in places, contains numerous crystals of garnets, andalusite and staurolite. See Specimen 61, State Collection, App. B, Vol. II., and Group H, Chapter III.

Near the centre of Sec. 25, at the west end of the lake, is a large mass, probably a ledge, of light-gray quartzite, which may fill in part at least, what appears to be a blank between the anthophyllitic schist XVII. and the mica schist XIX., just described. The number XVIII. is provisionally attached to this quartzite.

We have now described fifteen members of the Huronian series, from V. to XIX., both inclusive. This mica schist is the youngest member of the series, so far as my observations extend, to be found on the Upper Peninsula. It is proper to remark, however, that equivalency, member for member, of the Marquette rocks with the L'Anse, Gogebic and Menominee series, has not been established ; they are all Huronian, and it is doubtful if any are younger than XIX.

With regard to the strata below V., there is less certainty as to their order and equivalency. I believe, that the iron ore and associated rocks, to be seen at the **Magnetic, Cannon, and Chippewa** locations, belong here. They are in any event the equivalents of each other, and are very near the base of the Huronian series. See Geological Section, No. 10, map of the Marquette iron region, which extends from the Cannon to the Chippewa. At the latter location is a considerable deposit of ferruginous, silicious schist, or lean flag ore, in which occurs, in what I understand to be an irregular pocket-like mass, a peculiar specular ore of fair percentage, greenish-gray color, and containing numerous bright facets, which resemble scales of mica. This is in comparatively low, wet ground, and the extent of the deposit has not been determined. It resembles the Gilmore ore at north side, Sec. 26, T. 47, R. 26, Cascade range, the two being unlike any other ores in the region.

About 100 tons of 55 per cent. ore was taken from the latter location several years since, but work was not continued. The Gilmore deposit, as well as the Chippewa, is nearly in contact with the Laurentian.

At the **Cannon** location is a banded jaspery rock, holding thin layers of specular ore, which bears a striking resemblance to the rock of formation XII., and even to some varieties of "mixed ore." See Specimen 16, State Collection, App. B, Vol. II. A seam, several inches thick, of pure specular ore, was found here, but did not enlarge on being followed downward. The remarkable characteristic of this schist is the fact, that on following the range northwest and southeast, mica replaces the ore, and we have a micaceous quartz schist, or mica schist depending on the quantity of the latter mineral. These facts, already noticed, possess interest in their bearing on the nature of the Felch mountain ore deposit of the Menominee region, hereafter to be considered.

By far the most promising mine of this group, so far as existing explorations reveal, is the **Magnetic**, in south ½ of northwest ¼ of Sec. 20, T. 47, R. 30. The existence of a workable deposit of magnetic ore of medium richness has been proven. This ore, although highly magnetic, differs entirely in its character from those already described, as will be seen by inspecting Specimen No. 17 of State Collection, App. B, Vol. II. It is very hard, exceedingly fine-grained, and breaks into cubic or tabular pieces. Its structure is more like the flag ores than the first-class magnetites. It should yield about 55 per cent. in the furnace, although none has as yet been worked. The gangue is largely actinolite, instead of the more common quartz, which will help the reduction of the ore.

The relative geological position of this ore is shown in the accompanying north and south section, in connection with Map No. III., already referred to. As to the age of the series represented, I have but little doubt on account of their proximity to the Laurentian, and on lithological grounds, that they are the equivalents of the lowest rocks of the Republic mountain series, and are probably older than the lower quartzite V.

FIG. 6.

Geological Section (looking west).
Magnetic Mine. Sec. 20, T. 47, R. 30.

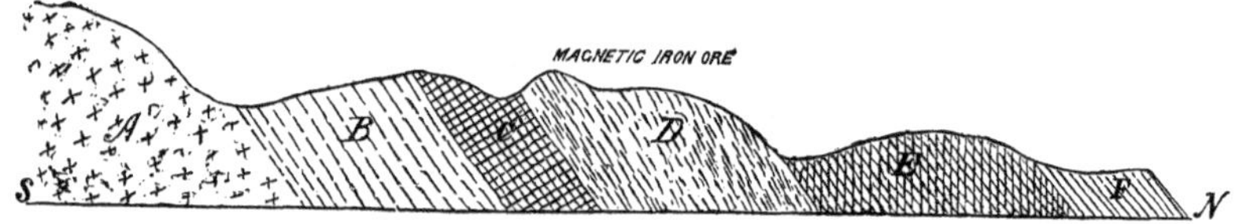

Level of water in Lake Michigamme 950 feet above L. S.

SCALE OF FEET.

A. Granite. B. Micaceous Quartz Schist. C. Quartzite and Quartz Schist. D. Banded Magnetic Schist (ore). E. Greenstone or Diorite. F. Dioritic Schist.

B, C, D are undoubtedly the equivalents of the specular and micaceous schists of the Cannon series.

The line of magnetic attraction, running southwest and south, and finally south by east from the Magnetic mine, which has been traced to Sec. 9, T. 45, R. 30, is one of the longest and most persistent belts of attraction in the whole Lake Superior region. The maps of the United States Linear Surveyors mark its position very plainly, as is shown in the chapter on the Magnetism on Rocks, Plate v. Comparatively little exploration has been made on this range; but I see no reason why deposits of the character and equal in value to the magnetic, may not be found along it.

A large amount of very poor ore, and a small amount of very good ore, has been found in south part of Sec. 7 and the north part of 18, T. 47, R. 28; and quite recently a workable deposit of first-class specular ore is reported to have been found there, the locality being known as the **Michigan Mine.** Specimen No. 2, State Collection, App. B, Vol. II., is from this deposit.

Clarksburg, Geological Section No. 6, map of Marquette iron region, records the leading facts to be observed in this vicinity. The Roman numerals marked on the several formations express their *relative* ages correctly; whether they also express the equivalency of these rocks with the Washington and other series previously described, I am not quite certain. Specimen No. 3, of State Collection, from formation marked III., possesses lithological interest, as being a Huronian rock allied to the Laurentian gneisses.

2. NEGAUNEE DISTRICT.

Following the same principle here that guided us in describing the mines of the Michigamme district—that is, beginning with those simplest in geological structure—we find on the **Saginaw and New England** range of mines (being the most westerly of this district), a structure almost identical with that of the Champion and Spurr mines. Referring to Geological Section No. 4, map of Marquette iron region, the rocks in the vicinity of the New England mine are represented as follows:—The ore formation XIII. is made up, as at the Republic mountain, of "mixed ore" (banded ore and jasper), magnesian schist and pure specular slate ore; magnetic ore being absent here, as in all the mines of this district. The quantity of specular slate ore at this mine is, so far as known, small; the small lens-shaped mass, that was formerly worked, having been abandoned.

Overlying the ore formation is the Upper Quartzite, XIV., dipping at a low angle to the north, as may be seen just north of the Parsons mine. This quartzite again comes to the surface about half a mile north, in a flat synclinal, where it again dips north and does not rise until we reach the New Excelsior mine, owned by the Iron Cliff Co., which is shown on the section.*

Returning to the **New England mine**, we find between the ore XII. and the quartzite XIV., a mass of specular conglomerate, somewhat similar to that described as existing at the Republic mountain, where it was regarded as belonging to the ore formation. The fact that it overlays the pure ore at this locality, and has lithological affinities with some of the conglomeritic varieties of the Upper quartzite, leads me to doubt in which formation it should be included. I incline to the view, that it belongs in XIV.

* This general section was constructed more than a year before ore was found at this locality, but it has not been found necessary to make any changes in it.

Formation XII., underlying the ore, is here widely different in its lithological character and economic value from the corresponding formation of the Michigamme district, where, it will be remembered, it was a valueless reddish quartz schist, containing thin lamina of iron. If we suppose tepid, alkaline waters to have permeated this formation, and to have dissolved out the greater portion of the silicious matter, leaving the iron oxide in a hydrated earthy condition, we would have the essential character exhibited by this formation as developed on the New England-Saginaw range, and as will be afterward seen at the Lake Superior mine. This is not offered so much as an hypothesis to account for the difference, as to illustrate the facts observed. The prevailing variety of rock in this formation is a brownish silicious schist, containing a considerable amount of iron (Specimen 26, State Collection, App. B., Vol. II.). Scattered through this formation are here and there large and small pockets of soft earthy hematite ore, having usually the most irregular forms, that can possibly be conceived. This subject was discussed under iron ores, Chapter III. Specimens 34 and 35, State Collection, are ores of this class.

The **Winthrop and Shenango mines** are in this formation, and are producing hematite ores as rich as any now worked in the district, and excepting perhaps the Lake Superior and McComber, richer than any other of this class, as indicated by analyses, Chapter X.

Underlying this hematite formation is a diorite, XI., similar in its general character to the rock, having a corresponding number in the Michigamme district; below this and south, are various ferruginous schists and diorites, corresponding in a general way with the Michigamme series, but which have not been carefully examined in the vicinity of the New England mine. Recent explorations afford opportunities for study, which did not exist when this section was made.

The series at the **Saginaw** and intermediate mines, as well as further west, is so near an exact duplicate of what has been given above, as to require no further mention than to state, that the deposits of specular ore are larger than at the New England, which has been mentioned as being rather small for profitable working. There has been too little work done at these new mines, to determine the extent of the deposits, but I see no reason to suppose that any of those now worked will prove very large. The fact that Sec. 16, the Parsons and New England mines, have produced specular ores and have been abandoned, is significant. No doubt, considerable amounts of first-class ore will be taken out on this range at a profit. The only question is, whether they will continue to produce such ore in quantity for a series of years, at a fair cost for mining.

This range of ore has been traced westerly into the northeast ¼ of Sec. 24, T. 47, R. 28; west of this the drift becomes very deep and the ore range is lost. A shaft 67 feet through the sand in this vicinity found no ledge. Whether there is any stratigraphical connection between this ore formation and the Washington, six miles distant west by north, is not determined. So far as is now known, it is economically a blank in the Marquette iron belt. Work now in progress at the new Michigan mine, already noticed, may throw light on this interesting and important question. It is not at all improbable, that the Negaunee and Michigamme districts may be independent ore basins, in which case the intervening rocks, which are all Huronian, would consist of the lower members of the series, that is below XIII. Even should this be the case, valuable hematite and flag ores may be found in this now barren district.

The new **Excelsior Mine,** previously mentioned and shown on the New England section, is near the southeast corner of Sec. 6, T. 47, R. 27, and is, as will be seen, the opposite cropping of the basin. There is so much drift between these ranges, that not much can be said definitely about the nature of the intervening rocks; but it seems probable that we have here a great basin, underlaid by ore at an unknown depth, and that the New England and Excelsior deposits are related to each other in the same way, as it was assumed are the Champion and Michigamme deposits. This could be cheaply tested, and possibly an important discovery of ore made, by a drill-hole through the quartzite, near the railroad on the west side of Section 16. All efforts to find an extension of the Excelsior deposit east and west have so far failed.

Returning to the New England range and following it eastward, we find that near the south ¼ post of Section 16, it bends suddenly to the northeast, making its way diagonally across this section to the **Lake Angeline Mine,** which produces specular ore, having such admixture of jasper, as to cause it to rank intermediate in the market between first and second class ores. Whether the deposit worked at this mine belongs to bed XII. or XIII., I have not determined, the ore partaking somewhat the character of each. The overlying rocks on the north are covered by the waters of Lake Angeline.

To the south is a high ridge of diorite, XI., on the south side of which is an extensive deposit of soft hematite, owned and worked in part by the Lake Angeline and Iron Cliff Companies.

I suppose this hematite to belong to formation X., and therefore of the same age as the Negaunee and Foster hematites, which will be fully described below. It will be borne in mind, that the hematite ores on the Saginaw range occur in formation XII.

Without attempting to point out at present the structural relations of the Lake Angeline and Lake Superior ore deposits, we will pass at once to a consideration of the latter mine, one of the most extensive, productive and geologically interesting in the Marquette region.

The accompanying map, No. IX., representing the **Lake Superior** specular and hematite workings, together with the **Barnum mine**, is intended to give the geological facts to be observed in considerable detail, as well as the condition of the workings in 1870. The structure of the east half of this mine is more complicated, than that of any other in the district, and some questions connected with it remain unsolved.

Regarding for the present the west half of the mine only, we find presented on a small scale about the same structural phenomena, which is so prominent a feature in the Republic mountain rocks. The basin, or trough, in this case, however, abruptly narrows up, the sides and bottom being as it were gathered in, as if to be tied, at a point just south of the engine-house ; to the west the outcropping edges of the basin diverge rapidly, and its bottom sinks into the earth in the same degree. If we suppose the frustrum of a hollow cone, lying with its axis horizontal and its small end towards the east, to be cut in two by a horizontal plane, representing the surface of the ground, the lower half will represent my conception of the form of the Lake Superior-Barnum ore basin. Conceive now this cone to be made of sheet-lead, and to be considerably bent and dented, and the illustration will be still more applicable.

A study and comparison of sections D—D′, C—C′, B—B′, and A—A′, in connection with the plan of the mine (Map IX.) will, I think, render it plain that this conception of the structure is in accordance with the facts ; although the minor folds and faults con

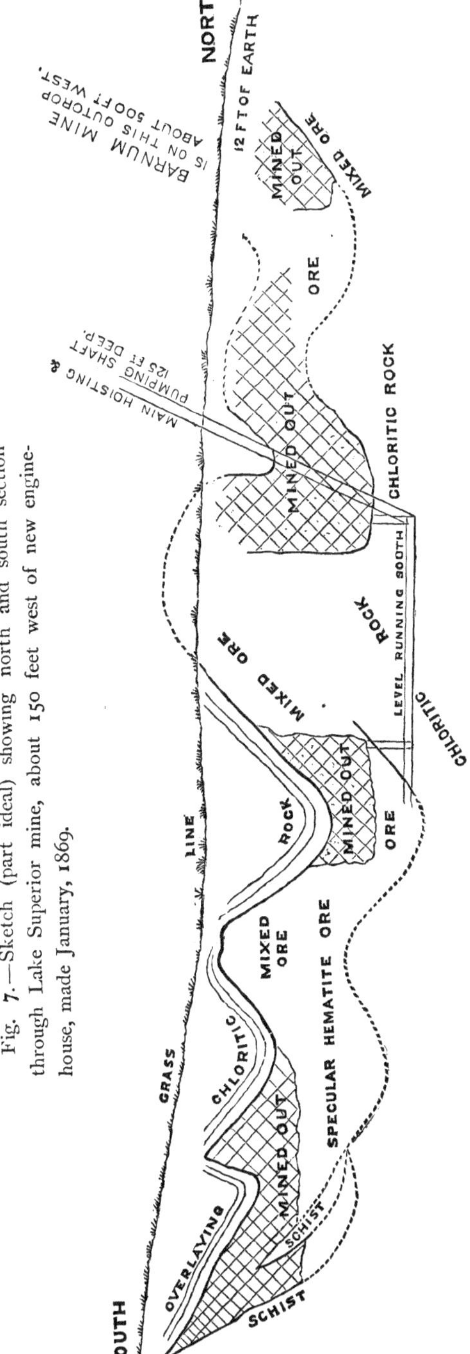

Fig. 7.—Sketch (part ideal) showing north and south section through Lake Superior mine, about 150 feet west of new engine-house, made January, 1869.

siderably obscure and confuse the general structural question. Of course, it is not absolutely proven, that the Barnum deposit dipping south, and the continuation of the main Lake Superior deposit, now worked in Pit No. 25, which dips north, are opposite croppings of the same bed, and that the intervening space is underlaid by the ore formation, and that, therefore, if work continue long enough they will eventually connect under ground; but certainly all the facts point to this conclusion. The importance of this theory in

Fig. 8.

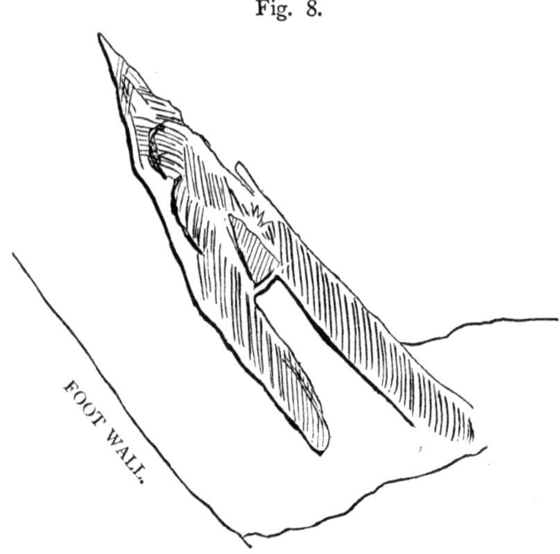

Fig. 8, represents on a large scale the south or left-hand end of the section represented in Fig. 7, and brings out the peculiar form of the "horse" of magnesian schist, which is shaded, the ore being white.

its bearing on explorations for ore, mining and valuing ore deposits, is very apparent. It shows, that such formations are not vein or dyke-line deposits, but true stratified beds, like the rocks by which they are enclosed. Their structure is therefore essentially the same as the coal, limestone, sandstone, and slate-beds, which are regarded as sedimentary deposits from water, subsequently more or less altered by heat pressure, and chemical waters acting during immense periods of time.

The Lake Superior-Barnum deposit evidently has a *bottom*, which will be reached within a period, of which it is worth while for the present generation to take some heed. So of many other deposits in the region.

As we go westerly from these mines the basins become, as we have seen, wider and correspondingly deeper. A depth of 300 feet in the Edwards mine reveals no essential change in the dip of the deposit, as will be seen by reference to the plans of the mine. The same is true of the Champion mine.

The time may come when, having worked out the steep upturned edges of the basins, and the flatter or deeper portions of the deposit are reached, ore properties will be valued somewhat according to the number of acres *underlaid by ore*, as coal now is.

Passing to the east portion of the Lake Superior mine, I confess myself unable to give any intelligent hypothesis of its structure. The facts observed are in part recorded on the Map of the mine on section E—E′, and on the accompanying sketch, in part ideal, which represents on a small scale a section near E—E′. There seems to

Fig. 9.—Sketch showing Geological Section of the Lake Superior mine (looking west), near Sec. E—E′, Map IX.

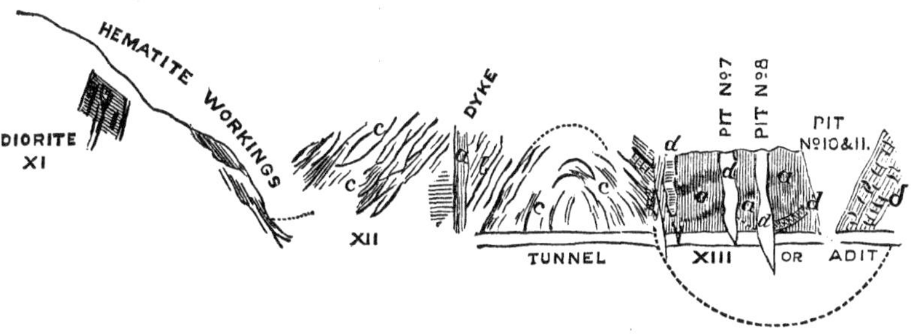

a. Chloritic schist. *b*. "Mixed ore." *c*. Limonitic schist (hematite rock). *d*. Pure Ore.

have been such a gathering together, crumpling, squeezing and breaking of the strata, as to nearly obliterate the stratification. An attempt has been made to represent the present condition of things, so far as revealed, by the workings. The remarkable features are the great masses of light grayish-green chloritic schist, having a vertical east and west cleavage, no discernible bedding planes, and holding small lenticular masses of specular ore, which conform in their strike and dip with this cleavage, and which seem to have no structural connection with the main deposits. They appear like dykes of ore, squeezed out of the parent mass, which we may suppose to have been in a comparatively plastic state, when the folding took place ; or they may have been small beds, contained originally in the chloritic schist, and brought to their present form and position by the same causes, which produce the cleavage in the schist. A comparison of these sections, showing effect of the folding on a large scale, with the figures (19 to 29, Vol. II.) representing the contorted lamina of the mixed ore of Republic mountain, will be found instructive. Indeed the same phenomena may be observed abundantly at the Lake Superior mine, and still better at the Cleveland knob.

Lake Superior mine sections E—E′, and Fig. 9, may almost be said to represent a huge breccia.

The peculiar nature of the hanging wall of the Lake Superior mine deserves further notice. Instead of the quartzite, which we have hitherto found overlying all the deposits of rich ore, we have here a magnesian schist very similar to, if not identical with, that already mentioned as being associated with the ore, as will be seen by reference to the geological sections, and to Spec. 55, State Collection, App. B, Vol. II. These rocks are given, however, different colors on the maps. The hanging wall of pit No. 25, Section A—A′, it will be observed, is made up of this schist and of layers of quartzite. Whether the Upper Quartzite is replaced by this schist, making it belong to XIV., or whether it is a member of the ore formation XIII., in which case XIV. would be wanting at this locality, I am not able to determine, but incline to the first opinion.

The hematite formation XII. is fully developed at this locality, producing an excellent ore which is extensively worked. The relation of this formation to the overlying and underlying rock is obscure, as has already been pointed out. This relation was very plain, it will be remembered, on the Saginaw-New England range.

The structural hypothesis by which I have attempted to connect the Lake Superior deposit with the Lake Angeline on the south, and Marquette, Cleveland and New York mines on the east, need not be further described here, but will be understood I think, by those interested in the question, from an examination of the following figure in connection with the maps.

Fig. 10.—Sketch (part ideal) showing position of ore basins at Ishpeming.

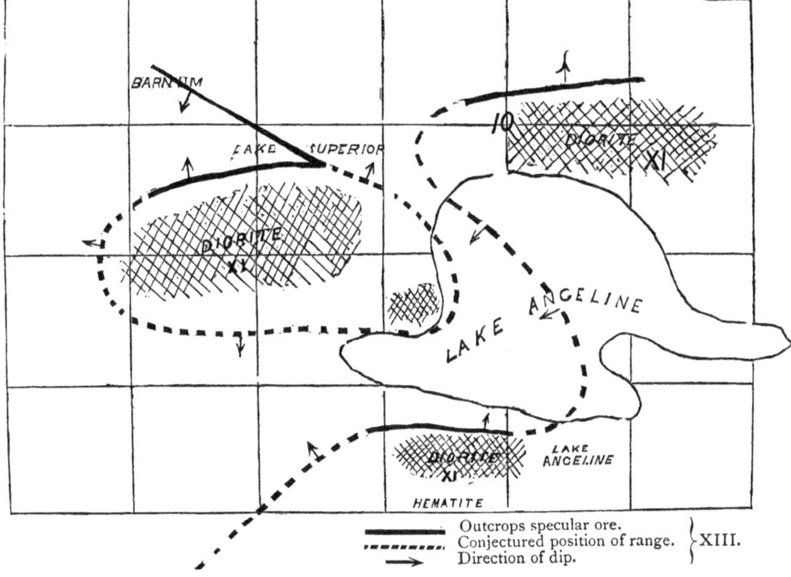

New York, Cleveland and Marquette Mines.

The geological facts to be observed, the general structure, nature and extent of the workings of the **New York mine,** which is one of the most regular deposits in the district, are so plainly set forth on the accompanying Map, No. X., that but few words of description are necessary. It will be seen to be a monoclinal deposit, in every essential particular, like the Barnum, Champion and Spurr. Two interesting facts will be observed: 1st. The absence of formation XII.; the pure ore, with its associated chloritic schists, seems to occupy the whole space between the Upper Quartzite, XIV., and the diorite, XI. It may be here observed that, as a rule, the purest ores are found in the upper part of the ore formation, that is, nearest the Upper Quartzite; the New York mine presents an exception. 2d. The deposits on the north side of the railroad, worked by Pits No. 3 and 4, have a striking resemblance to the small deposits, Pits 16 to 21, of the Lake Superior mine, just described. The facts to be noted at the Collins location, just east, taken in connection with Pits 3 and 4 of the New York, point plainly towards the existence of a small independent trough, north of the Cleveland-New York deposit. Explorations and mining operations so far, do not indicate the presence of a large amount of first-class ore here.

I made no special survey of the **Cleveland mine,** the fund at my disposal not permitting it ; the main object of the survey in this direction being, to represent in detail a sufficient number of typical mines, to cover the various structural phenomena to be found in the district. . The sketch of the Cleveland and Marquette mines, Plate II., from A. Heberlein's map, in connection with the New York mine (Map No. X.), will give a good general idea of this group. It will be seen, that the most northerly pit (Gents, No. 3) of the Cleveland mine, is a continuation of the New York deposit, having the same strike and dip. Gents pit is in one of the largest deposits of pure specular ore in the whole Lake Superior region. It dips south, forming the northerly edge of a narrow synclinal basin, which immediately comes to the surface again in the Swedes pit, where the ore has a northerly dip. These two pits produced in 1872 over 100,000 tons of ore. The ore basin widens and deepens to the west in a similar manner to the Lake Superior, and undoubtedly underlays the swamp, on which the village of Ishpeming is built. The connection of these deposits with those worked in the more southerly Cleveland and Marquette openings, has not received that attention which would enable me to express an opinion on the subject.

There can be little doubt, but that the Cleveland mine promises as well, if not better, for the future production of first-class specular ore, than any one of the older mines.

Jackson Mine and Negaunee Hematite Deposits.

No special survey was made of the **Jackson mine** ; but the accompanying Plate (iii.), from O. Dresler's map and Atlas map of the iron Mines at Negaunee (No. V.) will make known the general structure of the mine, which is essentially similar to that of the Cleveland and Lake Superior. This mine, although it produces first-class specular ore, will be here considered in connection with the hematite deposits, because they are adjacent, and their geological structure can be most conveniently described together. The Jackson mine, so far as is known, is the extreme east end of the

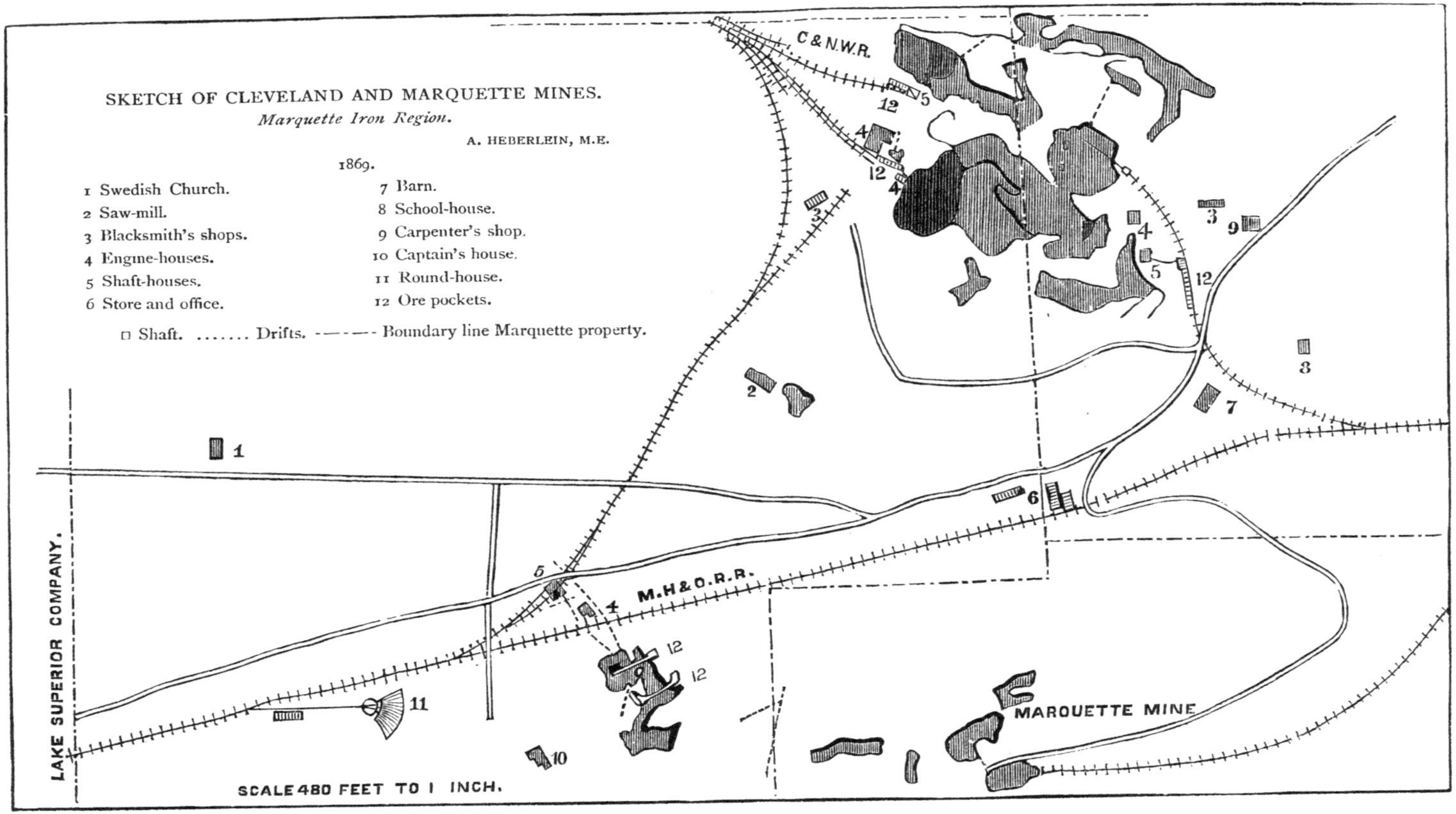

SKETCH OF CLEVELAND AND MARQUETTE MINES.

Marquette Iron Region.

A. HEBERLEIN, M.E.

1869.

1 Swedish Church.
2 Saw-mill.
3 Blacksmith's shops.
4 Engine-houses.
5 Shaft-houses.
6 Store and office.
7 Barn.
8 School-house.
9 Carpenter's shop.
10 Captain's house.
11 Round-house.
12 Ore pockets.

□ Shaft. .... Drifts. —·—·— Boundary line Marquette property.

C & N.W.R.

M.H.& O.R.R.

MARQUETTE MINE

LAKE SUPERIOR COMPANY.

SCALE 480 FEET TO 1 INCH.

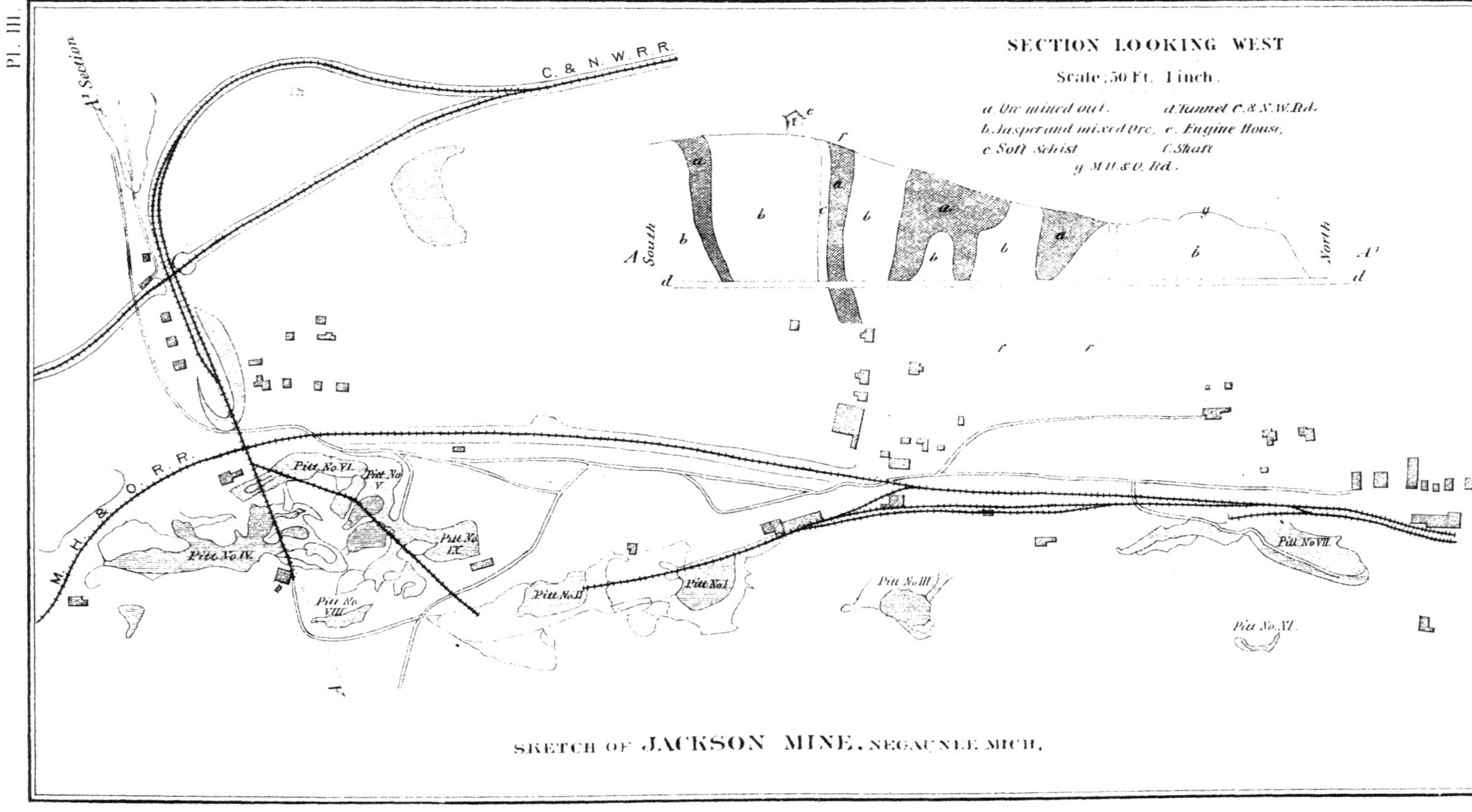

SKETCH OF JACKSON MINE, NEGAUNEE MICH.

rich ore basin formed by bed XIII. No workable deposit of ore of any kind has been found north and east from this locality, and the ores to the south are believed to belong to a lower horizon, and to be, on the whole, inferior in quality.

Looking back over the field we have now hastily surveyed, and assisted by the map of the Marquette iron-region, it will be seen that, while there are many minor irregularities, on the whole the ore basin gradually widens towards the west, from a mere point at the Jackson mine to a width of fully five miles at the west end of Michigamme lake, beyond which too little is known, to enable us to accurately define its limits. It follows, therefore, that all the Huronian rocks north, east and south from the Jackson mine, are below, or *older than the ore formation* (XIII.) and all the rocks to the westward and inside of the ore-basin are *younger*, hence above it.

The large amount of exploration work, done in the vicinity of Negaunee, in searching for hematite within the last few years, has aided greatly to develop the geological structure of that locality. But unfortunately, the money I had to expend here was more than exhausted, before this work began, so I have been enabled only in part to avail myself of it.

The facts observed are mostly recorded on the local map, mentioned above, and on the general map of the region. By reference to the former it will be seen, that a belt of country, about one mile wide, extending southeast from the Jackson mine, is dotted over quite irregularly with hematite workings, which are mostly on lands leased from Edward Breitung, as is explained in a note on the map. These mines produce dark-colored earthy hematite, containing metallic manganese, often up to an average of 5 per cent., varying considerably in the amount of metallic iron, but on the whole averaging lower, than the hematite ores heretofore mentioned, as will be seen from the chapter on analyses. I believe these ores all belong to one formation, No. X., in which, up to this time, no merchantable ores, except the Lake Angeline hematite, have been mentioned as occurring; it is at least certain, that they are older than formation XII., which embraces the Lake Superior and Winthrop deposits.

The geological sections A—A′ through the Himrod and Green Bay mines, and B—B′ through the Jackson Company's new hematite and old specular ore workings, fully illustrate the hypothesis of structure adopted. It will be seen, that the ore is contained between two beds of diorite, IX. below and XI. above, and that there is associated with the ore, chloritic schists and various ferruginous schists and flag ore. These last-named rocks, it will be remembered, made up this entire formation in the Michigamme district, where hematites are wanting, as are magnetic ores in the district we are describing. Underlying the lower diorite mentioned, is a clay slate, which is in turn underlaid by a gray quartzite, to be seen outcropping near the centre of the north half of Sec. 8, and represented in Sec. A—A′ under the number VIII. This is undoubtedly the same quartzite to be seen in the railway cut near the northwest end of Goose lake, where it is overlayed by a soft schist. See formations VIII. and XI., Geological Sec. No. 1, Map III. The clay slate on south shore and near west end of Teal lake, and exposed in railroad cut one mile east of Negaunee, is also believed to be of the same age.

The lithological character of the several formations, mentioned above, will be better understood by an examination of the following specimens of the State Collection: No. 21 quartzite from VIII.; No. 20 is a clay slate also from VIII.; No. 31 is from diorite IX.; Nos. 24 and 25 are hematite ores from formation X.; No. 26 is a specimen of ferruginous silicious schist from the Foster mine, which is also regarded as belonging to the same formation (X.); Specimen 28, from the same formation, is a magnetic, chloritic, silicious schist.

Referring again to Map No. V., it will be observed, that the Jackson Company's hematite workings, the McComber, Maas and Lonstorf's most northwesterly opening, the Rolling Mill, Himrod, Spurr and Calhoun, and Iron Cliff Co.'s Sec. 18 mines, are all in a rude curve, skirting the great development of diorite, which seems to limit these deposits on the southwest, and under which they all dip. The remaining openings are mostly contained in a narrow belt, which extends east-southeast from the Grand Central, diverging from the other range, which curves to the south. The diorite ridge which runs through the centre of the latter range is apparently a synclinal ridge underlaid by ore, which should therefore dip towards it from all directions, as is the fact so far as known. Undulations in the bed now unknown, may very likely bring the ore to the surface at several other points.

There can be no doubt of the great extent of this ore; it certainly can be on the average more cheaply mined and shipped than any other ore in the region, except perhaps the hematites of the Taylor and S. C. Smith mines. Location at the junction of two railroads, and contiguity to a prosperous village, are additional advantages, which will go a long way towards offsetting the disadvantages of lower percentage. The presence of several per cent. of manganese in this ore helps its working in the furnace, rendering it a desirable mixture. The McComber mine was first opened, and its ore is well and favorably known to many furnacemen. My analyses indicate, that this is a richer ore than the other mines of this group, but this cannot be established without further developments, as work has but just begun at most of them.

The **Teal Lake** ore deposit belongs to the same formation, as may be seen by an inspection of the map and sections. I have not been able, however, to find any good hematite in the old exploration pits, now nearly filled ; a lean flag ore is very abundant.

The **Foster mine,** near southwest corner of Sec. 23, T. 47, R. 27, is another hematite deposit belonging to formation X. It has produced a considerable amount of hematite ore of medium grade, which contains no manganese ; the deposits, or rather pockets, are pre-eminently irregular in form and uncertain in extent. The geological position of the Foster range is shown on Map No. III. and accompanying sections.

The Cascade Range.—The deposits on this range are the only ones now wrought, which remain to be described in the Marquette region. Like nearly every other described in this report, this ore was known to the United States linear surveyors, and afterwards examined and commented upon in considerable detail by Foster and Whitney. The range extends east and west through the south part of T. 47, R. 26. See Map III. The locality known as the **Gilmore mine,** at ¼ post between sections 23 and 26, is the most easterly point at which ore has been seen in quantity. This, it will be observed, is about three and one-half miles east, and two miles south, of the Negaunee hematite mines. The range has been traced west by south from this place for five miles, or to a point just four and one-half miles south of the Jackson mines. This country has recently been opened up by a branch of the C. and N. W. road, which closely follows the ore range. The principal openings have been made by the **Cascade, Pittsburg and Lake Superior, Carr and Gribben** Iron companies, who shipped an aggregate, in 1872, of over 40,000 tons, nearly all of which was by the first-named company and its lessees. The last two named companies —Carr and Gribben—have done too little work, to enable us to speak with much certainty about their deposits. (See tables, on Sheets XII. and XIII., Atlas.) By reference to the chapter on analyses, which is quite full regarding these ores, it will be seen that they have, on the average, less metallic iron and more silica, than the standard hard ores of the district. The West-End mine, however, worked by the Cascade company, and which produced last year about one-third of their product, appears to be an exception to the above rule, and to rank nearly with the first-class specular ores ; certainly considerable amount of high grade ore was taken from this pit last year, but whether it was kept separate from the leaner varieties in the shipments I do not know. The ore which largely prevails is a silicious or quartzose, or jaspery (practically these words have the same import) red oxide, having a characteristic coarse, slaty, or *flaggy* structure ; hence the name by which they are known throughout this report. They correspond nearly in composition, although not in their appearance and geological position, with the second-class ores of the old mines, as the analyses referred to prove. See Iron Ores, Chap. III. Some varieties closely resemble, if they are not identical with, certain varieties of the high grade ores ; but as a rule they are lighter in weight, duller in color and lustre, are harder under the knife, and pre-eminently flaggy or slaty in structure. I have not been able to obtain a statement of the working of these ores in the furnace. Further information regarding their lithological character may be obtained from descriptions of Specimens 5 and 6 of the State Collection, App. B, Vol. II. ; the latter is the beautiful "Bird's-eye" slate ore from the Bagaley and Wilcox pit. Specimen 7 is from the diorite bed, which overlays the West-end mine, and is interesting from its resemblance to granite in outcrop. *

The structural position which these ores seem to me to occupy is shown on geological section No. 2 of Map No. III. They are near the Laurentian, and the whole series is overlaid by a talcy quartzite, which I believe to be the equivalent of No. V. of the Re-

* Mr. Julien has determined the feldspar in this rare variety to be orthoclase.

public mountain series, and to be the same bed, which outcrops so conspicuously on the north side of Teal lake, and is calcareous at the Morgan furnace and at the Chocolate flux quarry, where it strikes the shore of Lake Superior. This rock varies more widely in its lithological character, than any other in the region, as will be pointed out elsewhere. If this hypothesis is correct, it will follow, that these ores are the equivalents of the Michigan and Magnetic ores of the Michigamme district, and are older than any iron bed made out in the Republic mountain series. The fact, that no iron in quantity has been found north of Teal and Deer lakes under quartzite V., where we should expect to find the opposite cropping of the Cascade series, is to be regarded in considering this question. The shortness of this range, which appears to terminate abruptly to the west, has not been found far east, and has altogether a local and isolated character, is significant. A hasty examination will satisfy any one that the *quantity* of ore in these deposits is very great, and that it is very favorably situated for mining and transporting. The accompanying north and south sec-

Fig. 11.—Geological section across Cascade range, looking west.—Part Ideal.

a. Flag ore or silicious hematite schist, in places quite rich. *b.* Banded jasper and specular ore with flag ore. *c.* Hematite rock or hematitic silicious schist. *d.* Diorite and dioritic schist. *e.* Quartzite. *f.* Conglomeritic and brecciated quartzite.

tion represents the different rocks to be seen outcropping on this range, projected on one plane. No attempt has been made to group them under formations I. to IV., to which they are supposed to belong. The general section No. 2, Map III., which has been mentioned, should be examined in connection with this sketch.

The **Iron Mountain, Ogden and Tilden** mines, not now worked, produced flag ores similar to those of the Cascade range, but not so rich on the average. These deposits belong, as will be seen by Map No. III., to formation X.; the Iron Mountain and Tilden mines being in opposite croppings of the same basin. The **Foster mine**, as has been observed, is also in the same formation, being overlaid and underlaid by flag ores. The Negaunee hematite and Teal lake ores being also in X., make that formation remarkably fruitful in the quantity and variety of ore, which it contains; but it does not, so far as known, hold the high grade specular ores in quantity.

Lower Quartzite, embracing Marble and Novaculite.

A brief consideration of the question of materials for *furnace flux* may come within the limits determined for this report. The subject, so far as the Silurian limestones are concerned, has been fully considered by Dr. Rominger, in Part III., who gives many analyses. The Menominee marbles will be mentioned in Chapter V. on that region. No calcareous, or other rock suitable for flux, has yet been found in the Laurentian system of the Upper Peninsula, although in Canada large beds of marble occur in this oldest series. It remains only for us to consider the silicious variegated marbles, found in the eastern part of the Marquette region, none having been worked west of Goose lake, which happens to mark the most easterly show of iron. The purest stone is found at the Morgan furnace, seven miles west of Marquette, where a heavy east and west bed of silicious marble, with vertical dip, and having associated with it clay slates, is prominently exposed. The prevailing colors are light-gray and pink. Specimens 11 and 12, State Collection, are from this locality; and Specimen 70, from the Gorge, represents the chloritic schist, which underlies the marble on the north.

The Chocolate Flux quarry on the shore of Lake Superior, three miles south of Marquette, is another locality, from which a small amount of furnace flux has been obtained. But the admixture of quartzose matter is here so great, that its use has been abandoned. Specimens 9 and 10, State Collection, represent the so-called "marble" and slate from this locality. It and the associated rocks are fully described in the extract from Dr. Houghton's unpublished notes, given in Appendix E, to which a sketch is appended. Mr. Julien examined a full suite of specimens from this locality, which are described in App. A, Vol. II., Nos. 106 to 113. No other marble locality possesses sufficient interest, to warrant mention, although flux has been quarried at several points near

Goose lake. It has been mentioned that the *novaculite* quarry, just east of Teal lake, from which whetstones were taken more than twenty years ago, is in the same formation. These stones are not now worked. See Specimen 13, State Collection, App. B, Vol. II.

During the past season several car-loads of quartzite were quarried in the same vicinity, and used as lining for Bessemer steel converters, at Capt. E. B. Ward's works, for which purpose it answered well.

The various marbles, slates, and quartzose rocks described above, are all believed to belong to one and the same formation, the Lower Quartzite (No. V.), which, it will be remembered, underlies the Republic mountain series, and overlies the Cascade series. This formation is one of the most interesting, geologically, in the Marquette region, and is worthy of a far more careful study than I have been able to give it. Specimens 8 to 13, inclusive, State Collection, App. B, Vol. II., represent several varieties of rock from this formation ; as many more varieties could easily be procured, including some very fair specimens of iron ore from south and east of Goose lake.

A brief description, in addition to what has already been given, of the great geological basin formed by this quartzite, which embraces within its folds the great mass of the Huronian rocks, and nineteen-twentieths of all the ore, will possess interest. Like the ore horizon XIII., which we saw came to a point at the Jackson mine, and widened to the west, so the opposite croppings of this quartzite converge to the east and come together at the Chocolate Flux quarry, already described. From this starting-point the *south rim* of the basin bears away towards Goose lake, where some minor folds and low dips make it the surface rock for a large area northeast of the lake. From the south end of the Lake west, the formation has a prevailing talcky character, often argillaceous and sometimes conglomeritic ; it has a great thickness and strikes west by south. West of the Cascade it seems to assume more the character of a chloritic gneiss and protogine, or at least a well-defined bed of protogine rock occupies the position in which we would expect to find the quartzite. See Map No. III. and sections.

The *northerly rim*, starting also from the Chocolate quarry, maintains a nearly due west course, crossing the railroad at the

Morgan furnace (where it holds the maximum amount of lime), forms the barrier rock in the Carp at the Old Jackson forge, passes north of Teal lake and south of Deer lake, occasionally at various points further west, and last, so far as I know, north of the Spurr mountain, nearly 40 miles west of Lake Superior.

3. ESCANABA DISTRICT.

The most southeasterly deposit in the Marquette region, and one which is entirely isolated from the localites already described, is the **S. C. Smith Mine**, producing soft hematite ore; it is located on Sects. 17, 18, and 20, T. 45, R. 25, and connected by a branch with the C. and N. W. railroad. It is but 42 miles from Escanaba, giving it a great advantage in distance over any mine, now shipping ore through that port. The geographical position is less remarkable than what might be called its geological isolation, for it appears to be in a small patch of Huronian rocks, in the midst of a great area of barren territory, underlaid by the Laurentian and Silurian systems. See Map III. The discovery of this deposit, a few years since, by Silas C. Smith, Esq., reflects great credit on his knowledge of the nature and distribution of ore deposits, and his perseverance in searching for them. Mr. Smith also first directed attention to the Republic mountain, which was, until within a few years, called by his name; he also made the first explorations in the Menominee region.

The few outcrops about the S. C. Smith mine, and the small amount of work done, when my examinations were made, enable me to say very little about its geological structure. The ore range runs northwest and southeast, approximately parallel with the Escanaba river, and cuts the southwest corner of Sect. 17. Contiguous on the northeast (whether underlying or overlying I am unable to say) is a bed of black clay-slate, in places identical with the so-called "plumbago" of the L'Anse range, which has been heretofore considered. Numerous fragments of a similar slate, probably belonging to the same formation, are found on the east side of Sec. 29. Laurentian granite is seen on both sides of the river, just east of this locality, away from which we have a right to assume the slate dips, rendering it probable, that the whole series dips southwesterly, in which case the slate would form the foot-wall of the ore deposit, as on the L'Anse range. On Section 20, west of the river, a talcky schist, holding grains of quartz, was observed, but its relations with the other rocks were not determined.

Near the west ¼ post of Section 20, and at other points in the vicinity, a flag-ore of good quality has been found ; a specimen from one of the test-pits gave Mr. Britton 56 per cent. of metallic iron ; whether there is any considerable amount of ore of this degree of richness has not, I think, been determined. Hand specimens of very fair specular ore could be found, but, as a whole, it seemed to me to be much more closely allied to the flag ores. Small boulders of this kind of ore had been found in this vicinity by C. E. Brotherton, some years ago.

Lapping over the upturned edges of the black slate on Sec. 17, and extending towards the east, is a horizontal Silurian limestone, which is, however, cut off by the river, beyond which numerous outcrops of granite and gneiss rear their heads above the flat sand plain. Silurian rocks are also seen on parts of Sec. 19, but west and northwest the country is all Laurentian, so far as I have been able to learn. South and east is a great plain, undoubtedly underlaid by Silurian rocks, but affording no outcrops, except near Little lake, where an isolated hill, apparently Huronian, rises out of the plain ; I have not learned that any indications of iron have been found there.

I regret not having had the time and means to make a re-examination of this interesting and important district, after last season's extensive developments, and reluctantly present this imperfect sketch for want of fuller and more complete data.

4. L'Anse District. (See Plate IV.)

The United States surveyors marked "iron ore" in two places on the line between Sects. 4 and 9, T. 49, R. 33. A quartzose or silicious brown and red ore can be seen outcropping, at several points in this vicinity. These facts early drew the attention of explorers to this district, and a considerable amount of land was bought from the government, for iron, as early as 1864. The fine harbor at the head of Keweenaw bay, only seven miles distant, and the abundance of excellent hard wood, tributary to this bay, have long caused it to be regarded as one of the best points in the northwest, at which to make charcoal pig-iron, and establish other manufactories related thereto. The soil along the protected shores of Keweenaw bay is good, which led to the establishment of Indian missions there many years ago. A circle having the village of L'Anse as a centre, and a radius of 35 miles, would embrace the Washington, Edwards, Champion, Republic, Michigamme, Spurr Mountain, Magnetic and Taylor mines, with others less promising, together with all the copper mines in the Portage Lake district, the Hecla-Calumet mine, as also the principal mines in the Ontonagon district. It would also embrace all the roofing slate territory to which attention has already been directed, and an immense sandstone area, about which little is known. The amount of hard wood within the circle would be surpassed by very few equal areas on the Upper Peninsula, and the quantity of pine is large. A railroad running west, tapping the Ontonagon copper region, and continuing through the Gogebic and Montreal river mineral region, so as to connect with the Northern Pacific road, would, with existing roads and the excellent water communication, make the greater part of the area described easily accessible from L'Anse. If the advantages of the geographical position of L'Anse have not been here overstated, it is somewhat remarkable that the locality should have remained so long undeveloped. The want of railroad communication with the outside world was, undoubtedly, the main reason. What effect the very heavy grades, encountered within ten miles of the town, will have on the amount of ore which will be carried there from the Michigamme district, remains to be seen. The ore from the Taylor mine, and others that may be opened on the L'Anse range, can be put on board vessel at L'Anse at less cost for transportation, than any equally good ores with which I am acquainted, on the entire chain of the Great Lakes.

As has been before remarked, the L'Anse iron range, so far as made out, lies in the north part of T. 49, R. 33, the best ore being in Secs. 9, 8, 4, and 5; it has a general easterly and westerly trend, like nearly all of the iron ranges of the Upper Peninsula.

The **Taylor Mine,** the only point where the existence of a workable deposit has been demonstrated by actual exploration, is near the centre of the northeast ¼ of northwest ¼ Sec. 9, T. 49, R. 33.

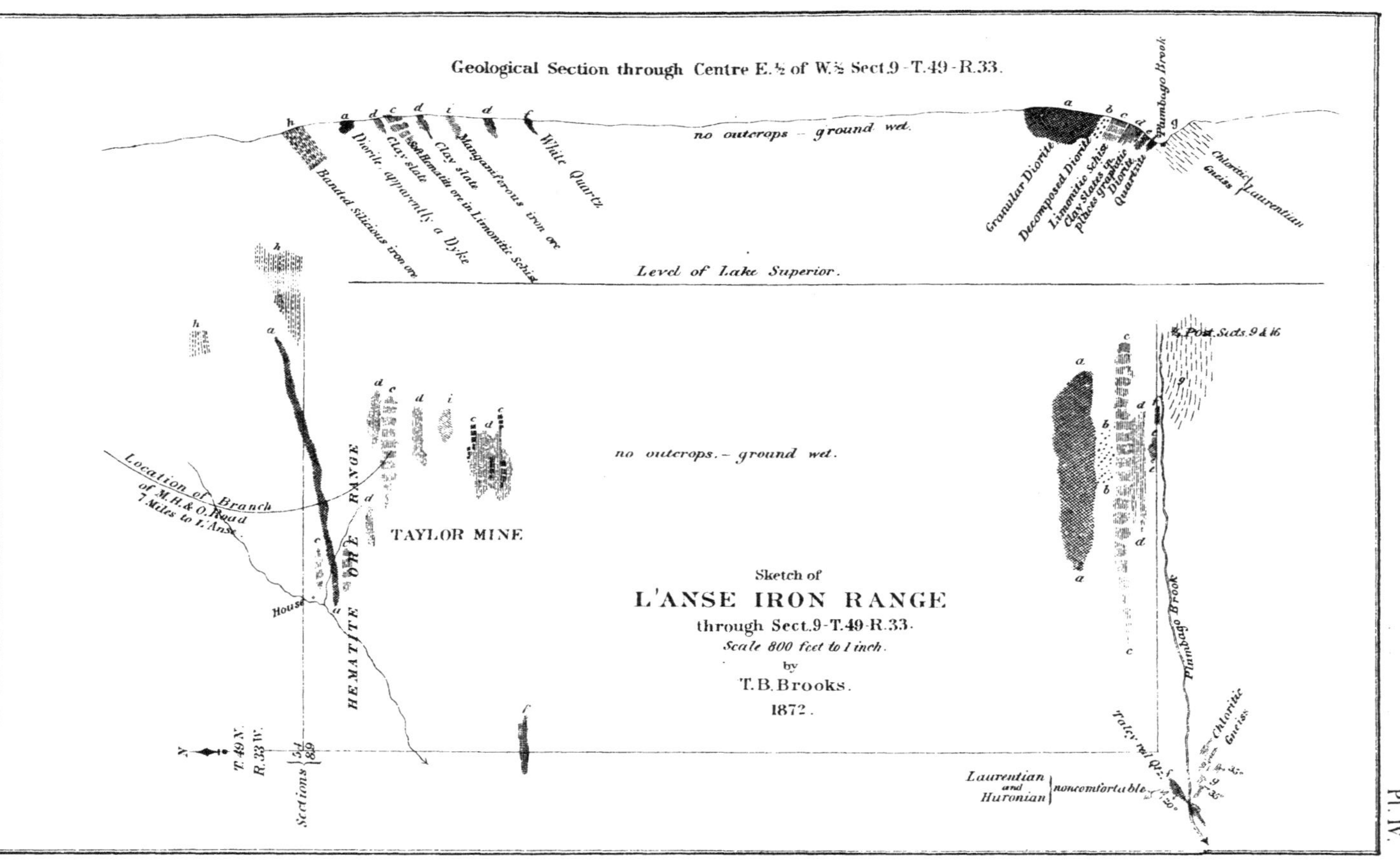

Geological Section through Centre E.½ of W.½ Sect.9 - T.49 - R.33.
no outcrops - ground wet.
White Quartz
Manganiferous iron ore
Clay slate
Soft Hematite ore in Limonitic Schist
Clay slate
Diorite, apparently a Dyke
Banded Silicious iron ore
Granular Diorite
Decomposed Diorite
Limonitic Schist
Clay Slates in places graphitic
Diorite
Quartzite
Plumbago Brook
Chloritic Gneiss
Laurentian
Level of Lake Superior.
no outcrops. - ground wet.
¼ Post Sects. 9 & 16
Location of Branch of M.H. & O. Road 7 Miles to L'Anse.
TAYLOR MINE
HEMATITE ORE RANGE
House
Sketch of
L'ANSE IRON RANGE
through Sect.9 - T.49 - R.33.
Scale 800 feet to 1 inch.
by
T.B.Brooks.
1872.
Plumbago Brook
Talcy red Qtz.
Chloritic Gneiss
Laurentian and Huronian
noncomfortable
N
T. 49 N.
R. 33 W.
Sections 5|4 8|9

This ore deposit is 950 feet above the surface of Lake Superior, and seven miles from L'Anse by railroad, built or building. The ground slopes gently to the west, affording an excellent opportunity for attacking the ore, which is covered by but a few feet of earth. The timber in the vicinity is first-rate hard wood.

The prevailing variety of ore at the Taylor mine is a soft hematite, similar in character to that of the Lake Superior and Winthrop mines. A number of analyses of average specimens, the results of which are given in full in Chapter X., varied from 44 to 57 per cent. metallic iron, with a remarkably small percentage of silica for an ore of this class. I see no reason to doubt but that a hematite can be mined here, which will yield an average of 55 per cent. of pig-metal in the furnace. Cross trenches and drifts show the deposit to have a maximum thickness 20 to 25 feet free from rock, and three or four times this thickness of such mixtures of ore and rock, as usually occur at hematite mines. The distance between the most easterly and westerly points at which ore has been found, is about 1,000 feet, but up to this time the explorations made have not demonstrated the deposit workable, as to quantity and quality, for more than about one-fourth of this distance. The oft-mentioned irregular pocket-like character of these deposits makes it difficult to predict, with any degree of certainty, regarding them, beyond what can be actually seen. But the heavy bed of hematitic rocks, which show a constant tendency by their decomposition to pass into ore, together with what has been actually developed by the workings, leaves no reasonable doubt but what there is here a large workable deposit of ore.

About 200 feet south of this ore deposit, and overlying it (the whole series dip south), is a bed of highly manganiferous iron ore, average specimens of which have yielded as much as 44 per cent. of the oxide of manganese; such ore must, of course, be comparatively poor in iron; this subject was considered under iron ores in Chapter III. The deposit is of uniform quality for a thickness of ten feet, and was penetrated by a shaft for the same distance. One per cent. of oxide of manganese was reported in some of the analyses of soft hematite mentioned above, showing the general dissemination of this substance, which seems to have its greatest concentration at the point we are describing. Whether this ore would possess value in the manufacture of metallic manganese, I am not able to say, but its presence, undoubtedly, gives additional value to iron ores, in improving the quality of the metal produced, and causing the ore to work more easily in the furnace, besides especially adapting the metal for steel manufacture.

Several other "shows" of iron in this vicinity are worth mentioning. Near the south ¼ post of Sec. 4, being on the north face of a high hill, is an extensive outcrop of several varieties of flag ore, more or less mixed with rock, in the vicinity of which considerable exploration work has been done. Some rich hand specimens of specular ore have been procured at this locality, but the great mass of the material to be seen is made up of layers of silicious ore, banded with quartzose material, the latter greatly predominating. The indications of hematite to be seen here are not promising. I see no reason why a flag ore yielding from 40 to 50 per cent., may not be sought for with reasonable chances of success. A similar ore was found several hundred feet farther north. The quantity of this mixed material existing in the S. ½ of S. ½ Sect. 4 is undoubtedly very great.

In the S. ½ of the N. E. ¼ of Sect. 8 are outcrops of hematitic rocks, which point towards the continuation of the Taylor mine series, making this a promising ground for exploration. Further west and southwest the ground falls off, the drift deepens, and no outcrops of any rock, so far as I know, are to be found, except in the immediate valley of Plumbago brook, where in Sect. 13, Town 49, R. 34, is an outcrop of argellite, which suggests a possibility of there being roofing-slate in the vicinity. Three miles west of the Taylor mine is the east edge of a treeless, sandy plain, which occupies nearly the whole of T. 49, R. 34, and extends into the townships south and west.

A similar desert country is passed through by the Peninsula Railway, commencing 7 miles from Negaunee. This latter, however, is underlaid chiefly by Silurian rocks, while the other is believed to be Huronian.

On the south side of Sect. 9, between Plumbago brook and the diorite ridge, which extends easterly and westerly more than one-half way across T. 49, R. 33, is a range of hematitic rock, similar to that at the Taylor mine, but which is not so promising for ore, so far as explorations have revealed. It has been traced for a distance of more than half a mile, and is the rock which immediately underlies the diorite, being itself in turn underlaid by clay-slate, the whole series dipping to the north, as will be seen on Plate IV.

Before dismissing the economic consideration of this district, it would be proper to notice the so-called "plumbago," found so abundantly in the north bank of Plumbago brook; but as this subject has been fully treated under the head of Carbonaceous Shale, Chap. III., it need not be further referred to here.

The **Huron bay slates** with associated rocks, may be regarded as belonging to the L'Anse series, although more than ten miles away in a northeasterly direction.

This district, which is now being explored for roofing-slate, affords indications of iron at several points, which I have not had such opportunity to examine, as would enable me to make any definite statement about them. So far as I can learn, those best acquainted in the district are not sanguine as to the existence of workable deposits of merchantable ore. At the end of Chap. I. will be found brief statements, regarding the slate companies now at work in this little-known district.

An inspection of Plate IV., in connection with what has been said, makes it necessary to add very little, regarding the structure of this range. The absence of outcrops through the central portion of Sec. 9, leaves the geological section quite incomplete. There can be little doubt, however, but that the quartzites, diorites, clay-slates and hematitic schists, so well exposed on the north side of Plumbago brook, where they dip north,are the equivalents of the Taylor mine series, which dip south, although the sequence is not exactly the same; and the diorite, so conspicuous on the south rim, is not exposed on the north side of the basin, unless the dyke-like mass of greenstone north of the Taylor mine represents it, which I do not think probable. The absence of outcrops also makes it impossible to determine whether there are any minor folds between the two croppings of the basin. If there are no such folds, then there is room for a considerable series of rocks above or younger, than those enumerated; and among them should occur, if it exists here at all, the rich hard ore of the Marquette district. It is assumed in this hypothesis, that the rocks to be seen are the equivalents of formations I. to X. of the Marquette series; this assumption is based chiefly on lithological grounds. Any rich hard ores found must be specular or red oxides, as there is an entire absence of magnetic attraction in the L'Anse district. Magnetic ores have not as yet been found associated with soft hematites, so far as I am aware, in the Upper Peninsula.

The diorite immediately north of the Taylor mine has been mentioned as *dyke-like*. Whether it actually cuts the series of clay and ferruginous slates and schists at an acute angle, was not determined, but in places it certainly has that appearance. If it does so, it is the only case that has come under my observation, in which the Huronian diorites (often termed greenstones and traps) do not conform with the schistose and slaty strata, with which they are associated. This locality, in connection with others which show *unmistakable dykes* of magnesian *schist* cutting various rocks, is worth the study of the geologist, but is comparatively not of much importance to the explorer and miner. Mr. Julien, as will be seen by reference to App. A, Vol. II., Specs. 342 to 353, regards the L'Anse greenstones as a peculiar variety of diorite.

Another point of considerable interest, in connection with the diorites of this locality, is the *dioritic sand*, which forms the base of the great south bed, and separates it from the underlying hematitic schist on the south. This material is an angular, coarse, dark, greenish sand, and has evidently been produced by the disintegration of the rock, which is in places quite friable.

But by far the most interesting geological fact to be observed at this locality, and one, the importance of which can scarcely be overestimated in considering the grand subdivisions of the Azoic rocks, is the *nonconformability* of the Huronian, or iron-bearing series, with the older Laurentian, which can be observed in the gorge formed by Plumbago brook, about 400 feet southwest of the southwest corner of Sec. 9, T. 49, R. 33 (See Plate IV.). Here a talcky, red, quartzose rock, dipping at a low angle northwest, and which is unmistakably Huronian, is seen nearly in contact with a Laurentian chloritic gneiss, which dips at an angle of about 35° south-southwest. The same phenomena can be noted at a point near the Republic mountain (see page 126); and the nonconformability is further proven by the fact that the Laurentian generally abounds in dykes of granite and diorite, which are almost entirely absent from the Huronian.

CHAPTER V.

MENOMINEE IRON REGION.*

THE centre of this region is about 40 miles west by north from Escanaba, 50 miles south-west from Marquette, and 50 miles north from Menominee, as the bird flies. (See Map, No. II.) The area known to bear iron is embraced within a square of 16 miles, being portions of Towns 39, 40, 41 and 42, Ranges 28, 29, 30 and 31. This does not include the iron deposits west of the Paint river, nor the Michigamme mountain, owned by the Republic Iron Co., in Sect. 4, T. 43, R. 31.† The iron ores in the Menominee region occur in two approximately parallel E. and W. *belts*, each probably composed of two distinct *ranges* or horizons of ore; these belts are separated by a broad granite area, in which a little unpromising iron has been found on Sects. 10 and 15, T. 41, R. 29.

This granite area narrows towards the west, caused by the convergence of the iron belts, and has nearly the shape of a flat-iron. The region is drained by the Menominee river, which skirts its W. and S. sides, and by the Sturgeon, a branch of the Menominee, which winds through the eastern part of the iron-fields.

---

* The facts contained in this chapter, as well as on Map No. IV. of Atlas, are largely from the Surveys and Explorations of Prof. R. Pumpelly and his assistant, Dr. H. Credner, made for the Portage Lake and Lake Superior Ship Canal Co. Prof. Pumpelly placed his private notes and sketches at my disposal, and added most valuable explanations. A valuable paper on this region is "The pre-Silurian formation of the Upper Peninsula of Michigan, in North America, by Dr. Herman Credner, Leipsic, illustrated by maps, diagrams and geological sections found in Plates VIII. to XII. (from the Journal of the German Geological Society)." Prof. Pumpelly and Dr. Credner are not in any way responsible for the hypothesis of structure here employed, nor for the views expressed as to the quality of the ores.

† A large amount of silicious iron ore occurs at this locality on the S.W. side of a high hill. Marble is found south and west, but in greatest abundance to the north, between Deer and Fence rivers, and on the upper waters of those streams. This district possesses much geological interest, and quite possibly economic importance, but means were not available for its examination.

1. South Iron Belt.

The South and, geologically, uppermost iron range of this Belt is probably the most regular and one of the most extensive iron deposits on the Upper Peninsula. The most easterly exposure of ore in this range is at the Breen mine on N. ½ of N. W. ¼ of Sec. 22, T. 39, R. 28. This location is 34 miles from Escanaba, and 45 miles from Menominee, in a bee line. The air-line distance from the elbow of the C. & N. W. R. R., now in operation, is 12½ miles.

Travelling from the Breen mine on a course N. 74° W., which is parallel with the general course of the river, we find on S. ½ of Sects. 11 and 10, N. ½ of Sect. 9, and S. ½ of Sect. 6, T. 39, R. 29, large natural exposures of ore, which have been still farther developed by recent explorations.

In the N. ½ of Sect. 2, T. 39, R. 30, are boulders of iron-ore, and near the S. ¼ post of Sec. 34, T. 40, R. 30, magnetic attractions, which indicate the presence of the iron range. Near the S. ¼ post of Sec. 30, T. 40, R. 30, is a large exposure of ore; thence, following a line of magnetic attraction which leads about W. by N., we find in the centre of the S. E. ¼ of Sec. 25, T. 40, R. 31, another exposure of ore, and a continuation of the local magnetic variations, westerly towards the Menominee river, two miles distant. A range of iron ore, corresponding with this and probably its continuation, has been made out in Wisconsin, between the Brulé and Pine Rivers. Here are no less than nine large exposures of ore, the extreme ones 16 miles apart, which lie in one straight, narrow belt.

Immediately N. of this iron range is a broad belt of impure marble, equally regular, of greater thickness, but which apparently widens towards the W.

North of this, in the vicinity of the Sturgeon River, on Secs. 7 and 8, T. 39, R. 28, and Sec. 12, T. 39, R. 29, are local magnetic attractions and iron boulders, which are believed to mark the position of another geologically lower iron range, although no outcrop has been seen in this vicinity; but near the centre of N. ½ of Sec. 20, T. 40, R. 30, just N. of Lake Antoine, is an outcrop of silicious ore.

Strong magnetic attractions can be observed near the S. W. cor. of Sec. 22, and iron boulders in Sec. 27, and also on north shore N. of Lake Fumée, in T. 40, R. 30.

These indications make certain the presence of a second iron range, although it cannot be demonstrated that these several shows belong to one horizon.

These two ranges, separated by the marble, constitute the South iron belt. North of and underlying both, is an immense bed of quartzite, which is well exposed at the falls of the Sturgeon river, Sec. 8, T. 39, R. 28; also on Sec. 1, T. 39, R. 29, and Sec. 28, T. 40, R. 29, and at the southwest ¼ of Sec. 23, T. 40, R. 30, as will be seen by the map. This quartzite, although believed to be geologically conformable with the ore formations, is not parallel with them, running more northwesterly, and dividing in T. 40, R. 30, into two and perhaps three ranges.

North of this quartzite, and underlying the whole series already described, are the Laurentian, granites, gneisses and schists, which make up the *granite area*, already referred to as probably being barren in workable deposits of ore, and which, therefore, our investigations do not embrace.

South of the south iron range, already described, is a bed of chloritic schist, well exposed on the south shore of Lake Hanbury, Sec. 15, T. 39, R. 29, and on the Sturgeon river in Sec. 13. Immediately south is a second quartzite, which is quite different in its character from the bed already described.

Next south is a broad belt of argillaceous slate, running parallel with the iron range, and exposed at several points in T. 39, Ranges 28 and 29. (See map.) South of this, and embracing portions of the Menominee river, is a broad well-defined belt of chloritic, hornblendic and dioritic rocks, running parallel with the iron range, the harder members of which form the barrier rocks of all the falls in this part of the Menominee, and probably those of Pine river in Wisconsin. This series are perfectly exposed at Sturgeon Falls, Sec. 27, T. 39, R. 29, and at the great and little Bequensenec Falls, and Sand Portage, in T. 39, R. 30.

2. NORTH IRON BELT.

The North iron belt or range has a course nearly due east and west, and is all embraced, so far as known, in the south tier of Secs. of T. 42, Ranges 28, 29, and 30. The most easterly discovered exposure of ore, known as the Felch mountain, is in the N. ½ of Secs. 32 and 33, T. 42, R. 28, and is sixteen miles north and three miles west from the Breen mine, the position of which has been defined. Travelling due west, fragments of iron ore are found in N. E. ¼ of Sec. 31, T. 42, R. 28; after which no absolute proof of the presence of iron is found (although it is probably continuous) until we reach Sec. 31, T. 42, R. 29, where, in the centre of the section, is an immense exposure of iron ore in an E. W. ridge, which can be traced westerly half-way across Sec. 36 of the next Township. The natural exposure of ore on Sec. 31 is larger than at any other point in the Menominee region, and the quality is as good, if not better, so far as can be judged by surface indications. Magnetic attractions and iron boulders, found farther west and southwest on this range, prove its extension in that direction. Whether the westerly course continues, or whether it curves to the southwest, as seems probable from the position of the lower quartzite and local magnetic attractions in the northwest part of T. 41, R. 30, has not been determined. The latter hypothesis is most in accordance with the known facts, although the southeast dip of the quartzite on Secs. 17 and 18, observed by Dr. Credner, is not explained. If this hypothesis is true, the iron range should cross the Menominee somewhere in Secs. 24 or 25, T. 41, R. 31, into Wisconsin. There can be little doubt but that the North and South belts belong to one geological horizon, hence somewhere come together.

The existence of two distinct iron ranges in the North belt, does not admit of so easy proof as in case of the South belt. The facts which point towards this are the following: About one-fourth of a mile north of the iron range, already described as existing on Sec. 36, T. 42, R. 30, is a bed of marble running east and west, parallel with the iron, on both sides of which are slight magnetic attractions. Prof. Pumpelly found, "about 80 paces south of this marble, an outcrop of strata made up of layers of quartz, magnetic iron and chlorite," probably of no economic value.

Again, in the E. ½ of Sec. 35, are two parallel lines of feeble magnetic attractions, several hundred feet apart, and to the north are some large, angular boulders of magnetic ore; similar smaller boulders are found between Secs. 33 and 28, still farther west.

South of the iron deposits on Secs. 31 and 36, is a bed of marble, somewhat similar to the one already described as underlying the south iron range of the South belt, and possibly the equivalent of it, as the two have the same relative geological position. Farther south, immediately adjacent to, and overlying the granitic rocks, is a heavy bed of quartzite, which is undoubtedly the equivalent of the lower quartzite, already described as forming the base of the South belt. This quartzite at the S. ¼ post of Sec. 31, T. 42, R. 29, is characterized by the presence of mica scales in the bedding planes, and might be denominated a micaceous quartz schist. It has considerable resemblance to the rock, associated with the Cannon ore in the Marquette region. This fact possesses considerable geological interest in connection with the relative age of the Felch mountain ore deposit, which, I think, belongs in this lower quartzite. See Chap. III., Group H. mica schists, and below.

The Huronian rocks in the N. ½ of Sec. 31, are covered with horizontal layers of Silurian sandstone, hence cannot be seen. North of the iron on Sec. 36, is the marble already mentioned, which is peculiar in being filled in places with crystals of kyanite, giving the gray weathered surface of the rock a rough jagged character, like a coarse rasp.

Just N. of the N. ¼ post of Sec. 31, T. 42, R. 29, is an east and west range of gneiss rock, and still farther north a heavy bed of hornblendic schist. At numerous points east and west, through the centre of T. 42, Ranges 28, 29, and 30, are outcrops of similar hornblendic rocks, together with beds of mica schist and gneiss, traversed in places by dykes, and perhaps by beds of granite. This broad belt of hornblendic rocks is apparently represented in its westerly extension, where it crosses the Michigamme river, by the mica and chloritic schists and gneisses, so well exposed at the Falls of the Michigamme, Cedar Portage, Long Portage, Norway Portage and intermediate points in Towns. 41 and 42, R. 31. Similar rocks cross the Paint river, a few miles farther west. This series would correspond in their geological position, as they do partially in their lithological and topographical characteristics, to the hornblendic and chloritic series, already described as forming the southernmost formations of the South belt, and which there, as here, produce numerous waterfalls.

Near the centre of this hornblendic belt, in the north part of Secs. 21, 22, 23, and 24, T. 42, R. 29, is a line of comparatively feeble magnetic attractions, which seems to have no equivalent in the

South belt, unless it be in Sec. 28, T. 39, N. R. 18, E. Wisconsin; or in one of the beds of hornblendic rock at Little Bequensenec Falls, to be described hereafter, which contains many specks of sulphuret of iron and of magnetic ore.

This line of attractions, noticed in T. 42, R. 29, may represent the north edge of a basin, of which the North iron belt, already described, is the south edge; but I incline to the hypothesis, that it is an independent ferruginous range. No outcrop or boulder of iron has been seen upon it in Michigan, and it is doubtful if it is of any economic importance, although of much geological interest, as helping to elucidate the structure.

Returning to the most easterly exposure of iron on the North belt, the Felch mountain, we find a different and less complete sequence of rocks. Except some boulders about one mile west, no marble can here be seen. The Felch mountain ore rests immediately upon, and is bounded on the south by hornblendic, micaceous and gneissoid rocks, which are undoubtedly Laurentian, thus shutting out the marble and quartzite, already described as existing under the iron to the west. No indications, which would suggest the presence of a second iron range, can be found here. Within half a mile north the hornblendic schists are to be seen. At the N. ¼ post of Sec. 31, about 1½ miles westerly, is a large exposure of quartzite, running east and west, and apparently dipping to the north, although the bedding is indistinct. This may be the equivalent of the north marble range, Sec. 36, T. 42, R. 30, for quartzites sometimes pass into marbles in the Marquette region.

The Felch mountain ore, so called, is in reality a dull red jasper-like quartzite, containing numerous thin lamina and minute gash veins of very pure specular ore. It has somewhat the appearance of the "mixed" or second class ore of the Marquette region (see Chap. III. A), differing in containing less iron, and in the fact, that the ore lamina have less continuity. Considerable amount of a similar rock can be seen on the Penokie iron range, Wisconsin. I have a two pound specimen of specular ore from the Felch mountain, which is as rich as any I ever saw. The deposit is somewhat magnetic, the east and west belt of magnetic influence having considerable breadth.

It is not at all improbable, that better ores may be found adjoining this on the north, or possibly still further north, in a geological position corresponding with the ore on Sec. 31, T. 42, R. 29.

In the south half of Sec. 36, T. 42, R. 29, about two miles west of the Felch mountain, Prof. Pumpelly and Dr. Credner observed a variety of the lower quartzite, the character of which is important in connection with the age of the Felch mountain deposit. It has been described as containing mica enough on its planes of stratification, to make it semi-schistose, is porous, and contains thin streaks of magnetic iron in crystals, with here and there cubes of iron pyrites.

The above facts lead me to accept the hypothesis already advanced, that the Felch mountain ore deposit is itself in the Lower Quartzite. If we suppose the mica contained in the quartzite exposed at S. ¼ post of Sec. 31, and in the S. part of Sec. 36, to be replaced entirely by specular ore, a Felch mountain ore would be the result. This hypothesis is supported by the fact, that the Cannon ore, Sec. 28, T. 47, R. 30, is a quartz schist, having specular ore in its bedding planes, and which in a short distance changes into mica. (See Chap. III., Mica schist.) It should be noted, however, that while the Cannon ore is micaceous, the Felch mountain is eminently granular. The Cannon, like the Felch deposit, is at the base of the Huronian series, resting immediately on the Laurentian.

It has already been mentioned that *Silurian sandstone* capped the iron bearing rocks on N ½ of Sec. 31, T. 42, R. 29; the same is true in places on Sections 34, 35, and 36, in same Township, as also in Sections 31, 32, and 33, in the Township east. Passing to the South belt, we find the sandstone covering the iron series in Section 25, T. 40, R. 31, in Secs. 30, 29, 23, and 36, T. 40, R. 30; also in Sections 9 and 10, T. 39, R. 29, and in Sec. 15, T. 39, R. 28 immediately north of the Breen mine, as well as at numerous other points, which it is not necessary to mention.*

Explorations eastward on the two iron belts of the Menominee region, reveal the presence of this sandstone and its accompanying overlying limestone (calciferous sand rock), in greater quantity, even to the point of entirely covering up the Huronian and Laurentian rocks, which is done, so far as known, from near the east side of the Menominee iron region, all the way to the Canadian line at the Sault Ste. Marie. Local magnetic attractions, discovered by

* These irregular patches of sandstone are not represented on the maps.

United States surveyors at various points in this Silurian area, render it likely that the iron-bearing or Huronian rocks extend far to the eastward, connecting probably with the similar rocks of the north shore of Lake Huron, where they were first studied and named by the Canadian geologists. Pine explorers inform me, that they.have observed dark-colored heavy rocks, which were somewhat magnetic, in the eastern portion of the Upper Peninsula. These may have been Huronian islands in the sea, in which the sandstones were laid down. This subject is discussed in Chap. II.

Like their equivalents in the Marquette region, the ore strata and accompanying rocks of the Menominee region usually conform in their strike with the general trend of the belts and ranges, and dip at high angles, thus presenting their upturned edges to the observer, and affording, where exposed, the best possible opportunity to observe the thickness of the beds and their mineral composition. But highly inclined strata, especially if they should be overturned, as is occasionally the case, are not favorable for making out the structure and sequence of the various beds. This question is farther complicated by the difficulty of distinguishing, in the case of the clay and chloritic slates, between the cleavage and bedding planes. The latter are sometimes very obscure, and have been confounded with the other, thus leading to erroneous results.

The geographical distribution of rocks in the Menominee region which has already been given in a general way, in connection with what has been said in Chapter II. concerning the structural relations of the Laurentian, Silurian and Huronian systems, leaves but little more to be said regarding the structure. The Laurentian area is the broad backbone of the great E. and W. anticlinal, on and against the north and south sides of which the iron series repose, dipping away from the axis; that is, the South belt south and the North belt north. This general structure, it will be observed, is similar to that presented by the Michigamme district on the south and the L'Anse-Huron bay districts on the north of the Marquette region, separated as they are by a great Laurentian anticlinal. It is probable that the Laurentian area of the Menominee region may wedge out at a point just west of the Menominee river, in the same way as do the Laurentian rocks of the Marquette region in the west part of T. 49, R. 33. (See Map I.)

In order to bring out the structure more fully for the information of the explorer and miner, three geological sections will be given, two on the South and one on the North belt. Like most geological sections, they are to a certain extent ideal, but are intended to correctly present the facts, together with such inferences as seem to be warranted. I should note that Dr. Credner's corresponding sections differ considerably in the hypothetical parts from mine, as will be seen by reference to his paper already mentioned.

Geological Sections, Menominee Iron Region.

Section A.

Projecting the more important rock exposures of the eastern portion of the South belt on one plane, which may be taken at right angles with the strike of the rocks, that is, N. 16° E, through Sturgeon Falls, Sec. 27, T. 39, R. 29, the following series will be found (See Map No. IV.) :—

At the falls of the Sturgeon, Sections 8 and 9, T. 39, R. 28, is a group of strata, which divide rocks unmistakably Laurentian on the N., from the lower Huronian quartzite on the S., and which Prof. Pumpelly and Dr. Credner regard as of Laurentian age, but which seems to me to admit of some doubt, as they conform with the bedding of both systems (all being conformable) and have lithological affinities with both.

Prof. Pumpelly describes them as follows, beginning with the uppermost strata :—

1. Talcose slates, soft, light-greenish, gray, with distinct ripple-marks.

2. Four beds of conglomerates, consisting of more or less rounded fragments of quartz, granite and gneiss, 15 to 30 feet wide. See Spec. 65, State Coll., App. B, Vol. II. This conglomerate has not been observed elsewhere, although a somewhat similar rock outcrops on Sec. 10, T. 42, R. 28.

3. Underlying the series are two beds of protogine gneiss, of reddish color, separated by a bed of chloritic schist; the upper one of the beds of protogine encloses a segregated vein, two feet wide, of a mixture of magnetic iron and sulphuret of iron, which does not promise to make a workable deposit.

North of this series, at the head of rapids on Sec. 9, T. 39, R. 28, unmistakable Laurentian rocks occur, but which appear to be conformable with the Huronian. The chief varieties found here as well as elsewhere in the Menominee region are,—a granite (in places porphyritic) syenite, mica-gneiss, with some mica-schist, hornblendic-gneiss and schists, chloritic and talcose gneiss, with some chloritic and talcose slates.

I. The lowest, geologically, and most northerly formation which is unmistakably Huronian in the South iron belt, is a *quartzite*, which outcrops conspicuously at the Falls of the Sturgeon river, Sec. 8, T. 39, R. 28 (not Sturgeon Falls), where it is not far from 1,000 feet thick, and rises to an elevation of over 200 feet above the river. It is usually light-gray, massive, compact, and often semi-vitreous, with indistinct bedding; has more the appearance of vein quartz than the Marquette quartzites. In places it shows ripple-marks with great distinctness; the weather has no appreciable effect on it.

This formation outcrops conspicuously, forming high ledges on Sec. 9, T. 39, R. 28, on Sec. 1, T. 39, R. 29 and Sec. 28, T. 40, R. 29. A quartzite, believed to be the equivalent of this, outcrops near the N. W. cor. Sec. 26, T. 40, R. 30. The Felch mountain iron deposit is also supposed to belong to this formation, as has already been explained.

II. A quartzose *sandstone* and conglomerate rock, which has a lithological character more allied to the Silurian than the Huronian, seems to overly this quartzite on the S., outcropping near the S. W. cor. of Sec. 2, T. 39, R. 29, and on the E. bank of Sturgeon river, on Sec. 8, T. 39, R. 28. But little is known about it, and its existence as a member of the iron series is not absolutely proven. From its soft, friable character it would more likely be found under swamps than on elevations.

The marble outcropping in Sections 24 and 25, T. 40, R. 30, would appear to occupy the same horizon. The same marble may exist on this geological section, but it has not been seen; the formation we are describing may be its equivalent.

III. The existence here of a range of slightly *magnetic* ore is indicated by angular boulders of lean ore in the valley of the Pine river, Sec. 12, T. 39, R. 29, and by magnetic attractions, Secs. 7 and 8, T. 39, R. 28. It does not, however, outcrop in this vicinity.

The hypothesis assumed for the structure of the South belt would make this ore the equivalent of the range known to exist north of Lakes Antoine and Fumeê, in T. 40, R. 30. It is possible, as will be seen hereafter, that this conjectured iron range may be the equivalent of the main iron deposit of the North belt.

IV. Crystalline *limestone or marble.*—This formation has an immense development in the South belt, far greater than in the other, its thickness being probably greater than that of the quartzite I. It is generally thinly bedded, and usually of a light-gray color, but is sometimes reddish, yellowish, or bluish.* The upper portion contains thin bands of slate, in which it resembles the marbles of the Marquette region, but differs from them in being freer from silica, less variegated in color, having fewer joints, as well as in being immensely greater in its extent, and more dolomitic. The Marquette marbles are indeed but calcareous beds in the Lower Quartzite (V.) of that series, there being no proper marble formation in the rocks of that region.

A piece of marble from near the Breen mine gave Dr. Rominger carbonate of lime, 61 per cent.; carbonate of magnesia, 34 per cent.; hydrated oxide of iron and manganese, 1 per cent.; and silicious matter, 0.25; which composition would make the rock rather a dolomite than a limestone. Specimen No. 66, State Collection, App. B, Vol. II., came from Sec. 11, T. 39, R. 29. Five specimens from this locality gave an average specific gravity of 2.81, approximately determined. Dr. Rominger gave attention to the value of this rock for building. (See his Report, Part III.) Large outcrops of marble occur on the south side of the Pine river on Secs. 11 and 12, T. 39, R. 29, and on the Sturgeon river, Secs. 17 and 18, T. 39, R. 28.

V. The principal *iron ore formation* of the South belt overlies, on the south side, the formation just described. It is made up chiefly, so far as is now known, of silicious specular slate ores, corresponding nearly with the so-called flag ores of the Marquette region. There is generally such admixture of magnetite as to produce moderate variations in the needle, but no evidence of the existence of a large body of magnetic ore. Specimen 68, State Col-

* The weathered surface is often rough, from minute ridges, caused by the more silicious layers, which best resisted the weathering.

lection, App. B, Vol. II. is from Sec. 11, T. 39, R. 29. At the Breen mine some very good soft hematite occurs in the same formation, which promises to be in workable quantities. See Specimen 67, State Collection, App. B., Vol. II. This ore would probably be found elsewhere if sought for, but it never outcrops. A blackish, porous ore, hematitic in its character, containing 56 per cent. of iron and nearly 1 per cent. of manganese, was found in a pit at the ¼ post between Sections 9 and 10, T. 39, R. 29, but its extent was not determined. Boulders of the same ore were seen in other places on the range.

The best exposures of the hard ores of this formation in the vicinity of the Sturgeon river, besides the Breen mine, are in Secs. 11, 10, 9 and 6, T. 39, R. 29. These ores will be described more fully, and analyses given hereafter.

VI. On the south shore of Lake Hanbury, which lies in Secs. 9, 10, 15 and 16, T. 39, R. 29, is an extensive outcrop of *chloritic schist*, the most easily splitting planes of which strike west by north, and dip south at a high angle. A similar rock, believed to be the same bed, can be seen on the Sturgeon river, near centre of Sec. 13, T. 39, R. 29. South of Lake Hanbury, 200 steps, is a rock partaking of a dioritic character, but which is probably a harder granular form of the same schist. Such rocks often graduate into each other in the Marquette region (Chap. III.). This schist may probably underlie Lake Hanbury and the swamps easterly and westerly from it.* It is represented on the section as following in its foldings formations VII. and VIII., described below. It is at least possible that this formation may be the same as the Menominee river diorites and chloritic schists, IX. and X., there brought to the surface by another series of more southern folds. But this hypothesis is not assumed in this discussion.

VII. *Clay-Slate.*—At 350 steps south of Lake Hanbury, on lines between Secs. 15 and 16, T. 39, R. 29, is a bluish and greenish gray slate, showing indistinct contorted bedding, with prevailing dip to *north*; the cleavage planes of which strike about north 70° west, and dip 80° to south. Veins of white quartz occur in

* Since the above was written Professor Pumpelly has informed me that he observed a large outcrop of marble south of the iron formation III., in T. 40, R. 30, which will be described below under Section B. This marble may fill the apparent blank existing at Lake Hanbury.

these planes. At 550 steps south of the lake, a similar slate is found dipping *north* under the quartzite VIII., next to be described. It is believed that these two outcrops of slate, are the opposite sides of a synclinal trough, which holds the quartzite.

In the N. E. 1/4 of Sec. 20, T. 39, R. 29, is an outcrop of talcose clay-slate. In Secs. 29 and 39, T. 39, R. 28, are several outcrops of dark colored, finely cleavable, but indistinctly bedded clay-slates. It is assumed that all these outcrops are parts of bed VII., which is folded into a synclinal and partial eroded anticlinal, as represented on section A of Map IV.

I am not in possession of sufficient facts to demonstrate the precise relations of these beds to each other, but the general fact is established by the northerly dips observed by me on Secs. 14, 15 and 16, that there are at least two folds between the iron range and the Menominee river, which probably reduces the estimated total thickness given in Dr. Credner's paper (18,000 feet), one-third. See page 175.

VIII. Associated with the clay-slates south of Lake Hanbury, is a bluish gray *quartzite*, which weathers into a brown, friable sandstone,* and in places reticulated with fine veins of quartz. At 550 steps south of Lake Hanbury, on line between Secs. 15 and 16, T. 39, R. 29, this quartzite is underlaid, as has been mentioned, by the clay-slate, VII., the division plane dipping plainly to the north at an angle of from 45° to 75°; the same rocks with the same northerly dip were observed farther east, on Secs. 15 and 14. This quartzite may be simply a local bed in the clay-slate formation, hence not entitled to a distinct number. The marked contortions both in the clay slate and quartzite are noticeable, and point unmistakably to the presence of a great fold. The cleavage planes maintain their east-west strike and southerly dip.

IX. This number is intended to include the soft *magnesian schists* (chloritic, talcose, and probably argillaceous) occurring so abundantly along the Menominee river, in the vicinity of the mouth of the Sturgeon, as well as at the several falls above. They will be more particularly described under geological section B.

---

* "Iron slate" is marked on the United States plats at this locality. The brown color of the quartzite has something the appearance of iron rust. The very feeble magnetic attractions existing along this range, indicate the presence of magnetite.

X. This formation is designed to embrace the granular *dioritic* rocks which form the barrier of the Sturgeon and other falls above, for 20 miles. It varies considerably in character, but on the whole bears a strong family resemblance to the granular diorites of the Marquette region. A peculiar gray variety, occurring at Sturgeon Falls, Sec. 27, T. 39, R. 29, is illustrated by Specimen No. 65, State Collection, App. B, Vol. II. This is the formation, it will be remembered, which in its supposed westerly prolongation into Wisconsin, produces the falls in the Pine river, and near them becomes iron-bearing. If the hornblendic schists mentioned as occurring in T. 42, are Huronian, they are probably the equivalents of this formation.

XI.—South of X., on or near the Menominee river, in south part of T. 39, R. 29, are several exposures of what appear to be *magnesian schists* and *protogine*, the structural relations of which to the rocks already described have not been made out. A rock similar to the protogine was observed in Sec. 13, T. 42, R. 30, and would there seem to have about the same relative position to the North belt that this has to the South belt.

Geological Section B runs northeast by north, across T. 40, R. 30, cutting Lake Antoine, and passes near the head of Great Bequensenec Falls. (See Map IV.)

I. Lower *quartzite*.—This formation appears far more conspicuously in this section than in A, owing to the double fold hypothetically introduced to cover the facts observed in the N. ½ of T. 40, R. 30. The large exposure of quartzite lying against the Laurentian, on Secs. 1 and 2, and the numerous angular boulders on Secs. 7 and 8, with the outcrop of quartzite near S. W. cor. of Sec. 23, taken in connection with the granite exposures on Secs. 4 and 9, lead one to the conclusion that one bed of quartzite, forming a synclinal basin under the Pine river and an eroded anticlinal to the south, best reconciles the facts observed. The lithological and topographical characteristics of this quartzite have already been given under A, and need not be repeated.

II. This formation was represented on A by friable sandstone and conglomerate, not observed near this section; the blue and pink *marble* outcropping near centre of Sec. 25, and the marble at the N. W. cor. of Sec. 24, are assumed to belong to one horizon (as shown by map and section), which is supposed to immediately overlie the quartzite. There is no reason to believe that this formation has any great thickness.

III. The "shows" and "signs" of ore to which this number was attached on section A, have developed into certainty on this section, where, near the centre of the N. ½ of Sec. 20, T. 40, R. 30, a considerable outcrop of *iron ore* is seen in the bottom of a small ravine. It is a silicious, red oxide, resembling in its general character the great ore formation of section A. Its continuation eastward is made certain by the magnetic attractions on the south line of Sec. 22, by the iron boulders of N. E. ¼ of Sec. 27, and on the north side of Lake Fumeê, on Sec. 26. Except the slight attractions noted by United States surveyors, at N. E. cor. of Sec. 30, T. 40, R. 29, there is no connecting link, so far as known, between this deposit and the indications of this bed on A. It is not proven that they are identical. Dr. Credner, as will be seen by reference to his paper, believes the ores on the north side of the lakes are the equivalents of those on the south, the two being connected by a synclinal fold.

IV. Crystalline *limestone or marble.* There are immense outcrops of this rock in the S. part of Secs. 34 and 35; large exposures on the S. shore of Lake Antoine; boulders on the W. side of Sec. 30, all in T. 40, R. 30, and a continuation of the boulders in Sec. 25, in the Township west. The apparent thickness is greater than was shown on A., which may be owing to a crumpling or short abrupt folding of this part of the formation; or, it may be due to an actual thickening of the formation to the westward.

Two outcrops referred to, deserve especial mention: that in the N. W. fractional ¼ of Sec. 29, contains beds of a sandy and almost conglomeritic rock, which is associated with thin beds of dark-gray argillaceous limestone. The outcrop on Sec. 35 is the largest marble outcrop in the Menominee region, it being over 1,200 feet wide. As the dip is at a high angle to the S., the perpendicular thickness of the bed cannot be less than 1,000 feet. The S. part of the outcrop shows bands of limestone alternating with thin seams of quartz.

V. The *main iron formation* is marked by an outcrop in the centre of S. E. ¼ of Sec. 25, T. 40, R. 31, and by another which forms the west end of a high ridge on line between Secs. 30 and 31, T. 40, R. 30, the two being connected by a line of magnetic influence.

Attractions also exist near the south ¼ post of Sec. 34, T. 40, R. 30, and in the N. W. ¼ of Sec. 2, T. 39, R. 30, are iron boulders. There is at present (October, 1872) no reason to believe that the ore in Towns 39 and 40, R. 30, is less in quantity, or differs in quality from that already described under the corresponding formation of geological section A.

VI., VII. and VIII. The hypothetical place of these formations on section B, is covered by deep drift—constituting the sandy terraces of the Menominee river. No outcrops of any kind can be seen on this belt of rocks, either in Ranges 30 or 31, except a large exposure of marble observed by Prof. Pumpelly, just south of the ¼ post, between Secs. 32 and 33, which corresponds in strike and dip and in general lithological character with marble formation IV. Reference to the map will show that this rock has no observed equivalent on A, where, if it exists at all, it should be found under Lake Hanbury.

I must confess that the existence of this marble, but lately made known to me, points to the existence of folds in the neighborhood of Lake Antoine, not suggested by my geological sections.

IX., X. The chloritic, hornblendic, and dioritic rocks embraced under these two formations are well exposed at the Great and Little Bequensenec Falls, and at Sand Portage, all in T. 39, R. 30. These falls afford an unsurpassed opportunity to study this series, which was carefully done by Dr. Credner, who made out the following section at the upper fall from north to south :—

a. Crystalline hornblendic rock, consisting of light to dark-green hornblende in crystalline masses, white feldspar, a little chlorite and some quartz.

b. Talcose rock, consisting only of fibrous talc, which forms a kind of soapstone in three heavy beds.

c. Fissile talcose silicious slates, of a reddish color, with small crystals of orthoclase.

d. Soft talcose slates of light green color.

e. Chloritic slates, dark green, with spots and layers of clayish red oxide of iron.

f. Hornblendic rock, dark green, crystalline, coarse-grained to aphanitic, with specks of sulphuret of iron.

By the Little Bequensenec Falls the following series of strata is laid open, from north to south :—

a. Talcose chloritic slates, with a great many segregations of quartz.

b. Hornblendic rocks, with much dark-green chlorite, and many specks of sulphuret of iron and magnetic iron ore, 35 feet.

c. Soft fibrous soapstone in two heavy beds, with some sulphuret of iron, 8 feet.

d. Talcose slates, fissile, with many layers and segregations of white quartz and red limonite.

e. Chloritic slates, 10 feet.

f. Bed of hornblendic crystalline rock, 12 feet.

g. Chloritic slates with seams of iron pyrites, 30 feet.

h. Fibrous talcose slates, reddish, with bands of green color.

i. Chloritic slate.

Geological Section C. (North Belt). On line between Ranges 29 and 30, T. 42.

I. A *quartzite*, which is micaceous at S. ¼ post of Sec. 31, and in south part of Sec. 36, T. 42, R. 29, and ferruginous at the Felch mountain. The lithological character and stratigraphical position of this formation have been fully considered. Although it differs considerably in its character from the equivalent formation of the South belt, there can be little doubt but that it is the same.

North of this quartzite is a considerable breadth of low damp ground, with no outcrops.

II. Crystalline *limestone or marble*, of a quite pure snow-white, to reddish granular variety, outcrops immediately south of the iron on Sec. 31. In the southeast ¼ of Sec. 35, T. 42, R. 30, is an outcrop of marble presenting very distinct bedding planes, which dip to the north. These two outcrops define a range parallel with the quartzite, and probably belong to this bed, II. Another outcrop of marble near the centre of Sec. 35 cannot be reconciled as belonging to this formation, and there is some uncertainty as to whether it lies above or below the iron formation. If below, then it would have the same relative position to the iron as the outcrop first mentioned above. More facts are needed to establish the relations of these marbles. As will be seen by comparing sections C and B, it is assumed that the limestones marked II., on each, are equivalents of this bed.

III. The great *iron-ore formation*, which extends easterly and westerly across Sec. 31, half way across Sec. 36, and probably much farther each way, has already been partially described. This bed is apparently the equivalent of III. of the South belt, but it is certainly more extensive, and, so far as can be seen, contains better ore. If this hypothesis be correct, then the upper and main iron formation of the South belt has no representative in the North belt, unless it be indicated by the slight magnetic attractions already mentioned as having been observed in the north part of Sec. 36. The strongest indication of the continuance of this formation eastward is to be found, so far as known, just six miles due east, in the N. E. 1/4 of Sec. 31, T. 42, R. 28, where Prof. Pumpelly observed numerous large angular fragments of specular iron ore, associated with fragments of marble. This deposit should, on this hypothesis, pass just north of the Felch mountain, in its eastward prolongation.* The quartzite near the north 1/4 post of Sec. 31, T. 42, R. 28, would, on this hypothesis, be the equivalent of the before mentioned marble in Sec. 36, seven miles west.

IV. Crystalline *limestone or marble*, containing crystals of kyanite, outcrops about 300 steps south of the north 1/4 post of S. 36, T. 42, R. 30. Several outcrops of the same rock occur a short distance to the west, and a little south, indicating the probable existence of a large deposit of this rock. Except in the presence of the kyanite crystals, which gives to a weathered surface the rough character heretofore described, this rock has much the character of the marble, with corresponding number of geological sections A and B. Whether these marbles are equivalents is not proven, but it is assumed as being more in accordance with the facts than any other hypothesis.

V. An interesting fact in connection with the limestone outcrops on Sec. 36, just described, is the presence of a very noticeable magnetic attraction on both sides of the marble, or rather associated with it.

Prof. Pumpelly observed south of one of these outcrops of marble "strata made up of layers of quartz, magnetic iron and chlorite, containing garnets, and resembling some of the strata at Republic Mountain, Marquette region." These attractions

* The blank space north of and above the iron formation III., on section C, is marked by no outcrops except Potsdam sandstone, which covers the Huronian rocks on Sec. 31, as has been already stated.

are probably due to this rock, which is certainly but a poor representative of the great upper iron bed of the South belt.

VI., VII., VIII. No other rock was observed on this section for several hundred paces; this space may or may not be filled by these formations, which, so far, have only been seen on geological section A. The numbers are introduced here, in order to carry along the hypothesis of structure which will best reconcile and present the observed facts.

IX., X. Just north of the north ¼ post of Sec. 31, T. 42, R. 29, is a large outcrop of gneiss, with thin layers of granite, and adjoining this on the north is the most southerly observed outcrop of the great hornblendic and mica schist series, the geographical extent and general structure of which have been fully considered. Whether this series of schists are the equivalents of beds IX. and X., which occupy the immediate valley of the Menominee, cannot be established. They have the same relative position to the iron ore, marble and quartzite series, and similarity in their lithological character. It must be admitted, however, that the lithological affinities of this series of rocks of the north belt are decidedly Laurentian rather than Huronian. The gneiss and granite outcrop, above described, may be almost regarded as a typical Laurentian rock in its appearance. If future investigations prove them to be Laurentian, a very troublesome structural problem would be presented here, as we would have Laurentian rocks conformably *overlying* beds, unmistakably Huronian. There seem to be fewer difficulties in supposing that the Huronian rocks of the Menominee region embrace lithological families not, so far, found represented in the equivalent series in Marquette region.

An important observation may be made here bearing on the variable thickness of the Huronian series, or else pointing unmistakably to tremendous folds in the rocks of the South iron belt,—it is this: the superficial breadth occupied by formations I. to VIII. inclusive, is nearly four times as great in the South belt as in the North. A portion of this difference may be accounted for by the thinning out of this series to the north; but the folds figured in geological section A, and possibly others not determined, would, I think, account for the greater part of this discrepancy.* There are no evidences of any folds in the corresponding series in the North belt.

---

* See page 169.

A range of marble associated with quartzite, chloritic and talcose rock, and overlaid by a chloritic gneiss, with beds of chloritic schist and gneissoid conglomerate, the whole dipping at a high angle to the south, passes about five miles north of the North belt. These may represent the north side of the trough or basin, of which this iron belt is the south outcrop. No iron has, however, been found, as far as I know, on this range.

Along the Menominee river, where it crosses this broad schistose belt which lies north of the North belt, is a series of north and south dips, observable at the Cedar, Long, and Norway portages, which point unmistakably to intermediate folds in these rocks, whose thickness, therefore, may not be very great.

Nothing remains to be said regarding the Menominee iron region which is of practical importance to the explorer, miner, or capitalist, and which would properly come within the scope of this work, except a statement as to the *quality of the ore.* The quantity has already been described as great, and the chances to mine all that could be desired. The distances by rail from shipping port and grades are most favorable. If the ores are of first quality, this region has a future which will only be surpassed, if it is surpassed, by the Marquette region, now developed to that extent that its ores produce nearly one-fourth of all the iron made in the United States.

Unfortunately at this time the question of quality cannot be fully answered, for the simple reason that up to the date of my last visit, in October, 1872, comparatively little exploring had been done, and iron deposits very seldom expose naturally their best ores; these have to be found by digging. This subject is fully treated in Chap. VII.; but I will repeat here that ninety-nine hundredths, if not nine hundred and ninety-nine thousandths, of all the ore outcropping in the Marquette region (and there is an immense amount of it) is not merchantable, according to the present standard for shipments. Soft hematite ores never outcrop; therefore if pure high grade ores be abundant in the Menominee region, they might not yet have been found from the little work that has been done.

The facts observed by me are as follows, taking the several iron locations in succession:—1st, The *Breen mine* on N. ½ of N. W. ¼ of Sec. 22, T. 39, R. 28, **South belt.** Three kinds of ore occur at this locality, the predominating variety (constituting perhaps four-fifths of all exposed) being a lean, silicious, slaty or flaggy ore, resembling the Iron mountain and Teal lake ores of the Marquette region. It varies in quality from a ferruginous quartz schist, containing but a few per cent. of iron, up to masses as good, if not better, than the second-class or flag ores of the Marquette region, with occasional richer streaks. Careful mining and selecting would produce an ore of this kind that should yield say 45 per cent. in the furnace, but it would be apt to "work hard," from the large amount of silica, and produce a hard iron, suitable, perhaps, for rail-heads. (See Iron Ores, Chap. III.) What percentage of the whole mass would be of this degree of richness, practical mining only can determine; from what could be seen in October, 1872, I should say not exceeding one-third.

The next variety in abundance is a soft, earthy, dark-colored hematite, resembling in its general appearance the Negaunee hematite ore of the Marquette region. A sort of irregular pocket of this ore was found lying in the first described variety, appearing as if it may have been produced by a partial decomposition and disintegration of the flag ore,—that is a secondary form of it. This hematite pocket, so far developed by the shafts and trenches, is of sufficient size to work advantageously, but is divided through the centre by a bar of very silicious ore. Several "shows" of this ore were found in other places, but none were proven to be of workable extent. See Spec. 67, State Coll., App. B, Vol. II.

The third variety of ore is best in quality, but, so far as known, least in quantity. It can be seen near the mouth of a drift on the south side of the ridge next the swamp, where a bed two or three feet thick was passed through, flag ore being found to the north of it. This is a hard, more or less porous, bluish, heavy, red ore, of a hematitic character, and has considerable resemblance to the so-called Jackson "hard hematite." It would undoubtedly work well in the furnace, and would yield not less than 60 per cent. of metallic iron. There are reasons to suppose that there may be a workable bed of this ore on the property; but judging from what is to be seen at the drift above mentioned, it may be under wet ground.

On the whole, it may be said of the Breen location, that the great amount of ferruginous schist there developed, and the tendency shown by it to pass into soft hematite, render it very probable that a considerable quantity of workable ore of this kind may exist. The absence of local magnetic attractions, and of boulders of rich hard ore, leads me to consider it doubtful whether any rich specular and magnetic ores, such as are now produced in the Marquette region, will be found here.

The ore range probably extends east and west, the entire length of the "80," or one-half mile, forming a ridge where the explorations have been made, from 20 to 30 feet high, bounded by a swamp on the south side. The whole iron series dip south, and are underlaid on the north by soft shaly magnesian and argillaceous rocks.

Sections 6, 9, 10 and 11, T. 39, R. 29. The ores on these sections form what appears to be a continuous deposit, and are so much alike in their general character that they can be more commonly and briefly described together. Except a few trenches dug by the Canal Co. on Secs. 9 and 11, and some test-pits sunk this season on Sec. 6, no work had been done on this range at the time of my last visit. Here, as at the Breen, the prevailing variety, in fact the only variety which I saw in quantity, was the silicious flaggy ore already described. The quantity of this ore is enormous, forming as it does the south face, and, perhaps, the great mass of a considerable ridge running west by north. The opportunity for attack by open cuts into the south face of this ridge is unsurpassed. Like the hard ores at the Breen, they vary greatly in richness,—from a quartz schist slightly impregnated with iron up to specimens, and even considerable masses which will yield 50 per cent., and occasionally a specimen that contains 60 per cent. of metallic iron. The prevailing variety, however, is represented by Specimen No. 68, App. B, Vol. II., from Sec. II., which contains from 25 to 45 per cent. of iron.

Dr. Credner reports having found, in "Cut D, on Sec. 11, 28½ feet of good fine-grained, steel-gray iron ore, with here and there a narrow streak of silicious ore, but in such a small proportion as not to spoil the good quality of the mass. The whole series gives a dark-red streak." Specimens designed to represent the average of this deposit gave Dr. C. F. Chandler 52 per cent. of iron. In another place he found a bed "6 feet thick, supposed to be very rich ore." I did not find these trenches (as afterwards appeared), although I designed to see all, and had with me two men, who helped to dig them. Dr. Credner further reports an aggregate of 139 feet in thickness of "workable ore" on Sec. 11, but my own observations lead me to question this, unless the standard of furnace-yield be put considerably lower than at present. It is unwise, however, to predict at this time what thorough explorations may reveal.

The ore on Sec. 9 is very similar to that on 11, but on the whole (so far as can be seen) not so good: the same may be said of that on Sec. 6. Two smaller boulders of rich specular slate ore were found on the latter section, but no large ones. Occasional narrow seams of tolerably rich ore were found, one of them over one foot thick, but nothing that looked like a workable deposit. At the ¼ post between Secs. 9 and 10, north of Lake Hanbury, are to be seen several boulders of a black, porous earthy ore resembling somewhat varieties of the Negaunee manganiferous hematites; the same ore was found in place in a pit near by, and a large boulder of it near the center of S. ½ of N. W. ¼ of Sec. 6, and at other points. A hand specimen gave Mr. Jenney 56.44 per cent. of metallic iron, less than 16 per cent. of insoluble silicious matter, and nearly 1 per cent. of manganese. It is unlike the Breen mine hematite, and, in fact, unlike any Lake Superior ore I have seen. It is not improbable that workable deposits of it may exist, which being soft would not be likely to produce outcrops or boulders. I think it is well worth investigation. I have some reasons for supposing that this ore may be Silurian.

The next exposure of ore west of Sec. 6 on the south range is near the ¼ post between Sections 30 and 31, T. 40, R. 30. This ore is softer and more slaty than those already described, although belonging to the flag ore family. It is apparently more argillaceous, and outcrops conspicuously in several places west of the ¼ post, dipping at a high angle to the *north*, which would necessitate an *overturned dip* in order to harmonize with the hypothetical geological sections given on the map. The exposed bedding-planes are bright and specular, giving the ore the appearance of being richer than it really is. The ore exposed here may yield 45 per cent. in the furnace; see analysis No. 254, Chap. X.

From this locality we are led by a broad belt of very moderate magnetic attractions west by north for half a mile, to the iron ore exposed in the centre of S. E. ¼ of Sec. 25, T. 40, R. 31, where the Canal Company have done some trenching; the exposure here is not great, the ore being in a small ravine on high ground. It is intermediate in character between the flag ores noticed, but most like the last. I followed the attractions about one-eighth of a mile west, to a point where the hill seemed to be capped with Silurian sandstone.

I have now mentioned in order, beginning at the east, all the main exposures of ore in the south range of the South belt, which has already been referred to as the most regular and one of the most extensive deposits of ore in the Lake Superior region; whether it is absolutely continuous for the 16 miles intervening between the extreme exposures, can only be determined by expensive explorations or actual mining.

Passing from the south to the north range of the South belt, we have but one exposure to consider, that near the centre of N. ½ of Sec. 20, T. 40, R. 30. This is in a small ravine, down which, to the south and toward Lake Antoine, a rivulet has its course in wet weather; the water has uncovered a narrow surface of flag ore similar to that seen on the south side of Sec. 30, but less slaty. Iron boulders are strewn along the ravine for over 100 feet. This ore is a red oxide, but holds enough magnetite to give it a moderate magnetic power.

Ten miles northerly across the granite region, from the last mentioned locality on Sec. 20, bring us to the main deposit of ore in the **North belt**—that on Secs. 31 and 36, of T. 42, and Ranges 29 and 30. The great extent of this deposit, and its favorable situation for mining, have already been commented on; it only remains to notice the quality of the ore. It is more granular and massive than the flag ore of the south range, and, as a whole, contains less silica and more metallic iron. The natural exposures of ore in the ledge are greater, no digging or uncovering at all being required to reach a great quantity of the ore. The best ore to be seen outcropping, is just southeast of the centre of Sec. 31: the top of the cliff is here about 100 feet above the low ground at its base on south side; and for about one-third of this height is a ledge of ore, from the foot of which the surface slopes rapidly to the low ground, affording the best possible opportunity for mining. This outcrop was carefully examined for a distance of several hundred feet in length, and from the richest places to be found in it, 29 specimens of ore, of about one pound each, were collected, no two being broken from the same place. The specific gravity of these specimens was approximately determined on the ground, and was found to vary from 3.26 to 4.15, the mean of the 29 specimens being 3.71 ; this multiplied by 12, according to the empirical rule given under Explorations (Chap. VII.), gives 45 as the average percentage of the whole. An ore which actually analyzes 45 per cent. of metallic iron should yield say 47½ per cent. in the furnace, which is about what I consider this ledge of ore would work, if mined and sorted with ordinary care. Several ounces, chipped from five of the best hand specimens I could find, gave Dr. Wuth, of Pittsburg, 54.81 per cent. of metallic iron (See Analysis No. 98, Chap. X.). Separate analyses of ten hand specimens, selected from same locality by Prof. Pumpelly and Dr. Credner, gave Dr. Chandler from 49 to 64 per cent. of metallic iron, the average being 53.74 per cent. If this higher grade can be found in workable quantities (which is probable), then we should have a 55 per cent. ore, which, considering its granular and semi-porous nature, and the fact of its being a red oxide, would indicate an ore not difficult to reduce, and one which would sell in the present market.

No boulders were observed in this vicinity which would indicate a richer ore than the above of the red oxide variety, and no magnetic attractions were observed which would suggest a workable deposit of magnetic ore, although all the ores of this region are slightly magnetic. As hematite ores do not outcrop, and as no explorations have been directed to finding such ores, nothing can be said regarding them. My impressions are that they will be found on Secs. 31, 32, or 36 of the North belt.

The Felch mountain ore was fully described when considering the lower quartzite. It is totally unlike either of the preceding varieties, and more closely resembles the "mixed ore" which accompanies the rich specular ores of the Marquette region. The laminæ of ore are very rich, analyzing from 63 to 67 per cent. of metallic iron ; but the large admixture of quartzite (at least three quarters of the whole) would render it unmerchantable at present. It is by its constitution particularly well adapted to *stamping* and *washing*, and on account of its proximity to several rapids and falls in the Sturgeon river, is well situated to be worked in this way, when the market drives miners to this means of production, as it will sooner or later.

3. Paint River District.

Too little is known about the remote Paint river district, in Towns 42 and 43, Ranges 32 and 33, to enable me to give anything of interest regarding its geological structure. The Huronian rocks are extensively developed there, and contain deposits of hard hematite ore. I had the opportunity to examine only two localities, at the Paint River Falls, Sec. 20, T. 43, R. 32, and on Sec. 13, T. 42, R. 33. The ores are identical, and unlike any in the more easterly part of the Menominee region, in being richer in iron, freer from silica, and in containing more water. (See Analysis 68, Chap. X.)

Explorations now in progress will determine many of the unsettled questions regarding the ores of the Menominee region, especially of the South belt. I regret that I cannot embody their results in this Report, and thus give it a completeness that in the present state of my information is impossible.

CHAPTER VI.

LAKE GOGEBIC AND MONTREAL RIVER IRON RANGE.

An examination of this but little known iron-field was not contemplated in the original plan of the survey. But, having had occasion in the line of my profession to make some explorations there, a few of the general results obtained will be given, with a view of aiding future explorations, and of calling attention to a comparatively unexplored region. The probability of there being early railroad communication through this country, connecting the existing system of roads of the Upper Peninsula with the North Pacific, Minnesota and Wisconsin systems, now radiating from the west end of Lake Superior, attaches additional interest to this most western portion of the Upper Peninsula.

The facts observed and conclusions formed are the joint work of Prof. Raphael Pumpelly and myself, and have, so far as they bear on the stratigraphical relations of the four great systems of rocks, been in substance given to the public, in the American Journal of Science and Arts, Vol. III., June, 1872. Many rock specimens, gathered by us are minutely described by Mr. Julien, in App. A, Vol. II.

The iron range under consideration may be regarded as the eastern prolongation of the Penokie range of Wisconsin, as well as the western extension of the Marquette series, the whole being Huronian. The position of the range is tolerably well defined by magnetic observations and notes on the U. S. land office plats; on these we find mention of iron and magnetic attractions on Secs. 7 and 8, T. 47, N., R. 45, W., as also in Secs. 13 and 14 of the Town west. The belt of Huronian rocks, as made out by us, extends nearly east and west, through the north part of T. 47, Ranges 44, 45, 46 and 47, crossing the Montreal River in Secs. 16 and 21, of the last-named Township. Going east, the range was lost before it reached Lake Gogebic.

The geological boundaries of this range are fortunately of the most unmistakable nature, and render a detailed description of its position unnecessary. (See Map I.)

On the north is the high, broad, irregular ridge, or series of ridges, constituting the South Copper Range, the rocks of which are greenish and brownish, massive and amygdaloidal copper-bearing traps, their bedding being exceedingly obscure, with occasional beds of sandstone and an imperfect conglomerate. The strike of these rocks, so far as it could be made out, was east and west, with a dip to the north at a high angle, thus *conforming* with the Huronian rocks underneath.

Against and over the copper series on the north, abut the horizontally bedded lower Silurian sandstones, which are beautifully exposed on the west branch of the Ontonagon river, in Sec. 23, T. 46, R. 41. These sandstones form the surface rock, and occupy the broad belt between the two copper ranges from the region we are describing to Keweenaw bay, but taper to a point before reaching the Montreal river, in going west.

On the south of the iron-bearing rocks are a series of granites, chloritic gneisses and obscure schists, which, except the latter, are unmistakably Laurentian in their lithological character, and are *non-conformably* overlaid by the Huronian rocks. The general structural relations of the four great systems here enumerated are shown in the accompanying diagram. As the *non-conformability*

Fig. 12. Sketch showing Geological Section—looking west, between Lake Gogebic and Montreal River (in part ideal).

L. Laurentian rocks—gneiss, granite and schists, which are *non-conformably* overlaid by, H. Huronian—Clay slate, ferruginous and jasper schists, flag ores, quartzites and diorites, say 4,000 feet thick, which are *conformably* overlaid by, C. Copper-bearing rocks, chiefly greenish and brownish, massive and amygdaloidal traps, with occasional sandstones and conglomerate layers, which are *non-conformably* overlaid by, S. Lower Silurian sandstone, coarse quartz sandrock.

of the copper-bearing rocks and sandstones is doubted by some geologists, it should perhaps be stated that the actual contact was not seen. But the sandstones were observed lying horizontal, and affording not the slightest evidence of disturbance, within a few miles of highly-tilted copper rocks, which gave every evidence of having been elevated before the deposition of the sandstones. So far as my observation has extended, this rule is general; that is, no Lake Superior sandstone, which is unmistakably lower Silurian, has ever been found in any position other than nearly horizontal; and no rock which was unmistakably of the Copper series has been seen which was not considerably tilted. The fact that certain sandstones belonging to the copper series are very similar, if not lithologically identical with some of the lower Silurian sandstones, has helped to complicate this question. An interesting locality for study in this connection is the west fork of the Ontonagon river, just south of the Forest Copper Mine. I am not sure but that it affords an exception to the rule above stated, as at that point sandstones, *apparently* Silurian, dip south at an angle of 45°.

The best locality in which to study the character of the iron series in the West region, is on Black river and its tributaries, especially on the outlet of Sunday lake, T. 47, Ranges 45 and 46. Here will be found banded ferruginous jaspery schists, chloritic greenstones, brown ferruginous slates, black and gray banded silicious slates, silicious flag ores, several varieties of quartzites and clay slate. The whole series strike east and west, and dip north away from the granites and gneisses and under the copper rocks, at an angle of from 40 to 90°. Several varieties of the Huronian and Laurentian rocks of this vicinity have been examined by Mr. Julien, for descriptions of which see Appendix A, Vol. II. It will be observed from these descriptions that these rocks, although somewhat different from the Huronian series of the Marquette region, are still essentially the same; and I know of no good reason why merchantable ores may not be found amongst them. No ore, however, was found either in place, or in the form of boulders, which would pass for shipping ore in the Marquette region at this time. The absence of strong magnetic attractions renders it improbable that pure magnetic ores will be found here. The most encouraging indications observed pointed towards the existence of soft hematites, which may very likely be found of a quality and in quantity to pay for working. The best "show" observed was in the south ½ of the S. W. ¼, Sec. 18, T. 47, R. 46. It is on the north-easterly side of an east and west ridge, where there is a large exposure of highly ferruginous quartzite in places holding hand-specimens of hematite ore of fair quality. As this kind of ore never outcrops, on account of its soft, earthy character, and as we had no facilities for digging, nothing more definite was determined.

CHAPTER VII.

EXPLORATIONS (*Prospecting for Ore*).

1. How Failures have occurred, and how to avoid Them.

THE history of the development of a good many of our iron mining enterprises has been somewhat as follows:—The deposit is found, sometimes by accident, but often by systematic explorations made at the expense of corporations, firms, or individuals, by a class of men known as *explorers;* who are acquainted with woodcraft, are often miners, and who always have some knowledge of structural geology, the different varieties of ore, and the use of the miner's compass. A boulder of ore, red soil in the roots of a fallen tree, the variation of the magnetic needle, the proximity of rocks supposed to belong to the iron range, and often the outcrop of the ore itself, determines where digging shall be commenced.

If the indications are promising, before many marks are made the land is secured, if not already owned or controlled by those interested in the explorations. If government land, it is "entered" at the land office at $1.25 per acre, or $2.50 if within the limits of some railroad grant. If the land is "second-hand," already entered, it may be bought outright, or if the price be regarded as too high, a refusal is often taken with the privilege of exploring.

If the discovery is on the land of some railroad or mining company, it usually cannot be bought. In this case, all trace of the work done is often concealed, secrecy enjoined on all concerned, and the explorer lives in the vain hope that he may sometime have the opportunity to buy the land, an expectation in which he usually dies, as large corporations do not often sell iron deposits for small prices, if at all. Instead of this unwise course, explorers often sell their information to the companies owning the land, which they can usually do at a fair price. Our supposed exploring party having secured the land, begin to dig test-pits and trenches openly and systematically. The solid ledge is usually soon found, which may prove to be some variety of iron ore, perhaps pure, but far more likely a "mixed ore" or lean flag ore, hence not merchantable.

Specimens (which I am sorry to say are apt to be the best that can be found) are sent in as *averages* of the deposit. Experts pronounce them shipping ore, and common talk asserts that So and So have a "good show" for a mine.

Soon the test-pits, trenches and drifts develop a workable width and length of what seems to the explorers to be merchantable ore. "Mixed with a little rock perhaps in places," but this occurs in most mines at the start. Experienced mining men visit the new deposit, examine it carefully, and assert honestly that "it looks better than did the Champion or Barnum locations when they first saw them."

The explorers select what they believe to be strictly *average* specimens of the ore (an impossible thing as will appear), which are sent to some distinguished chemist who reports, perhaps 65 per cent. of metallic iron, and only traces of sulphur and phosphorus, and expresses the opinion that the ore will *work well* in a blast furnace, and is identical with other well-known Lake Superior ores. This report, with the certificates of good practical mining men, and the opinion of some geologist who may have examined the locality, satisfies the owners that they have a workable deposit of "shipping ore."

Next in order, if it has not proceeded simultaneously with the above, is the organization of a company under the general mining law of Michigan,* which prescribes not to exceed 20,000 shares at $25 per share, par value. The property above mentioned is put into the new company at a moderate price; some prominent man of character and means is found to take the presidency of the company, his friends, with others, being "let in" on the "ground floor," and the None-such Iron Co. is organized and at work.

Building up a location is the next thing in order. To this end a contract is usually let to some French Canadian to build a dozen log houses for miners' families, a company's store, barn and shop. For this purpose the contractor lays out *fifteen different lines* on which to put the buildings, being governed in each instance by the ease with which the logs can be got together. In clearing for the foundations it is usual for the Frenchman to find a new deposit of ore

---

* App. I., Vol. II., contains an abstract of the Mining Laws of Michigan.

better than the one first found, to which a part of the mining force is at once transferred, the location of the buildings being changed so as to avoid the fragments which blasting has already begun to throw. The condition of affairs at the new location is at this period about as follows :—houses are going up rapidly, stripping is being pushed to the utmost, several "pairs" of Cornish men are sinking shafts or blasting off the "cap rock" so as to get at the ore. The contract for a first-class wagon road to connect with the State road has been let at $2 per rod, and a party of engineers are at work locating a branch railroad to the mine, and it is confidently predicted that a considerable amount of ore will be shipped from the mine that season.

About this time the president of the company—an old iron man, who has made a fortune by smelting 40 per cent. ores with anthracite coal in Eastern Pennsylvania—and a part of the board of directors visit the mine. One of the directors is an eminent lawyer who helped to "place" the property, another is a stockbroker who had made a fortune in Wall Street, a third is a railroad king, and another a successful whisky distiller. None but the president knew anything of iron before they came into the company. He is of course amazed at the richness of the ore, and tells the captain in charge of the mine truthfully, that he is throwing away as good ore as he ever used in his Pennsylvania furnaces. All collect and examine numerous specimens, which are submitted to the president and captain for their judgment as to richness. Nothing less than 50 per cent. is found, and the average is much higher. The lawyer who has fine muscular sense and a consciousness of its possession, soon discovers that he can judge accurately of the percentage of iron by handling the pieces of ore, and speedily becomes an authority with the broker and distiller. Specimens are hefted which contain 59, 61, 62½, 68, and finally one fine-grained fragment of steely ore, which, after careful manipulation in each hand, it is decided contains 75 per cent. of metallic iron. The captain unhesitatingly admits that to be richer than anything in the Jackson mine. Rock is found in several pits, but the captain explains that it is only greenstone which "caps" the ore, and proves by the magnetic needle which is "dead 90," that the ore is there. Being in a hurry he may not have faced the instrument exactly east and west.

Having spent one half-day in the examination of their property, and becoming satisfied that it is first-class and will prove a profitable investment for themselves and friends, the company leave, having first instructed their superintendent to bend all his energies to getting out ore, without reference to quality, cost, or future condition of the mine—though the whole is not, of course, directly expressed. On their way East, the president perhaps sells a thousand tons or more to some furnace man who is a stockholder in the new company, and telegraphs back to the superintendent to ship it at once.

The foregoing sketch contains the elements on which many Lake Superior iron mining enterprises have been organized, and at the start operated. It is needless to remark that many such undertakings result in utter failure. In the copper region the proportion of failures is far greater, and in oil, gold, and silver enterprises overwhelmingly so. The average human imagination becomes temporarily diseased when stimulated by the chances of possessing hidden mineral wealth. Iron, being the least valuable of the metals, has less of this influence than the others, but is not entirely free from it.

It may interest those who are disposed to identify themselves with Lake Superior iron mining enterprises (and I believe no equal investment has paid better in past time or promises better for the long future) to know the cause of failure in such enterprises. Classifying them carefully, I find that about two thirds of the disastrous enterprises were based on deposits of ore the *quality* of which was not merchantable: they were not rich enough in metallic iron. The extraordinary richness of Lake Superior ore is not generally known. I have reports from 40 furnace stacks in which these ores are smelted, which show that the average furnace yield of 250,000 tons of magnetic and specular ore for 1870 was 65 per cent.

The amount of high grade hard ore is so great that consumers can usually get all they require, and will not buy an inferior grade. For this reason experienced iron men from other regions have often been deceived; they had not a sufficient realization of this question of quality. Marquette ores—which were rich compared with what they were used to—could not be sold on account of their leanness. The soft hematite ores are not considered in this connection.

The remaining third of the failures have come from a lack of *quantity*, the quality of the ore being satisfactory. It follows, therefore, that the question of first importance in a new iron mining enterprise is to know—First, the *average percentage* of metallic iron in the deposit. What will the ore, *mined in the usual way, yield on the average when smelted in the blast furnace?* Second, approximately or relatively, *how much is there of it?* The failure to answer these questions correctly at the start has caused the loss of over one million dollars in the Marquette region during the last ten years, and the business is still going on. Experience is an expensive school, but is always full; no sooner does one class graduate than a new crop of "freshmen" take their places.

I believe it is not impossible nor even difficult to ascertain, at a moderate cost, the average amount of metallic iron, in any given deposit, sufficiently near for all practical purposes, and whether there is enough ore to pay for working.

It is the business of the explorer to find ore deposits and to determine approximately their extent and richness, thereby avoiding such failures as have been described above. This subject will now be considered under the several following heads:—

2. Prospecting and Woodcraft.

As considerable part of the iron exploration work now being carried on in the Lake Superior region involves camping out and a knowledge of woodcraft, some facts regarding this part of the business will not be amiss here, and are the more necessary because very little reliable information on this subject can be found in any book with which I am acquainted. There are no roads through large districts of country, which, in consequence, can only be reached by boats or walking; in either case a considerable part of the labor is *packing*, which means transporting everything on the backs of men. This mode of transportation costs about $9 per ton per mile at the present time, which is twenty-seven times as much as it costs to move freight on wagon-roads; it is, therefore, important to carry only such articles as are needed. Many an exploration enterprise has practically failed because the chief energies of the party were expended in carrying supplies and material which were not needed, while necessary things were left behind. It is safe to say that two times out of three, even in the case of experienced explorers, supplies do not come out equal. The party will be out of pork and have an abundance of flour, or the converse; will travel in a leaky canoe for the want of a little pitch, or be barefooted because they had no awl; or ragged for want of thread; or suffering for food, where there is plenty of fish and game, because the salt had failed; or have their supplies wet for want of a piece of oilcloth. I have been in all these straits.

Organization of the Party.—Take the ordinary case of searching for mineral or timber, when an explorer and two men constitute the party. As packing is the heavy work, it is indispensable that all hands understand it. An average packer will carry 70 to 80 pounds and his blankets, but loads of 50 to 65 pounds are more common; across portages men often carry 100 pounds, and sometimes a barrel of flour weighing 200 pounds; but the packer who carries 70 pounds and his blankets, 10 to 15 miles per day, on a trail, or 5 to 10 miles through ordinary woods, has earned the $2.25 clear per day, which is the present average wages.

Next to packing, cooking is an indispensable qualification. No man is fit to go in the woods who cannot cook; and many a woodsman, with a frying-pan and two tin pails, will, over his camp-fire prepare a better cooked meal, and in less time, than can be produced in one-third of the kitchens of the country, with all the appliances that belong to modern housekeeping.

An ability to handle a canoe in rapid water is almost as indispensable as the others. Three men with a month's supplies will require a 16-foot canoe, which will weigh, when dry, about 125 pounds, and can easily be carried across a portage by one man; such a canoe will cost, in the Menominee waters, at this time, $15 to $30. The Bad water Indian village is the chief source of supply.

Next to packing, cooking, and canoeing, an ability to travel through the woods, and locate himself, by the United States Land Office plats, or maps made from them, aided by a pocket-compass, is essential. A man who possesses these qualifications is a woodsman, and has a calling which, if he is honest and intelligent, will be profitable in the Lake Superior region for a long time to come. If, in addition to these requirements, he is a judge of timber, and can keep simple accounts, write letters, and locate himself by the "40," then he is fit to lead a party, and become a "pine-looker," or "cruiser." If he add to this, a knowledge of the more common rocks and minerals, and an ability to make rough maps or plans of ground, then he is an explorer. Such men can command from $4 to $6 per day clear, with full time, and often an interest in what they find besides; or if they choose to examine lands (either timber or mineral) on their own account, they can usually sell their "notes" at so much per acre, subject to re-examination; or some one may purchase the land, paying the explorer for his services in an undivided interest in them. Notes of pine lands now sell readily at from 50 to 75 cents per acre.

Supplies.—Pork, flour and tea embrace all that is absolutely essential in the way of supplies, though sugar, beans and dried fruit are usually added; rice, oatmeal or wheat grits are also generally carried, and a little hard bread is convenient, to which a few pounds of cheese may be supplemented. Pickled ham, especially in summer, may take the place of part of the pork, and smoked beef is sometimes used.

The following table of supplies has been prepared with considerable care from actual experience:—

Rations Required for Three Men, One Month.

Rations.	Pounds.	Amount in percentage of the flour.*
Flour, biscuit or crackers, rice, grits or oatmeal, but at least ¾ self-raising flour (equal to 1⅓ lbs. per man, per day)	125	1.
Extra heavy clear mess pork about ¾; pickled ham, say ¼	82	.650
Beans or peas	20	.160
Sugar (coffee A)	18	.140
Tea (good young Hyson)	3	.024
Dried apples	10	.080
Cheese	4	.032
Salt	2	.016
Pepper	¼	.002
Baking powder (Durkee's or Royal), if self-raising flour is not used	2½	.020
Equal to $2\frac{85}{100}$ lbs. per man per day, or total	266¾ lbs.	

* Supplies purchased in the proportions given in this column should come out even.

Equipment.—A shelter or bake-oven tent is preferable, although a closed A tent is often used in "fly time" (June and July): the former is more cheerful, healthier and warmer, because it lets the fire shine in. The style sketched will hold three men with supplies: it requires 12 yards of cotton drilling, 36 inches wide.

FIG. 13.
Explorers' bake-oven tent.

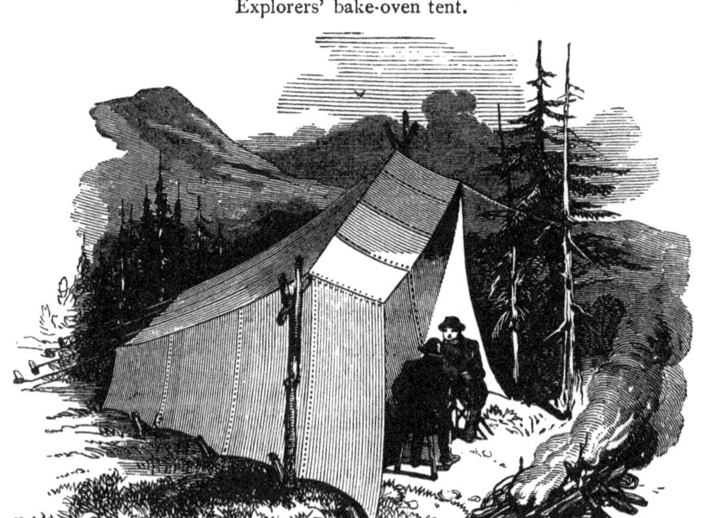

Two light explorer's axes, weighing with handles 2¾ lbs. for summer use and 5 lbs. for winter, each, are needed; if the exploration is for mineral, the backs or poles should be of steel. For three men a nest of two or three oval tin pails with covers, the largest holding 5 quarts, one frying-pan with socket handle, one 2 or 3 quart tin basin, one large spoon, one butcher or sheath knife, and a tin cup, plate, knife, fork and spoon to each man in the party, is all that is required.

If the party be large, a tin bake-oven will pay; it should be hinged so as to fold up. Canoes have already been mentioned: they are best for most kinds of river and lake service on account of their lightness, which makes them easy to portage, the ease with which they can be repaired with canvas and pitch (or resin and pork fat), and their suitableness for running rapids. But sometimes they

NOTE.—The stools shown in Fig. 13 do not belong to a camp outfit. They were introduced inadvertently by the engraver.

cannot be procured, and in low water are more liable to injury from rocks than are boats ; a skiff 2½ fathoms long, pointed at both ends, with flaring sides, and made of ½ inch boards, is a good substitute. Each man in the party should have a pocket compass, water-proof match box, and sheath knife, and there should be at least one leather and one tin map case in each party. Should the exploration be for minerals, a dip compass, and at least one exploring pick ought to be added. A small shovel will pay in such a party, but is seldom carried. A dial compass for use in traveling when there is local attraction, or in discovering the same, is often advantageous. I have found a small horse-shoe magnet and a pocket lens useful. Every party going in the woods should be supplied with the best maps that can be procured (Farmer's are the best I have seen), and always with exact tracings of the U. S. Land Office plats or maps of the Townships they propose visiting ; these plats can be obtained at any U. S. Land Office and cost, if they show variations of the needle and geological notes, about $2.25 each at Marquette. The following are the locations of all the U. S. Land Offices in Michigan, with names of officers.

U. S. Land Offices in Michigan.

District.	Office.	Register.	Receiver.
Detroit........	Detroit........	F. Morley......	J. M. Farland.
East Saginaw...	East Saginaw...	Wm. R. Bates..	A. A. Day.
Ionia..........	Ionia..........	J. H. Kidd.....	J. C. Jennings.
Traverse City...	Traverse City...	Morgan Bates...	Perry Hanna.
Marquette......	Marquette......	A. Campbell....	J. M. Wilkinson.

The explorer cannot too carefully study his maps ; next to personal examination in the field they are his great original sources of information. The surveys of the Upper Peninsula, as is explained in Chapter I., were made with great care, and embrace topography, timber, soil and geology.

Under sundries which will be found useful in camp, may be mentioned: Soap and towels, thread and needles, buttons, awl, strong twine, some cotton cloth, a file to sharpen axes, a few wrought nails if a boat is used, some extra pairs of moose-skin moccasins (for summer), fish-lines and hooks, extra compass, resin or pitch, blank U. S. plats, and fly-nets or "fly-medicine," or both in "fly-time." A large, stout, water-proof, tin match-box, extra note-book and pencils, paper and envelopes, are desirable. A short, light, single-barreled shot-gun, with bore large enough to chamber buck-shot, may be carried to advantage after the middle of August.

Mode of Working.—Mineral explorations, and especially those for iron, will only be considered under this head. The leading idea is, of course, to make a systematic and exhaustive examination of the surface for the mineral sought: to this end all outcrops of rock of whatever kind, and all boulders must be examined for some "sign" or "show" of mineral. As has been elsewhere remarked, the upturned roots of trees afford one of the best sources of information: the beds of rapid streams, which usually contain boulders and often expose the solid ledge, should be carefully examined. Any indication at all favorable should be followed up by digging. Next in importance to this kind of search is the use of the magnetic needle in discovering local attractions due to iron-ore; it is safe to assume that more than one-half the iron in the Lake Superior iron region is sufficiently magnetic to produce appreciable variations in an ordinary compass; and as magnetic ore will attract the needle at the same distance with equal strength when covered by rock, earth, air or water, this instrument is of great service to the explorer. Its use is fully considered elsewhere, as well as the geological principles applicable to this kind of work.

An explorer should make a careful sketch or map of each section examined, on a scale of 4 inches to 1 mile: on such a scale "a 40" is one inch square. On this should be marked in their proper places all streams, lakes, swamps, hills, etc., and all outcrops, with a name or sign indicating the kind of rock; colored pencils are convenient for delineating the different varieties of rocks. Opposite each such sketch should be a full written description of the rocks and minerals found, as well as notes on timber and soil.

The accompanying sketch (Fig. 14) of Sec. 29, T. 50, R. 30, from the note-book of the late A. M. Brotherton, a perfectly honest and thoroughly competent explorer, will serve as an illustration. To it is appended a map of the same section (Fig. 15), from the U. S. Surveys, which shows, valuable as these surveys are, and reliable, so far as the section lines go, they often are considerably in error in their representations of the interior of sections.

Fig. 14. Sec. 29, T. 50, R. 30. Explorer's Sketch.

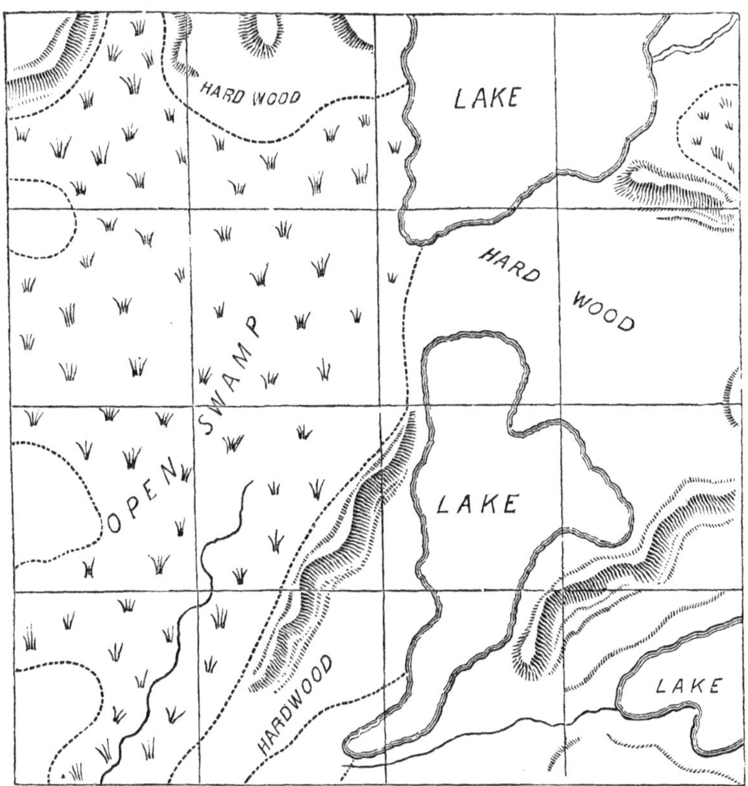

Fig. 15. Same Section, from U. S. Linear Surveys.

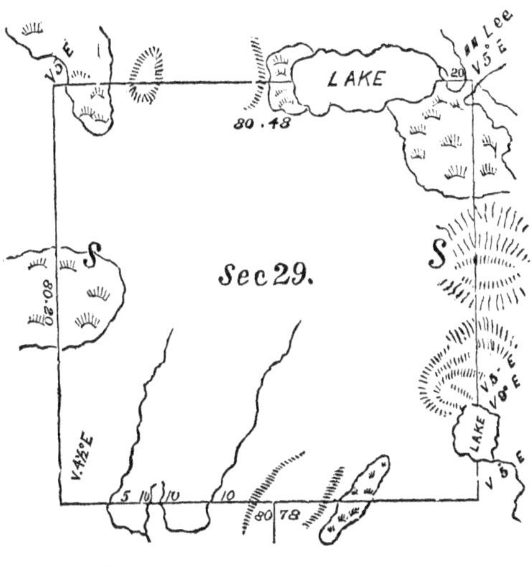

How to Recognize Iron Ores.—As a large majority of the explorers now employed are timber-hunters, they need not necessarily have a knowledge of minerals. I have, however, generally found these men more or less interested in rocks, and often very desirous of knowing how to determine the more common ores, so as to be able to note any they might find. To obtain a good knowledge, the study of a complete collection, or a residence at a mine, is indispensable. A few brief characteristics, only, will here be given, by which explorers may generally recognize iron ores in the woods.—First.—They are considerably *heavier* than any other rocks with which they are associated. Rich, magnetic, and specular ores, like those of the Marquette region, are nearly twice as heavy as the same bulk of the more common rocks, and five-sevenths as heavy as a piece of iron or steel of the same size. The soft hematites are much lighter, but are still appreciably heavier than the heaviest rock. As fine muscular sense and much practice are necessary in this business, the inexperienced explorer is advised, in every instance, to break pieces of rock of the same size as the supposed ore specimen, when, by lifting them together and changing from one hand to the other, the difference in weight will at once be felt if one of the specimens be iron ore. If the explorer is provided with a pair of balances, as is explained hereafter, he may determine, not only as to whether the substance is iron ore or not, but also approximately the percentage of metallic iron.—Second.—As to color, *magnetic* ores are black, and when pounded with the axe give a black powder, which will adhere to the axe or pick. Red *specular* ores are often bright and shining on their weathered surface, almost like polished steel; they give a red powder when pulverized, which does not adhere to the axe. Soft *hematite* ores are reddish and brownish in color, are generally porous, and often soft and earthy, in character; when pulverized they give a brownish and sometimes a yellowish powder, which does not adhere to iron or steel. These characteristics are possessed by none of the rocks of the Marquette region.—Third. Magnetic ores attract the needle of the compass strongly, often causing the north end to point south. Other ores and rocks do not attract it, but a little magnetic ore is often disseminated through rocks, especially greenstone, thereby producing more or less variation of the needle, which may not indicate valuable ores.

The rock which is oftenest mistaken for iron ore is Hornblende, and the related Diorites or Greenstones. These rocks are heavy and dark colored, and often contain enough magnetite to give them some influence on the needle. Many an explorer has carried heavy pieces of this rock many miles through the woods, only to throw them away in disgust on meeting some one who had, perhaps, only so much knowledge of ores, as it is expected these few facts will impart. Some have persisted in their folly, and bought lands on which experienced iron explorers could only find hornblendic rock. This rock differs from the ore, which it most resembles, in being *lighter*, and in giving a *light colored powder*, which does not adhere to iron or steel, as well as in other less important particulars, as may be seen by comparing the two, which should be done.

The text relating to the magnetism of rocks and use of the needle in finding ore might properly have been inserted here as a division under Exploration, of which subject it forms properly a part. But the amount of material which had been prepared on that subject, and other reasons, determined me to place it in a distinct chapter (VIII.), which follows.

3. Digging for Ore.

The exploration work above described is superficial, and will not usually determine whether a certain piece of land contains workable deposits of ore or not. Such examinations are usually made to determine whether lands are worth buying at government price, or as preliminary to a more thorough exploration. When we consider that soft hematite ores never outcrop, and that pure hard ores rarely do, it is evident that something more than looking over the surface is necessary. The excavations of earth and rock required in an exhaustive exploration of a piece of land are mining operations, and will be considered in another chapter. Only a few points will be presented here which bear especially on work of this kind.

This work is simply sinking test-pits and shafts, and opening trenches (costeaning) and drifts to expose the solid ledge. It rarely happens that such work need be prosecuted into the solid ledge. As has been before remarked, if there be pure ore at the locality, i will be almost certain to come to the surface of the ledge somewhere, and will there be found by digging through the earth. This may not always be the case, but it is safe to say that, as a rule, nine-tenths of all the money to be expended in exploring at any given locality, had best be expended in earth excavation.

There is a great deal of vague talk among miners and explorers of the Marquette region about "*cap rock;*" one would get the impression, from much that is said on this subject, that pure ores were always overlaid by rock. The fact is, however, that there are very few workable deposits of ore but what come to the surface, or, at least, connect with those that do. I should distrust any locality where "cap rocks" prevailed to any great extent; our iron-ore deposits are comparatively thin beds, which sit on edge, and come to the surface without wearing any "cap."* There are places, however, where the solid ledge has to be penetrated; when this is necessary, I think it had usually best be done by drilling. By means of hand drills, holes can be sunk 22 feet, and by means of the appliances used in sinking oil-wells to any required depth; an experienced miner will have little difficulty in judging of the material passed through by the drill mud, and if there is any question as to richness, it can easily be settled by an approximate analysis which will be described hereafter. The diamond drill gives the most valuable results, and has been used to some extent in this region, and still more extensively in the Lake Champlain region.

Exploring excavations should always be done by contract; a large amount of "test-pitting" has been done in the Marquette region at seventy-five cents per foot in depth for a 4 × 6 shaft, the miner being paid only for such shafts as were "bottomed," *i. e.*, the solid ledge reached and uncovered, whatever the depth or difficulties. For drifts 3 × 6 which bared the ledge, $1.50 was paid, and for open trenches a price proportionate to depth and width. Good miners can find themselves and make good wages at these prices in much of the ground in the Marquette region. Pits are sometimes sunk 35 feet, but the average depth does not exceed 12 feet. Mr. Colwell sunk 67 feet through sand on Section 24–47–28. Large

* In the Menominee region true "cap rocks" are found in the horizontal sandstones which overlie some of the ore, see page 68.

boulders and water are the difficulties usually encountered ; beyond 10 feet a windlass is necessary. A portable forge and mass of iron for an anvil are desirable, but picks can very well be heated in a hard-wood camp-fire and sharpened on a rock.

With regard to the significance of the material passed through, but one remark will be made ; mixed drift, that is, large and small boulders, sand, clay, etc., is usually not very deep, 40 feet being the greatest depth I have observed, the average being less than 10 feet. Sand with no boulders is usually deeper and sometimes very deep.

4. Quality and Quantity.—Sampling.—Approximate Analysis.

Up to this point we have considered chiefly the question of finding ore regardless of *quality* and *quantity*. These are, after all, the vital questions, and their importance is rendered still more conspicuous by the statement, that there is at least twenty times as much ore in the Lake Superior region that is worthless from a lack of metallic iron, as there is of merchantable ore, according to the present standard for shipment; and further, it is easy to find specimens of pure ore in almost any body of worthless ore.

To determine approximately the average percentage of metallic iron, proceed as follows:—Open two or more trenches or drifts entirely across such portion of the ore formation as is regarded fit to work. In the region we are considering, the ores usually dip at a high angle, so that the edges of the beds or strata are exposed by such cross cuts ; free the solid ledge from all earth and loose material ; then, with a heavy hammer, break off small fragments *every two inches across the entire bed*, without reference to whether the pieces are ore or rock. Wash all of those pieces, break them all into fragments of the size of grains of wheat, mix them up thoroughly, send a tea-cupful to a reliable chemist, and his return will be the practical average of metallic iron in the whole bed from which the pieces came.

Of course, in mining, the ore is sorted, so that we should expect to get a somewhat better yield from working the ore, than that found as above, but it is not wise to count much on this. If, after trying, say half a dozen cross cuts in this way, an average yield of fifty per cent. (50%) of metallic iron is not found, the deposit is doubtful; if less than forty per cent. (40%) it is of no value in the present market, should the ore be specular or magnetic. Nineteen times out of twenty, such *mechanical averages*, when honestly taken, would show a yield of less than forty per cent. (40%.)

The plan above described is somewhat expensive and consumes time, which is an important element where one is maintaining an exploring party in the woods. A method which can be used on the ground, and which will give results, according to my experience, within a few per cent. of the above in the case of the silicious or quartzose hard ores (the kind usually found), is the following:—Provide an ordinary swing balance which will sustain at least two pounds, and weights, the smallest of which should not exceed five grains, the whole costing less than $5. Break up numerous hand specimens across the ore deposits as before, wash and dry them. Suspend each in turn by a fine fish-line and weigh it in the air, afterwards weigh it when immersed in water. Divide the weight in air by the difference between the weight in air and the weight in water. The quotient will be the *specific gravity* of the specimen, and will range from 3.17 for very lean ores to 5.13 for very rich compact ores. The specific gravity so obtained, multiplied by thirteen, if the ore be rich (*i.e.*, above 55%), and by twelve, if the ore be lean (*i.e.*, from 40 to 55%), will give the approximate percentage of metallic iron in the specimen.

The mean of a large number of determinations, made with specimens selected promiscuously from the deposit, will give a close approximation to the average percentage of metallic iron in the bed. According to my experience, the error will fall within five per cent., which is nearer the truth than any man can determine by simple inspection. It must be borne in mind that this purely empirical rule applies only to Lake Superior *magnetic and specular* ores, and only to such as contain some form of quartz as gangue, which is true of nearly all. The numbers 12 and 13, given above, as multipliers, were derived from numerous analyses and specific gravity determinations made by Dr. C. F. Chandler, of New York, and J. B. Britton, Esq., of Philadelphia. This plan is not offered as a substitute for chemical analysis, but I believe will often prove useful in the woods, and may sometimes help in deciding whether it is worth while to have an analysis made. As has been before stated, unless the deposit is proven by analysis to contain an average of 50% of metallic iron, if specular or magnetic, and not less than 40%, if soft hematite, it is of doubtful value at the present time.

It would seem as if sufficient experience should enable us to judge of the quality of an ore at sight, or at least enable us to select an average specimen for analysis, without the laborious plan above described; but this is not the case, as is well known to those who have had experience in iron ores. It may be stated as an economic and psychological axiom, *that no man, however honest or skilled, can, on his judgment alone, select an average specimen of ore from a deposit; he will always choose a richer specimen than the average.* This would, of course, be very difficult from the technical stand-point, on account of the delicacy of muscle and skill of sight required; but the greater and insurmountable difficulty is in the human mind. We cannot help feeling that at a new opening there must be somewhere under our feet, or near by, better ore than we can see and the specimen selected is designed to be rather what we suppose, believe or hope the deposit to be, than an average of what we actually see and feel. I have numerous facts under this head, and am able to give an approximate mathematical expression to this form of human hopefulness. In eleven instances the difference between the *average by judgment*, and the *mechanical average* obtained as above described, varied from 6 to 24 per cent., averaging 11; the mechanical average being least in every instance; in each case I had reason to have confidence in the honesty and skill of the parties. It does not seem possible that such errors in average could exist, but they are constantly made, and will continue to be as long as iron ores and human minds are constituted on the present plan.

One of the fallacies which have caused innumerable disappointments in iron mining is the belief, almost universal, that ores grow richer in depth. This may be true of certain ores in some regions, but it is not true of the iron ores here being considered. They are just as good on top as in any part of their extent, and it may be stated as an invariable rule that if there be any good ore in a given deposit which is available for mining, it will somewhere come to the surface, except the earth covering in the Marquette region and the sandstone in the Menominee, which of course have to be removed when found. Hence a sufficient number of earth test pits, trenches and drifts will usually find it, if it exists, without penetrating the rock. I do not mean to say that a deposit of ore may not grow thicker in depth; they often present this feature, and on the other hand sometimes grow thinner, and wedge out entirely. As has been before stated, by far the larger part of the money available for the exploration of any given locality should be spent in earth work.

While it is not difficult to determine with sufficient accuracy for all practical purposes the quality of a deposit of iron ore, as has been above shown, it is often impossible within a reasonable cost, to form so reliable a judgment as to the *quantity*. But a sufficient amount of judicious exploration will usually settle the all-important question as to whether the deposit is large enough to warrant development as a mine, future operations alone determining whether it will prove a great or small one. The method of doing this is obvious; many test-pits and trenches must be dug and drifts made where the earth is deep, the ledge of ore being thus laid bare in as many places as possible. No one engaged in making an exhaustive exploration of an iron-ore property should neglect the advantages of deep drill-holes; these can be sunk 20 feet with the ordinary drills employed at the mines. An inspection of the mud, and especially an analysis of an average of it, will prove of great value.

The annular diamond drill was introduced in 1870, at the Lake Superior mine, and gave very satisfactory results; the core gives almost as good an idea of the nature of the rock passed through as a shaft, and the cost is far less,—about $5 per foot. But being propelled by a steam engine, it is only adapted to work near communications; it cannot be taken into the woods.

In the case of magnetic ores great assistance in determining the extent and position of the bed can be derived from a proper use of the magnetic needle, which subject is considered in the following chapter. Attention will, in this connection, only be directed to one important fact; *worthless ores often attract the needle just as strongly as merchantable ones.* Now, as there are many times more lean magnetic ores than rich, it follows that a variation or dip of the needle may not, probably does not, signify a workable deposit.

CHAPTER VIII.

MAGNETISM OF ROCKS, AND USE OF THE MAGNETIC NEEDLE IN EXPLORING FOR ORE.*

1. Elementary Principles.

A FEW of the elementary principles of the science of magnetism, made use of in the following investigations, will first be given.

Magnetite, or magnetic iron ore, contains, when pure, about 72 per cent. of iron and 28 per cent. of oxygen. The unmixed mineral is black, or blackish in mass and streak, has a specific gravity of 4.9 to 5.2, and hardness of 5.5 to 6.5, which is somewhat less than that of quartz; its crystals are usually octahedrous, and in the massive state it is often granular, and sometimes friable. Magnetite is one of the most abundant ores of iron in the United States, and, besides occurring in workable masses, is often disseminated through certain rocks, in grains, or in bunches and thin seams or laminæ, thus constituting what will be called "magnetic rocks" in this paper.

Its home is in the oldest rocks:—the primary (azoic, eozoic or archæan), as they have been successively termed. When it occurs in younger rocks, its origin can generally be traced to local metamorphism. The characteristic property of this mineral is its *magnetism*, with reference to which it is sometimes called *lodestone*. When brought near to pieces of iron or steel it often manifests an attraction for them, as it always does for another magnet. It hence causes the magnetic needle to deviate from its normal direction when brought near it. This property does not belong, in any marked extent, to any other mineral, and is the one which we have here chiefly to consider.

A piece of magnetite, broken from its parent bed, and suspended

---

* A part of this paper was read before the American Philosophical Society, Philadelphia, and published.

by a thread, will take a position, as near as the mode of suspension will permit, corresponding with its original one. If a north and south line be marked on a specimen thus suspended, it would rudely and imperfectly answer the purpose of the magnetic needle; if with this piece of magnetite we rub, in a certain way, a slender bar of hardened steel, it in turn becomes magnetic, and, if properly mounted, will point north and south, and constitute a compass. Mounted in another way, so as to admit of vertical motion, the magnetic needle will, while pointing north, incline downward at an angle of about 76° at Marquette. This "dip," as it is called, increases to the north and decreases to the south.

Two magnetic needles made in this way present these phenomena: their north poles or south poles repel each other, while the north pole of one will attract the south pole of the other, and conversely. The same is, of course, true of two pieces of magnetite, or of a piece of magnetite and a magnetic needle; *opposite poles attract, and similar poles repel.* This property is termed *polarity.* From this it appears that the north magnetic pole of the earth must, in the light of the science of magnetism, be regarded as a south pole, because it attracts the north end of the magnetic needle. The *poles* of any magnet are understood to be those points opposite each other, and near its surface, where the attractive and repulsive power may be supposed to be concentrated. Any magnet, natural or artificial, exerts its influence or sends out its rays in every direction, like a luminous point. The limit of this influence may be designated as the *sphere of its attraction.* A magnetic needle within this sphere, and uninfluenced by other force, would point directly to the centre of the sphere or focus of attraction. The force which holds it in this direction varies inversely as the square of the distance from the centre; hence practically (on account of this rapid diminution of power) we soon get beyond the influence of even a great natural magnet, like a hill of magnetic ore.

All the properties above designated, and numerous others not necessary to our purpose, appertain in general to a mountain of magnetic ore or rock, as well as to the delicate needle of a miniature compass. It is therefore evident that the magnetic needle should assist in determining the position and magnitude of rock formations containing magnetite. It has been extensively used in numerous places in finding iron ore, and to a far less extent, if practically at all, in this country, by field geologists, in determining the geographical extent, and, in part, lithological character of formations containing too little magnetite to give them commercial value, and which have already been designated *magnetic rocks.* The fact that all substances usually encountered in magnetical observations are transparent to the magnetic rays, or permeable by them, enables us to be certain of the existence of magnetic rocks or ores, though they be covered with water, earth, or non-magnetic rocks, to the depth of many feet, or even fathoms. *A given magnetic force affects the needle just as much through one hundred feet of granite as through the same distance of the atmosphere.* Dr. Scoresby gave a fine illustration of this fact, and an important application of the science of magnetism, by measuring, with great precision, 126 feet through solid rock, by observing the deviations in a needle, caused by an artificial magnet.

The earth itself may be regarded as a great magnet, which has the power of inducing this force (all magnets have a similar power) in masses of magnetite, and in all forms of iron and steel. We may suppose the force we have described above, as existing in the magnetic rocks and artificial magnets, to have been derived from the earth. An unmagnetized mass of steel or iron always manifests polarity induced by the earth, the upper or southerly portion being the *south pole*, and the lower or northerly end the *north pole*, in accordance with the law already stated. If the mass of iron or steel be elongated in form and made to stand nearly vertical, or to lie nearly in the plane of the meridian, this force is more manifest. To illustrate:—The upper end of all cast-iron lamp-posts attracts the north end of the needle, and the lower end the south. The magnetism thus induced in the wrought-iron pipes, lining the so-called magnetic wells of Michigan, would probably explain all the phenomena actually observed there. The law is, briefly: *the upper part of every mass* (of whatever form and size) *of iron, steel or magnetite, is a south pole, and the lower part a north pole.* This is, of course, true of magnetic rocks; hence almost universally the north end of the needle is attracted by such rocks, because it is the south pole of the rock which is uppermost and nearest. South pole or *negative* attractions, which are occasionally observed, come usually from faults or other divisional planes in the rocks; opposite poles being produced on opposite sides of such breaks which sever the mass; a precisely similar phenomenon can often be observed on opposite sides of the joints in railroad tracks.

From this cause several natural magnets are often encountered in a short distance; and a needle, passing in a few feet from the sphere of the attraction of one of them, will turn round and point toward the pole of a neighboring mass which more strongly attracts it. Hence, in magnetic surveys, we have not the simple focal point first considered to deal with, but often several local centres of attraction, positive and negative, in addition to the directive force of the earth, all influencing the needle at the same time. The recent investigations in the use of "magnetism in testing iron for flaws" would undoubtedly aid in the study of the effect of faults on the magnetism of rocks. See Engineering (London), 1867, p. 550, and 1868, pp. 297 and 440. The magnetism of iron ships should also possess interest in the same connection.

The *direction* which a magnetic needle takes (allowing it to have universal motion), under the circumstances supposed above, and the *power* with which it holds to that direction, must be the mechanical resultant of all the forces acting on it. It cannot point in two directions at the same time, hence stands between, inclining to the greater force. The principle of the parallelogram of forces makes it easy to determine the direction of this resultant, and to measure with mathematical precision the power which urges it. To do this we must know the direction and intensity of all the forces.

As an example, suppose a magnetic needle which, uninfluenced by other force than the earth's attraction, points due north and vibrates 10 times in one minute, to be placed due east from a south pole in a magnetic rock; and that, in this position, the earth's directing force be exactly neutralized by an artificial magnet, placed south of the needle,—it is evident that a needle so situated will point due west, urged by the local force alone, and that its vibrations will be solely due to this force. Suppose, for example, these vibrations to number 20 in one minute, or twice as many as were due to the earth's force. Now remove the artificial magnet; what will be the direction of the needle, and what number of vibrations will it give, urged by the local and cosmical forces?

It is a law of magnetism that the force urging a magnetic needle is proportional to the square of the number of vibrations made in a given time; $10^2 = 100$ and $20^2 = 400$, hence the local force is four times as great as the earth's. Lay off in Fig. 16 the line x N due north, making it equal 100 on some chosen scale: lay off the line x W due west, making it equal by the same scale 400; complete the parallelogram by drawing the lines N y and W y parallel with the first lines. Draw the diagonal x y, it will be the resultant

Fig. 16.

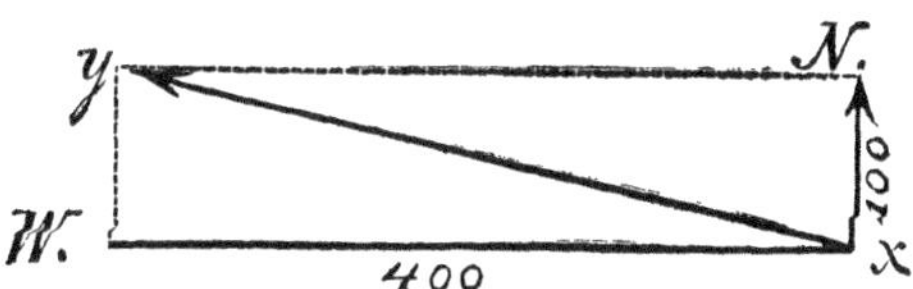

sought. Applying the protractor and scale we find its course to be N. 75° 53 W., and length to be 412.31, the square root of which is 20⅓, which would be the number of vibrations.

Suppose that in another locality the same needle pointed N. 45° E. and vibrated 14¼ times in one minute, what would be the direction and intensity of the local force? In Fig. 17 lay off the line x y N. 45° E., its length equal to the square of the number of vibrations = 200; complete the parallelogram as before. It is evident that the line x E represents the direction and intensity of the local force, which in this case is due east, and has a power just equal to that of the earth. Unfortunately the simple cases here presented

Fig. 17.

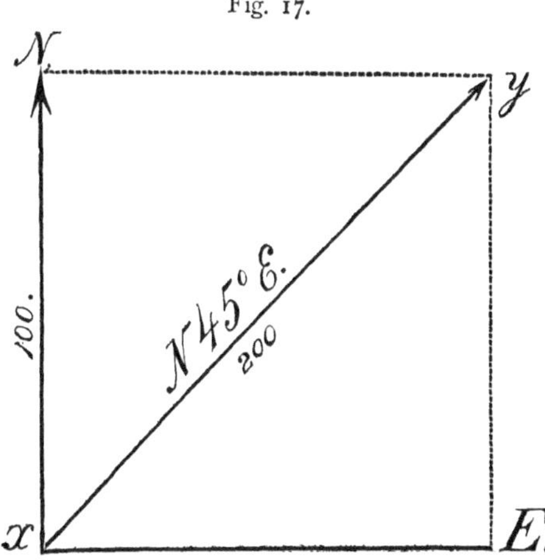

seldom occur,—usually two or more local forces act on the needle at the same time.

In a similar manner any number of forces acting in as many different directions can be resolved. It follows that a magnetic needle, influenced by the earth's force, can never point directly toward a local magnetic pole, but will, with two exceptions which need not be named, always incline to point to the north of it.

It is evident that the degree of magnetism possessed by a needle, while it makes no difference with its direction, will affect the number of vibrations. Take the needle in the last case, and suppose it more highly charged; it will still point N. 45° E., but its vibrations will be increased in number just in proportion to the additional power imparted. Hence, in determining *absolute* terrestrial or local intensity, a standard for comparison is necessary; but this is not required in the work under consideration.

2. Magnetic Instruments—Dip Compass.

As the instruments employed in these observations are quite different from those used in Terrestrial Magnetism, which are described in the works on this science, a brief account of them will be given.

The Dip or Miner's Compass is a circular brass box, a common form being 3¾ inches in diameter, and ¾ inch thick, having a circular glass on each side, which permits a perfect view of the needle. The needle is 2⅞ inches long, weighs 13¾ grains, and is counterpoised so as to stand horizontal where there is no local attraction, the needle being permitted to *swing in a north and south vertical plane*, which is the position in which it is ordinarily used. The axis of the needle is of hard steel, its points resting loosely in conical cavities in agates, fixed in two arms projecting from the sides. Outside is a ring for supporting the instrument when observations are made, so placed that the weight of the suspended instrument brings the zero line of the graduated circle to a horizontal position. Although designed to be used chiefly for determining dips or inclinations of the needle due to local influences, it answers passably well for taking magnetic bearings when laid on its side, and is frequently used in this way in rough work.

As there is usually no means of throwing this needle off its points of support, the wear is great, and the instrument is often out of order. A person going out of the way of shops where repairs can be made, would do well to take two, and then have the means at hand for making ordinary repairs. These compasses generally possess each an individuality of its own, and one must know his instrument before placing much confidence in his results: they will seldom reverse, 30° difference in the two readings being not infrequent. A New Jersey iron explorer informed me that his Dip Compass always indicated 90° when faced west, and the true dip due to local attraction when faced east. He is said to have used one position in buying and the other in selling iron lands very successfully.

My compass was made by Messrs. W. & L. E. Gurley, of Troy, N. Y. I have since seen one made by H. W. Hunter, of N. Y., which promises well. A reliable dip compass is a desideratum.

This is exclusively a hand instrument, and has no support; nearly all the magnetic observations recorded in this paper were made on instruments held in the hand. This may seem rude and unscientific to precise observers of physical phenomena; but it was found by trial that the average error by this mode of observation was less than 3°, which was comparatively small in localities where changing the position of the instrument only a few feet often made 50° difference in the direction of the needle, and deviations of 180° from the normal direction were common. It is not necessary to observe the direction of the wind to the degree to construct a useful theory of storms. Had the accurate instruments and precise methods of terrestrial magnetism been employed, not more than 50 stations could have been occupied with the time at my disposal, while with my rude methods over 1,000 stations were observed at.

The miner's compass above described is now in very general use in the magnetic iron-ore regions of the United States. The object here sought is to endeavor to point out new and perhaps better modes of using that instrument in finding iron ore, and incidentally to ascertain if it has any place in general geological field work. I have long believed that the magnetic needle can be so used as to give more definite information regarding magnetic ores and rocks than has yet been done to my knowledge. I did some rude and incompleted work in this field, at the Ringwood Iron Mines and elsewhere in New Jersey and Southern New York, the results of which are in part published in Prof. Cook's Report on the Geology of New Jersey. The observations of Prof. Cook and Dr. Kitchell on the magnetism of the iron ores of New Jersey, and the use of the magnetic needle in finding them, possess interest; see pp. 532–538 of their report. The map of the Ringwood Iron Mines, accompanying that report, exhibits a part of my own observations above referred to.

The idea of applying Magnetic Science to Geology is not at all new; years ago Bischoff, after citing numerous observations that had been made in various parts of the world by different observers in regard to the influence of mountains on the magnetic needle, concluded as follows: "Assuming that it is magnetic ore alone, either as masses or disseminated through the rocks, to which the magnetic influences are to be ascribed—and in my opinion this is quite unquestionable—it would seem that magnetic observations instituted with the same degree of care as those made by Reich, would be well adapted for the discovery of hidden beds of magnetic iron ore. Such observations might therefore prove eminently serviceable to the iron industry. Certainly it would be requisite first to ascertain whether mountain masses containing only disseminated magnetic iron ore, but extending over a considerable surface, would not produce as great an effect as beds of magnetic iron ore. Sabine's observations do not appear to favor this; but, however this may be, the magnetic needle indicates the presence of magnetic iron ore where it cannot be recognized mineralogically, and demonstrates the very general distribution of this mineral."

My mode of observing was as follows:—To determine "variations" east or west,* the bearings of a standard line were taken as in ordinary surveys. Sometimes a solar compass was used, but oftener a pocket compass. The variations as shown by the miner's compass, termed "dips," were observed on this compass held in the hand generally in the plane of the meridian, hence the instrument would face east and west. Sometimes observations were made with the compass held at right angles with this position; that is, facing north and south. The instrument was always held in the hand and levelled by its own weight.

The *intensity* of the magnetic force for the three positions of the compass above designated, was measured by the number of vibrations† made by the needle in a unit of time, usually taken at ¼ of a

---

* Declination, or the cosmical deviation of the needle from the true meridian, is not here considered.

† Half-vibrations would be the proper term, as the time from one point of rest to the next was counted and not the complete vibration.

minute. The vibrations varied from 0 to 60 in this time, 6 being the normal for my compass, due to the earth's influence. No attempt was made to eliminate the earth's attraction by neutralizing it with a magnet when the observation was made, or by computation. Of course, when the compass faced north or south, this was partially accomplished, because the earth's attraction would then be nearly in the direction of the axis of the needle. It must be borne in mind that the great amount of friction in this form of compass renders the number of vibrations only a rude approximation to the number which would be indicated by a delicately mounted needle.

The short needle of an ordinary pocket or dip compass, if in good order, will vibrate quickly and for some time where there is no local attraction. This motion is sometimes termed "working," and such normal "working," due simply to the earth's attraction, has often been mistaken by inexperienced persons for an indication of ore.

There is no better instrument for observing variations accurately than Burt's Solar Compass; but it is too heavy for explorers' use. I have found a convenient substitute for rough observations in the Pocket Dial Compass, which, used with a watch indicating local time, is rapid and sufficiently precise. This instrument, or an ordinary portable sundial, can also be used for running lines where there is local attraction; for rough work I have used it instead of the Solar Compass.

I hoped to have made some observations with properly constructed instruments, such as are used in determining the elements of terrestrial magnetism, in order to institute a comparison between accurate results and my own rude work; but the nature of such investigations requires more time than I have thus far had at my disposal. Fortunately Dr. John Locke made complete magnetic observations at several points in the Marquette Iron Region, which are recorded in "Smithsonian Contributions to Knowledge," vol. 3, pp. 25-27. One station was over magnetic rocks in Section 18, Town 47 north, Range 26 west, the geology of which he thus describes: "A loadstone in place broken into sharp angular fragments; here were two poles, 17.67 feet apart, one attracting the north, the other the south pole of the needle." Dr. Locke found the dip to be 42 deg. 53 min., when it should have been about 76 deg. The duration of 500 vibrations was 822 sec., when it should have been about 1,500 sec., and the calculated horizontal intensity was more than four times the normal force computed for that station. If Dr. Locke had occupied 500 stations on that section of land, he would have obtained different results at each, often differing more from each other than the foregoing do from the normal forces.

These observations, like all recorded ones that have come under my notice, have had *terrestrial magnetism* as their chief object; therefore the observers have avoided the very localities which to the geologist and explorer possess the greatest interest—those where local magnetic attractions exist. Dr. Locke calls attention to the importance of magnetic science to the geologist, and gives many interesting isolated facts bearing on the subject, particularly regarding the existence of magnetite in volcanic rocks, where it usually occurs.

Before dismissing the subject of instruments suited to magnetic surveys, I will call attention to a patent mariner's compass made by E. S. Ritchie, Esq., of Boston, in which the needle is entirely supported by a liquid having the same specific gravity, thus giving it universal motion. A needle so mounted and having the earth's attraction neutralized by a magnet, should point directly towards a local magnetic pole when brought within its influence, thus accomplishing with one observation and no calculations what requires at least two with the ordinary compass. For intensity Mr. Ritchie suggested the following mode:—Time the needle from the instant of its being let off at 90 deg. to its passing the resting point. I am of the opinion that a valuable instrument for miners and explorers could be made on Mr. Ritchie's plan.

A modification of the ordinary compass has been made which accomplishes the same thing in part. The agate support is fitted to the needle by a sort of universal joint, which gives the needle a vertical range through half a quadrant in addition to its horizontal motion. The only one I ever saw was made from the design of the late Wm. J. Amsden, Esq., of Scranton, Pa., who made some valuable magnetic surveys.* A pocket compass on a similar idea has lately been patented. A somewhat similar instrument has, I understand, been used for a long time in Sweden and Norway. On the same principle the ordinary surveyor's compass indicates dips rudely. At the west quarter post of Section 7, Town 46

* Messrs. Gurley now make a dip compass which gives the needle limited lateral range.

north, Range 29 west, being on the east side of Republic Mountain, I find marked on the U. S. Survey plat: "End of needle dips ¼ inch, variation 62 deg. west."

C. F. Varley, Esq., the English Electrician, suggested to me that a portable electro-magnetic apparatus could be constructed, with which might be determined the direction and distance to the pole of a magnetic rock by some simple observations and computations. An instrument of this kind would have considerable value in connection with magnetic needles, especially where the magnetic ore or rock was covered with considerable thickness of other material. In 1867 Mr. Varley, with a view to detecting electric currents, if any existed, made some observations both in the copper and iron-bearing rocks of Lake Superior; he found such currents in the mines of native copper, but none in the iron mines. The instruments employed were rude, having been extemporized on the spot. I do not know whether he has published anything on this subject.

Professor Joseph Henry has suggested in a letter that it is "highly probable that the abnormal variations of the magnetic elements in our iron ores are due to *electro-magnetic* action rather than to magnetic."

3. Geological Sketch of the Magnetic Rocks.

In order to make the perusal of this subject to a certain extent independent of the remainder of this report,* a few facts regarding the geological position and lithological character of the magnetic rocks of the Marquette region will here be repeated, the subject having been more fully considered elsewhere.

Rocks of the four oldest geological epochs yet made out on this continent are represented on the Upper Peninsula of Michigan; two belonging to the Azoic, one to the Lower Silurian, and one between these, of questioned age. The equivalency of these with the Canadian series has not been fully established, but the nomenclature of the Canadian geologists will be employed provisionally.

The Laurentian of the Upper Peninsula is like that of Canada in being largely made up of granitic-gneisses, but differs in containing no limestone so far as I have seen, and little, I may say practically

* Many persons have asked for copies of this chapter who do not expect to get the whole Report.

no iron ore, and very little disseminated magnetite. Next above the Laurentian, and resting on it non-conformably, are the Huronian or iron-bearing rocks; these are also called by the Canadian geologists "the lower copper-bearing series." This series comprise several plainly stratified beds of iron ore and ferruginous rock, varying in the percentage of metallic iron from 15 to 67 per cent., interstratified with greenish tough rocks, in which the bedding is obscure, which appear to be more or less altered diorites, together with quartzites (which pass into marble), clay slates, mica schists, and various obscure magnesian schists. The maximum thickness of the whole in the Marquette region is not far from 5,000 feet.

While the great Huronian area of Canada north of Georgian bay bears, so far as I am aware, little or no workable iron, and derives its economic importance from its ores of copper, the Marquette series, supposed to be of the same age, are eminently iron bearing, and have as yet produced no copper. It is doubtful if in the same extent and thickness of rocks, anywhere in the world, there is a larger percentage of iron oxide than in the Marquette series. In the order of relative abundance, so far as made out, the ores are the *flag*, the red *specular* hematites, soft or brown *hematites*, and *magnetites*. These all exist in workable beds, and all as disseminated minerals in rocks usually silicious. The geological distribution of these ores of iron in the Huronian series will be considered in another place. The geographical distribution is less understood; so far there seems to be the greatest concentration of magnetic ores in the Michigamme district of the Marquette region. From this, the relative proportion of magnetite seems to decrease as we go east, north, west and south, although there is a considerable magnetic attraction in the Menominee or southern iron region.*

Next younger than the Huronian are the copper-bearing rocks of Keweenaw peninsula, which extend westward into Wisconsin, the age of which has led to much controversy; good authorities having placed them in different epochs, from the Azoic to the Triassic. Recent observations made by Prof. R. Pumpelly and myself go strongly to confirm the view, if we have not positively demonstrated it, that they are non-conformably overlaid by the Silurian, and are therefore related to the Azoic. The relations of the copper-bearing

* See Appendix H., Vol. II.

rocks to the Huronian are not fully made out. In tracing the dividing line from Bad river in Wisconsin to Lake Gogebic, Michigan, last fall, a distance of sixty miles, we found them nearly, if not precisely conformable, but widely different in lithological character.

With regard to the magnetism of the copper-bearing series, the United States surveyors mark considerable variations at several points on the Land Office plats, due in all probability to disseminated magnetite in the trappean members of the series, although good authorities have ascribed these variations to electric currents. My own observations on the magnetism of these rocks have been limited, but lead me to believe that it is far less in amount and less persistent in character than is usually the case in the Huronian, indicating that the magnetite (to which I ascribe the attractions) is perhaps an accidental rather than essential constituent, and small in amount. Macfarlane found less than one per cent. in one of the Portage lake traps.

The next series of rocks in ascending order are the horizontally-bedded Lower Silurian sandstones, which skirt the south shore of Lake Superior nearly its whole length, called by Foster, Whitney, and Dr. Rominger, Potsdam, and assigned by the Canadian geologists, under the name St. Mary's, to a later period. They have not been proven to be magnetic, although strong magnetic attractions have been observed over this Silurian area, as will be explained hereafter.

To recapitulate, we have: 1. The Laurentian granite and gneiss, practically non-magnetic; 2. The Huronian iron-bearing rocks, often highly magnetic; 3. The copper series, slightly magnetic; and 4th. The Silurian rocks, without magnetism. This classification is intended to apply more particularly to the rocks of the Marquette and Menominee regions proper, embracing the central and southern portions of the Upper Peninsula; and even here, as has been noted above, there are exceptions. This sketch of the Marquette rocks, in the light of the distribution of magnetite, would be incomplete, did I not mention the fact that this mineral is very generally present in the form of fine sand in the drift in the region I am describing. If one moves a magnet about in the sand of a creek it is rarely that *magnetic sand* will not be found adhering. I have never seen it accumulated in quantities that would point towards its being utilized; nor have I ever observed a local variation which I ascribed to the mineral in this form.

We will now return to the Huronian or highly magnetic series, taking up its structure in some detail. About nineteen lithologically distinct beds or strata make up the series; of these, six and probably seven are generally so magnetic as to cause considerable variations in the needle. These beds vary from forty to several hundred feet in thickness, and strike and dip in all directions, and at all angles. The prevailing strike, however, is easterly and westerly, and the dip at high angles, often vertical. These rocks frequently outcrop, when we have no use for the magnetic needle in their study. Again, they are covered by deep drift, where magnetic observations, or workings, can only reveal them.

In order to study the magnetic characteristics of these rocks more minutely than could be done in the field, two hundred and twenty-two specimens, covering all the more common varieties, were collected and are deposited in the cabinet of the University of Michigan; they are fully described under lithology in this Report. Fifty-four, or twenty-four per cent., were found to possess some degree of magnetic power as manifested by their influence on a magnetic needle; each specimen being in turn made to touch each end of a mounted needle. If it had the power to lead it 20 deg. from its normal direction, the specimen was said to be feebly magnetic, and strongly magnetic when the needle followed the specimen round the circle if held about half an inch from it. Of these fifty-four specimens, thirteen were feebly magnetic, twenty-nine magnetic, five decidedly magnetic, and seven strongly magnetic.* None would, however, lift ordinary carpet tacks. Twenty-four, or nearly one-half, possessed polarity in some degree. Thirty were simply magnetic, with no *polarity* that could be detected by the rude means employed: in some instances the specimen would repel the needle at half an inch distance, but would attract it if placed in contact. Such specimens were rated as possessing polarity. All of the strongly magnetic specimens were rich in magnetite and possessed polarity, and it is not improbable that

---

* Appendix H gives the percentage of material lifted by the magnet in twenty-one specimens of Lake Superior ore, together with the color of the powder.

all would have been found to possess it if tested by more delicate means. Von Cotta, however, speaks of magnetic iron ore which possessed no polarity. The specimens generally attracted the south pole more strongly than the north. When examined, they had been collected about three months. Whether they would have shown more or less magnetic power if tested when freshly broken, I do not know. Dr. Kitchell says that under certain circumstances fragments gain magnetism.

In 1860 I saw a powerful loadstone for its size, in the possession of Professor Trego, of Philadelphia, which he had picked up in New Jersey twenty-two years before. I once collected a number of pieces of loadstone in the Bull Mine, New York, which in the mine would lift small nails; in a few days two-thirds of them had lost this power. This may have been due to the fact that in the mine the nails themselves were made magnetic by induction.

Regarding the *location of the poles* in magnetic rocks, the laws of magnetism would place them near the surface, or next divisional planes or terminations of masses. Observers are generally agreed that iron ore is most magnetic near dykes or volcanic rock. Quoting again from Dr. Kitchell, "Geology of New Jersey," p. 535: "The extent of the magnetic qualities of iron ores depends on their position with respect to the surface; the nearer to the surface the greater will be their magnetic properties. This appears to depend on the action of surface water and atmospheric agents, for it has been frequently observed that ore, when first taken out of a mine at a considerable depth, possessed but slight magnetic properties, but on being exposed to the atmosphere for a few months or years it would increase so much that excellent specimens of loadstone for experimental purposes could be selected therefrom. Seams of ore that contain numerous joints and fissures, through which water and atmospheric agents pass, possess more decided magnetic properties than those which are more compact and free from crevices and fissures." *

These remarks of Dr. Kitchell possess much interest. I have but one fact that bears on this question;—an average sample made up of numerous fragments collected by myself of the Iron Moun-

* If a fact, is this due to the contact of air and water, or is it because the seams necessarily produce small independent magnets.

tain Missouri "surface," or boulder ore, contained only about one-fourth as much magnetite (as measured by the amount lifted with a horse-shoe magnet) as did a specimen of "quarry" (ledge) ore selected at the same time and in the same way.

Classifying the magnetic ores and rocks of the Marquette region economically, the merchantable ores, according to the present standard of richness, would not constitute two per cent. of the whole; the balance being ferruginous quartzites and schists possessing no present value as ores. The merchantable magnetic ores have so far all been found in one formation near the middle of the series, and that is not all pure ore by any means; therefore, when an ore-hunter finds an "*attraction*" in the Lake Superior region, the chances of his having found a mine are not more than one in fifty. Neither the strike nor dip of the formation seems to affect its magnetic power. This depends, so far as my observations throw any light on the question, chiefly on the percentage of magnetite entering into the composition of the rock. Prof. Cook—"Geology of New Jersey," pp. 537–8—says that the magnetism of iron ores was influenced by the "pinch and shoot" structure so prevalent in the iron mines of New York and New Jersey. He points out the analogy between these regular pod-shaped masses—"shoots" of ore,—pitching downward in a northerly direction and an iron bar in the same position; both become magnetic and have polarity.

The "pinch and shoot" structure exists in the magnetic ores of the Marquette region, but is obscure, and in strike and dip there is no parallelism between our rocks and those of New Jersey, as is shown elsewhere. Yet our ores must usually be more strongly magnetic than those of New Jersey; for Prof. Cook says: "It is generally conceded that ore, covered by thirty feet of earth, will attract the needle, and 'large veins' have disturbed it when covered by fifty feet of earth." Now at five and even fifty times these distances horizontally, the needle is often deflected in the Marquette region, and at the Spurr Mountain the needle indicates a dip of 70 degrees at an elevation of 94 feet above the ore.

With regard to the *associations of the various ores* it may be said, that magnetic and specular ores are often found together, as are also the specular and soft hematite ores; but so far the magnetites and hematites have not been found in juxtaposition. If we suppose all our ores to have once been magnetic, and that the red specular was first derived from the magnetite and the hydrated oxide (soft hematites) in turn from it, we have an hypothesis which best explains many facts, and which will be of use to the explorer. As a rule it may be assumed that the hard ores of the Lake Superior region, even although they be rated as red specular, contain a sufficient amount of magnetite to cause some local disturbance in the needle; there are exceptions to this rule, but they are rare. In some instances, especially in the Menominee region, the disturbance is slight, but enough to be noticed by careful observation. It should be noted that the L'Anse Iron Range, so far as known, contains no magnetic ore whatever.

4. Explanation of Magneto-geologic Charts, Plans and Sections.

Having now briefly stated those elementary principles of Magnetism which are involved in our subject, described the instruments employed and their use, and sketched the geology of the rocks whose magnetic forces we are to study, we are fully prepared to examine the results of the observations made, and to draw such conclusions and make such applications as the facts seem to warrant.

It has been found necessary to introduce a few terms which may be new in describing the graphical representations of the phenomena observed. No work to which I could gain access contained expressions such as portions of our work seemed to require. Figures 1 and 2, Republic mountain chart (No. XI. of Atlas), are copied in part from the geological and topographical map of Republic mountain, which see for explanation of geology, relief of ground, and geographical position.

Magnetic observations were made across the entire Huronian series lapping on the Laurentian on each side, along survey lines 26 and 30, which run N. 53° E.; the observations being taken for a considerable part of the distance every 25 feet. The arrows in Fig. 1 indicate the directions which the needle actually pointed under the combined influence of terrestrial and local attraction. The angle between these arrows and the meridian is the *variation* in Azimuth (called simply variation) and ranges, as will be seen, from 0 to 180°. The direction of the arrows, although sometimes irregular, leaves no doubt as to which are the magnetic rocks.

The full significance and value of the common compass in locating magnetic rocks and ores is better shown in Plate V., which represents variations observed at the west end of the Washington mine, embracing the West Cut or Pit No. 10. The stations indicated on the Plate refer to survey lines shown on the map of the mine, No. VIII., to which reference is made for information regarding the geology and topographical features of the locality. A glance at this figure will bring to the mind of all familiar with magnetic experiments, the plumose forms assumed by magnetic sands or iron filings resting on paper and influenced by the magnet. Our figure may be regarded as representing the laboratory experiment greatly magnified. As to the irregularities shown by some of the arrows, it is probable that if the magnetism of ordinary magnets could be studied minutely, as with microscopic needles, that corresponding irregularities would be observed in the directions and polarity of the forces, not unlike those seen on this magnetic plan of the Washington mine. If we admit, as we are forced to do from these facts, that magnetic rocks present phenomena entirely analogous to artificial magnets, then it is not difficult to decide as to the cause of the phenomena exhibited on the sketch before us.

The dotted line is designed to indicate the position of maximum variation, or rather the position of the force which causes the variation. The observations made for *intensity* along this line, indicated by vibrations (six being the normal number), confirm the indications of the horizontal compass. There can be no doubt but that nearly under this line, at no great depth, is a large amount of magnetite; whether free enough from rock to constitute a merchantable ore, explorations only can establish. Since this plan was made, work has been resumed at Pit No. 10, and a tolerably regular bed of ore revealed, having the strike and dip marked on the plan, which coincides closely with what might have been predicted. The relationship of this deposit with the others constituting the mine will be considered elsewhere. This magnetic plan, as well as Fig. 1, Republic mountain chart, shows, that while the variations are governed by a uniform law away from the lines of maxima, within these lines great irregularities of direction exist.*

* Since the above was written, I have, by the kindness of Mr. F. Firmstone, of Easton, Pa., been able to inspect some magnetic charts of New Jersey localities, made by the late Mr. Amsden, of Scranton, which are excellent.

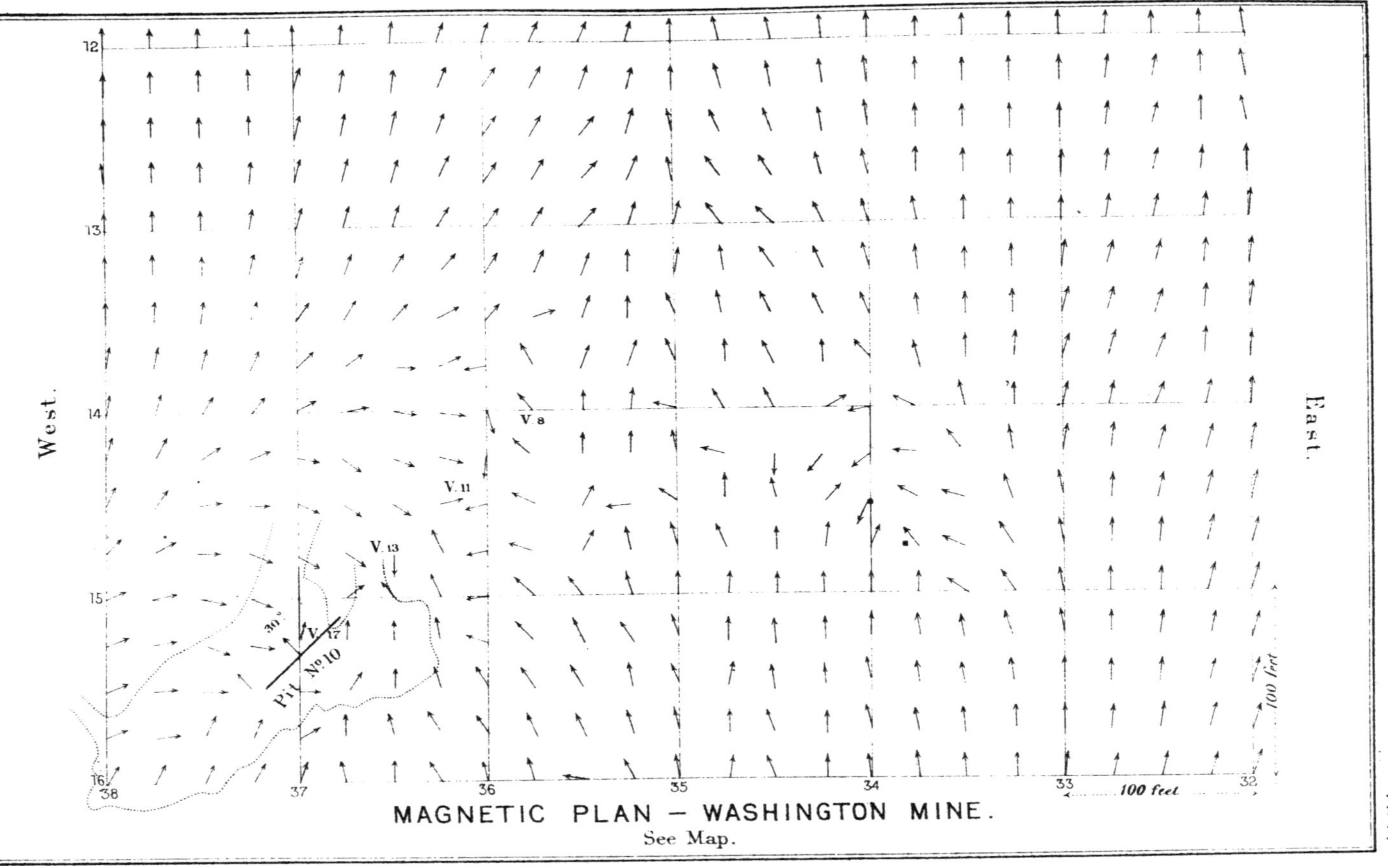

MAGNETIC PLAN – WASHINGTON MINE.

See Map.

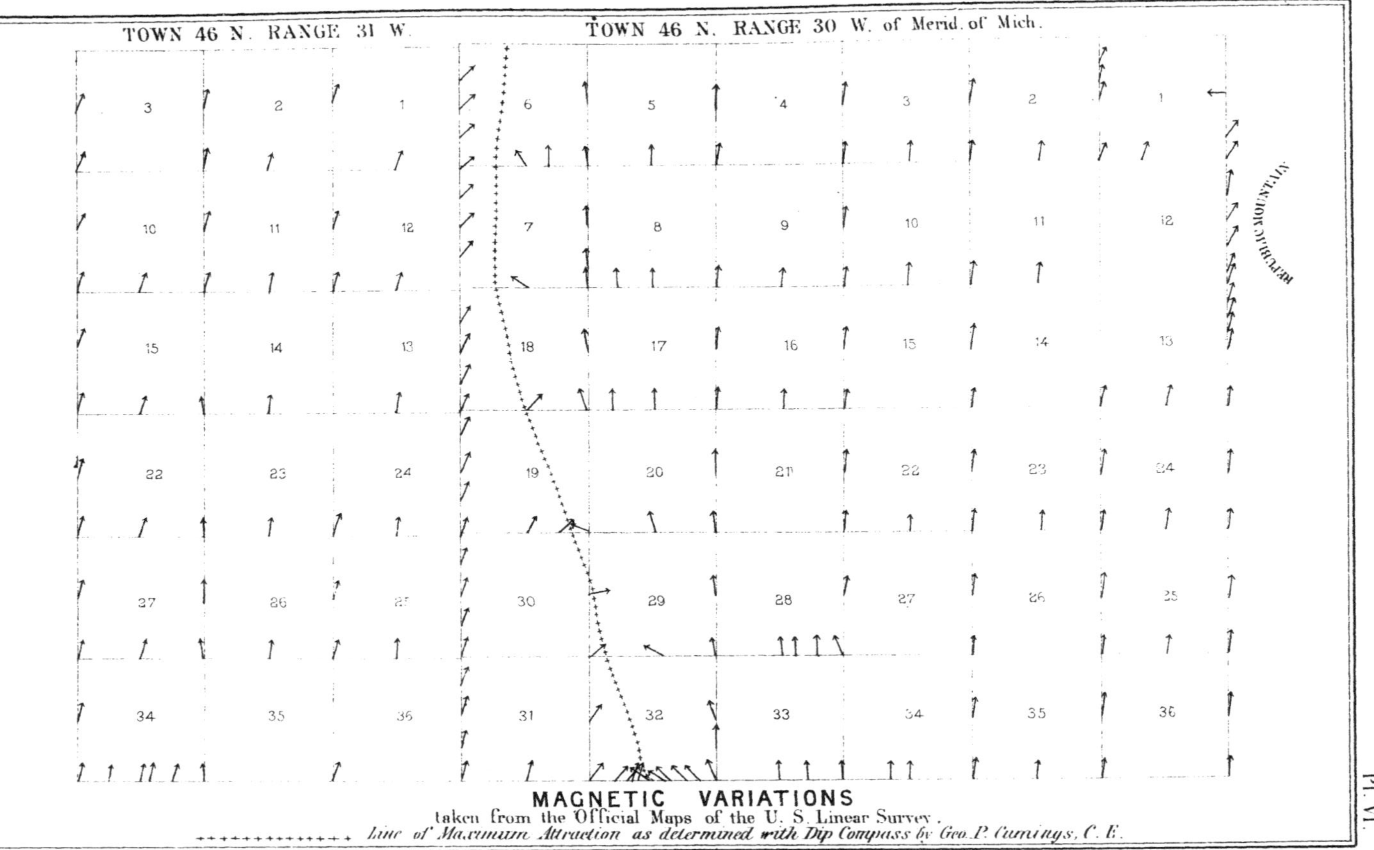

MAGNETIC VARIATIONS

taken from the Official Maps of the U. S. Linear Survey.

+++++++++++++ *Line of Maximum Attraction as determined with Dip Compass by Geo. P. Cumings, C. E.*

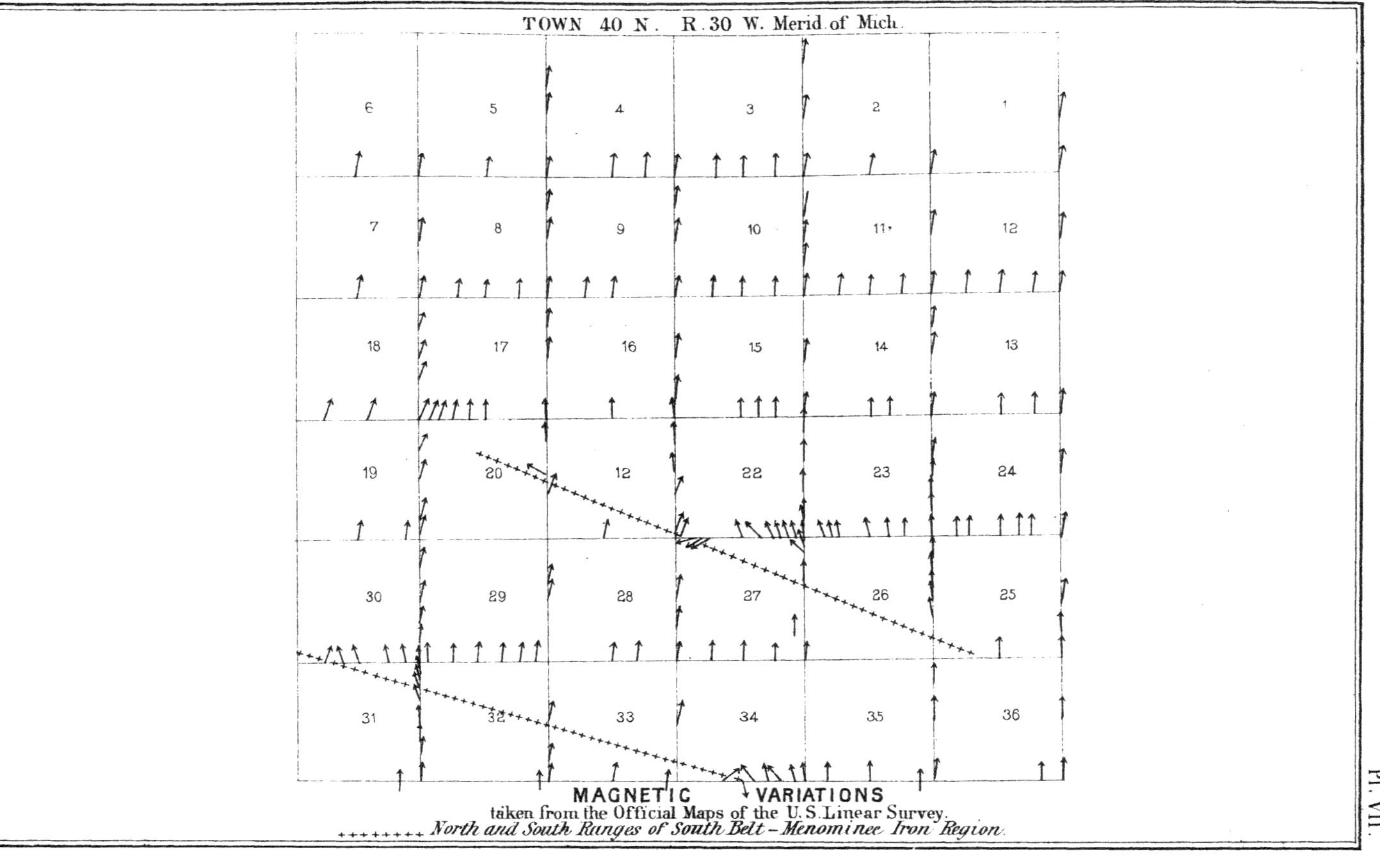
TOWN 40 N. R. 30 W. Merid of Mich.
6
5
4
3
2
1
7
8
9
10
11
12
18
17
16
15
14
13
19
20
12
22
23
24
30
29
28
27
26
25
31
32
33
34
35
36
MAGNETIC VARIATIONS
taken from the Official Maps of the U.S. Linear Survey.
++++++++ North and South Ranges of South Belt - Menominee Iron Region.

Passing from Plate V., which represents but a small area, over which the magnetic observations have been very numerous, to a magnetic plan of a large surface, with widely separated observations, we have in Plates VI. and VII., copied from the United States Land Office books, a fine exemplification of the significance of local magnetic variations.

In Plate VI. the magnetic rocks run nearly north and south,—which direction, as has been heretofore stated, produces the maximum variation. It will be seen that the needle is influenced at a distance of nearly, if not quite two miles, and that the variation diminishes rapidly as we depart from the line of maximum attraction. The disturbances recorded on the north-east part of this plan are due to Republic mountain.

Plate VII. represents one of the iron townships in the Menominee region. The variations are scarcely so great, nor do they extend so far as in the other. As the two iron ranges represented run much more nearly east and west in this case, it is interesting to observe the difference in the behavior of the needle. These plans are additional proof of the value of the Linear Surveys to the explorer, a point to which I have often referred.

Figures 3 and 4, Chart XI., Atlas, are *magnetic sections* along lines 26 and 30 of plan. The arrows indicate the direction of the dip-needle vibrating in the plane of the meridian. The normal direction is the horizontal line ; the arrow head indicating north end of needle should therefore normally point to the right hand side of the chart. It will be seen that the dip, like the variation, often attains the maximum of 180°, that is, the north end points south.

The colored curved lines express approximately the *intensity* of the local magnetic force ; their ordinates being the number of vibrations made by the needle in one quarter of a minute, on a vertical scale of eight vibrations to the inch. The *blue* line records the observed vibrations of the *horizontal* needle, the others of the dip-needle. The *black* line refers to the needle vibrating in the plane of the meridian (compass *facing west*). The *red* line refers to the needle vibrating in an east and west plane (compass *facing* south.)

Fig. 2 is a magneto-geological section on the line A—A′ of Fig. 1. The upper curve represents a projection on one plane of the maximum intensities of all the curves of Figs. 3 and 4. The lower curve, Fig. 2, has reference to variations and dips, its ordinates being proportional to the maximum variation in direction of the needle, caused by the magnetic rocks. It is intended as a sort of summary of the facts expressed by all the arrows denoting directions, as the upper curve is a general expression of the intensities. It will be observed that the summits of the lower curve, Fig. 2, which indicates maximum variation, are always northerly from the centre of the magnetic bed. This is as it should be, because the greatest *variation* takes place before we reach the local magnetic pole, when approaching it from the *north*. The intensities, on the other hand, are greatest directly over the magnetic rocks. It should be borne in mind that the intensity of a magnetic force is really proportional to the square of the number of vibrations in a given time; but in these investigations the actual number of vibrations has been used in constructing the sections, as being more convenient.

In addition to the facts observed during this survey, which are recorded on the Republic Mountain Chart, and various figures in this volume, certain others, obtained from the United States Land Office, plats of Towns 46 and 47 north, Ranges 29 and 30 west, will be employed, besides those already given from the same source.

The discussion of the facts in our possession falls conveniently under two heads:—First, Regarding the entire Huronian series as a unit, and the comparison of its magnetism with the Laurentian system. Second, A study of the magnetism of the individual beds of the Huronian or iron-bearing rocks, in detail. Republic mountain and vicinity afford an excellent opportunity for both these investigations.

The Magnetism of the Laurentian System or Granitic Rocks.

The Federal township plats above referred to, cover an area of, say twelve miles in diameter, of which Republic mountain is the centre; at least nine-tenths of this territory is Laurentian. The variations of the needle noted are from two to six degrees east, averaging four and a half degrees, which may be regarded as the *declination* of the needle at the date of the surveys of this locality, due to cosmical causes. From this and similar facts covering the whole Marquette region, we may conclude that this oldest system of all known rocks has here no beds of magnetite, nor does it now contain magnetite as an essential constituent mineral, nor indeed oxide of iron in any form. Prof. Pumpelly and myself found slightly magnetic rocks in the Laurentian south of Lake Gogebic, and the professor mentions in his report to the Portage Lake and Lake Superior Ship Canal Company "a deposit of iron ore in the Laurentian gneiss and hornblendic schist series on Sections 10 and 15, T. 41 N., R. 29 W.," in the Menominee Iron Region, from which I have seen specimens which do not look very promising. One or two other places are mentioned where magnetic beds occur in the Laurentian, but they are exceptional, the rule being as has been stated. But everywhere in the region we are considering, over or near the Huronian Series, the Government surveyors note variations. The approximate boundary between these two systems of the Azoic in some parts of the Upper Peninsula could indeed almost be delineated from their surveys by magnetic variations alone.

Magnetism of the Huronian Series as a Unit—Republic Mountain.

No special observations were made to determine the extreme limit to which its magnetic influence extends. The Federal surveys would make the distance over one mile, and Durocher mentions that he was told in Sweden that "important beds of iron ore produced deviations in the needle up to the distance of nearly two kilometres," or over one mile—*Annales des Mines*, 5 Series, Vol. 8, p. 220. The Federal surveyors note a variation at the north-east corner of Section 7 (See Fig. 1, Republic Mountain Chart) of 25° west, agreeing very nearly with my observations corrected for the change in declination since the survey was made. This corner is at least 600 feet from the nearest Huronian bed, and probably 900 feet from any member of the series containing magnetite. Judging by the direction and intensity of the magnetic force as exhibited by the needle, as we approach the mountain from the north-east (see Figs. 1, 3, and 4), it seems probable that the bed which chiefly produced the effect was No. VI., and still more distant ores. If this be a correct inference, we have the phenomenon of a magnetic needle deflected 25° from its normal direction by a bed of rocks containing not to exceed 33 per cent. of magnetite, distant 1,500 feet horizontally. The facts from the U. S. surveys given above show that the needle is sometimes influenced to a much greater distance.

Passing to the south-west side of the Huronian basin we find the influence exerted by the magnetic rocks to gradually diminish as we recede from their edge, which is believed to be under the Michigamme river. See Fig. 1. Here we find the needle varying 15° at a distance of at least 800 feet from the nearest magnetic rocks.

An inspection of Fig. 1 shows that the variations of the needle are much greater on the north-east than on the south-west side of the mountain, which should evidently be the case from the fact that to the south-west the terrestrial and local forces are more nearly in the same line than on the north-east side; hence in the latter case the mechanical resultant (direction of the needle) would form a greater angle with the direction of the earth's force (magnetic meridian) than in the former.

The question of the distance to which magnetic ore and rocks will attract the needle receives some additional light from the Champion Mine, Plates VIII. to XV. It is evident in this case that the magnetic force of the ore is felt to a distance exceeding 700 feet to the north of the mine. To the south there is less certainty, because of the other magnetic rocks (see sections) which underlie the ore in that direction. It is probable that careful observations would detect the influence of this remarkable deposit of ore through an east and west zone, which in places would attain a breadth of 2,000 feet or more, one-fifth of this area showing a magnetic dip of 90°; but this does not prove the existence of 400 feet of magnetic rocks or ore, by any means, as will be seen below.

At the Spurr Mountain, which is an east-west deposit of highly magnetic ore like the Champion, Mr. Lawton observed just south of the range 23 vibrations in a quarter of a minute; going south the vibrations diminished somewhat regularly, until at 600 feet the needle vibrated but *ten* times in a quarter of a minute. At 300 feet north of the mountain the needle settled indifferently in any direction, owing to the fact that the terrestrial and local forces just balanced each other at that point; further north the vibrations increased somewhat irregularly, owing to the presence of slightly magnetic rocks, until at 1,400 feet *six* vibrations were observed in a quarter of a minute. There must of course be points north and south of all magnetic belts where the vibrations would be equal and normal, but these limits were not reached, the observations proving only that the magnetic belt at Spurr Mountain is over 2,300 feet wide.

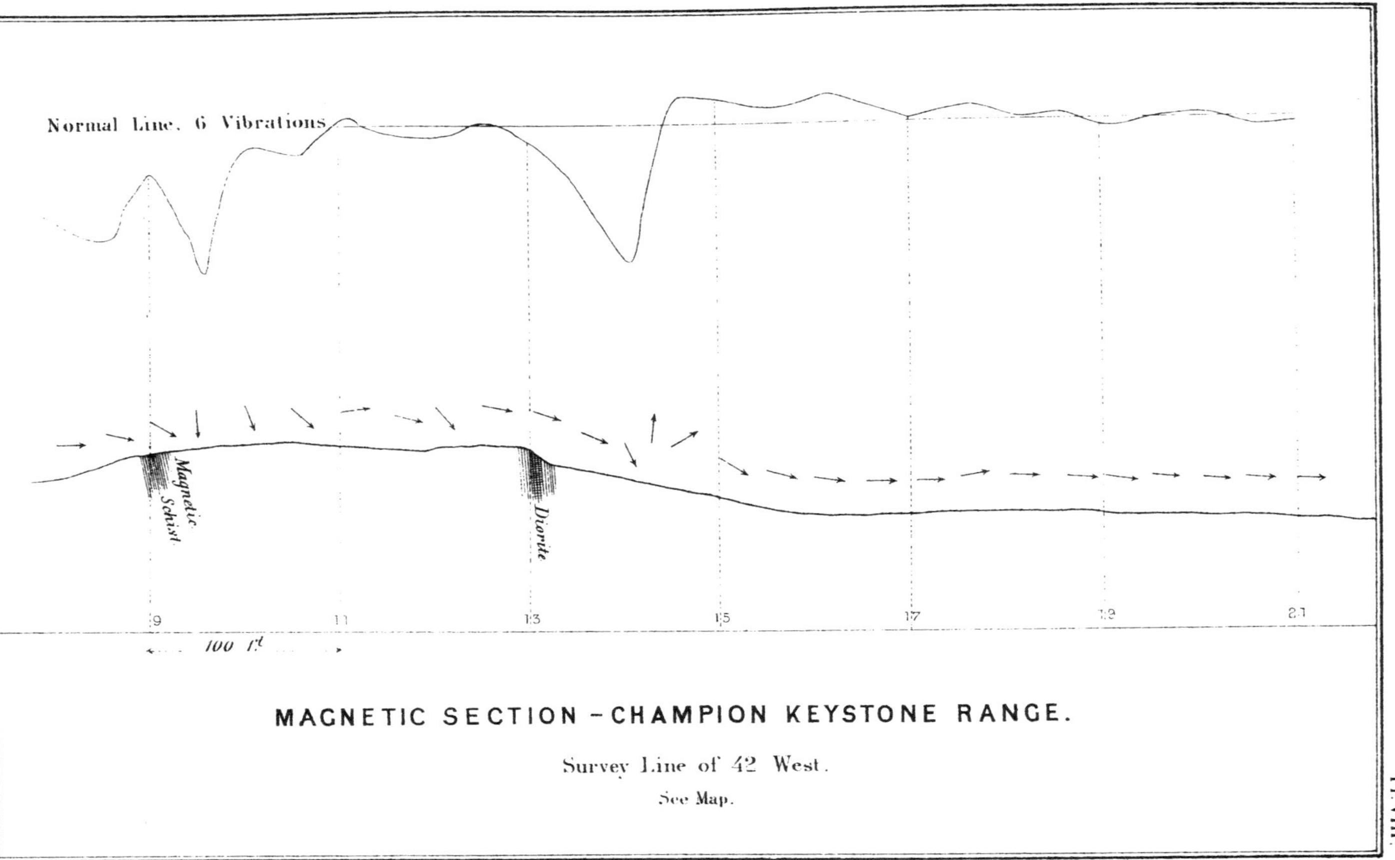

MAGNETIC SECTION - CHAMPION KEYSTONE RANGE.

Survey Line of 42 West.

See Map.

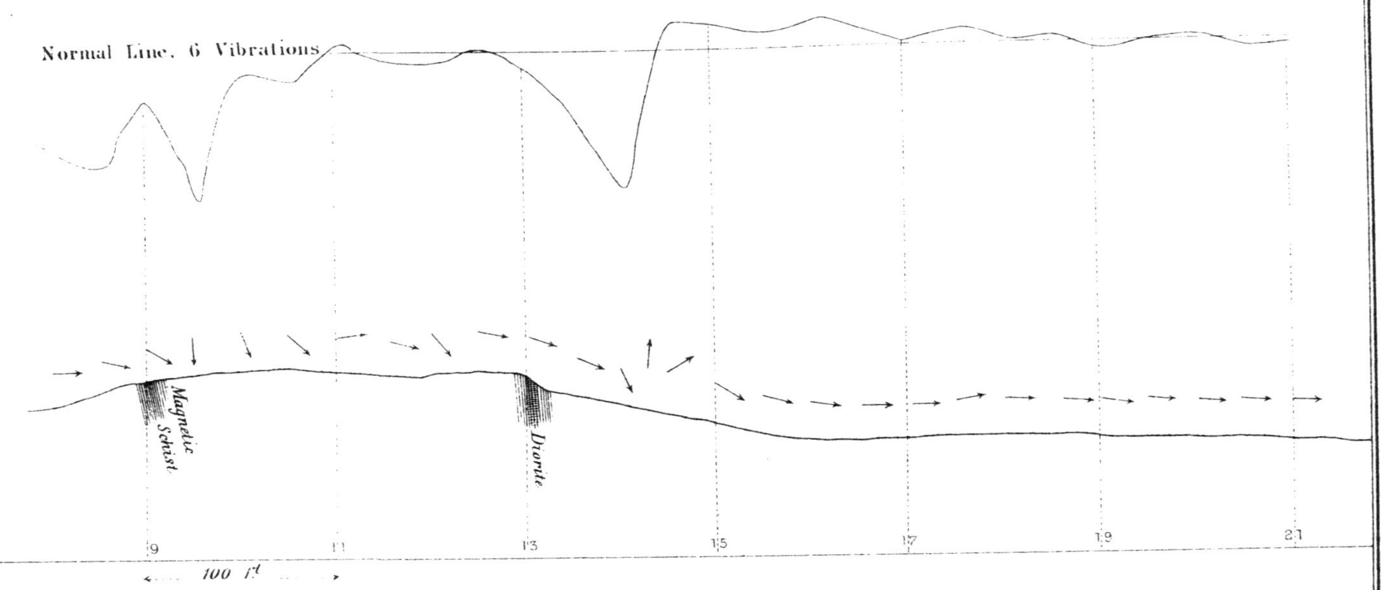

Normal Line, 6 Vibrations

Magnetic Schist

Diorite

9 11 13 15 17 19 21

100 ft

MAGNETIC SECTION – CHAMPION KEYSTONE RANGE.

Survey Line of 42 West.

See Map.

Pl. IX.

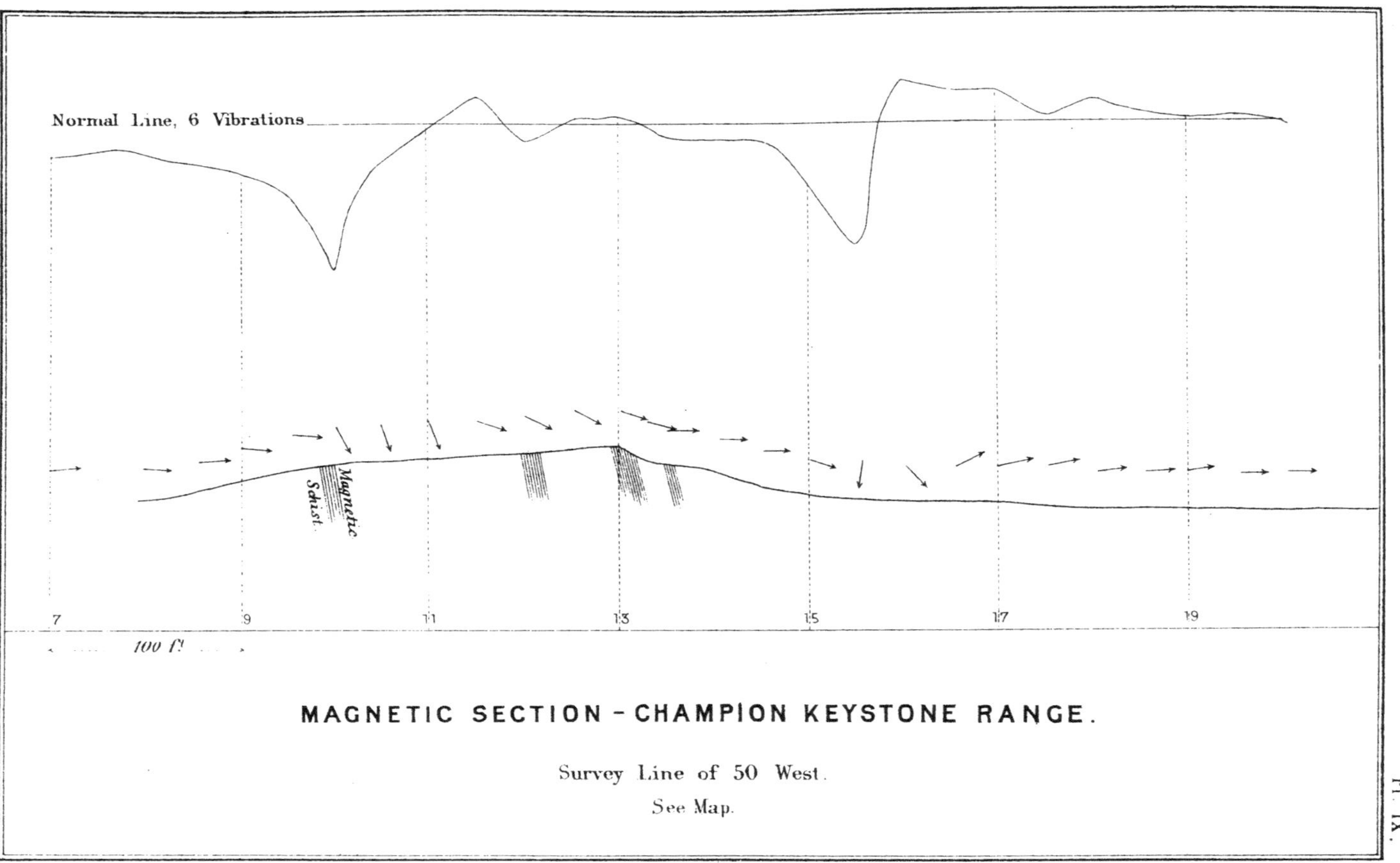

MAGNETIC SECTION - CHAMPION KEYSTONE RANGE.

Survey Line of 50 West.

See Map.

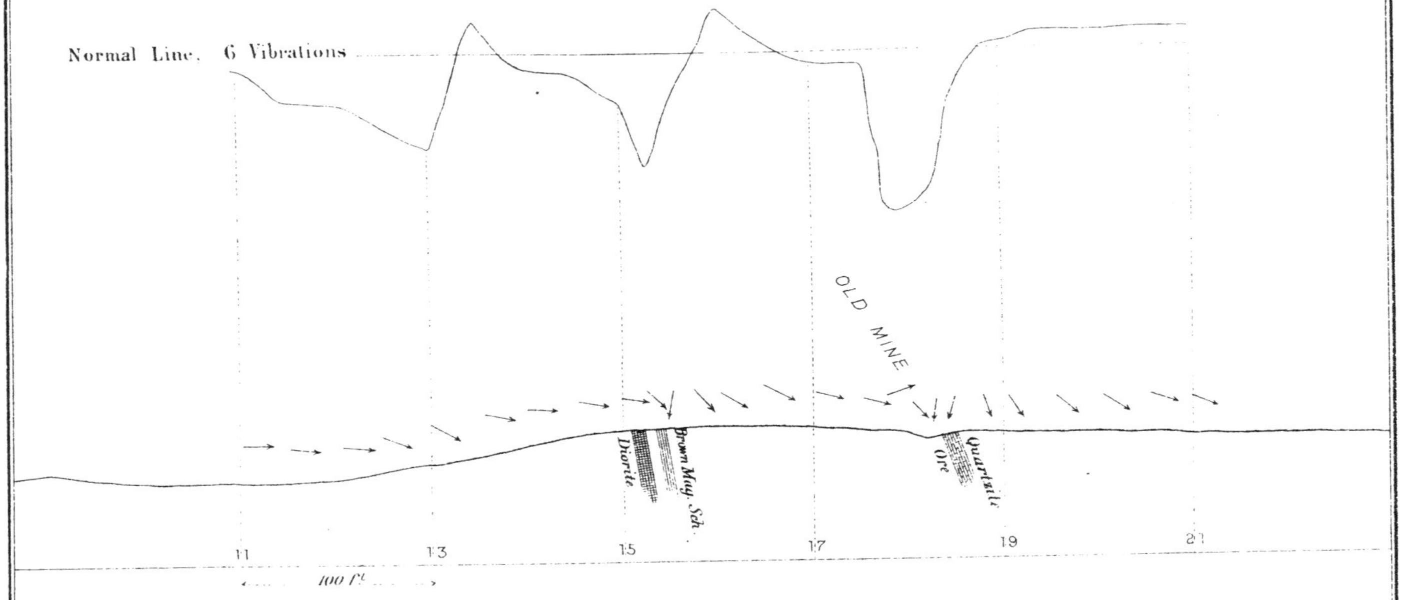

Normal Line. 6 Vibrations

OLD MINE

Diorite

Brown Mag. Sch.

Ore

Quartzite

11 13 15 17 19 21

100 ft.

MAGNETIC SECTION – CHAMPION KEYSTONE RANGE.

Survey Line of 54 West.

See Map.

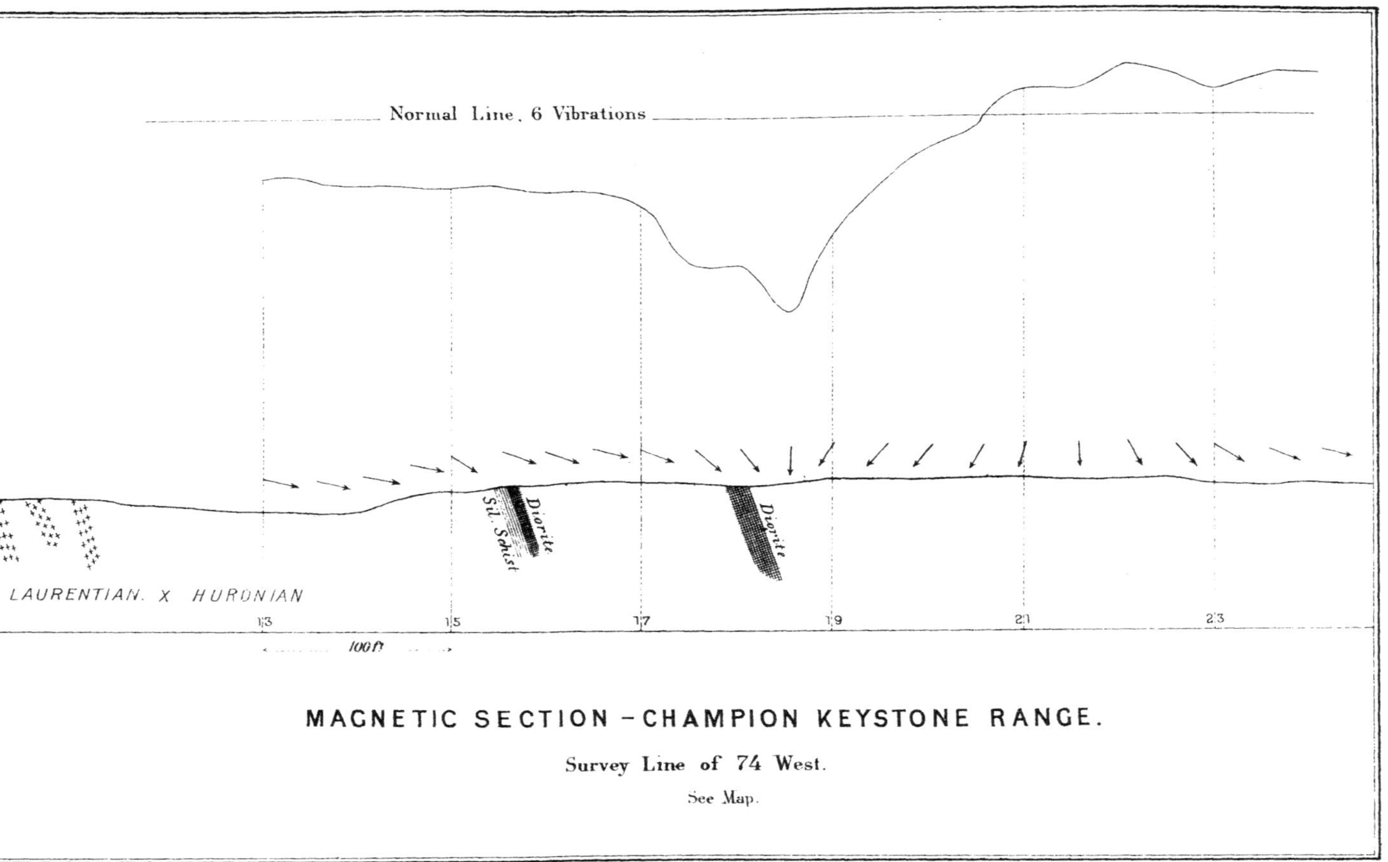

MAGNETIC SECTION – CHAMPION KEYSTONE RANGE.

Survey Line of 74 West.

See Map.

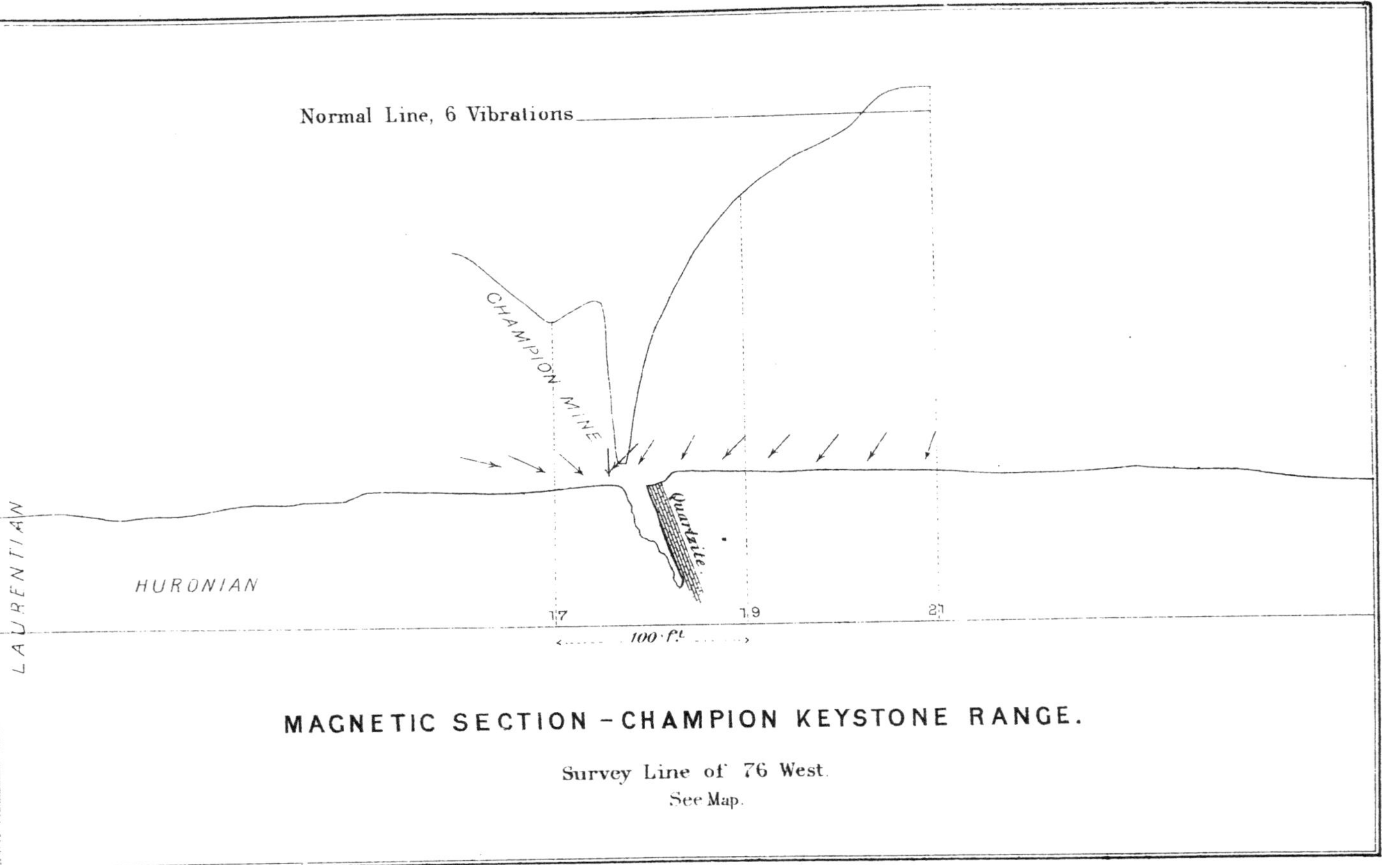

MAGNETIC SECTION - CHAMPION KEYSTONE RANGE.

Survey Line of 76 West.

See Map.

Pl. XIII.

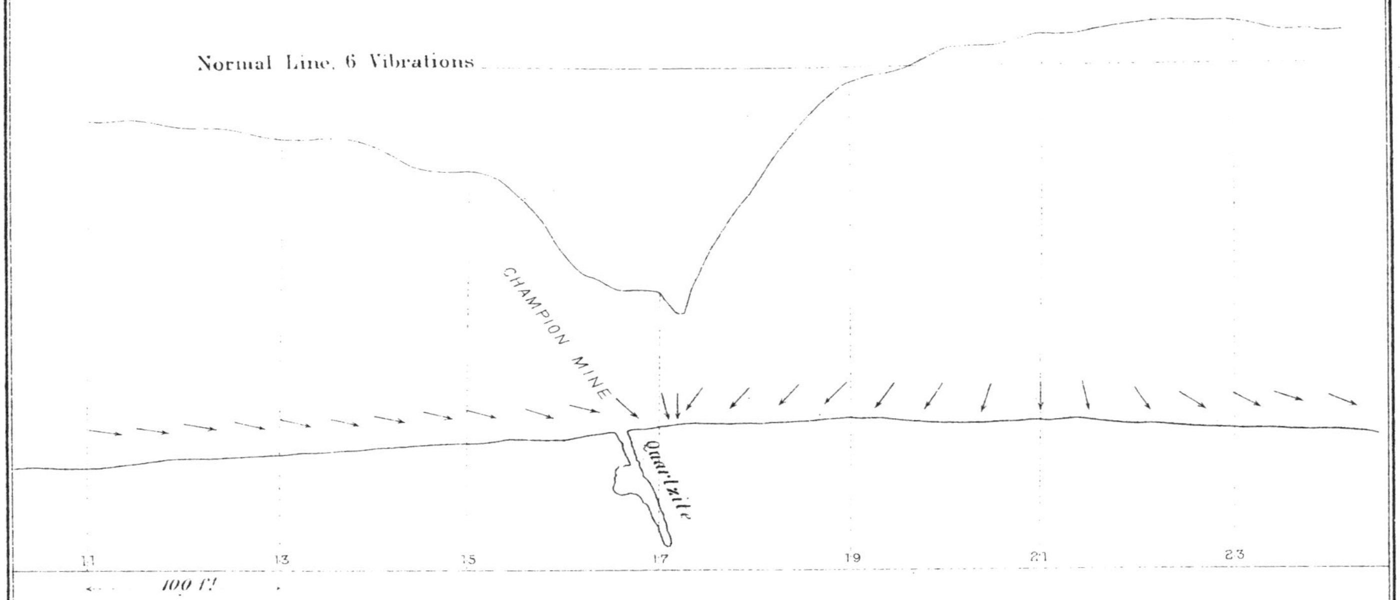
Normal Line, 6 Vibrations
CHAMPION MINE
Quartzite
11
13
15
17
19
21
23
100 ft

MAGNETIC SECTION - CHAMPION KEYSTONE RANGE.

Survey Line of 78 West.

See Map.

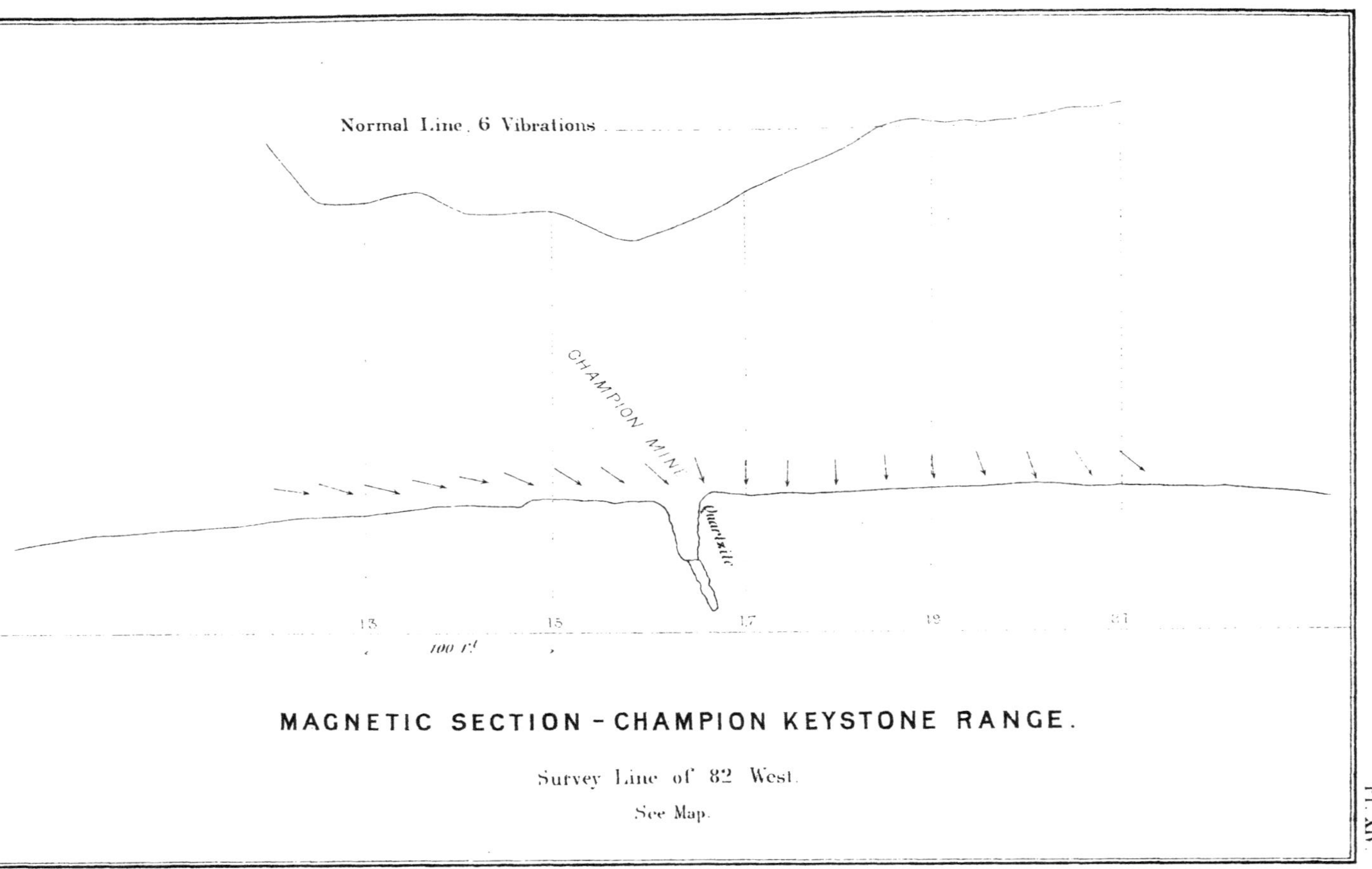

MAGNETIC SECTION - CHAMPION KEYSTONE RANGE.

Survey Line of 82 West.

See Map.

It may be asked why the very silicious magnetic rocks of the Republic Mountain influence the needle at a greater distance than the pure ores of the Champion Mine. It is not at all certain that this is the fact; the limit of the influence has been determined in neither case. The stratigraphical conditions, however, are quite different. The strike of the Republic mountain rocks being north-westerly, is far more favorable for producing variations than is that of the Champion deposit, which is east and west. It is quite evident that a north-south deposit of ore would cause greatest variations (see Plate VI.) and an east-west deposit least. If, in the latter case, we conceive the power to be equally distributed along an east and west mathematical line, there would be produced no variations at all in a horizontal compass. Again, there are four highly magnetic beds at Republic Mountain, while at the Champion there is only one.

Regarding the polarity of the magnetic force: (1) In every instance the north end of the horizontal needle was drawn towards the magnetic rocks; hence, north-easterly of Republic Mountain, the variation was west; and south-westerly, the variation was east. (2) With the dip-needle vibrating in an east and west plane, the north end pointed westerly, or towards the mountain on its north-east side. (3) With the dip-needle vibrating in the plane of the meridian, on the north-east side of the mountain, the south end inclined downward, producing a "negative dip," as shown in Figs. 3 and 4, and this increased as the magnetic rocks were approached until the needle turned entirely over. This apparent *negative* attraction was probably in reality only the effect of an attraction for the north end of the needle, which inclined to the magnetic rocks by the shortest road. Why the north end of the needle moved upward instead of downward (which was apparently just as short a road) as it approached the magnetic rocks over the non-magnetic Laurentian, I can only explain as follows,—which hypothesis may also explain instances other than this where slight negative attractions have been observed over granitic rocks, for example, south and south-east of the Champion mine. My needles were always counterpoised near Negaunee or Marquette, which towns are built on the Huronian. Of course an effort was made to get away from the magnetic members of the series; but this evidently would be impossible if their influence extends to the distance of one half mile.

Magnetic rocks would probably be found throughout the Huronian belt by boring less than 1,000 feet into the earth, owing to the basin-like structure of the series. It is probable, therefore, that my needles were counterpoised under the influence of some *positive* magnetic force ; hence, when taken over Laurentian rocks containing no magnetite, they would show "negative" attraction. If this hypothesis is correct, then the negative attraction referred to above is explained.

Regarding the *intensity of the magnetic force* exerted by Republic mountain as a whole, but one observation need in this place be made. The vibrations are greater on the south-west than on the north-east side, or exactly the converse of the variations. The Magneto-Geologic Sections of the Champion and Keystone Range (see Plates VIII. to XV.) present the same phenomenon.* As the needle is carried north from the Champion bed, its vibrations rapidly diminish in number until they become *less* than the normal number due to the earth's magnetism ; after which, on going still farther, the vibrations will increase until the normal number is reached : but in going south, the diminution is far less rapid, and the number of vibrations never falls below the normal number. The same was observed at the Spurr as is noted on page 226.

The obvious reason is this : when the needle is south of the local force, both it and the terrestrial force act in the same direction, producing a maximum effect ; but when the needle is north of the local force, it can evidently be influenced only by the greater force less the smaller. In the first case the mechanical resultant is the *sum*, in the other it is the *difference* between the two magnetic forces. This readily explains the difference in the slope of the curve of intensity north and south of the magnetic poles, so noticeable in the magnetic sections.

Republic Mountain.

A glance at the directions of the needle as indicated by the arrows in figures 1, 3, and 4 of Chart XI., will impress one with the conviction that there is no direction in azimuth, or inclination which

* The survey lines on the Magnetic Sections, Plates VIII. to XV., refer to Map of the Champion Mine, No. VII., which should be examined in connection with them.

the needle does not assume in crossing the series of rocks. The north end of the needle never points north, often east and west, and sometimes south; while in the dip-compass it turns a series of somewhat irregular somersaults, pointing habitually downward, but often towards the zenith. The needle may be said to "box the compass right and left," as we may suppose that feat accomplished by a drunken sailor. A second glance at the arrows will show us that there is much method in the madness of our ge-go-sence;* the needle very generally tends to point toward the blue or red-colored rocks, which contain magnetite, while it is comparatively indifferent to the green, gray, and salmon colored, which contain little or none of this mineral. The particular significance of the variations and dips will be more fully discussed below.

We will leave for the present the consideration of the direction of the magnetic force expressed by the arrows, and return to the subject of the *intensity of the force as expressed by the colored curves* (see page 223). Nothing is more evident on the chart than that these curves indicate with great certainty the position of the magnetic beds over which they are more or less convex, producing summits; and more or less concave or flat over the non-magnetic rocks, pointing literally as a finger in some instances to the location of the magnetic force. Comparing the three curves in figs. 3 and 4, it appears that:—(1) The red line (compass facing south) oftenest rises higher than any other over the magnetic rocks; and sinks lower away from them. It has also fewer changes in direction than the others. (2) The black line (compass facing east-west) falls lower than either of the others over the magnetic rocks. (3) The blue line (compass horizontal) often has an extreme depression, where the others have an extreme elevation.

These, the most obvious generalizations from the curves, are explained by the principles of the mechanics of forces already mentioned.

Fearing there may be some confusion from representing the same element-*intensity* by three curves, I suggest the following conception: Suppose an observer to be provided with a horizontal com-

* A Chippewa word for magnetic needle, signifying "little fish," in allusion to its wiggling motion.

pass having a blue needle and two dip-compasses, one provided with a black and the other with a red needle. Suppose, further, these to be mounted for observing at the same station, but so far apart as not to influence one another; the blue needle moves in a horizontal plane, the red needle in a vertical east and west plane, and the black needle in a vertical north and south plane. Suppose, further, a powerful magnet to be placed (1) directly under or directly over the station, it is evident that only the black and red needles will be influenced. (2) If placed north, the blue and black needles only will be influenced. The directive force in this case would be a maximum; because the magnet's power is added to the earth's, both acting in the same line. (3) If the magnet be placed directly south, the red needle will again be uninfluenced, but the black and blue needles will indicate a minimum of intensity instead of a maximum, for their directive power will be the difference between the force of the magnet and that of the earth. (Places have been observed where the needle gave us no vibrations in any position from this cause. A fine illustration occurs in Fig. 3, Chart XI., Station 24, where there must have been a very strong pole to the south of the station; but this pole is evidently north of Station 24, Fig. 4, where the greatest intensity was observed.) (4) If the magnet be placed east or west of our supposed station, the effect will be the same; the red needle will be most influenced, blue next, and black not at all.

We are now fully prepared to explain the phenomena presented by the colored curves.

(1) Why does the red line usually rise higher over the magnetic rocks, and sink lower away from them, and why does it fluctuate least? When the needle vibrates in an east and west plane, its axis points north,—that is nearly in the line of the directive force of the earth, which it thus partially neutralizes; giving the local forces full power. As these are much stronger than that of the earth at short distances, we should expect the result observed over the magnetic rocks. Away from them, the earth's force being nearly neutralized, we should have the minimum of intensity as is shown by the red line. That the changes in direction in this line are less frequent and less abrupt than the others, indicates, I think, that if the earth's attraction was entirely neutralized and the error of observation reduced to a minimum, the curve derived from the magnetic force resident in the rocks on any particular cross-section might be more

regular than any shown in the chart. It is reasonable to suppose that the red curve has most significance in our investigations. (2) Why do the black and blue lines fall as a rule lowest over the magnetic rocks? Suppose a local force, about equal to the earth's, to exist directly south of a dip-compass placed in the plane of the meridian, or of a horizontal compass; we should evidently have a minimum of intensity, because the terrestrial and local forces would balance each other. The marked exception to this rule over formation XI., Fig. 4, is evidently due to the fact that the magnetic power resident in beds X. and XII. just balance each other, and as the directive power of the earth is neutralized in the case of the red line by the direction in which the needle is held, we have a point of comparative equilibrium. (3) Why does the blue curve sometimes present depressions opposite the summits of the others? This is readily explained by supposing the local force to exist directly under the station; its force would then be entirely neutralized by the centre-pin of the horizontal compass, while having its full effect on the dip-needle in both positions.

5. Diminution of Intensity due to Elevation.

All the observations for intensity above considered were taken at an elevation of about 4 feet from the surface. Sometimes the rocks came to the surface, sometimes there were several feet and perhaps yards of drift between; it is therefore an important practical question to ascertain what effect the elevation of the needle has on the number of its vibrations.

The difficulty of attaining any considerable elevation at which to observe intensity, renders our observations on its rate of diminution due to elevation or vertical distance of little value. The theory of the sphere of attraction and law of decrease of force, as the square of the distance from the centre, has been mentioned; but with several local forces acting on the same point (the case usually presented in nature), the law is greatly modified, the decrease being in a less ratio. This subject possesses especial interest in connection with the determination of the depth at which magnetic rocks, producing a given disturbance, will be found; therefore, the few observations made, unsatisfactory though they are, will be given. At Republic Mountain a staging was erected in the windfall, by means of which eight equi-distant observations were made; the lower one on the magnetic schist, the upper one 14 feet above it. The results were as follows:

Elevation in feet.	Vibrations.		Remarks.
	Facing west.	Facing north.	
0	56	53	On surface of schist.
2	41	41	
4	33	30	
6	27½	30	
8	19	23	
10	15½	24	
12	18	24	
14	12	20	

At another point near the above, and over the same magnetic rock, the following vibrations were observed:

Elevation in feet.	Vibrations.		Remarks.
	Facing west.	Facing north.	
0	60	60	On surface of schist.
3	50	49	
6	36	37	
9	25	26	
12	18½	18	

The observations have all been represented graphically, but as no law was apparent, and as the figures can be easily reproduced, they are not given. The first table gave the most regular curve, but still too angular to attempt the application of a mathematical formula. They do not seem to me to afford a basis for calculation, as to how high the appreciably magnetic influence of these rocks would extend. I have an impression, however, without being able to give any reason, that it would be considerably less than one half mile, which was shown to be the distance to which the influence of the same rocks extended horizontally. I cannot consider it probable that a needle would dip where an earth covering of over 2,000 feet exists, if such a case were possible. At the Champion mine, by the aid of shaft house No. 2, an elevation of 44 feet above the ore was attained, and the following observations made :

Elevation in feet.	Vibrations.			Remarks.
	I.	II.	III.	
0	18½	17½	23	Level of surface of ore in shaft.
18	19	17	17	Surface of ground.
32	16½	16½	16½	Girder of shaft house.
44	15½	..	15	Girder of shaft house.

At other points at the Champion mine, 25, 32, 33 and 40 vibrations were observed, the compass being within 5 feet of the ore. The diminution here is quite regular and nearly as the distance. If the rate continue, the vibrations should reach the normal number (six for the instrument used) at about 150 feet ; but it is highly improbable that this law would hold for the whole height.

The difference between the rate of diminution at the two localities is very marked ; at Republic Mountain an elevation of 12 feet in one instance reduced the vibrations from 60 to 18½, in another 14 feet elevation reduced the number from 56 to 12. At the Champion 44 feet elevation made an average of less than 4 difference in the vibrations. In this comparison the following geological differences must be borne in mind.

The Champion deposit at shaft No. 2 is a heavy bed of nearly pure black oxide running east and west and dipping north at an angle of 68 degrees, and it is the only magnetic rock in the vicinity. The Champion deposit loses its magnetism in going west, specular slate taking the place of the magnetite in that direction. The Republic Mountain bed over which the observations were made (No. X.*) is, on the contrary, a silicious schist, containing not to exceed 33 per cent. of magnetite, (the merchantable ores of Republic Mountain, of which there are large deposits, are in bed No. XIII., and are mostly specular hematites.) This magnetic bed X. is associated with others of a similar character, all striking north-west and south-east and dipping nearly vertical. The specimens of these magnetic schists which were examined possessed marked polarity. The Champion deposit evidently contains far more magnetite within the same sphere of influence than the Republic Mountain.

There is no doubt that variations and dips are a much more delicate and ready means of observing slight magnetic attractions, than vibrations when observed with the hand instruments employed. In one instance at Republic Mountain the dip at 12 feet elevation was 30 degrees, at 9 feet 50 degrees, at 6 feet 70 degrees, at 3 feet 77 degrees, at 0 or on surface of rock 105 degrees. It appears that the magnetic poles of the Champion bed are more deeply seated than those at Republic Mountain, which seem to be at the surface. This may be due to the fact that the upper part of the Champion deposit is mined out. Sets of careful observations made for considerable heights, both for dip and vibrations, would possess great interest, especially if made over beds of ore or rock, the position and character of which were known. In a record of over three thousand magnetic observations made by me in Michigan, Missouri, New York and New Jersey, I have not in more than six instances found the needle in the dip-compass above described to vibrate over 40 times in a quarter of a minute, and in no instance in which this rate was observed was the needle removed more than 5 feet from the magnetic mineral. Of course in the same needle the vibrations will vary with the degree of magnetism that has been imparted to it, and the condition of the instrument in other respects. I have had a rude standard, and when my needle fell below that it was overhauled, so that the numbers are relatively correct. I do not remember to have observed over 15 vibrations in a quarter of a

* The Roman numerals refer to the order of the beds of the Huronian series, counting upwards from I. to XIX.

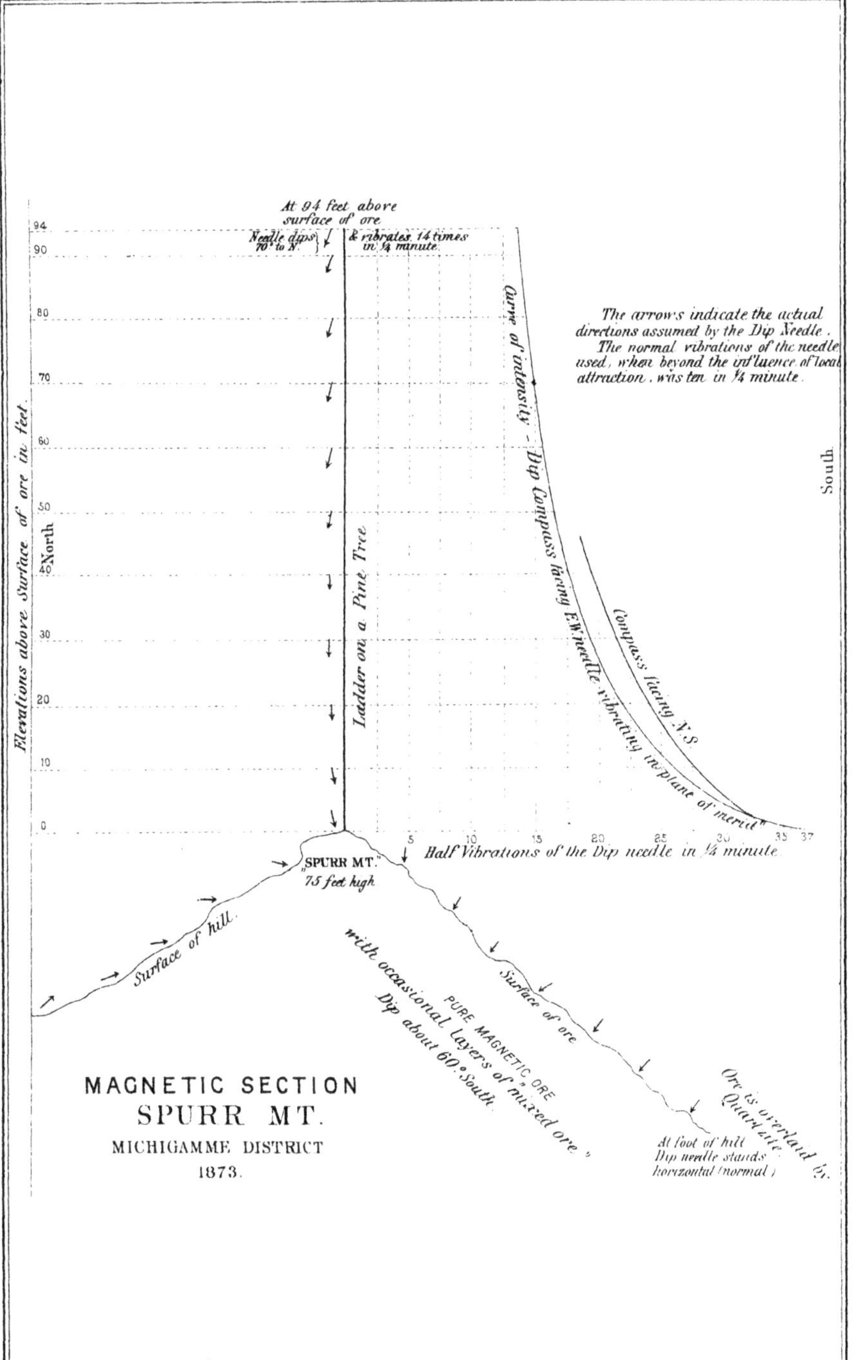

MAGNETIC SECTION
SPURR MT.
MICHIGAMME DISTRICT
1873.

minute, or one per second, at a greater distance than 50 feet from a magnetic bed, and usually this number of vibrations would indicate a distance not exceeding 25 feet in the Marquette Iron Region.

Since the above observations were made and recorded, the development of the Michigamme district has permitted observations to be made at the *Spurr Mountain* which throw much light on the subject of the diminution in dip, and intensity due to elevation. The following table records the observations made,* and Plate XVI. represents the general law of diminution graphically. The observations were carried to an elevation of 94 feet by means of a fortunately situated pine-tree, up which a ladder was constructed. While there are minor irregularities, due wholly or in part to errors of instrument, the presence of nails in the ladder, and personal error, the average curve is remarkably regular, and points, as most of the other facts do, to a far more rapid rate of diminution near the surface than at a considerable elevation.

It is not to be expected that the law of decrease of magnetic force would hold at this locality. Had the local force been concentrated in a focal point directly under the tree, and the force of the earth been neutralized, then we might expect the law to be discernible. Some useful practical rules may be readily drawn from the table and plate under consideration.

1. If, in a locality where magnetic attractions prevail, we find considerable difference in the number of vibrations between the compass, when in contact with the ground, or held six feet above it, we may conclude the ore is very near the surface; if there is but little difference, then the ore is probably deep. 2. The amount of the dip gives but little clue to the depth of the ore. If the Spurr Mountain had been covered by a hundred feet of earth, water, or non-magnetic rock, we would have found at the surface a dip of about 70°, and it is probable, if not certain, that if it were possible to make observations to the north of the mountain, at the same elevation, a greater dip than 70° would be found, due to the changed direction of the local force.

---

* Mr. C. M. Boss rendered great assistance in these observations.

Observations for diminution of magnetic force in vertical direction—(Needle vibrating in north-south plane)—Spurr Mountain.

Height.	Dip.	Vib. in ¼ min.	Remarks.	Height.	Dip.	Vib. in ¼ min.	Remarks.
0	100°	37	On surface of ore.	25	93°	20½	
2	100°	33		26	93°	20	
4½	100°	30		27	92°	20	
6	100°	28½		28	92°	19½	
7	100°	27		29	92°	19½	
8	100°	27		30	92°	19¼	
9	100°	27½		31¼	91°	19	
10	100°	26		32½	90°	18½	
11	100°	25½	26 facing south.	33½	90°	18½	
12	96°	24½		34½	90°	18	
13	100°	24		35½	88°	18½	
14	96°	24½	24½ facing south.	36½	88°	19	
15	98°	23		37½		18	
16	96°	23½		41	88°	17½	
17	95°	23½		42¼		17	
18	95°	23		45½	86°	17	
19	94°	22½	23 facing south.	48		17	
20	94°	22¼		52	80°	16½	
21	94°	21½		56	80°	16½	
22	93°	22		63	78°	16	15 vib., faced N., dip 86 E.
23	92°	21½		68	80°	15	15 Vib., faced N.
24	93°	20½		79	78°	14½	13 " " "
				92	72°	14½	13 " " S.
				94	70°	14	13½ " " S.

6. What is the significance of a dip of 90° or "dead 90°."

As there is a general impression among those who have made but little use of the dip-needle in exploring for iron ores, that a variation of 90° signifies merchantable ore directly under the feet, it is important to ascertain the exact purport of such great fluctuations in the direction of the needle. For the present we will leave out of the question the unpleasant fact that in 19 cases out of 20, if not 99 out of a 100, the mineral producing the dip would, if found, prove to be only a ferruginous schist or magnetic rock instead of merchantable ore, and consider the case often presented where there is *a dip of 90° at a place which is not underlaid by magnetic mineral*, or where there is none within several hundred feet. In such cases there are generally two, approximately parallel lines, of 90° dip, one over the ore, where the vibrations are very *quick* (always more than the normal number). The second line (the one we are now considering) will always be found north of the first, and along it the vibrations will be *slow*, always less than the normal number.

A moment's inspection of almost any magnetic section (Plates VIII. to XIV.) will illustrate the fact and suggest the cause. If we hold a dip-compass over a highly magnetic bed the needle will indicate 90°, pointing directly towards it. Moving north, the needle will continue to point towards the ore, that is, be turned backward, thus varying or dipping more than 90° from its normal direction. Continuing north, we soon get so far from the local influence, that its power ceases to entirely overbalance that of the earth, and the needle commences to return to its normal direction. In doing so it must evidently somewhere stand again at 90°, which means simply, that the local force to the south and the earth's force to the north, are so related in intensity, that the resultant is a vertical line. Still going north, the dip grows less and less until the boundary of the local attraction is past, and the needle returns to its terrestrial allegiance. It is evident that no such phenomena can occur to the south of the magnetic bed, for the terrestrial and local influences acting in the same direction, no "dead" points could occur.

This "dead 90°" line, then, instead of proving the immediate presence of ore, proves just the reverse if the phenomena are presented as above, which is the case at the Magnetic, Champion, Spurr, and Michigamme mines, and at one place at the Washington mine. There may be ore under this line, but it will always be deep and have little or no influence in producing the phenomena observed. Rule:—When there is a dip of 90°, and the vibrations *exceed* the normal number, we may conclude that the magnetic mineral is under our feet, or very near us to the south. If, with the same dip, the vibrations are *less* than the normal number, we may conclude that the magnetic bed producing the effect is south of us, and may be at considerable distance. This rule will evidently apply only where there is one strongly magnetic bed not very deep, which is the most common case. If there be several beds, as at Republic Mountain, the application of the principle is more difficult; but in the nature of force, some modification of the phenomena must be presented by all magnetic rocks.

It is worth remarking that the south belt of 90° dip, is more sharply bounded, especially on its south side, and usually narrower, than the north belt.

The lower curve of Fig. 2, Republic Mountain Chart, illustrates what has been said above; the summits of the curves showing the maximum dips are north of the magnetic beds, while the summits of the curves showing the maximum intensity (see upper curve, same fig.) are over the centres of the magnetic beds.

This subject would be incomplete without considering the case, quite common, where a zone of local attractions has but one line of 90° dip, or to make the case general, but one line of *maximum* dip whether it be 90° or less. It may be said that this last expression, covers the whole question, but with ore-hunters "dead 90" has a peculiar significance, and it is for them that I am writing. This case (one line of 90° dip) is illustrated in some of the Champion mine sections. A few words will explain how it flows out of the first case.

If we follow the two lines of 90° dip to where the earth covering becomes very deep, so that our distance from the magnetic mineral considerably reduces its influence, our two lines would evidently be merged into one, and continuing on to where the earth was still deeper, which has the effect of raising us above the ore deposit, this maximum dip would become less than 90°.

This maxima line would evidently correspond with the south line of 90° dip in the case first supposed, that is to say would lie nearly over the mineral producing it. With great depth of earth covering, it can be proven that it would lie to the north of the magnetic bed.

An inspection and consideration of the facts presented in the Spurr Mountain magnetic section given above, will, I think, convince any one of this without the aid of the rigid mechanical demonstration which the problem admits of.

I have seen large amounts of money unsuccessfully expended in digging for iron ore for want of a knowledge of the simple principles set forth above, hence I have dwelt longer on this point than its importance to the general subject would seem to warrant.

7. Additional Practical Suggestions and Rules.

The facts given above, with others in my possession, enable us to answer provisionally the following practical questions :

I. Can we by means of the magnetic needle determine the order of superposition or succession of beds of the iron-bearing rocks ?

Comparing the magnetic sections obtained at the Republic mountain and Champion mines, it is evident that, while there is considerable variation in the details, the salient features agree remarkably, pointing towards the same order and same lithological character in the rocks. A number of other sections made within 10 miles of the above-named localities, across the same belt of rocks, gave the same general result.

It is therefore asserted with much confidence that where a magnetic section similar to these is found in the Michigamme district, a corresponding geological section will be found beneath the surface; and that, as a rule, there will be less difference in the magnetic sections than in the topographical, which we know depends greatly on the underlying rocks. But whoever expects to find many places where so complete sections can be obtained as these localities afford, will be disappointed, for they present rare opportunities for studying the structure and magnetism of the Huronian series.

In places the covering of drift will be so deep as greatly to reduce the intensity, making it exceedingly difficult to observe with ordinary instruments, as was the case at the Cannon location. Again, the lower magnetic rock, beds VI., VIII., and X., are in places far less magnetic, containing sometimes very little magnetite, as is the case south of the Washington mine. In other places the lower magnetic rocks may be entirely wanting, owing probably to a fault, as at the west end of the Champion. On the north shore of Lake Michigamme there is a magnetic bed above XIII. (the ore formation), being therefore younger than any member of the Republic mountain series. In other places XIII. is wanting, and when present it is sometimes highly magnetic, as at the Champion, and again it holds very little magnetite, as at Republic mountain, the pure ore there being mostly specular hematite, as has been elsewhere observed.

With all these uncertainties, however, the results of magnetic surveys cannot but be valuable in the exploration and development of iron properties, and in the solution of all questions of structural geology in regions of magnetic rocks. In such rocks, I believe, their value to the geologist is only second to topographical work, and, considering the cheapness of magnetic surveys, they may often pay best if means be limited.

Detailed magnetic observations, if made with precision, ought to throw light on the lithological character and intricacies of structure of these rocks, and on the nature of the magnetic force resident in them. This could not, however, be undertaken ; the work done is more than was contemplated in my instructions and more than was justified by the means at my disposal.

II. Is it possible to determine quality—*i.e.*, the percentage of iron—in a magnetic rock by means of the magnetic needle ? In other words, can the needle alone make us sure we have a workable deposit of ore under our feet ?

This is the most important practical question connected with this subject, and is the one constantly presented to the miner and explorer. Magnetic observations should always be made in connection with topographical and geological surveys ; whether these take such names, and are based on instrumentation, or whether they be such rude work as the explorer is constantly doing, but which are as much topographical and geological as the other, and often quite as valuable. A judgment of the commercial value of a bed of magnetic ore should, of course, be based on all the facts available. *If nothing more was known than what the magnetic needle revealed, I would not venture an opinion as to whether it was merchantable ore or magnetic rock which produced the phenomenon.* In the Marquette Region, as has been before observed, the chances are at least fifty to one that a worthless ferruginous rock is the cause of any observed attraction. But this case never occurs ; we always know something more than the needle reveals. One of the most important uses of the needle, and one for which it can within certain limits be depended on, is in tracing magnetic beds in the direction of their strike *until some outcrop*, which may give us the information sought, is found. I have in this way traced magnetic beds for many miles both in the Marquette Region and in New York and New Jersey.

Preparatory to the examination of any particular range of ore, the exp'orer should thoroughly study up, with his own instrument, the phenomena presented at some exposed or developed part of the range he is exploring. This will give him data relating to variations, dips, and vibrations, which can be used where the rocks are covered and unknown. By means of the quickness of the vibrations, or of the rapidity with which they decrease as the compass is elevated, he may judge approximately of the depth of the drift, and so of other phenomena.

III. Does the magnetic needle afford the means of determining the absolute thickness of a bed of magnetic ore or rock?

My observations do not permit an affirmative answer to this question, especially if there be much earth covering. A study of all the magnetic sections which have come under my observation, indicates that, while in some instances the *comparative width* is plainly shown, the boundaries between the magnetic and non-magnetic rocks are not generally brought out sufficiently to warrant a definite expression as to thickness. We should expect this, because the magnetic influence is centred in the poles of the masses, and towards such foci the needle tends to point.

IV. Can we by means of the magnetic needle ascertain the direction and depth of a local magnetic pole? In other words, can we determine the thickness of rock or earth covering which overlies a given magnetic rock?

Often I think we can, with much precision, locate a point in the surface over the pole and determine its depth, by making what may be called a *magnetic triangulation*. Proceed thus: Remote from any magnetic rocks, neutralize, by means of a bar magnet, the earth's influence on the needle of a solar compass. The needle will then stand indifferently in all directions, and will not vibrate. Record carefully the distance and position of the neutralizing magnet; the compass is then ready for use. Set it up near the magnetic pole to be determined, and fix the magnet in exactly the same relative position it had before. The earth's directive power on the needle will again be neutralized, and the needle will point as nearly towards the local pole as its mode of mounting will permit; mark the line indicated by the needle on the ground; remove the compass to one, or, better, two other positions, and repeat the operation. If there is no other local force to interfere, the three lines must intersect in one point, which will be directly over the pole whose position is sought. By using a dip-compass in a similar manner, it is evident that the data to determine the depth, by the simple solution of a triangle, would be obtained. The fact that several local poles often influence the needle at each station renders this operation difficult in practice;—we should endeavor to find a place where but one strong pole exists.

A magnetic needle having universal motion, like Mr. Ritchie's, would evidently determine both position and depth at the same time; but a solar compass would have to be used to fix the position of the artificial magnet used in neutralizing the earth's force, unless it be fixed by an observation on the North Star, or by a meridian line brought in from a non-magnetic area.

V. When considering the magnetism of the rocks of the four great geological epochs represented on the Upper Peninsula of Michigan, I observed that considerable magnetic variations were noted by the Federal surveyors, over rocks of Silurian age, which had never been observed to be in themselves magnetic. In some instances these variations had been observed over a limestone, supposed to be Trenton, and at a distance of 75 miles from the nearest Huronian, or other (known to be) magnetic rocks.

This phenomenon may be due either: 1. To the presence of magnetite in such rocks, due to local metamorphism or other cause. 2. To accumulations of magnetic sand in the drift; or, 3. To the underlying Huronian rocks, which may be supposed to exert their influence up through the overlying Silurian.

Without having made a study of any of these localities, I incline decidedly to the latter hypothesis, as accounting for the known facts better than either of the others.

Should this prove true (and I hope to settle it at some future time) it may lead to a novel and interesting application of the science of magnetism to some important questions in geology—the determination of the thickness of sedimentary rocks by *magnetic triangulation* in places where it would otherwise be difficult to arrive at such thickness. It might also enable us to work out the structure and distribution, in a rough way, of these oldest rocks which underlie great Silurian areas, which would in no other practicable way be possible, thus throwing light on the nature of the rocky bottom of the ancient seas.

On the same principle we can, of course, trace magnetic iron belts under water. I have in many instances made very satisfactory magnetic observations from a canoe in the inland lakes of the Upper Peninsula. The bottom of Lake Superior may be thus partially mapped. Silt and sand will make no difference with the needle; it looks through everything but iron.

I have endeavored in the above to set forth plainly just what has been done in this comparatively new field, to give the results obtained, and to call attention to those principles which underlie the use of the magnetic needle in exploration for iron ores. The time and means at my disposal were meagre, my instruments imperfect, and I had no precedent to follow. I am persuaded that the subject is worth the attention of the explorer, miner, geologist, and physicist.

There has been a good deal written bearing on the subject of the Magnetism of Rocks, my references having very much increased of late. I had proposed to examine these authorities before writing this paper, but unfortunately the best libraries of Michigan do not contain any of the works referred to, and not being able to have abstracts made in Eastern libraries, I have derived no benefit from these authorities.* Could I have examined the results of the magnetic observations which must have been made in the great iron regions of Sweden, Norway, and Russia, I should probably have found my meagre results anticipated, and this article might not have been written. I am confident, however, that the Huronian rocks of Michigan have never been magnetically studied, and it may be that the methods that have been used in Europe are not such as would commend themselves to Lake Superior explorers, miners, and surveyors, who require cheap, light, and simple instruments that admit of rapid use.

The State of Michigan, or those interested in her Iron Regions, may at some future time see fit to have this subject thoroughly investigated. To that future investigator I commend my notes, trusting that he may find in them a reconnoissance of his rich field of labor.

---

* Gilbert's Annalen (German) contains several papers. See volumes 3, 4, 5, 16, 26, 28, 32, 35, 44, 52, 53, and 75.

CHAPTER IX.

METHOD AND COST OF MINING SPECULAR AND MAGNETIC ORES.*

THE iron ores of the Marquette region are mostly extracted in open excavations; hence the process is more nearly allied to quarrying. Several attempts at underground work have been made, which have not, on the whole, been successful. The Edwards mine has been almost entirely wrought by candle-light. The slate ore pit No. 1 of the New England mine was worked in the same way, as is also the Pioneer furnace pit of the Jackson mine.

The Champion mine was opened systematically for underground work, with two levels, sixty feet apart, and three shafts at distances apart along the bed of about 200 feet; but this idea has been so far modified that one-third of the ore of this mine is now extracted by daylight. The Cleveland mine has recently commenced to mine considerable ore underground.

Several other mines have, from time to time, worked underground stopes, but so far only temporarily; if such stopes could not be opened out to daylight, they have usually been abandoned. In brief, it may be said that no considerable amount of ore has as yet (1870) been mined underground in this region, and of that so mined very little has been taken out at a profit, and I may add that it seems to be the belief of the most experienced mining men that this state of things will hold for some time to come, for reasons which will appear.

Nearly the same remarks may be applied to the mines of the Iron Mountain region, Missouri, the ores of which are very similar in character to those of Marquette. Some of the New York and New Jersey magnetic deposits are also wrought open, but this is the exception, underground mining being there the rule.

---

* Two papers on this subject read before the American Institute of Mining Engineers and the American Society of Civil Engineers, and published, are embodied in this chapter.

The following brief sketch of the geological structure of the Marquette iron deposits will indicate some advantages of the method of mining employed ; the subject being more fully considered in the chapters on the geology of the Marquette and Menominee regions, and illustrated in maps Nos. III. to X. of Atlas. See also Plate VIII., representing Edwards mine.* The iron-bearing or Huronian series of rocks are stratified beds, the principal ore formation being overlaid by a quartzite, XIV., and underlaid by a diorite, or greenstone, XI. This ore formation is made up, first, of pure ore ; second, of "mixed ore" (*i. e.*, banded jasper and ore) ; and third, a soft, greenish schistose, or slaty rock (magnesian), which occurs in lens-shaped beds which alternate with ore, thus often dividing the formation into two or more beds of ore, separated by rock. Usually the beds of both ore and rock thin out as they are followed in the direction of the strike from a centre of maximum thickness, producing irregular lentiform masses. Since their original deposition, if we may assume they were laid down under water, the whole series, including the iron beds, have been bent, folded and corrugated into irregular troughs, basins and domes, which often present at the surface their upturned edges of pure ore, standing nearly vertical. A cross-section, finely illustrating this structure, can be seen on the west of the great south-west opening of the Lake Superior mine. It is locally known as the "Big W," which letter is plainly suggested by the sharp folding of rock and ore. See Fig. 7 and View IV.

The fact that, as a rule, the richest ore is found near the upper part of the formation, and the most jaspery part near the base, has led to the separation of this formation into two beds, Nos. XII. and XIII.

This structure, involving sudden changes in the amount and direction of the dip, from horizontal to vertical, would evidently necessitate, in the case of underground work, constant changes in the plan of attacking the ore, as well as in the mode of supporting the roof.

The magnetic iron deposits in the Eastern States may also be regarded as true beds, but are far more regular in strike and dip, extending downward at a high angle to an undetermined depth, and appearing more like veins. If folds exist, they are much deeper and more regular than in the deposits under consideration. The

* Many copies of this chapter will be distributed separately, rendering this geological *résumé* necessary.

Marquette ore deposits are often very thick, 50 feet being not infrequent, which makes ordinary timbering difficult, if not practically impossible; while the eastern deposits, so far as my observations have extended, are seldom over 20 feet, and average considerably less than that thickness.

The "pinch and shoot" structure, suggesting what are termed "chimneys" and "courses of ores" in some metalliferous mines and which is very apparent in the New York and New Jersey mines (practically dividing the ore into pod-shaped masses, the axes of which "pitch" in the planes of stratification in a direction quite different from the dip), can at this time be best observed in the Marquette region at the Edwards mine, Plate XIX. and Map No. VIII. Atlas. The intervening barren streaks where the hanging and foot-walls come near together, and which therefore divide the "shoots," form excellent supports to the overlying rocks and give the mine great security, as all who have worked deposits having this structure will testify.

The soft schist mentioned as occasionally bedded with the Marquette ores, often constitutes the hanging wall in parts of the mine, but does not possess the requisite strength to make a good roof. It is impossible to support such rock with occasional timbers or pillars, for it will scale off between the supports, demoralizing the men, if not actually endangering their lives. Even when the works reach the solid quartzite XIV., which, as has been stated, is the true hanging wall-rock of the ore formation, it is sometimes not safe, particularly near the surface. These facts make open workings a practical necessity at the start, and the great economy of breaking ore from high stopes with heavy charges of powder induces a continuation of the method, even when the rock covering has attained a thickness of many yards, and underground work would seem to be advisable. It is, indeed, hard to say what thickness of solid rock a Marquette mine-superintendent would hesitate to remove if it covered a large deposit of ore. Forty feet of earth and nearly as many of quartzite (as hard as granite) have been "stripped," and the thickness of rock is daily growing greater as the beds of ore are followed in depth.

It may be said, and I do not know but that it is a canon of mining, that all mines, which sooner or later have to be wrought underground, should be systematically opened as mines at the start, but this is not Marquette practice; and I have undertaken to describe, and, so far as I am justified, defend the methods there employed. It would be difficult to convince our people that, having a large deposit of pure ore before them of unknown form and size, covered often by but little earth, and backed by perhaps a small amount of money in the company's treasury, it is best to incur the delay and cost incident to sinking and drifting to open ground already opened by nature and ready to win. Wrought as open quarries, several of our mines have paid their way from the start, while, had they been opened on a regular system of mining, they would have required an investment of $50,000 in plant and improvements before shipments could have begun, and at least one year's time. Such facts settle such questions with American capitalists; and with the uncertainties which attend the opening of new mines in new districts, the high rate of interest in this country, and uncertainty of tariff legislation regarding iron, it may be a question whether this hand to mouth—quick return—let the future take care of itself—view of the question, is not in a certain degree defensible.

The appearance of our mines is anything but pleasing. They consist of several (sometimes of ten or more) irregular elongated pits, often very large and generally more or less connected, having usually an easterly and westerly trend imposed by the strike of the rocks. Everywhere are great piles of waste earth and rock, which are often in the way of the miner, and which in some instances have been handled over three times.

There are two principal advantages in open works. First, the preparatory work is all reduced to the simplest and safest kind of pick and shovel, hammer and drill, horse and cart business; such as can be let to the common run of mine contractors. On the other hand, underground mining involves sinking, drifting, timbering and elaborate machinery, all of which require skilled labor and large investments. In an isolated cold country like Marquette, the *quality* of the labor demanded is an important consideration. The second advantage, already mentioned, is the great economy in cost of drilling and explosives which high stopes in open works permit. These elements of cost are important items in all mining where hard ores are encountered. It is believed that they have been reduced to a minimum in the Marquette iron mines, where holes two inches in diameter are sometimes sunk 22 feet, and 15 feet is common. Such holes are not fired directly with the blasting charge, but are "shook" several times first, that is, fired with small charges which produce cracks and cavities about the bottom of the hole; when these are large enough to contain a sufficient amount of powder, the lifting charge is put in and the great mass thrown down. Twenty kegs of powder, of 25 pounds each, are sometimes fired at once, and from five to ten kegs is not an uncommon charge for a stope hole. By this method 5,000 tons of material have, in some instances, been removed at one blast, and one-third of that amount is quite common at some of the mines. In this way the entire cost for labor of drilling and explosives has been reduced, for a single blast, to less than three cents per ton. But the average cost is of course much greater, being at some of the mines 50 cents for all the drilling and powder consumed in the mine; about one-third of this is for block-holing the large masses thrown down by the stope holes, which are often so large that they have in turn to be broken by powder. The cost of powder and fuse for the hard ore mines, it is believed, does not exceed ten cents per ton. In some of the New York and New Jersey mines, which are worked underground, I am informed that these items cost much more. In the Persberg mines, Sweden, the drilling and explosives cost 65 cents per ton of ore in 1870.

It may be inferred, from the above description, that Marquette iron mining does not differ essentially from ordinary rock excavation on public works, being work that may be let by the cubic yard or ton. Until quite recently this has been very near the truth, the difference being in the skill and care required in separating the ore and rock which are often mixed together in the deposit. But these palmy days are rapidly passing for most of the mines now worked. An increase of water and greater cost of handling incident to increased depth, and, what is still more costly, the increase in thickness of the rock covering, will soon require, in fact does now (1870) really require, more expensive plants, different methods, and more skill.

The transition from the present system of quarrying to the future method of underground mining, which will have to be made in the Marquette region, will be a critical period, and will possess great interest, as affording a solution of a mining problem such as may not yet have been presented anywhere. Attempts at its solution have already been made, but, as has been remarked, very little ore has as yet been extracted at a profit by candle-light. To recapitulate, the system adopted will have to meet the case, 1st, of beds of ore varying, often abruptly, in thickness from 0 to 50 feet; 2d, of beds varying in dip from nearly vertical to horizontal, and passing by a curve of small radius from one inclination to another; 3d, of beds varying in character of hanging wall from a solid quartzite, which will stand with ordinary supports, to a soft schist, which can only be kept in place by a continuous support, or by actual filling in—"remblais." Again, the axes of the folds are not horizontal, but sometimes "pitch" at angles of 30 degs. or more in the direction of the strike, producing a fourth troublesome feature. See Map IX. Now, when we consider that the dressed ore is expected to yield 65 per cent. in the furnace, and is seldom worth on the average over $4 or $5 per gross ton on the cars at the mine, including royalty, the general character of the problem will be understood.

In New Jersey, with perfect regularity in the dip, better hanging walls, thickness within the limits of easy timbering, cheaper fuel and labor, and material which breaks easier than that of Lake Superior, the ores of several well-known mines, I am told, cost fully this amount.

Steam machinery for hoisting and pumping, which has cost from six to not less than fifty thousand dollars, has been erected at most of the Marquette mines, as shown by the table at the end of this chapter. In 1870, however, not much more than one-half of the entire ore product of the region was handled by steam, and much less than this proportion of all the material, the balance being done by horses, the use of which, however, is decreasing.

From these facts it may be inferred, that while the cost of breaking ore may have been reduced to a minimum by the system of mining employed, not so much can be said in favor of the methods of handling the ore from the miner's hands to the cars. The expensive horse and cart, swing derrick and whim, are in too general use, and the roads over which the loads are hauled are often not above criticism as to grades and surface. The causes which have led to this extensive use of horses are considered in another place.

The local staff of a Lake Superior Iron Mining Company usually consists of the *agent*, who is often secretary or treasurer of the company, and whose duty it is to take general charge of the company's business, except selling the ore, which is commonly done by a special agent in Cleveland, who may or may not be an officer of the company. This agent supervises the accounts, makes the payments, attends to shipping the ore and to ordering supplies, and often assists in selling ore. One man sometimes represents more than one company in this capacity. A majority of the agents reside in Marquette. The *superintendent*, who by custom has the title of captain, always resides at the mine, directs the work, and is in the main responsible for it. On him as much or more than on any other officer of the company does the success of its operations depend.

The offices of agent and superintendent are sometimes united in the same man. Large mines have a *chief clerk*, who is practically assistant superintendent. Next in order of rank are the foremen, master mechanics, and time-keepers. For names and addresses of agents, superintendents and managing officers, see Statistical Table, Plate XII. of Atlas.

The *organization* of the force of two large mines in the summer of 1870 is shown below. The first mine (I.) shipped the greatest amount of ore, and the second (II.) did most of its dead work in the winter, the aggregate shipments for the two, for that year, being 300,000 tons.

	I.		II.	
Contractors engaged in stripping, sinking, etc..	77		7	
Company account, men, laborers and mechanics on miscellaneous work....................	65		32	
Total employed in *dead work*............		142		39
Contractors breaking ore.....................	117		114	
Company account, men breaking ore..........			25	
Total at *mining* proper...................		117		139
Carpenters and wagon-makers................	6		6	
Blacksmiths and helpers......................	17		10	
Total mechanics employed in *repairing*....		23		16
Drivers and stable-men.......................	20		12	
Engineers and firemen........................	11		8	
Loading ore from stock-pile..................	18			
Total *handling* ore........................		49		20
Superintendent and clerks....................	3		3	
Foreman, blaster and watchman..............	6		7	
Total *staff* at mine.......................		9		10
Total force employed......................		340		224

This force was employed during the period of shipments, hence of greatest activity ; after the close of navigation, in November, it would probably be reduced 25 per cent. Less than one-half of the men employed have families, many single men going "outside" in the fall and returning in the spring.

One large mine, the best managed in the region, expended in 1872, 51,000 days' work all told, of which 48 per cent. was by contractors, and 52 per cent. by the day or on company's account : it produced about 2¼ tons of ore for each day's work.

The *wages* of the men employed in and about the mines, in 1869 and 1870, were about as follows : Common labor was nominally $1.80 per day for most of the time, but by far the largest part of the mining work was done under contracts. Contractors made, clear of costs, from $60 to $77 per month as high and low averages ; $70 is probably near the mean of the whole. It was not uncommon for a "pair" (two or more men working jointly) to make $100 per month each, and again the earnings will fall so low as barely to pay board ; but such are extreme cases. Leaving out the staff of the mine and the contractors, the wages of all others, mechanics, engineers, firemen, drivers, but mostly common laborers, averaged in 1869 and 1870 about $2.12 per man per day. Mechanics received from $2.50 to $4.00. In 1872 the wages of men and contract prices were from 25 to 50 per cent. above the figures here given.

The *nationality* at three mines, which employed an aggregate of over 600 men, was in 1870 as follows, expressed in percentages :

Irish	31
English (Cornishmen)	27
Swedes	18
Canadians (French)	5
Americans	5
Germans	4
Norwegians, Danes, and Scotch	10
	100

The relative proportion of the Irish element is decreasing ; a few years since nearly all the men employed at some mines being of this nationality. The percentage of Cornishmen is increasing, owing largely to a want of work in the copper region. These men are skilled miners, and do a large part of the sinking and drifting. Swedes are rapidly gaining in numbers, many of them having been miners in their own country.

The exodus of Swedes to the United States apparently threatens to depopulate that country. There can be little doubt but that a more genial climate and better food will improve the lower class, from whom the emigrants come. Statistics of the population of the Upper Peninsula are given in App. G, Vol. II.

The unit of measure and comparison in the following table is the *gross ton of merchantable ore.* The ore is the object of the miner's efforts, and the tons sold measure his business. The items of cost in all that follows express the expenditure per ton of ore mined, prepared for market, and loaded on the cars. In instituting a comparison between these figures and those obtained by the civil engineer on public works excavations, where the cubic yard of vacant space is the ordinary unit of work accomplished, it must be borne in mind that the labor incident to sledging up and sorting out the ore from the rock considerably enhances the cost of mining.

In order to more intelligently follow the methods of working the Marquette mines, we must classify the various items of cost under appropriate heads, and assume some absolute cost per gross ton, as near the actual fact as possible, as a basis of comparison of these items with each other, and with other mining regions.

No discussion of the question which leaves out the *cost*, would possess much practical interest; but all who have undertaken to obtain such facts for publication, know the difficulty, and will not place implicit reliance on the accuracy of what follows. $2.64 per gross ton will be assumed as the entire cost of mining the hard ore, and delivering it in the cars ready for shipment (in 1870); but this sum does not include interest on capital, expense of selling, royalty or mine rent, nor depreciation of the mining property. The cost of mining the soft hematite ores is considerably less, and the methods much simpler.

Royalties or mine rents have not become settled; there are not many leased mines; one of the best of its kind (the New York) pays but 20 cents per ton for first-class specular ore. In other instances 75 cents is paid for a lean hematite. Time and experience will settle these prices on an equitable basis. See Atlas, Tables XII., XIII.

Before dismissing the subject of royalty or mine rent, which is not again noticed in the following discussion, I will make a few remarks. Marquette mines, as has been stated, are generally owned and worked by the same parties, hence royalty does not enter directly as an item of cost, but it exists in substance, and may be called *depreciation of the mine*, an item in the cost of ore often not sufficiently considered. One of the best organized and successfully operated iron companies in eastern Pennsylvania place this item at fifty cents per ton of ore. That is to say, every ton of ore sent from a New Jersey mine (which they own) is charged with fifty cents over and above its cost, as shown by the mine accounts, and a like sum is credited to the capital stock account, or to a sinking fund. This fifty cents stands for the original cost of the ore in the ground, and is all the more real, that it was paid in advance in the price of property and improvements. Any mining company which fails to recognize this principle is doomed some day to serious disappointment. Whoever has had experience with charcoal blast furnaces, which so rapidly sink their capital by the consumption of timber, will be fully alive to the importance of this matter. It is a delusion to suppose that our mines will not eventually be *exhausted;* iron ores do not grow; a ton shipped from a mine is gone forever, and the property has one ton less remaining, and is therefore worth less money. Continued shipments will eventually exhaust any and all deposits. Abandoned pits, in which no ore can be found, now exist at all of our mines, and in this class are some that two years ago were the best. The Andover mine, New Jersey, once presented as good opportunity to break ore as any pit now worked in the Marquette region; but about 150,000 tons aggregate product exhausted the mine, and to-day the owners do not know where to find a ton of merchantable ore on the property. I do not wish to be understood as predicting the exhaustion of the whole region; I think Marquette will produce iron as long as that article is wanted. New deposits of rich ore will be found, and leaner ones, which now have no value, will be worked, and the old deposits will be followed deeper; but this implies new mines, the building up of new locations, new railroads, new men and more capital. What I wish to say is, that unless present holders of average Lake Superior iron mining stocks are receiving fair interest on their investments, and in addition are being paid back the capital they have invested at the rate of, say, 50 to 75 cents per ton of ore sold, they are not doing a good business.

Therefore the $2.64 assumed in the following table should be increased by this royalty, making it $3.14. Commission for selling, interest and exchange, insurance and expenses of the general office of the company (including salaries), will increase this sum to at least $3.50, which will more truly represent the actual cost per gross ton of ore on cars and sold. This, from the amount assumed before as selling price, leaves from 50 cents to $1.50 per ton for interest on all fixed capital invested; in an exceptional condition of the market, like 1872 and 1873, the margins are of course larger.

There may be no better place than in this connection, to speak of another fruitful source of the disappointments which are sometimes experienced by stockholders. I refer to those delusive "*permanent improvement accounts*," better named permanent disappointment accounts, which are too often kept open, and in which are too frequently placed awkward sums which should properly go to running expenses, and be paid for by the pig-iron, ore, lumber, or whatever is produced. After the necessary real estate is bought, the mining or manufacturing plant built, and the business of production actually commenced, the improvement account should be closed forever. Some kinds of business, in some places, under some managements, may permit an opposite course, but the above is the only safe rule. If in any particular year an extraordinary expenditure is made which is not likely to be repeated, a part of it may properly be held in some open account, in order that it may be distributed over more than one year's product. But this is a different thing from piling up a permanent account under the delusion that the property is enhancing in value.

There are few kinds of business in which there is more danger from this cause than in iron mining, for not only is an iron-ore property depreciating from the exhaustion of the ore, but at any time it may be still more depreciated by unfriendly tariff legislation, for which the iron-master must be prepared.

TABLE *showing the Approximate Cost of Mining the Specular and Magnetic Ores of Lake Superior, made in* 1870.

General heads under which cost of mining is classified.		Elements of cost, not including royalty or depreciation.	APPROXIMATE COST OF EACH ITEM. In per cent. of the whole. Items.	Totals.	Based on a total cost of $2.64 per ton. Items.	Totals.	Amounts. Labor.	Supplies.
I. Dead work (preparation).		1. Explorations	00.6	28.1	.015	.742	Eighty per cent. .620	Twenty per cent. .122
		2. Sinking shafts	01.5		.040			
		3. Drifts and tunnels.	06.1		.160			
		4. Roads...........	00.6		.017			
		5. Stripping earth and rock...........	13.2		.350			
		6. Miscellaneous work and minor improvements *	06.1		.160			
II. Mining proper (labor).	Drilling.	1. Ledge holes (in stope)..........	04.2	39.8	.110	1.050	1.050	....
		2. Block holes (in fragments)......	04.9		.130			
	Other work.	3. Sledging, sorting, and loading.....	13.3		.350			
		4. Handling rock....	09.5		.250			
		5. Miscellaneous work..........	07.9		.210			
III. Mining materials and implements ("mine costs").	Explosives.	1. Powder and fuse.	03.6	11.9	.095	.313	.103	.210
		2. Nitro-glycerine...	...†		...†			
	Tools.	3. Steel (drills)......	00.7		.018			
		4. Tools other than drills...........	01.6		.043			
	Repairs.	5. Blacksmiths' supplies...........	01.8		.047			
		6. Blacksmiths' labor.	04.2		.110			
IV. Handling ore from miners' hands to cars, and pumping.	By horses.	1. Teaming, labor of drivers and stablemen...........	05.7	15.6	.150	.413	.272	.141
		2. Forage..........	04.2		.110			
		3. Carts, sleds, harness, etc........	00.2		.006			
	By men.	4. Loading ore from stock pile.......	01.3		.035			
	By steam.	5. Labor, supplies, and repairs.....	04.2		.112			
V. Management and general expenses.		1. Salaries and office expenses.. 2. Tax of all kinds.	04.6	04.6	.122	.122	.062	.060
			100.0	100.0	2.64	2.64	2.107	0.533

* Does not include exceptional permanent improvements.

† No reliable figures obtained.

In order to institute a comparison between American open-excavation mining and the systematic underground work of Sweden, I append the following table, for which I am indebted to Prof. Richard Akerman, of Stockholm:—

COST OF MINING ORE IN PERSBERG MINES, SWEDEN, 1870.

In currency.

General heads under which cost of mining is classified.	Elements or items of cost, not including royalty or depreciation.	In percentage of whole.		Based on a total cost of $2.20 p. ton.	
		Items.	Totals.	Items.	Totals.
I. In the mine	1. Boring	22.73	38.66	.50	.85
	2. Powder	5.82		.13	
	3. Priming reed	0.84		.02	
	4. Clay	0.50		.01	
	5. Candles, augers, and sledges	2.33		.05	
	6. Charcoal	0.44		.01	
	7. Auger whetting	3.20		.07	
	8. Shooters' fees	2.80		.06	
II. Water drawing (or pumping)	1. Water drawing	3.50	3.50	.07	.07
III. Bringing up the mountain (hoisting rock and ore)	1. Putting into the ton	4.68	11.17	.10	.26
	2. Receiving	1.11		.03	
	3. Down freight	1.10		.03	
	4. Hoisting	2.74		.06	
	5. Oil and lines	0.28		.01	
	6. Mine tubs and ladders	1.26		.03	
IV. Dressing	1. Dressing	8.12	8.12	.18	.18
V. Picking and washing	1. Picking and washing	5.65	5.65	.12	.12
VI. Buildings	1. Buildings	16.45	16.45	.36	.36
VII. General expenses	1. General expenses	16.45	16.45	.36	.36
		100.00	100.00	2.20	2.20

Professor Akerman furnished also these explanations:—

a. Our drill holes are about one inch in diameter and cost 7½ to 12 cents currency, per foot, when boring downwards, and twice as much when boring upwards.

b. Powder costs 11½ cents, dynamite 43 cents, and ammonium powder 40½ cents per Swedish pound (the Swedish lb. equals .93 of the English).

c. The reason why blasting with us is more expensive than with you, must partly depend upon stronger mountain ground and partly upon the small diameter of our augers.

d. "Dressing" on the Persberg table is to be understood as sledging and sorting.

e. "Picking and washing" is a kind of after-sorting by hand of the smaller pieces (of which about a third of the ore consists), got partly by blasting and partly by the first sorting.

f. "Buildings" include timbering in the mines and all buildings made for pumping and hoisting.

g. "General expenses" include some benefits for the laborers, such as domiciles, potatoes, gardens, expenses for schools, medicine, administration, etc., etc.

h. "Down freight" is the cost for bringing down the ore a short distance from the mines to the lake-shore, where it is sold.

i. Water power is used at Persberg both for pumping and hoisting.

j. Our miners receive from 48 to 75 cents per day, besides what I above called benefits.

k. The mining costs at Persberg are among the highest in Sweden.

The titles of the several heads under which mining costs may be divided, and the number of the items, depend on the object sought: the classification employed in the Marquette table, seemed best adapted to the presentation of the facts in hand. It will be observed that the form of the Swedish table differs materially and is of course better adapted to underground work, and to a more careful and laborious selection of ore.

I believe that considerable advantage would accrue to many of the Marquette mines, if the accounts were so kept that cost sheets similar to the foregoing could be prepared from time to time. It is well known that the cost of mining varies greatly in the different mines, some costing twice as much as others. This difference is often largely owing to natural causes, but sometimes it is, in part at least, in the management. There is no better way, in fact there is no other way, of stopping "leaks" of this sort, than by first finding where they are.

A comparison of such cost sheets from different mines, for the same time, or from the same mine for different periods, would indicate at once to which items the excessive cost belongs, and thereby direct the attention of the management to the leak. I therefore venture the opinion, that a carefully prepared cost sheet is one of the first steps in attempting to reduce the cost of ore.

In the detailed description of methods which follows, the items will be taken up in the order of the table.*

I. Dead Work.

This general head embraces all the work and costs incident to getting ready to mine the ore, and is subdivided into—1. Explorations (embracing only such searches for ore as are in progress from year to year about the mine). 2. Sinking shafts. 3. Drifts and tunnels. 4. Roads for wagons. 5. Stripping earth and rock, or uncovering the ore. 6. Miscellaneous work and minor improvements. The entire expenditure for dead work is 74 cents per ton of ore produced, which equals 28 per cent. of the whole cost.

1. **Explorations.**—More or less digging of test-pits, sinking shafts, drifting, trenching, and sinking drill holes is constantly in progress at most of the mines. My facts indicate that this work varies in amount from one-half to three cents per ton at the producing mines, being of course greatest at the new locations. It is not carried on systematically, being pushed when there is an increased demand for ore, or some old pit shows signs of failing, and again entirely discontinued. The price paid for pits 4 feet by 6 feet, and not over 10 feet deep, is from 30 to 60 cents per foot, depending on the ground; when so deep as to require a windlass, 50 to 75 cents and up to $1.25, if the shaft reach the depth of 30 feet and is wet. Drifting in firm earth will cost about the same per foot, depending

* For detailed descriptions of all the mine workings as they were at the close of the season of 1872, see "Appendix to A. P. Swineford's History of the Lake Superior Iron Region," being a review of its mines and furnaces for 1872, published by the Marquette Mining Journal.

on the depth below the surface and nature of the earth. Drill holes sunk by hand, material 15 feet deep, will cost from 75 cents to $1.00, and if deeper, considerably more per foot. There seems to be no reason why more use should not be made of the drill in this work. By means of a simple spring pole, such as was used in early days in the oil region, holes could be easily sunk 100 feet, which is as deep as it is usually necessary to go at this time. An experienced miner will judge very accurately of the ground passed through by the mud, and if there was any doubt, chemical analysis would determine the nature of the material; the mud furnishing a strictly average specimen, so desirable in an analysis for practical purposes. As has been mentioned, the *annular diamond drill* was introduced last season (in 1869) at the Lake Superior mine with success. A hole 130 feet deep was sunk at a cost of about $5 per foot; the core produced furnished very satisfactory knowledge of the substance passed through. The drill did not perform as well at the Washington mine, where several holes were sunk, the deepest 96 feet. In two instances the annular diamond bit got fast in an oblique seam and two were lost; not counting loss of diamonds, the work cost about $1.50 per foot: whether larger bits, a different setting of the diamonds, or more experience would overcome this difficulty, I do not know. It is a matter of great importance, and is worth thoroughly working out. As the subject of exploration for ore has been fully considered in another chapter, it is not necessary to treat it farther here.

2. **Sinking Shafts.**—This work, which forms so large an item of cost in some underground mines, varies in the Marquette Region, so far as I have ascertained, from 1½ to 5½ cents per ton of ore. Our open and comparatively shallow workings do not call for many shafts or winzes; the deepest shaft in the region is now (1870) not over 200 feet. The prices for this work range from a mean of $22.50 to $31.50 per foot in depth, depending on the hardness of the ground. In some mines, extreme prices range from $15.00 to $40.00, and even more if the shaft be very wet. Miners are often permitted to select the size most advantageous to themselves, which may be four feet by six; but eight by twelve feet is more common. The material is generally hoisted with the ordinary hand windlass, but sometimes with a horse-whip or whim, the miner having to deliver the stuff at the mouth of the shaft. From 10 to 15 per cent. of the

price received by the miner for sinking has to be expended in *mine costs; i.e.*, powder, fuse, candles, steel, tools, etc. No charge is made against him for smith's work. Sometimes the contract is let at so much per foot of shaft and so much per ton of ore, which gives the miner an interest in separating ore from rock.

3. **Drifting and Tunnelling.**—This element of cost varied more widely than any other, and might have been divided into two: (1) Drifts designed to open ground for stoping; and (2) Tunnels or adits for drainage and transportation of ore, the latter being of the nature of a permanent improvement. But on the principle that permanent improvement accounts are often permanent disappointment accounts, and to be avoided, and considering the fact that this kind of work is actually going on year by year, and must do so as long as the mine is worked, it does not seem wise to separate it from the current cost of getting ore. Ordinary 4 × 7 drifts cost, in hard ore, from an average of $22.50 to $24.50 per foot, the miners delivering the material behind them, and paying their own costs, as in the case of shafts.

Tunnels large enough to admit railroad cars and small locomotives cost from $30.00 to $50.00 per foot. The Washington tunnel, now over 1,100 feet long, and timbered a considerable part of the way, cost an average of about $40.00, not including rails. The timbered portion is twelve feet wide at the bottom, ten feet at the top, and ten feet high in the clear. No machinery has yet been brought to bear on either sinking shafts or drifting; the labor required is more than one-half expended in drilling holes for blasting. The subject of drilling is fully considered under its proper head.

4. **Making Wagon-Roads.**—The great amount of team-work employed about the mines requires a complete system of roads for summer and winter use. These are sometimes expensive on account of rock-cuts, costing, in some instances, as high as four cents per ton of ore in the early stages of work.

5. **Stripping Earth and Rock,** or uncovering the ore. This constitutes on the average nearly one-half of the dead-work, and is one of the largest single items in the whole cost of mining. So far as my inquiries extended I found it to vary from 20 to 52 cents per ton of ore. This cost is necessarily increasing at all of the mines worked as open cuts. It is simple rock and earth-work, the material being removed on wagons, carts, or sleds, drawn by horses.

The advantages of light railroads and small locomotives do not seem to have commended themselves for this work. There would, of course, be considerable danger of destroying tracks from blasting, and it often happens that not much work has to be done in one place; still there is no doubt but that a large saving would be effected by substituting steam for horses in portions of this work, as will be more fully considered hereafter.

The aggregate amount of material which has been handled in stripping is very great. Thirty and even forty feet of earth have been removed, and nearly as great a depth of rock; but this is the experience in open workings everywhere. I have seen twenty-one feet of earth and soft, shaly rock stripped from a nearly horizontal bed of 44 per cent. Clinton ore in Western New York, which did not average over thirty inches thick. In South-eastern Kentucky I found the rule among the miners of sub-carboniferous ores to be, that it would pay to remove a foot of earth for the sake of an inch of ore, which does not differ widely from the Western New York practice. In both of these instances the stripping was nearly the entire cost of mining, and labor was much lower than in the Marquette region. The usual contract price for removing ordinary earth (sand, clay, and boulders mixed together) is fifty cents per cubic yard, the digging costing about one-half, and the hauling one-half. Hauls vary from 100 to 800 feet. The highest price paid for excavating any considerable quantity of rock in open cuts, which has come to my notice, was $3.00 per cubic yard, equal to $24.00 per fathom, or about $1.00 per ton. This was a very hard jasper rock, containing but little ore. Large quantities of rock have been excavated and hauled over 500 feet at the Lake Superior mine for $2.50 per yard. The soft greenish schist, so common at all the mines, can be moved for from $1.00 to $1.40 per yard, including hauling. When a good face can be obtained on the overlying quartzite, which is likely to constitute the greater part of the rock to be moved in future, it should be broken down and loaded on wagons for from $1.50 to $2.00 per cubic yard.

The amount of money which it will pay to expend in stripping of course depends chiefly on the quantity of ore uncovered. If we assume fifty cents to be the maximum expenditure per ton of ore for this work (this amount has been greatly exceeded), the problem of what thickness of rock may be stripped admits of an easy theoretical solution. One cubic yard of solid ore (allowing for wastage on account of associated rock) may be considered to yield three tons of merchantable ore, which, at the allowance above assumed, would give us $1.50 to be expended per square yard in stripping a bed of ore only one yard thick. Hence in this case it would pay to remove nine feet in thickness of earth, or about three feet in thickness of rock. But suppose we have a bed of ore twenty-four feet in vertical thickness, which is a more common case, what amount of earth or rock would it pay to remove under the assumed limit of expenditure? Twenty-four feet of ore will yield twenty-four tons per square yard of surface, which, at fifty cents per ton, gives $12.00 available for stripping per square yard. This sum would remove twenty-four feet thickness of solid rock; or a foot in thickness of rock may be stripped for every foot in thickness of ore uncovered, at a cost of fifty cents per ton of ore. The same expenditure will remove three times this thickness of earth.

An important and often neglected question connected with this subject is, *where to deposit waste*, that it may be out of the way of future mining operations. Some material has been already handled twice in the Marquette region, and I know of a mine in Southern New York where the same earth was three times handled before it was finally permitted to rest. In a new region, like Marquette, where comparatively little thorough exploring has been done, it is often difficult to decide where waste piles will be out of the way for all future time. If a drill hole were put down for fifty feet in rock, and no ore found, it would be safe to say, that if ore existed under that spot, it would have to be mined under ground; hence, that so far as future stripping was concerned, a waste pile placed there would be out of the way. A very common practice in under-ground work, in some mining regions, is *to fill up the worked-out places with the waste*, and this can undoubtedly be done to advantage in some instances in open works, although it has not as yet been practised in the Marquette region. The trouble is to find out when a pit is exhausted—it is so common to break through a thin layer of rock and find a bed of workable ore behind it. But there are parts of most mines where the foot-wall has unquestionably been reached, and if any doubt exists, a few deep drill-holes will settle the point. When this is the case, and the foot-wall has a sufficiently gentle slope to permit of its holding materials deposited on it, it will, I think, be often found advantageous to use it to support a waste pile.

For the sake of illustration, take the New York and Cleveland Mine workings, which are adjacent. In this instance the slope of the foot-wall is so steep that it would probably be necessary to cut in it a rude step on which to rest a rough retaining wall, which could be built of blocks of quartzite swung across from the hanging-wall by means of a derrick. The triangular space thus formed would hold all the waste rock for a long time to come, and would afford a minimum haul. It might not answer to deposit earth in such positions, as heavy rains would be likely to wash it into the pits. The dip of the foot-wall in this, as well as in most cases, will, I think, become flatter in depth, so that a better opportunity will be afforded for a second similar waste receptacle at greater depth, if one should be required.

6. **Miscellaneous Dead Work.**—Under this head are included several items which were not of sufficient importance to require separate treatment. Improvements such as dwellings, shops, fences, tracks, trestle-works, pockets, docks, whims, skip-ways, pumping-fixtures, etc., etc., occurring from year to year, are embraced here. These items are in part embraced under "Building" in the Swedish table. This head was originally also designed to cover those exceptional expensive improvements which are of occasional occurrence only, and the cost of which might properly be distributed over several years' product. Additional facts, however, lead me to believe that the amount given (16 cents per ton) is too small. The expensive pumping and winding plants now being erected, and which will continue to be built for a long time to come, increase the cost of the ore materially unless we charge them to permanent improvement accounts, which is not altogether a safe course, as has been already pointed out.

II. Mining Proper, or Breaking Ore.

This general head embraces all the labor incident to blasting the materials down from the solid ledge, breaking it up into fragments that may be easily handled, the separation of the ore from the rock by hand and loading. The average cost of this is $1.05 per ton of ore produced, which equals forty per cent.

of the whole. The character of this work will be sufficiently well understood from the table and the following explanation:—

1. **Ledge or Stope Holes.**—The drilling or rock-boring is now (1870) entirely done by hand. The steel used for drills is 1¼ inch octagon, with a bit 2 inches, making a hole nearly 2¼ inches in diameter. Drills vary in length up to 24 feet. English steel is used at some mines, but a majority use American steel, and the most experienced men who have employed both, inform me that the drill steel made by Hussey & Wells and Parke Bros., Pittsburgh, answers as well as the best imported steel, and much better than the average. The drill is turned by one man sitting and struck by two standing, with eight-pound hammers, at the rate of about thirty-six blows per minute each. In this way from nine to eleven feet of hole are sunk per day, the men working usually on contract. The price of stope holes ranges from 60 to 80 cents per foot in depth, the mean being not far from 75 cents; no mine costs have to be paid out of this price. When there is a large proportion of block holes, which admit of the use of smaller steel, the whole drilling of a pit is often let at from 60 to 65 cents. Very deep holes, say from fifteen to twenty-two feet, are sometimes sunk with still larger bits, which about doubles the cost. In these cases two men are required to turn the drill and three to strike.

The cost of drilling ledge-holes per ton of ore, varies from a mere trifle in the case where one twenty-two foot hole throws down 4,000 tons, as has been done, to a very large item on low stopes with perhaps tight, hard ground. From 3 cents to 25 cents per ton may be regarded as extreme averages, although 35 and even 48 cents have been reached, for short periods, under very unfavorable circumstances. The price given in the table (11 cents) approximates to the average for hard ores; this number divided into 75 cents, the average cost of drilling per foot, gives, say 7, which should represent the number of tons of ore broken per foot of stope-hole drilled. The data obtained directly under this head confirm this amount, which is also equivalent to about two cubic yards per foot of hole.

The depth of stope-holes varies from two to twenty-two feet, the short ones being employed in "taking up bottom," that is, in squaring the stope so as to give the best chance for the deep holes. The average of 1,500 holes of all kinds in one part of the

Washington mine was four feet nine inches, but the stopes which furnished this result were below average height. It is believed that nine or ten feet would be nearer the average for deep holes, and say three and a half feet for the short ones.

2. **Block-Holes.**—The masses of rock and ore loosened by the heavy blasts already described, are often so large that they have in turn to be broken with explosives, which operation is termed block-holing. The amount of this work varies from almost nothing in some pits and in certain mines, to four-fifths of all the drilling required in others, the maximum being reached on high stopes of hard, tough ore. Over two hundred block-holes have been employed to one stope-hole in the Cleveland Mine, one hole being required to every two to four tons of ore. Block-holes sometimes produce fragments so large as to require block-holing in turn, before they are made small enough to be mastered by the sledge. These holes vary in depth from eight to twenty-four inches, the mean ranging near one foot. With nitro-glycerine the holes need not be so deep as for powder. One inch octagon steel is often used in this work, making a hole nearly 1½ inches in diameter. The drilling is performed as in the case of stope-holes, but usually only one man strikes.

In the same ground, the same drill-gang will sink more than twice the number of feet of block-hole in a day with small steel, than of stope-hole with large steel,—ranging from twenty-four to twenty-seven feet. In open mines of strictly hard ore, this work costs more than stope-holes, and is set down in the table at 13 cents per ton. This amount added to the 11 cents given as the cost of stope-holes per ton, equals 24 cents for the total cost of the labor of *drilling* required under breaking ore :—this would also equal about 70 cents per cubic yard, which would pay for one foot of two-inch drill-hole. But this is by no means the whole ; the work of sinking and drifting, which is set down as aggregating 20 cents, is more than half drilling ; and a part of the cost of rock-stripping is also for this work. I estimate that 40 *cents per ton of ore* is not far from the actual price paid for this kind of labor in the hard-ore mines, equal to fifteen per cent. of the whole cost. On this estimate, not less than $300,000 were paid out for drilling in 1870. This work, from the favorable circumstances under which much of it is done in open excavations, no scaffolding being required, is by far the most purely mechanical labor performed about the mines. While the absolute cost of this item of drilling is very large, and can undoubtedly be reduced by the use of the *power-drill*, it is, as compared with some other mines and regions, small. Our open cuts or quarries afford far better facilities for blasting than under-ground mines. In one Southern New York mine the drilling cost, in 1870, $1.25 per ton of ore, or forty per cent. of the whole cost of mining; in a large magnetic mine in New Jersey, it cost from 60 to 80 cents per ton of ore. In the Persberg mines, Sweden, when the ore cost, in 1870, $2.20 currency per ton, the drilling was 40 cents per ton, equal to twenty-three per cent. of the whole cost, being considerably more than ours, absolutely and relatively. When we consider that the average of wages in Sweden is not far from 65 cents per day, or say one-fourth of what is paid Lake Superior miners, it would seem as if Sweden would be a good field for a power-drill.

The facts relating to drilling have been given in much detail in the hope that inventors and owners of rock-drilling machines may become acquainted with the wants of the Marquette region in this regard. I have had my attention called to several of these machines, but have not had opportunity to make such investigation of their respective merits as would justify an opinion. I have no hesitation in saying that a machine which would do the work required at a less cost than it is now done (75 cents per foot) would find ready sale, and every facility would be afforded for experiments.

I need not here remark that a power-drill, adapted to Marquette iron mines, must be portable, as it would have to be shifted every few hours; and I should say that two men, or at most three, should be able to handle it on a ragged rock surface. Again, it must be capable of being set up anywhere, to accomplish which, I think that movable tripod, telescopic legs, like those with which engineers' instruments are often supplied, would be convenient.*

3. **Sledging, Sorting, and Loading.**—In considering this item, it must be borne in mind that the ore and rock have not only to be broken so that they can be removed, but must be made so fine as to

* Since the above was written the Burleigh Drill has been tried at several mines with varied success. My facts are quite insufficient to enable me to form a judgment as to its fitness to do the required work, or to know whether it has had a fair trial.

be easily separated, and so that the pieces can be fed into a Blake crusher. This work requires more muscle and as much skill and care as any other done at the mine. Eighteen to twenty-three pound sledges are employed, and the difference in results, between the experienced miner who strikes the lump of ore the right blow in the right place, with this immense hand hammer, and the tyro, is very great. Contracts for sledging and loading, which sometimes include a little block-holing and short tramming, have been let at prices varying from 20 to 50 cents per ton. The loading usually costs not to exceed 10 or 12 cents, the balance being chiefly sledging. There is a wide difference in the texture of ore, some kinds requiring five times as much sledging as others. On the whole, Marquette ores break with much greater difficulty than those of the Eastern magnetic mines. With poorer ground worked and the market more in favor of buyers (which makes them more exacting on quality), the cost of this element will be increased.

Drops, similar to those used at foundries to break old castings, have been employed to break very hard lumps of ore, but the expense of getting the lumps of ore to them has caused this plan to be abandoned. In the copper region powerful steam hammers have been used for a similar purpose, but the same objection as that given above would apply to their introduction at the iron mines. It must be borne in mind that a lump of iron-ore is not worth more than about one-hundredth part as much as a lump of copper of the same weight, and therefore will not bear as much handling.

A steam miner who can walk up to the lump of ore and sledge it to pieces where it lies is what is wanted. Nitro-glycerine or duallin breaks the material finer, producing by its explosion more of a smashing effect than powder, and thereby requiring less sledging. There is no doubt, as is elsewhere stated, about the advantage of employing these new explosives in block-holing.

4. **Handling Rock.**—In addition to the rock which overlies the ore, considered under stripping, at most of the mines more or less rock is found mixed with the ore through the mines, which has to be removed during the process of mining. The proportion varies from none up to one-half of the whole, and often for short periods more than this; the average at this time is believed to be twenty per cent. The 25 cents placed against this item in the table is intended

to cover the cost of sorting out and handling this rock under average circumstances. This cost will be increased as poorer grades of stuff are worked.

5. **Miscellaneous Work.**—The 21 cents opposite this item in the table is no more than sufficient to pay for foremen, repairs of tracks and roads, wheeling, tramming, blaster, sometimes hand-pumping, and such securing of the workings as may be necessary, etc.

III. Mining Materials and Implements, embracing "Mine Costs."

This general head is subdivided in the table into Explosives, Tools, and Repairs, which are in turn itemized, as will appear below. The expense incurred here is 31⅓ cents per ton of ore produced, equal to about twelve per cent. of the whole cost.

1, 2. **Explosives.**—Powder and fuse and nitro-glycerine. The present (1870) is an unfortunate time to collect statistics regarding the cost of explosives, for the reason that nitro-glycerine is to a certain extent on trial, and most of the mines employ both it and powder in the same pits, making it difficult to separate the results. The place of the new explosive cannot be said to be wholly fixed in our mines. It is more powerful than powder, bulk for bulk, or weight for weight; can be used in wet as well or better than in dry ground, which is very important in some places; it has so far proved no more dangerous than powder, and its fumes have not been found objectionable. As has been stated, the fragments resulting from its use are usually smaller, hence require less sledging, and, it being more powerful than powder, less drilling is needed.

In the case of wet holes intended for sand-blasting, nitro-glycerine can often be used in small charges to produce cracks which carry off the water and thus prepare the way for the powder. Overhanging loose rock can often be advantageously brought down by a flat cartridge of glycerine.

In short holes, 3 to 6 feet, glycerine will sometimes break two or three times as much ground as powder, thus making the saving on the drilling more than balance the extra cost of the explosive.

The quantity of glycerine used per hole, of course, varies with its depth and other circumstances, and is at the Washington and Republic Mines, according to Captain Peter Pascoe, as follows :—

Depth of hole.	Glycerine.
3 feet	¾ lbs.
4 "	1½ "
5 "	2¼ "
6 "	3½ "
8 "	5 "
10 "	7 "
12 "	10 "
14 "	14 "
16 "	18 "
18 "	21 "
20 "	24 "

There can be no doubt but that the use of this explosive hastens work. Sinking and drifting can be more speedily done with it than without.

Whether it is suited to breaking the great masses from the solid ledge remains to be seen. Certainly it cannot be used to fill the cracks produced by shaking, where heavy sand blasts are required; and it is doubtful whether drill-holes large enough to contain the requisite amount of the blasting oil can be profitably employed; two or more holes could be used, but this would greatly increase the cost of drilling. It certainly costs *more* per ton of ore mined than powder, but how far this greater cost is balanced by other advantages experience must determine. It is significant that in 1870, being the next year after its introduction, over $40,000 worth was sold in the Marquette region at $1.50 per pound. In 1872 about 40,000 pounds were used, the price being $1.25 per pound. The Painsville Ohio Co. erected (1871) a factory near Negaunee. Duallin and giant powder have recently been introduced.

The figures given in the table, and in what follows, refer exclusively to powder, the nitro-glycerine element having been eliminated as far as was possible. Fuse costs about ½ cent per ton, leaving 9 cents per ton for powder, which, according to the data obtained, varied from 7 to 10 cents. The price of powder ranged from $3.75 to $4.50 per keg of 25 pounds. Therefore an average of 45 tons of ore should have been broken with one keg of powder, or about ½ pound of powder to one ton of ore. This, it must be remembered, does not express the actual work of the powder, on account of the amount of rock moved in addition to the ore—in one instance 23,000 weighed tons of material required 320 kegs of powder, or 72 tons per keg. In another instance 31 kegs threw down 3,500 tons (approximate) of quartzite, or 113 tons per keg. One mine, which produced over 100,000 tons of ore in 1869, consumed for all purposes one keg of powder to every 43 tons of ore produced. The waste material in this case did not amount to over 20 per cent., hence about 52 tons, or, say, 18 cubic yards of material, were moved per keg of powder. The consumption of explosives per ton of ore must increase as the mines grow deeper, either by the greater amount required to remove the rock covering, or by the less favorable opportunity afforded for blasting, if the ore be won underground.

In one group of New Jersey mines, the powder and fuse in 1870 cost 18 cents per ton; in another mine in Southern New York, 14½ cents; in Sweden, at the Persberg mines, 15 cents. All of which figures considerably exceed those reached in Marquette, which is proof of the economy in explosives from working iron mines as open quarries as long as possible.

3. **Steel.**—The use of steel drills has already been described, and reference made to the brands in use. My data, which are far from complete, under this head, indicate that the cost of steel per ton of ore ranges from ¾ to $3\frac{3}{10}$ cents, averaging perhaps $1\frac{8}{10}$ cents; the price of steel being 20 cents per pound. This would give about 11 tons of ore, or about 3 cubic yards per pound of steel consumed, which is less than the data obtained direct on this point seemed to indicate.

It is the practice of some mines to charge the ore contractors 2 per cent. on their contracts for wear of steel, which agrees nearly with the above. At other mines the steel is weighed at the end of each month, and the contractor charged with the shortage, whatever it be.

4. **Tools, other than Drills.**—Cost about $4\frac{3}{10}$ cents per ton of ore.

The Ames No. 2 D-handled, square, and round-pointed, strap-backed, solid steel shovel is the favorite.

Washoe picks, Nos. 5 and 6, and Powell, same numbers, both

railroad (25 inches long), and pole (19 inches long) are extensively used. Certain mines make their own picks after a fashion of their own.

Solid steel crow-bars, both single and double-pointed, are used.

Solid cast-steel sledges, both American and chrome, weighing from 16 to 18 pounds, and often 25 lbs., are extensively used.

Solid cast-steel striking-hammers, 8 to 9 pounds, and in some instances 11 pounds, are employed.

5. **Blacksmiths' Supplies.**—This item is largely made up of coal and iron, steel being embraced under another head. Charcoal was formerly used exclusively for working steel; but mineral coal is now employed with good results at most mines. The table shows this item to be a trifle less than five cents per ton of ore.

6. **Blacksmiths' Labor.**—This is largely sharpening drills. The number dulled per day by a gang of three drillers will average about 75, in hard ore. One blacksmith and helper will sharpen about 275 drills per day of ten hours. The 11 cents marked opposite this item embraces all the blacksmiths' work done in and about the mine, for whatever purpose. Therefore strictly, it should have been divided, part going to dead work.

IV. Handling Ore from Miners' Hands to Cars, and Pumping.

Pumping, which has heretofore been a small item in the Marquette region, cannot well be separated from hoisting ore, as the same machinery does both. This item, in the case of some New Jersey magnetic mines, costs 75 cents per ton of ore: at the Persberg mines, Sweden, it costs but 7 cents. The entire cost under this head, in the Marquette region, including hoisting and pumping, is 41 cents per ton of ore produced, which equals 15½ per cent. of the whole. This work is done in part by horses, part by men, and part by steam.

1, 2, 3. **The Work of Horses in Handling Ore.**—The team work employed at the Marquette mines, apart from the stripping, amounts, according to my inquiries, which have been quite full on this point, to 10 per cent. of the whole cost of mining, or say 27 cents per ton of ore, the drivers' wages being the largest item. This cost is obtained by dividing the total expenditure for teaming, by the total number of tons of ore produced. If it was figured only on the ore actually handled by the horses, it would be much greater. If to this were added the cost of the team-work employed in stripping, the total would not be less than 30 cents per ton of ore, or, say $250,000 on the product of 1870, a sum sufficient in itself to supply all the mines in the region with all the additional steam-hoisting and pumping machinery and small locomotives required to do the work now done by horses, and at a very much less yearly cost. We may verify this almost incredible estimate in another way. The total number of horses employed at all the mines in 1870, including hired teams, was about 364, or an average of 30 to each mine, varying from 9 to 74. The best data I can get indicate that to work a lot of horses for one year, including wages of drivers, stable-men, smiths' work, forage, repairs of vehicles, and depreciation, in the years 1869 and 1870, cost an average of $650 per horse. The wages of hired teams, including drivers, for the same period, was $6 per day. At this rate, 364 horses would have cost nearly $240,000, a sum sufficiently near the other to confirm the general truth of the estimate.

These figures surely justify the prediction, that if there ever comes a period when our mines do not pay, it may be due largely to horses. In this age of steam, has a business any just right to prosper which employs horses to do work that can be more cheaply done by machinery? The average number of tons of ore handled per horse employed in and about the mines for all work in 1870 was 2,350, ranging from 1,150 to 5,300 tons. In considering these facts it must be borne in mind that the mines in question are not by any means without steam power. Twelve engines, varying in power from say 10 to 50 horse, were at work. To prove that this item of cost is unusually large in the Marquette region, I will give a few facts regarding the employment of live stock at mines, which have come under my notice elsewhere. While the cases cited do not present all circumstances like the Marquette mines, they are sufficiently near to afford interesting comparisons.

The Cornwall Ore Bank Co., Penn., shipped from their one immense deposit, in 1870, over 174,000 tons, employing no horses in the work. The ore was all handled by one locomotive, the cars being loaded by wheelbarrows. No pumping is required in this mine, and the facilities for reaching the ore with cars are unusually good. The ore is quite soft, so that the blasting does not endanger the tracks.

The Iron mountain mine, Missouri, shipped in 1870 more ore than any one mine in the Marquette region. It employed during the winter 68, and during the summer a somewhat less number of horses, mules, and oxen. One animal moved about twelve tons per day, or 3,600 tons per year; but more than three-fourths of this stock was employed in getting "surface ore," a feature which does not exist in Marquette mining. The bluff (quarried) ore moved per horse employed was more than five times the above amount. No steam-engine or locomotive was in use at the mine.

At the Caledonia and Keene mines, St. Lawrence County, New York, in 1869, three horses handled 27,500 tons of ore and waste, the average haul being over 700 feet, all up grade, in places steep. This gives over 9,000 tons per head; steam was not employed for handling material at either mine.

The Sterling mine, Orange County, New York, shipped in 1869 40,000 tons of ore, which was handled under circumstances quite similar to those encountered in the Marquette region, by two horses and one small stationary engine, which gives 20,000 tons per animal employed. The system of tramways and sidings at this mine is very complete.

Passing from American to Swedish mines, which are far deeper, and in which there is a larger percentage of rock mixed with ore, we find that in the Persberg mines, in 1870 (see table), the total cost for handling ore and water drawing was 14^2 per cent. of the whole cost, or 33 cents per ton of ore; and this amount included the handling of all the rock and other waste material which in our table is embraced under *Dead-work*. If we take out of dead-work 10 cents for handling this waste and add it to the amount found above, we have 51 cents as total cost of handling Lake Superior ores, equal to twenty per cent. of the whole cost, or about fifty per cent. greater than in the Swedish mines, but there water was exclusively used.

It is not difficult to understand how *horses** have come to play so important a part at our mines.

---

* It should be noted that oxen have been in use for some time at the Lake Superior mine, but, so far as I am informed, at no other.

The first operation in opening a new mine is, usually, to strip off the earth and rock covering, which can be best accomplished with the horse and cart. On the ore face thus exposed, mining is begun, the ore being hauled to the cars (often not brought very near to the pit), and such rock as is mixed with the ore is sorted out and hauled in another direction. It is very convenient and economical to back a cart directly to the miners' hands, and this was done until it came to be regarded as *the way* to get out ore. There was certainly no better way at the start in many cases; but when horses come to be used on hauls of over 500 feet and up grades, in places as steep as 1 in 10, the operation costing 25 to 30 cents per ton, it may be worth while to ask if such ore had not better be left in the ground until machinery propelled by steam can be brought to bear on it. Another cause which conspired to prolong this expensive mode, was the great demand for ore during the war and the consequent high prices. Mine superintendents were given no time to plan nor make improvements looking to future economy. Mine owners did not then want surveys, nor machinery, nor tunnels, nor anything that had reference to the future; they only wanted ore, nor did they care much what it cost, nor what the quality was (so consumers say): it was ore, ore, ore! Wherever three men could be set at work, a cart was backed up to them and shipments began from a new pit.

On short hauls, smooth roads, and light grades, horses can be used to advantage, and will continue to be so used, especially where there is more or less uncertainty as to the quantity of ore in the pit worked, which is often the case. But where there is a large mass of ore, rock, or earth to be moved under any other circumstances, it will usually pay to bring steam-power to bear upon it. Portable, or easily-to-be-moved railroads, and small locomotives for long hauls are in much favor at this time, and would have the advantage of utilizing existing wagon-roads. But the first step in many cases is undoubtedly to lay horse railways on the present roads. As is shown above in the remarks on the use of horses in certain New York iron mines, one animal can move from ten to twenty thousand tons on such roads in one year. If the horses at our Marquette mines can be made to perform one third this amount of work, the present cost of hauling will be reduced fifty per cent.

Portable hoisting-engines are extensively used in New Jersey and

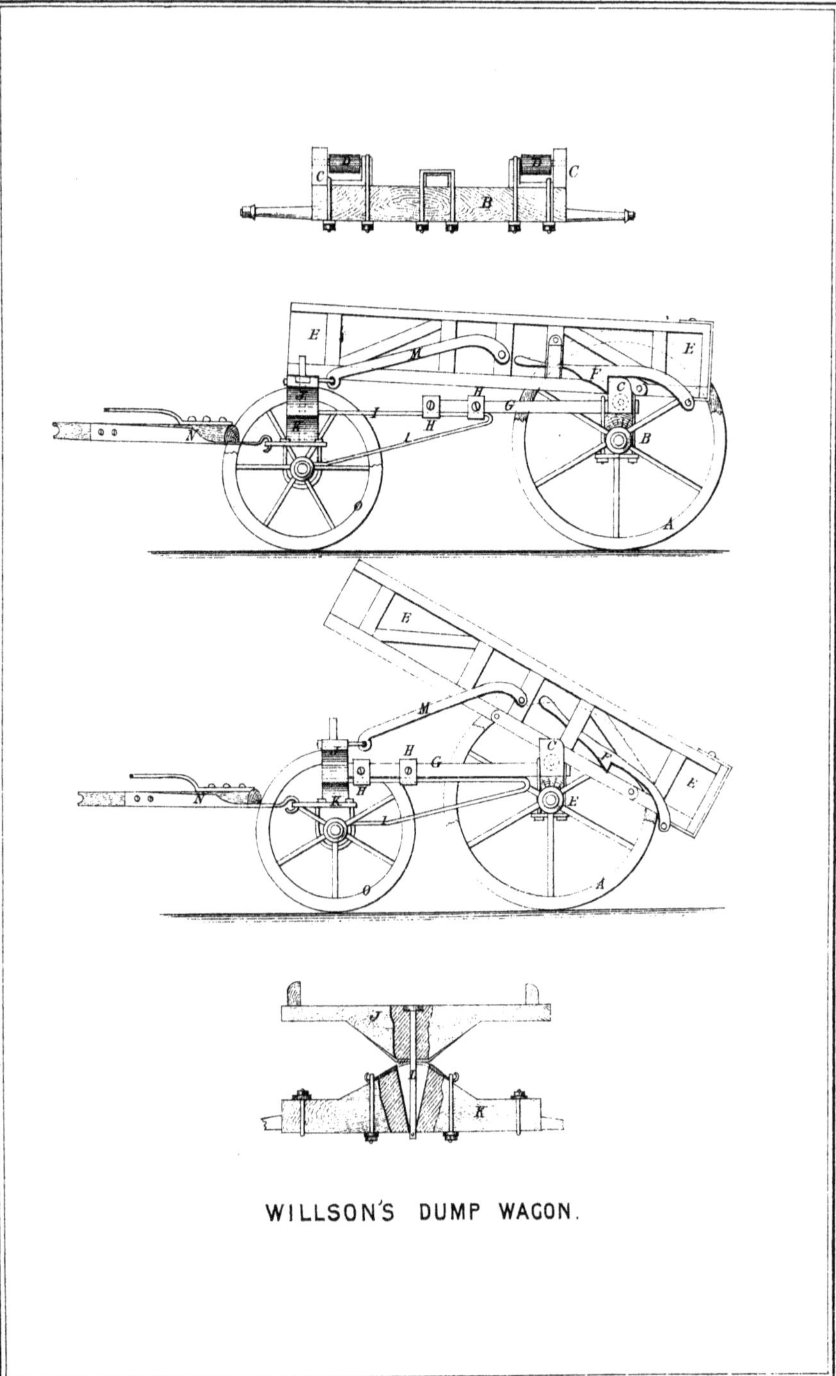

WILLSON'S DUMP WAGON.

Pennsylvania; they can be set up quickly just where wanted, and handle material rapidly and with great economy. A thorough system of under-ground communications which would bring all or most of the material to the main hoisting-shaft is always to be aimed at, as in this way the dead lift may be made by steam. At present, owing to the continued pressure for ore, it is not uncommon to see ore and rock carted up-hill, over abominable roads, from pits which in a few months, perhaps, will or could be reached by drifts along which the ore could be cheaply trammed to a steam hoisting-shaft.

As may be supposed, this extensive use of draught animals has led to great perfection in the carts, wagons, and sleds. A dump-sled for winter use, contrived by Captain Merry, of the Jackson mine, is a perfect vehicle of its kind. I am unable to give drawings of but one, known as Daniel Willson's Patent Dump Wagon, of which over 50 are in use in the region. See Plate XVII.

While harnessed to the cart or wagon is the favorite mode of using the horse, it is by no means the only way. Some pits in the course of mining became too deep for cart roads; these were in many instances worked by *swing derricks*, horses being the power employed; the long booms of these derricks made it possible to drop the bucket in different parts of a wide pit. This method is, however, very expensive, as the following figures will show. The total lift from bottom of pit to bottom of cart was in one case 79 feet; the cost being as follows:—

2 men filling	$4 00
1 man to land	2 00
2 derrick horses and driver	5 25
	$11 25

This sum paid for hoisting 45 tons in 10 hours, is equal to 25 cents per ton. In one case, where the hoist was 55 feet, the cost was 16 cents per ton.

In another case, with the ordinary two-bucket horse-whim, the cost of hoisting 65 feet, and landing, was 6 cents per ton; this did not include filling the buckets. In another case the ore was hoisted 40 feet, and landed for 5 cents per ton, not including the filling. Estimating the filling at 10 cents, these facts show that it costs in the cases cited an average of 1 cent to lift one ton of ore 7 feet, including the landing or dumping, which employs one man.

Without attempting to fully solve the important problem of the best mode of handling the material at Marquette mines, for that is beyond the scope of this report, I would suggest the following general policy as being safe for the mines to pursue :—

Let all large pits now worked, where a considerable amount of horse labor is required, be suspended until some form of steam machinery can be brought to bear on them. There are, of course, exceptions to this rule : for instance, where the other costs are unusually light, more money may be expended in handling the ore, as is often the case with the soft hematites ; but the principle is, I think, correct. It would not be difficult to find many instances of this kind ; for example, a given pit is worked, the ore being moved by horses, at a profit say of 50 cents per ton, which if left for one year could be reached by some tunnel or other improvement which would permit the same ore to be taken out at a profit of $1.00 per ton ; it would certainly pay to wait in such instances. In these cases it will usually be found that the superintendent has been persuaded into promising that his mine can be made to produce a certain amount of ore which may have been already sold, his attention being thereby fixed on a large product, rather than cheap mining. This subject will be considered more fully below. I will here only ask, if it is not better policy for a mine to net say $50,000 on 50,000 tons of ore, than to make the same sum on 100,000 tons. If the mines were inexhaustible it might not make much difference, but as it is, it may make all the difference there is between a profitable business and an unprofitable one in the end. It must be borne in mind, that while the ore business has been on the whole profitable, there are large mines that have been producing ore for years that have never returned a dollar to their stockholders.

Among the mining appliances which have been brought to great perfection in the Marquette region, are the various forms of pockets and shoots for transferring the ore, first, from the mine cars, buckets, and carts to the railroad cars, and second, from these to the vessel.

The magnificent ore docks at Marquette, Escanaba, and L'Anse belong to the latter class, and are undoubtedly the best of the kind

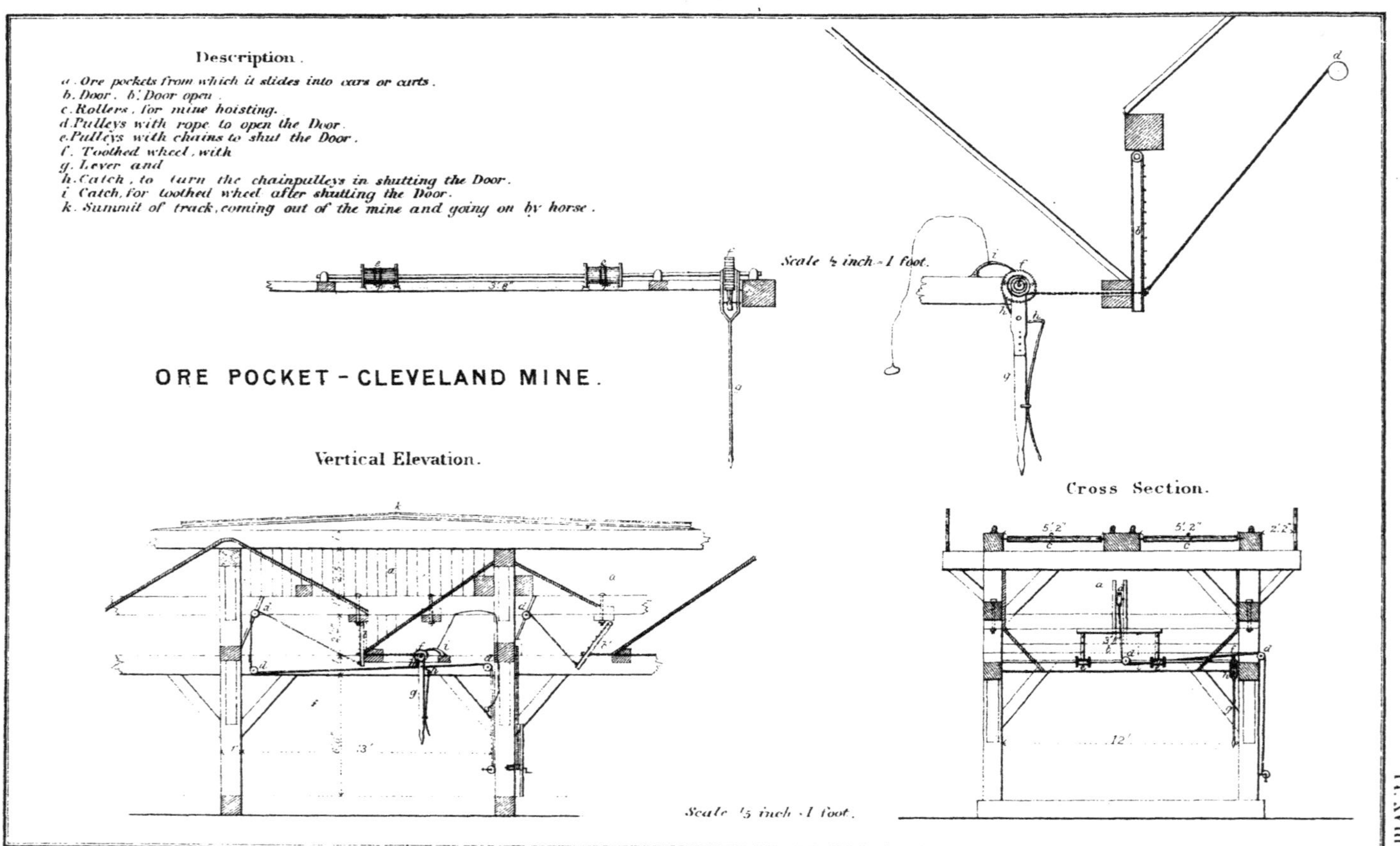
Description.
a. Ore pockets from which it slides into cars or carts.
b. Door. b'. Door open.
c. Rollers, for mine hoisting.
d. Pulleys with rope to open the Door.
e. Pulleys with chains to shut the Door.
f. Toothed wheel, with
g. Lever and
h. Catch, to turn the chainpulleys in shutting the Door.
i. Catch, for toothed wheel after shutting the Door.
k. Summit of track, coming out of the mine and going on by horse.
ORE POCKET - CLEVELAND MINE.
Vertical Elevation.
Cross Section.
Scale ½ inch = 1 foot.
Scale ⅕ inch = 1 foot.
3' 8"
5' 2"
2' 2"
3' 2"
12'
13'

in the United States if not in the world. They are described and illustrated in Chapter I., and in Appendix F. of Vol. II.

Of the first class there are numerous varieties, from the simple log crib built up alongside and above the track, into which the ore is dumped from elevated railways, and from the sloping bottom of which it is "shot" through holes closed by rods into cars at a cost of not over 3½ cents per ton, to the more expensive and perfect contrivance employed at the Cleveland mine, which is shown in Plate XVIII.

The mine car in this case passes over the centre of the pocket, which dumps its ore in turn into a car or cart below, by an ingeniously arranged door which is shown on an enlarged scale.

4. **Loading Ore from Stock Pile.**—During the winter no shipments are made from the mines, hence the product has to be piled up. It is the policy of some mines, and I think it is the best, to do most of their dead work in the winter, hence to stock but little ore; others maintain nearly the same rate of production in proportion to the force employed, winter and summer. Stocked ore has to be loaded in cars by hand, which is always contract work and costs from 9 to 12 cents per ton, the mean being, say 11 cents, including all costs connected with it. This amount, distributed over the whole product for the year, was found to average for the cases inquired into, $3\frac{5}{10}$ cents per ton.

5. **Machinery for Pumping and Hoisting.**—Notwithstanding the great cost of the work of horses, a large amount of machinery, as has already been remarked, is now in use, as the following statements will prove :—

The introduction of machinery has so far seemed to make but little relative diminution in the number of horses employed, because of the greater amount of waste material which has to be moved in the later years. The amount given in the table, opposite this item, $11\frac{2}{10}$ cents, is designed to be an approximation to the cost of running the machinery of such mines as have plants distributed over the entire product of those mines. I estimate that less than one-half of the product of such mines was handled by machinery in 1870. The actual cost of moving the ore so handled, including the *pumping*, varied from 14 to 21 cents, the mean, as shown by my data, being about 18 cents. This cost is made up of wages of engineers and firemen, say fifteen per cent.; fillers, landers, and surface tramming, sixty per cent.; fuel, repairs of machinery and supplies, say twenty-five per cent. This covers the cost from miners' hands to cars or stock pile.

While this sum is materially less than the cost of the same work by horses, it is much greater than in the Copper region of Lake Superior, where this work is brought to great perfection. Some of the appliances employed in the Copper region cannot be used at iron mines on account of the greater irregularity of the deposits. But time will introduce many economies which will reduce this item below the figures given. It must be borne in mind, in comparing the cost of steam machinery with horses, that in the case of the engines all the pumping is included, while the horses handle only the ore and rock. Making this correction, it is safe to say that it costs at least four times as much to handle the same material by horses as by machinery.

The following description of recently erected plants will give a good idea of the machinery now in use at the iron mines, it being essentially such as is employed at the copper mines.

The *Macomber mine machinery* consists of one steam-engine with cylinder 18 × 24 inches, with bed cast solid in one piece. Valve is of the kind known as the H valve, and is worked by link motion; steam pipe 4 inches in diameter; exhaust pipe 6 inches in diameter; engine supplied with the Judson governor. Pump for feeding boiler is worked from cross-head; also an auxiliary for fire protection, etc. Main shaft is 5 inches in diameter, of hammered iron, and 16 feet long. One boiler 48 inch shell, 26 feet long, with two 18-inch flues. Smoke-stack is 40 feet high and 24 inches in diameter. The winding drums are 4 feet in diameter, and of sufficient capacity to contain 525 feet of 1¼ inch wire rope. They are worked by a friction movement, thrown in and out of gear by means of eccentrics with lever attachments. The brakes are known as band-brakes, which clamp the entire surface of the drum, 5 inches in width, and are of sufficient power to hold a loaded skip at any point in case of accident. They are worked by levers with hand or foot, as may be desired. The drums make about 13½ revolutions per minute, the engine making 80, which gives the skip a speed of a trifle less than 3 feet per second. The skips are of heavy boiler iron, each having four 12-inch wheels. The capacity of each is 35 cubic feet, equal to about 2½ tons of ore. The pump is 10 inches in diameter by 6 feet stroke, capable of discharging 660 gallons of

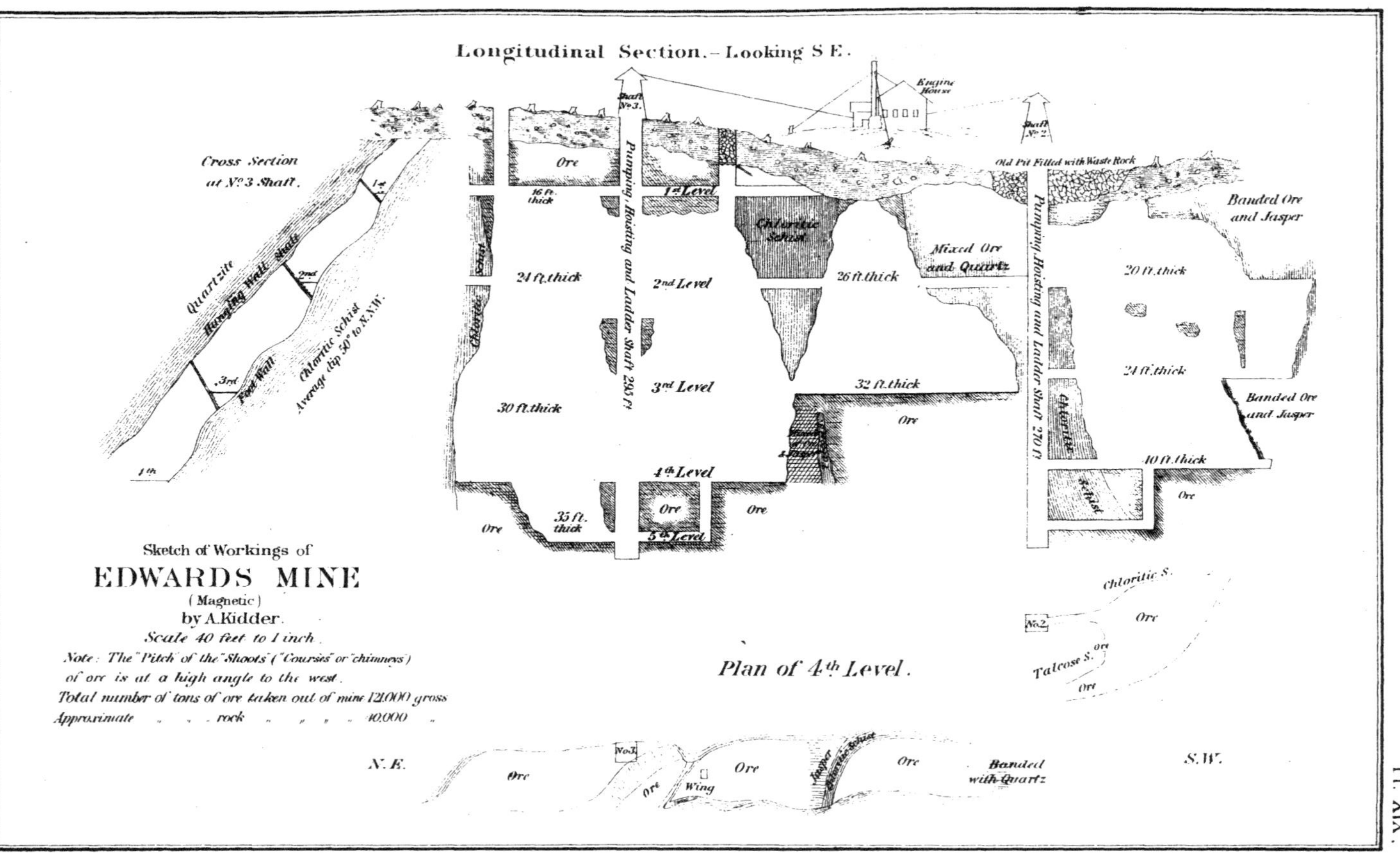

Longitudinal Section.—Looking S E.
Shaft No. 3.
Engine House
Shaft No. 2.
Old Pit Filled with Waste Rock
Cross Section at No. 3 Shaft.
Quartzite
Hanging Wall Shaft
Foot Wall
Chloritic Schist
Average dip 50° to N.N.W.
1st
2nd
3rd
4th
Ore
16 ft. thick
1st Level
Pumping, Hoisting and Ladder Shaft 295 ft
Chloritic Schist
Mixed Ore and Quartz
Pumping, Hoisting and Ladder Shaft 270 ft
Banded Ore and Jasper
Schist
24 ft. thick
2nd Level
26 ft. thick
20 ft. thick
Chloritic
3rd Level
32 ft. thick
30 ft. thick
24 ft. thick
Banded Ore and Jasper
Ore
Chloritic
4th Level
10 ft. thick
Schist
Ore
Ore
Ore
35 ft. thick
5th Level
Ore
Sketch of Workings of
EDWARDS MINE
(Magnetic)
by A. Kidder.
Scale 40 feet to 1 inch.
Note: The "Pitch" of the "Shoots" ("Coursės" or "chimneys") of ore is at a high angle to the west.
Total number of tons of ore taken out of mine 121,000 gross
Approximate " " rock " " " 40,000 "
Plan of 4th Level.
Chloritic S.
No. 2
Ore
Talcose S.
Ore
Ore
N. E.
No. 3
Ore
Ore
Wing
Ore
Jasper
Chloritic Schist
Ore
Banded with Quartz
S. W.

water per minute. It is worked from a slotted crank arm, on end of main drum shaft, which admits of lengthening or shortening the stroke at pleasure. The pump is double acting, with single valve on a new plan. It is furnished with rods, travellers, connections, balance bobs, etc. This machinery was furnished complete in all its parts, and set up at the mine in working order for pumping and hoisting by the Iron Bay Foundry, Marquette, Mich., 1872.

The *Barnum mine plant* consists of one horizontal high pressure steam-engine of 20 inches diameter of cylinder and 30 inches stroke; steam furnished by two tubular boilers, each 48 inches in diameter and 14 feet long, and each containing 50 tubes, three inches in diameter. Maximum power of this engine is 120 horse, but is working at present at one-third its capacity. There are two winding drums, each 5 feet in diameter; speed of engine about 60 revolutions per minute, and of drums about 12. Drums are attached to main shaft by cone-gears, which are operated by steam cylinders and levers; screw-levers control the brakes and drums during the descent of the skip.

Engine is connected to the drum-shaft by spur-gearing in the proportion of one to five; speed of skip in shaft, about 3 feet per second; load of ore, 5,000 pounds; weight of skip, which is self-dumping, is 2,400 pounds, making the total load 7,400 pounds. Actual power employed, about 47 horse; engine also draws water with a 6-inch Cornish pump. Total weight of this machinery about 42 tons, and total cost about $10,000. Built at the Michigan Iron Foundry, Detroit, in 1869.

The foregoing described plants, together with those given in the subjoined tabular statement (pages 280 and 281), embrace over three-fourths of all the machinery employed in hoisting and pumping in the entire region.

V. Management and General Expenses.

This covers only such expenses as are incurred in the mining region, and not salaries of officers above the superintendent, nor the cost of selling the ore.

1, 2.—**Salaries, Office Expenses, and Taxes.**—This element of cost constitutes less than 5 per cent. of the whole cost of the ore,

DESCRIPTION OF STATIONARY ENGINES, WITH THEIR

NAME OF MINE.	Number or name of Pit or Shaft.	Size of Cylinder, Length and Diameter.	No. of Cylinders.	Number, size, and kind of Boiler.	Average working-pressure.	Nominal horse-power.	Kind of work, as pumping, hoisting, etc.	Height to which ore is lifted in feet.	Average number of tons hoisted in 24 hours.
Jackson	Pit No. 4.	13″x 30″, one 40 horse, Root's pat'nt trunk engine	2	Steam supplied for this double and single engine from two of Root's patent boilers, 50 horse-power each, connected together.	70 lbs.	140	Hoisting.	125 feet.	120
	Pit No. 6.	13″x 30″, one 40 horse Root's pat'nt trunk engine	1	do. do. do.	70 lbs.	40	Hoisting and pumping.	From 80 ft. to 125 ft.	200
	Pit No. 7.	8″x 12″	2	One boiler, 42″ diameter x 12 feet long, tubular, 40–3 in. flues.	70 lbs.	20	Hoisting and pumping.	50 feet.	50
	Pit No. 5.	5″ x 8″	2	Tubular boiler, 40 in. diam. x 13 ft. long, 40–3 in. tubes.	70 lbs.	8	Hoisting.	50 feet.	40 tons of ore, rock and water.
	Machine shop.	8 x 16 inches.	1	Tubular boiler, 60 in. diam. x 25 ft. long, 121–2 in. tubes.			Running machinery in shop.		
Champion	4 shafts now worked by main engine. 2 new shafts now being sunk.	One horizontal engine, 14 inches bore, 20 in. stroke of piston.	1	Two return flue boilers, 42 inches diam., 28 ft. long, 2 flues in each, 16 inches diameter. One locomotive boiler, 28 inches diam. of shell, 26 x 30 in. fire-box, 36–2 in. flues, at 1st level of No. 3 shaft.	65 lbs. to the sq. in.	60 on hoisting drums	One 6-inch plunge pump. One No. 7 Earle pump, at 3d level of No. 3 shaft; elevating water to surface; supplied with steam from boiler at 1st level.	180 feet.	400 from 4 shafts.
Edwards.	Nos. 2 & 3.	24 x 36 inches.	1	Two. 5 ft. diam., 27 ft. long, with return flues each.	70 lbs.	150	Pumping and hoisting.	300 feet.	200
Lake Angeline.......	2 Pits.	16 x 24 inches.	1	One. 42 in. shell, 20 ft. long, with 2–14 in. flues.	60 lbs.	60	Pumping and hoisting.	75 feet.	150
Washington.	At No. 7 opening, known as No. 1 & 2, skip roads.	16 x 24 inches.	1	One boiler, 2 flues, 24 ft. 6 in. length, 44 in. diameter.	90 lbs.	50	Hoisting.	No. 1 skip, 130 feet. No. 2 skip, 55 feet.	44 / 35
Lake Superior..	Main shaft.	20 x 30 inches.	1	Two boilers, 3 flues, 43 x 6 feet.	60 lbs.		Hoisting and pumping.	160 feet.	350
	Hematite.	12 x 20 inches.	1	One boiler, 2 flues, 3½ x 24 feet.	65 lbs.		Hoisting and pumping.	130 feet.	100
	Portable engine & boiler—"Sect. 16."	10 x 18 inches.	1	One boiler, flue.	30 lbs.		Hoisting and pumping.	60 feet.	
	Sect. 21.	10 x 12 inches.	1	One boiler, upright flue.	35 lbs.		Hoisting.	60 feet.	

WORK, AT SIX MARQUETTE MINES, JANUARY, 1873.

Kind of Skip and its load.	Diameter of Barrel-pump in inches.	Kind of Pumps.	Revolutions of Engines per minute.	Hours per day that Pump is worked.	Shaft.		Kind and quantity of fuel used in 24 hours.	REMARKS.
					Vertical.	Inclined.		
Two 5 ft. drums, with 4 wheel, self-dumping. Skip-car 2½ tons.			75			2	One cord of wood per day; don't run at night.	There are also two (2) 12-horse power locomotives, which are used for distributing cars in the tunnels during the shipping season.
Two 3 ft. drums, one hoisting skip-car 2½ tons, 4 hoisting patent dump buckets 1 ton each.	8	Cornish jack-head.	100	10	1	1		
Inside dump-car 3 tons.	8	Cornish jack-head.	100	12		1	One cord of wood per day; don't run at night.	Also four (4) steam pumps, which are used in various parts of the mine, viz.: 1 No. 9 Earle steam pump; 1 No. 8 Knowles steam pump; 1 No. G Cameron steam pump; 1 Worthington duplex pump; also one 8 (eight) inch double-acting bucket pump.
Bucket 1 ton.			100	10	1		¾ cord per day.	
			80				One cord per day.	
Wrought-iron skips, 42 inches long, 30 in width and depth. Hold 3,000 lbs. of ore.	6	Plunge-pump, 6 in. diameter of cylinder and 6 in. column, elevating the water to the surface 180 feet.	20	22		incl'd	Mixed wood, four cords in 24 hours.	Makers—Hodge & Christie, Detroit, Mich. This one engine does all the work of this mine.
Cornish skip 1½ tons.	Two 6 in. One 7 in. One 8 in.	Two 6-in. draw-lifts from 5th to 4th levels, at Nos. 2 and 3 shafts. One 8-in. draw-lift, at No. 2 shaft, from 5th level to 2d. One 7-inch plunger-pole, from 4th level at No. 3 shaft, taking also No. 2 water to surface.	30	20		incl'd	Wood, six cords.	Makers—Hodge & Christie, Detroit. See plan of mine—Plate XIX.
Cornish skip 1½ tons.		One 10-inch double-acting pump.	30	10		incl'd	Wood, 2½ cords. Coal, ¾ ton.	Maker—D. H. Merritt, Marquette.
Iron self-dumper about 1 ton.		Earle. Nos. 4, 6, and 7.	see catalogue.	3	vert'l		Coal, hard & soft wood; about 1,500 lbs. coal in 24 h.; 4 cords wood in do.	Furnishing steam for Burleigh Drill Compressor, 3 Earle pumps (2 No. 4 & 1 No. 7), besides to hoisting engi's.
Iron skip 3 tons.	10	Plunger.	about 30	10		incl'd	Six cords wood.	Makers—Wash'n Iron Works, N'burgh, N. Y.
Iron car 3 tons.	8	Bucket plunger.	about 60	14		incl'd	Three cords wood.	
Iron skip 2 tons,	6	Bucket plunger.	about 40	10		incl'd	Three cords wood.	
Iron skip 2 tons.			about 80			incl'd	Three cords wood.	

amounting to about 12 cents per ton. I am happy to note here a much better showing than in the Persberg mines, Sweden, where this item, in 1870, cost 16½ per cent. of the whole, or 36 cents per ton of ore; nearly three times its cost with us. I presume the excess of this item in Sweden may be largely due to heavier taxes, and smaller production.

CHAPTER X.

CHEMICAL COMPOSITION OF ORES.—ANALYSES.

THIS chapter contains the results of over one hundred and fifty analyses, more or less complete, of iron ores from the Upper Peninsula of Michigan, mostly from the Marquette region, together with five analyses of pig-iron produced from these ores ; and several analyses of ores from other parts of the U. S., which are largely used with Lake Superior ores as mixtures. In order to bring out the variations in quality of the ores, and to obtain *reliable practical averages*, seldom less than two and in one instance eight samples were analyzed from the same mine.

By far the largest portion of the samples, the analyses of which appear in this Report, were selected by myself with a view to obtaining a fair and *safe average* of the ore sampled, one that would be borne out and confirmed by practically working the same ore in the furnace. I am well aware, from extended observation and practical experience, that a large majority of the published analyses of iron ores, not only have no practical value, but are positively detrimental to the best interests of the iron trade, representing as they so often do the ores to be richer in iron than they actually are, simply because the samples analyzed were not honestly or skilfully collected. Even the most skilful and conscientious men, if they err at all in collecting a sample from a new iron location, are almost sure to err on the side of finding too much, rather than too little iron. The chemist is often wrongly blamed for these false results. My experience with many analysts leads me to believe that they are, as a rule, thoroughly honest and painstaking men, who return correct results for the *samples sent them ;* the trouble is with the samplers. This point receives further consideration under Explorations, Chapter VII.

In earnestly endeavoring to avoid this rock on which so many mining engineers and geologists have wrecked their reputations, I may in some instances have gone to the opposite extreme and collected samples which were below the average richness—at least I am quite persuaded that I shall be charged with this—hence venture this explanation in advance of the charge. If such mistakes are found, I can only say myself and not the analysts are to blame, and I stand ready to make such corrections as lie in my power.

My *method of sampling* is as follows:—1st. To obtain an average of a producing mine; I found that the immense stock piles accumulated at Cleveland, Ohio, at the end of the shipping season, afforded excellent opportunities for sampling. The stock piles at the mines or a large number of loaded cars were often resorted to, and in many instances it was thought best to go into the mine and take the samples from the solid ledge or the loose ore as it was being taken out. In either case an ordinary shot bag, holding 4 *or* 5 *pounds of ore, was filled with small fragments, varying from the size of a pea to that of a walnut, of all kinds of ore, from all parts of the pile, together with the rock, if any, which was found mixed with the ore.* Some of these fragments were picked up and some were broken from larger pieces; the dust and mud over the ore made it often impossible to distinguish whether the pieces taken were ore or rock. These samples were all pulverized and thoroughly mixed, and from this the specimens were taken for the chemist, the same being forwarded by mail in small numbered tin tubes; and in each instance a pound or more of the pulverized ore was retained for future reference. The reserved portions are now in my safe in Marquette, from which samples will be furnished to any who may desire. 2d. To obtain an average sample from a new locality or from exploration pits is more difficult and unsatisfactory. This subject is fully treated under Explorations, Chapter VII.

With all this care my results varied, in extreme cases, from 10 per cent. below to 5 per cent. above the true average, but the common variation was not more than three per cent. Two or three of the extreme results, known to be wrong, are omitted from the tables. The name of the sampler is in every case given when known, and the circumstances of its collection are briefly stated in the notes. The samples collected by E. R. Taylor, of Cleveland, were, at my request, taken in accordance with the rules above given.

The surname of the chemists and date at which analysis was

made, as near as could be ascertained, are given under the result in every instance except one. The number of analyses made, with names in full and address of these gentlemen, are as follows:—

	No. Made.
Professor Oscar D. Allen, New Haven, Conn....	17
Professor Geo. J. Brush, New Haven, Conn.....	1
J. Blodgett Britton, Philadelphia, Pa............	56
A. A. Blair, St. Louis, Mo....................	2
Dr. C. F. Chandler, School of Mines, N. Y......	8
Dr. C. F. Chandler and F. A. Cairns, School of Mines, N. Y............................	12
Chandler and Schweitzer.......................	1
F. H. Emmerton, Chicago, Ill..................	1
F. B. Jenney, Marquette, Mich..................	8
Prof. Geo. W. Maynard, New York.............	5
Maynard and Wendel.........................	3
Ed. R. Taylor, Cleveland, Ohio................	14
Dr. A. Wendel, Troy, N. Y....................	20
Dr. Otto Wuth, Pittsburgh, Pa.................	30
Samuel Peters................................	1
T. G. Wormley................................	4

The metallic iron was usually determined by but one chemist, as the chances of difference on this element are small. Phosphorus determinations are more difficult, and considerable differences in the amount of this element found in the same sample by different chemists, will be observed. For this reason duplicates were often sent to two and sometimes to three; the results being given as returned by them. If any one supposes the differences to be due to errors in samples, which is improbable, I will gladly furnish duplicates for re-examination. The specific gravities of powder were mostly determined by Mr. Jenney, and not by the chemists over whose names they are sometimes placed.

The subjoined table contains an approximate general summary of the results, exhibiting the average composition of the four classes of ore now produced by the following mines:—

I. *Red Specular Ores.* Barnum, Cleveland, Jackson, Lake Superior, New York, Republic, and Kloman.

II. *Black Magnetic and Slate Ores.* Champion, Edwards, Michigan, Spurr, and Washington.

III. *Soft Hematites.* Foster, Lake Superior, Lake Angeline, Taylor, Macomber, New England, Shenango, S. C. Smith, and Winthrop.

IV. *Flag Ore.* Cascade.

Table No. XIII. of Atlas contains a somewhat similar summary so far as metallic iron and phosphorus are concerned. More facts are incorporated in this table, which has slightly changed the averages.

	I.	II.	III.	IV.
Protoxide of Iron		19.639		
Sesqui- or Peroxide of Iron	90.52	67.761	75.75	70.98
Oxide of Manganese	Trace.	0.13	0.80	Trace.
Alumina	1.39	2.13	1.536	2.01
Lime	0.70	0.68	0.36	0.45
Magnesia	0.42	0.69	0.294	0.20
Sulphur	0.05	0.132	0.110	0.03
Phosphoric Acid	0.258	0.199	0.185	0.13
Silicic Acid, Silica, or Insoluble Silicious Matter	5.892	7.828	14.035	25.12
Water, Combined			3.94	
" Uncombined			1.18	
" Total	0.77	0.811		1.08
Volatile Matter			1.81	
	100.000	100.000	100.000	100.00
Metallic Iron	62.915	62.930	52.649	49.332
Phosphorus	0.111	0.085	0.078	0.053
Sulphur	0.05	0.132	0.110	0.03
Metallic Manganese	Trace.	0.091	0.56	Trace.
Specific Gravity	4.74	4.59	3.88	4.09

A glance at this table shows us that, except the soft hematite III., which contains about 5 per cent. of water, all the ores are essentially and chiefly composed of oxide of iron and silica or insoluble silicious matter. The other elements, viz., oxide of manganese, alumina, lime, magnesia, sulphur, phosphoric acid, and water amount in the aggregate to only about 5 per cent. in the I., II., and IV. classes. So constant is this ratio that a valuable determination of iron in a hard ore, and one sufficiently accurate for practical purposes, can be made by ascertaining the percentage of insoluble silicious matter, adding 5 to it and subtracting the sum from 100. The result is the iron oxide, which, multiplied by .70 for red, and .72 for black oxides, gives the metallic iron.

Regarding the percentage of metallic iron, consumers of Lake

Superior ores will at once note that their furnace books very often show a higher yield than 62.9 per cent., which is given in the table as the average percentage for first-class ores. This may not have been the case in exceptional years, like 1872, when the consumption so crowded the production that mines had not the time nor skilled labor to make such selection as they usually make. But that furnaces running on first-class ores usually make a better yield than that given, is shown by "Table of Metallurgical Qualities of certain Lake Superior Ores by Consumers," Plate No. XIII. of Atlas, where various consumers credited these ores, in 1870, with an average of *over sixty-four per cent. of iron*, as shown by their furnace-books. This discrepancy is easily accounted for; the chemist's result is in *pure metallic iron*, the furnace man's is in *pig iron*, which contains several per cent. of carbon and silicon, and other substances,—see subjoined analyses. Therefore the chemist should always find *less* iron than is shown by the furnace accounts if he has an *average* sample of the ore. Just what this difference is depends on the grade of iron made, on the waste in the slag, and other things: good authorities have placed it at 2½ per cent.

Passing to a more detailed examination of the facts recorded in the table, we find, in descending order,—oxide of *manganese* has a maximum of nearly one per cent. in the hematite, and is nothing in the specular and flag ores. If the hematite was subdivided into manganiferous and non-manganiferous varieties, as suggested under Lithology, Chapter III., then one variety would contain only a minute quantity of manganese, while the other would reach an average of, say 3 per cent. of the oxide. The presence of manganese adds to the value of an ore, especially for making steel. *Alumina* reaches a maximum of over 2 per cent. in the magnetite ores, and is least in the specular ores. The earthy character of the hematites would lead one to expect more of this element in that class. *Lime* and *magnesia* aggregate a trifle over one per cent. in the high grade ore, and less than this amount in those of low grade. *Sulphur* is relatively most abundant in the magnetites; but, so far as I know, the minute quantity found has never been objected to by consumers of the ore. The quantity of *phosphoric acid* and phosphorus is of such moment in connection with the wants of the Bessemer steel manufacture, now rapidly developing in the West, that this subject will receive especial attention hereafter.

The distribution and relations of the *silicious matter* have been mentioned ;—it has its maximum in the flag ores where it reaches one-fourth of the whole weight, and is least in the rich speculars, which contain only about 6 per cent. on the average.

The total *water* in the hard ores is only about 1 per cent. In the soft hematites it rises to an average of over 5 per cent., and, as will be seen in the subjoined analyses, increases in a few instances to about twice this amount, the greater part of which is combined with the limonite, which largely makes up the soft ore. An appreciable amount of *volatile* matter, supposed to be mostly carbonaceous, occurs only in the hematite ores. The specific gravities given will be observed to have a very significant relation to the amount of iron, which subject is considered fully in Chapter III.

Phosphorus in Lake Superior Ores.

Pig-iron intended for the use of *steel* makers must be remarkably free from phosphorus, *one-tenth of one per cent.*, according to some authorities, being the maximum amount allowable for many purposes. As it has been found impossible, up to this time, to eliminate this element from the metal either in the blast furnace or in any of the various processes for making steel, it is indispensable, in steel manufacture, that we start with an ore comparatively free from it; and for the best bar iron, only a very small amount of phosphorus is admissible,—its effect being to produce cold shortness.

It is a safe practical maxim of iron metallurgy that all the phosphorus contained in the coal, limestone, and ore charged into a blast furnace will be found in the resulting pig-iron, and that the conversion of such pig-iron into steel will increase the phosphorus just in the ratio in which the metal is wasted in the process. It is therefore very evident, if say one-tenth of one per cent. only is admissible in steel, not only our ores but fuel and flux must be very free from phosphorus at the start. In considering the facts regarding this element here given, it must be constantly borne in mind that a rich ore may contain more phosphorus than a lean ore, and yet produce a pig-iron containing less phosphorus than the other, because *less of the rich ore is required* to make a ton of iron.

To illustrate: an ore yielding $66\frac{2}{3}$ per cent. in the furnace, and containing .06 of phosphorus, will produce a pig containing .09 of phosphorus; while an ore containing but 50 per cent. of iron and .05 of phosphorus will produce a pig containing .10 of phosphorus; therefore the amount of iron in the ore must be always considered in comparing the amounts of phosphorus. Applying this rule to the facts given in the foregoing table, we shall find that the apparent greater freedom of the hematite and flag ores from phosphorus is nearly balanced by their comparative poverty in iron.

The distribution of phosphorus among the Lake Superior ores, so far as my facts go, follows no obvious law; it seems to have little, if any, relation to the kind of ore. Some of the hematite ores are among the lowest and others among the richest in this element, and so of the specular and magnetic ores.

A rule, to which there are, however, several exceptions, seems to be that the ores poor in iron and rich in silica, contain least phosphorus; but the analyses of the Republic mountain ore show more iron and less silica than in any other, and that it is also very low in phosphorus. The table of analyses, in Plate No. XIII. of Atlas, presents most of the facts in a compact form; but as this subject is of peculiar interest at this time in connection with the Bessemer steel manufacture, I venture to incorporate a second tabular statement here, in which the mines are arranged in order of the quantity of phosphorus, beginning with the lowest. No mine is included from which less than two samples have been analyzed. The deposits and mines marked with a * are new, and not sufficiently developed to enable me to say that an average sample of the ore was obtained.

Mine.	Kind of Ore.	Phosphorus.	Iron.
Lake Angeline	Jaspery Specular	0.031	53.83
Winthrop	Soft Hematite	0.037	54.63
Republic*	Specular and Magnetic	0.040	66.51
Michigamme*	Magnetic	0.041	64.388
Silas C. Smith	Hematite	0.047	49.70
Cascade	Flag	0.053	49.332
Menominee Iron reg'n*	Specular & Hematite	0.054	48.209
Edwards	2d Class Magnetic	0.055	49.190
Macomber	Hematite	0.058	54.92
Cascade	Flag and Specular	0.061	51.253

Mine.	Kind of Ore.	Phosphorus.	Iron.
Jackson	Specular	0.066	63.715
Magnetic*	Magnetic	0.067	54.72
Edwards	Do.	0.067	61.60
Shenango	Hematite	0.070	56.315
Champion	Magnetic and Slate	0.072	63.55
Negaunee *	Manganifs. Soft Hem'e	0.074	44.29
Lake Angeline	Hematite	0.079	50.70
New England	Soft Hematite	0.080	48.24
Kloman*	Specular	0.089	63.55
Foster	Hematite	0.094	52.27
Spurr Mountain*	Magnetic	0.104	63.81
Lake Superior	Specular	0.104	62.11
Taylor (L'Anse)*	Hematite	0.107	52.88
Jackson	Hematite and Jaspery.	0.124	57.155
Cleveland	Specular	0.126	61.092
Lake Superior	Hematite	0.130	54.19
Saginaw*	Specular and Hematite	0.132	52.40
Barnum	Specular	0.134	61.69
Washington	Magnetic	0.141	61.305
New York	Specular	0.224	61.74

It has been stated that an inspection of the first table did not warrant us in asserting that either of the four classes of ore represented could be easily recognized as being comparatively free from phosphorus; so an examination of the above presentation of the facts forces us to the conclusion that the distribution is not geographical; for we here see widely-separated mines containing the same amount of phosphorus, whilst contiguous mines vary widely. In fact, in different parts of the same mine there is found a wide difference in the quantity of this noxious element; *e. g.:* The New York mine results show more than twice as much phosphorus in the ore from pit No. 1 as from pit No. 2; and the Lake Superior ore appears to contain less phosphorus than the Barnum, although they belong to one deposit. A part of this difference is undoubtedly due to errors in sampling and errors in the analysis; but the number of samples analyzed, the care taken in collecting them, and the reputation of the chemists, leave but little doubt that the relative and absolute average amounts of phosphorus in the ores from the developed mines are nearly expressed in the foregoing table.

At the suggestion of Mr. A. L. Holley, I selected, with much care, an average sample of the rock which occurs in the hard ores, more or less of which goes into the furnace, and had it analyzed; the result was less than the average amount of phosphorus. This fact, in connection with the low amount found in the second class and flag ores, leads me to believe that no care in selecting and sorting ore will diminish the quantity of phosphorus.

By way of verifying the amount of phosphorus in Lake Superior ores, here given, there are presented in the following table five analyses of pig-iron made from them with charcoal, and a flux containing no appreciable amount of phosphorus. They may, therefore, be said to indicate very accurately the amount of phosphorus in the ores, which, as will be seen, averages about the maximum amount given above as admissible in steel.

	1	2	3	4	5	Average.
Magnesia			0.47			
Silicic Acid, or Silica		1.16	1.83	3.21	2.91	2.28
Silicon	2.245					
Graphitic Carbon	2.88	3.72	3.35		3.61	3.39
Combined "	.80	0.30	0.00		.05	.38
Metallic Iron	93.201		93.49			93.34
Phosphorus	.138	0.104	0.082	0.126	.092	0.108
Sulphur	.011	0.045	trace.		.04	0.032
Metallic Manganese	.174					.174

No. 1 was chipped from many pigs of No. 1 gray foundry iron made at the Pioneer furnace Negaunee, of Jackson ore. Analysis by Dr. C. F. Chandler. No. 2 is a pig-iron made from assorted Lake Superior ores at the Appleton Furnace, Wisconsin. Analysis by Mr. Morrell. No. 3 is also a specimen of Appleton iron. Analysis by Dr. Wuth. No. 4 is No. 1 gray foundry iron made by the Jackson Iron Co. at Fayette, Michigan, of Jackson ore with charcoal, and is extensively used in the manufacture of Bessemer steel. Analysis by Mr. Morrell. No. 5 is a specimen of pig made by the Michigan Iron Co. in Marquette County, of a mixture of specular, magnetic, and hematite ores. Analysis by Mr. Morrell. The analysis of Pioneer pig was at the expense of the Survey; the others were furnished by Mr. Holley. It was proposed to carry this work much further, but the limited means would not permit.

For contributions in money, and valuable suggestions and encouragement in obtaining the results set forth in this chapter, I am under especial obligation to John Fritz, of Bethlehem, Pa., and S. P. Ely, of Marquette; A. Pardee, Daniel J. Morrell, A. B. Meeker, and W. H. Barnum also contributed liberally towards paying for the chemical work, which cost nearly $2,000.

The physical and mineralogical character of the following ores is given under Lithology, in Chapter III. For commercial statistics, and, incompletely, the metallurgical qualities, see Plates XII. and XIII. of Atlas.

(*The mines are arranged alphabetically. The upper line gives the number of the sample.*)

BARNUM MINE—*Specular Ore.*

	58.	14.*	14.*	262.*	262.*	277.*	277.*	*Averages.*
Sesqui- or Peroxide of Iron	93.40	86.71						
Oxide of Manganese	......	trace						
Alumina	0.33	1.92						
Lime	0.30	0.64						
Magnesia	0.15	0.53						
Sulphur	min'te trace.	0.04						
Phosphoric Acid	0.23	0.25	0.189	0.31	0.288	......	0.649	
Silicic Acid, or Silica	4.80	9.43						
Water, Total	0.29	0.46						
	99.50	99.98						
Metallic Iron	65.38	60.79	......	64.30	......	56.31	......	61.69
Phosphorus	0.10	0.11	0.083	.133	0.123	0.149	0.278	.134
Sulphur	......	0.04						
Specific Gravity	......	4.58						
	Chemist, Allen. Sept. 2, 1871. *Sampler*, Brooks.	*Chemists*, Chandler & Cairns. Mar. 4, 1872. *Sampler*, Brooks.	*Chemist*, Wuth. *Sampler*,	*Chemist*, Taylor. *Sampler*, Taylor.	*Chemist*, Wendel. *Sampler*,	*Chemist*, Britton. Dec. 31, 1872. *Sampler*, Brooks.	*Chemist*, Wendel. Feb. 6, 1873. *Sampler*,	

NOTES.—58. From three stock piles at mine. 14. Large stock pile at Cleveland. 262. Stock pile at Cleveland. 277. All parts of mine.

CLEVELAND MINE—*Specular Ore.*

	36.	36.	36.	260.	260.	271.	271.	272.	272.	273.	*Averages.*
Sesqui- or Peroxide of Iron	88.50										
Oxide of Manganese	trace.										
Alumina	1.84										
Lime	0.89										
Magnesia	0.75										
Sulphur	0.01										
Phosphoric Acid	0.46	0.229	......	0.178	0.14	0.343	......	0.218			
Silicic Acid, or Silica	6.40										
Water, Total	1.23										
	100.08										
Metallic Iron	61.95	......	......	......	62.10	......	56.590	......	......	63.730	61.092
Phosphorus	0.20	0.100	0.187	0.076	.061	0.147	0.168	0.093	0.154	0.111	0.119
Sulphur	0.01										
Metallic Manganese	trace.										
Specific Gravity	4.64	......	......	......	......	4.42	......	4.37	......	4.93	
	Chemists, Chandler & Cairns. Mar. 9, 1872. *Sampler*, Brooks.	*Chemist*, Wuth. *Sampler*,	*Chemist*, Britton. *Sampler*,	*Chemist*, Wendel. *Sampler*, Taylor.	*Chemist*, Taylor. *Sampler*,	*Chemist*, Wendel. Feb. 6, 1873. *Sampler*, Brooks.	*Chemist*, Britton. Dec. 31, 1872. *Sampler*,	*Chemist*, Wendel. Feb. 6, 1873. *Sampler*, Brooks.	*Chemist*, Britton. Dec. 31, 1872. *Sampler*,	*Chemist*, Britton. Dec. 31, 1872. *Sampler*,	

NOTES.—36. Large stock pile in Cleveland. 260. Stock pile in Cleveland. 271. Laurie Genth's Pit, No. 3. 272. Swede's pit. 273. School House opening. The last three were from mine.

* The occurrence of the same number more than once in this line, signifies that duplicates of the same sample were sent to different chemists.

CHAMPION MINE—*Magnetic and Slate Ore.*

	38.	38.	38.	227.	227.	228.	228.	*Averages.*
Protoxide of Iron	17.87							
Sesqui- or Peroxide of Iron	74.93							
Oxide of Manganese	0.05							
Alumina	1.15							
Lime	0.52							
Magnesia	0.92							
Sulphur	0.12							
Phosphoric Acid	0.28	0.116	......	0.021	0.337	0.161	0.316	
Silicic Acid, or Silica	3.70							
Water, Total	0.52							
	100.06							
Metallic Iron	66.04	......	......	......	57.97	......	66.65	63.55
Phosphorus	0.12	0.051	0.048	0.009	0.143	0.070	0.136	.084
Sulphur	0.12							
Metallic Manganese	0.03							
Specific Gravity	4.75	......	4.43	......	......	4.87		
	Chemists, Chandler & Cairns. Mar. 9, 1872. *Sampler,* Brooks.	*Chemist,* Wuth. *Sampler,*	*Chemist,* Britton. *Sampler,*	*Chemist,* Wuth. *Sampler,* Brooks.	*Chemist,* Wendel, Feb. 6, 1873. *Sampler,*	*Chemist,* Wuth. *Sampler,* Brooks.	*Chemist,* Wendel, Feb. 6, 1873. *Sampler,*	

NOTES.—38. Large stock pile in Cleveland, all varieties. 227. "Slate ore," Shaft No. 4. 228. "Black ore," Shafts Nos. 1, 2, and 3. The two last from mine.

CASCADE MINES—*Flag Ore.*

	17.	22.	22.	257.	257.	258.	258.	15.	*Averages.*
Sesqui- or Peroxide of Iron	71.98	83.70	......	......	......	......	......	66.20	
Protoxide of Manganese	0.01	trace.							
Alumina	0.68	3.34							
Lime	0.16	0.75							
Magnesia	0.06	0.34							
Sulphur	0.04	0.03							
Phosphoric Acid	0.07	0.24	0.248	......	......	......	......	.14	
Silicic Acid, or Silica	......	10.67							
Insoluble Silicious Matter	25.26	......	......	.....	......	......	......	31.02	
Water, Total	1.03	0.87	......	......	......	......	......	1.29	
Alkalies, undetermined and lost	0.71								
	100.00	99.94							
Metallic Iron	50.49	58.59	......	46.120	......	45.010	......	46.450	49.332
Phosphorus	0.03	0.10	0.108	.042	0.043	0.027	0.036	0.060	.053
Sulphur	0.04	0.03							
Specific Gravity	......	4.43	......	3.95	......	4.01			
	Chemist, Britton, Aug. 18, 1870. *Sampler,* Brooks.	*Chemists,* Chandler & Cairns, Mar. 4, 1872. *Sampler,* Brooks, J'y, '72	*Chemist,* Wuth, 1872. *Sampler,*	*Chemist,* Britton, 1872. *Sampler,* Brooks.	*Chemist,* Allen, 1872. *Sampler,*	*Chemist,* Britton. *Sampler,* Brooks.	*Chemist,* Allen. *Sampler,*	*Chemist,* Britton, Aug., 1870. *Sampler,* Brooks.	

NOTES.—17. Selected bird's-eye slate ore. Exploration pit. 22. The richest pieces from a small stock pile in Cleveland. 257. Emma mine. 258. Bagley mine; bird's-eye slate ore. The two last were obtained from the mine workings. 15. Old opening, north face ridge, S.W. corner. Sect. 29.

CASCADE MINES—*Flag and Specular Ore.*

	259.	259.	266.	266.	256.	256.	*Averages.*
Phosphoric Acid	....	....	0.16	0.096			
Metallic Iron	50.820	....	44.00	....	58.940	....	51.253
Phosphorus	0.078	0.073	0.069	0.041	0.055	0.055	0.061
Specific Gravity	4.13	....	....	....	4.44		
	Chemist, Britton. 1872. *Sampler,* Brooks.	*Chemist,* Allen. 1872. *Sampler,*	*Chemist,* Taylor. *Sampler,* Taylor.	*Chemist,* Wendel. *Sampler,*	*Chemist,* Britton. 1872. *Samplers,* J. Fritz & A. Pardee.	*Chemist,* Allen. 1872. *Sampler,*	

NOTES.—259. Saw-Mill opening, west of stream. 256. West End Mine (specular ore). Stock pile at Mine. 266. Stock pile at Cleveland.

CANADIAN ORES—*Magnetic.*

	222.	217.	216.	220, *b.*	220, *a.*	*Averages.*
Bisulphide of Iron	....	....	....	....	2.19	
Sesqui- or Peroxide of Iron	....	....	....	78.03		
Proto-sesquioxide of Iron	92.19	....	....	....	84.38	
Alumina	.68	....	....	1.17	2.86	
Lime	.28	....	....	....	0.74	
Magnesia	.83	....	....	....	5.61	
Sulphur	.78					
Phosphoric Acid	.14	0.21	....	0.077	0.087	
Silicic Acid, or Silica	3.55	....	....	6.10	4.13	
Water, Total (moisture)	.48					
Carbonate of Lime	....	....	....	13.71	....	
Carbonate of Magnesia	....	....	....	0.91	....	
Oxygen with the Sulphur and loss	1.07					
	100.00			99.997	99.997	
Metallic Iron	66.86	51.40	45.20	54.00	60.00	55.49
Phosphorus	.06	0.092	.037	.033	0.037	0.052
	Chemist, Britton. Nov. 17, 1870. *Sampler,* Brooks.	*Chemist,* E. R. Taylor. Jan. 2, 1873. *Sampler,* Taylor.	*Chemist,* Taylor. Jan. 2, 1873. *Sampler,* Taylor.	*Chemist,* Wuth. *Sampler,*	*Chemist,* Wuth. *Sampler,*	

NOTES.—222. Analysis furnished by Redington and Adams, Cleveland. 217. Stock pile at Cleveland. 216. Stock pile at Cleveland. 220. Analyses furnished by Dr. Wuth. *a.* Magnetic ore after roasting: *b.* Red hematite. 222 and 217 are Forsyth ore. 216 and 220 are Marmora ore.

EDWARDS MINE—*Magnetic Ore.*

	41.	41.	41.	199.	*Averages.*
Protoxide of Iron	21.60	....	....	9.98	
Sesqui- or Peroxide of Iron	55.80	....	....	85.41	
Oxide of Manganese	0.10				
Alumina	4.34				
Lime	0.77				
Magnesia	0.84				
Sulphur	0.16				
Sulphuric Acid	....	....	....	.03	
Phosphoric Acid	0.12	0.288	....	.07	
Silicic Acid, or Silica	15.41				
Insoluble Silicious Matter	....	....	....	2.43	
Water, Total	0.81				
	99.95				
Metallic Iron	55.75	....	....	67.45	61.60
Phosphorus	0.05	0.125	0.137	.030	.067
Sulphur	0.16				
Metallic Manganese	0.06				
Specific Gravity	4.24				
	Chemists, Chandler & Cairns, March 9, 1872. *Sampler,* Brooks.	*Chemist,* Wuth. *Sampler,*	*Chemist,* Britton. *Sampler,*	*Chemist,* Taylor. Jan., 1873. *Sampler,* Unknown.	

NOTE.—41. Large stock pile in Cleveland.

EDWARDS MINE—*Second-class Magnetic Ore.*

	265.	265.	286.	*Averages.*
Phosphoric Acid	0.10	0.136		
Metallic Iron	48.80	....	49.580	49.190
Phosphorus	0.043	0.058	0.061	.055
	Chemist, Taylor. *Sampler,* Taylor.	*Chemist,* Wendel. *Sampler,*	*Chemist,* Britton. Jan. 9, 1873. *Sampler,* Brooks.	

NOTES.—265. Stock pile at Cleveland. 286. From mine.

FOSTER MINE—*Hematite Ore.*

	49.	87.	270.	270.	26.	*Averages.*
Sesqui- or Peroxide of Iron	74.69	....	....	....	79.49	
Oxide of Manganese	.42	....	....	....	0.25	
Alumina	.50	....	....	....	1.19	
Lime	.37	....	....	....	0.27	
Magnesia	.63	....	....	....	0.33	
Sulphuric Acid	....	....	....	....	0.17	
Phosphoric Acid	.18	....	0.33	0.226	0.19	
Silicic Acid, or Silica	16.44	....	....	....	9.28	
Insoluble Silicious Matter	....	20.68				
Water, Combined	....	6.12				
Water, Total	7.16	....	....	....	8.74	
	100.39	....	....	....	99.91	
Metallic Iron	52.28	49.78	51.40	....	55.64	52.27
Phosphorus	.080	....	0.144	0.097	0.083	.094
Sulphur	....	....	....	....	0.068	
	Chemist, Brush. July 5, 1871. *Sampler*, Brooks.	*Chemist*, Britton. Nov. 4, 1871. *Sampler*, Brooks.	*Chemist*, Taylor. *Sampler*, Taylor.	*Chemist*, Wendel. *Sampler*,	*Chemist*, Chandler. May 14, 1866. *Sampler*, Brooks.	

NOTES.—49. Stock pile at Pioneer Furnace, Negaunee, Mich. 87. From mine, numerous fragments. 270. Stock pile at Cleveland. 26. From mine when first opened.

JACKSON MINE -*Specular Ore.*

	24.	24.	24.	51.	230.	230.	230.	*Averages.*
Sesqui- or Peroxide of Iron	93.75							
Oxide of Manganese	trace.	......	......	0.60				
Alumina	0.73							
Lime	0.61							
Magnesia	0.23							
Sulphur	0.03	......	......	0.18				
Phosphoric Acid	0.32	0.127	......	0.10	0.144			
Silicic Acid, or Silica	3.27	......	......	1.45				
Water, Total	1.09							
Alumina, Lime, Magnesia, Water, etc	......	......	......	1.67				
	100.03							
Metallic Iron	65.62	......	......	......	......	61.810	......	63.715
Phosphorus	0.14	0.055	0.069	0.04	0.063	0.078	0.073	.066
Sulphur	0.03	......	......	0.18				
Specific Gravity	......	......	......	......	4.95			
	Chemists, Chandler & Cairns. Mar. 9, 1872. *Sampler*, Brooks.	*Chemist*, Wuth. *Sampler*. Brooks.	*Chemist*, Britton. Dec. 20, 1872. *Sampler*, Brooks.	*Chemist*, Chandler. July 13, 1871. *Sampler*, Brooks.	*Chemist*, Wuth. *Sampler*, Brooks.	*Chemist*, Britton. Feb. 18, 1873. *Sampler*,	*Chemist*, Allen. *Sampler*,	

NOTES.—24. Large stock pile in Cleveland. 51. Stock pile at Pioneer Furnace, Negaunee, Mich. 230. Slate ore. West end of mine.

JACKSON MINE—*Hematite and Jaspery Ores.*

	231.	231.	231.	229.	229.	229.	*Averages.*
Phosphoric Acid	0.316	0.523	....	....	0.338	0.054	
Metallic Iron	....	59.30	54.530	56.590	58.20	....	57.155
Phosphorus	0.138	0.224	0.154	0.061	0.144	0.023	.124
Specific Gravity	4.20	....	....	4.59			
	Chemist, Wuth. 1872. *Sampler*, Brooks.	*Chemist*, Wendel. Feb. 6, 1873. *Sampler*,	*Chemist*, Britton. Feb. 18, 1873. *Sampler*,	*Chemist*, Britton. Feb. 18, 1873. *Sampler*, Brooks.	*Chemist*, Wendel. Feb. 6, 1873. *Sampler*,	*Chemist*, Wuth. *Sampler*,	

NOTES.—231. Hematite ore—west part of mine. 229. Old Pioneer opening—Jaspery ore. The Hematite and Specular ores occur together in this mine.

KLOMAN MINE—*Specular Ore.*

	235.	225.	*Averages.*
Metallic Iron	63.55	....	63.55
Phosphorus	0.097	0.081	.089
Specific Gravity	4 90		
	Chemist, Britton. *Sampler*, Brooks.	*Chemist*, Allen. *Sampler*,	

NOTE.—235. Fragments broken from outcrop, before work began.

LAKE SUPERIOR MINE—*Specular Ore.*

	37.	37.	37.	261.	261.	44.	274.	*Averages.*
Sesqui- or Peroxide of Iron	86.70							
Oxide of Manganese	trace.							
Alumina	1.64							
Lime	0.57							
Magnesia	0.24							
Sulphur	0.02							
Phosphoric Acid	0.14	0.075	......	0.24	0.239			
Silicic Acid, or Silica	9.82							
Water Total	0.61							
	99.74							
Metallic Iron	60.69	......	......	63.50	......	64.37	59.89	62.11
Phosphorus	0.06	0.033	0.046	0.103	0.102	0.10	.065	.078
Sulphur	0.02							
Specific Gravity	4.55						4.69	
	Chemists, Chandler & Cairns, Mar. 9, 1872. *Sampler*, Brooks.	*Chemist*, Wuth. *Sampler*,	*Chemist*, Britton. *Sampler*,	*Chemist*, Taylor. *Sampler*, Taylor.	*Chemist*, Wendel. *Sampler*,	*Chemist*, Britton. *Sampler*, John Fritz.	*Chemist*, Britton, Dec., 1872. *Sampler*, Brooks.	

NOTES.—37. Large Stock pile in Cleveland. 261. Stock pile at Cleveland. 44. Stock pile at Bethlehem Furnace. 274. Lower bed. Pit No. 1. Pennsylvania mine.

LAKE SUPERIOR MINE—*Hematite.*

	10.	10.	10.	269.	269.	276.	276.	87.	*Averages.*
Sesqui- or Peroxide of Iron	79.80								
Oxide of Manganese	0.10								
Alumina	2.05								
Lime	0.45								
Magnesia	0.53								
Sulphur	0.03								
Phosphoric Acid	0.30	0.104	.....	0.24	0.237	......	0.668		
Insoluble Silicious Matter	.....	.....	.....	.....	.....	.....	.....	15.42	
Silicic Acid, or Silica	12.52	.....	.....	.....	.....	.....	.....	.....	
Water, Combined	4.11	.....	.....	.....	.....	.....	.....	4.66	
" Uncombined	0.14								
	100.03								
Metallic Iron	55.86	.....	.....	52.00	.....	.....	.....	55.00	54.28
Phosphorus	0.13	0.045	0.066	0.103	0.101	0.131	0.286	.....	.130
Sulphur	0.03								
Metallic Manganese	0.07								
Specific Gravity	4.12								
	Chemists, Chandler & Cairns. March 4, 1872. *Sampler,* Brooks.	*Chemist,* Wuth. *Sampler,*	*Chemist,* Britton. *Sampler,*	*Chemist,* Taylor. *Sampler,* Taylor.	*Chemist,* Wendel. *Sampler,*	*Chemist,* Britton. Dec. 31, 1872. *Sampler,* Brooks.	*Chemist,* Wendel. Feb. 6, 1873. *Sampler,*	*Chemist,* Britton. Nov. 4. 1871. *Sampler,* Brooks.	

NOTES.—10. Large Stock pile at Cleveland. 269. Stock pile at Cleveland. 276. Hematite workings of mine.

LAKE ANGELINE—*Specular Ore (Jaspery).*

	21.	21.	267.	267.	34.	*Averages.*
Sesqui- or Peroxide of Iron	72.00	.....	.....	.....	85.43	
Oxide of Manganese	trace.					
Alumina	0.92	.....	.....	.....	1.89	
Lime	0.33	.....	.....	.....	0.24	
Magnesia	0.34	.....	.....	.....	0.13	
Sulphur	0.02	.....	.....	.....	none.	
Phosphoric Acid	0.08	0.101	0.04	0.083	none.	
Silicic Acid, or Silica	25.09	.....	.....	.....	12.31	
Water, Combined	1.09					
" Uncombined	0.12					
	99.99	.....	.....	.....	100.00	
Metallic Iron	50.40	.....	52.00	.....	59.08	53.83
Phosphorus	0.03	0.044	0.017	0.036	none.	.031
Sulphur	0.02					
Specific Gravity	3.97					
	Chemists, Chandler & Cairns. March 4, 1872. *Sampler,* Brooks.	*Chemist,* Wuth. 1872. *Sampler,*	*Chemist,* Taylor. 1872. *Sampler,* Taylor.	*Chemist,* Wendel. 1872. *Sampler,*	*Chemist,* Wuth. Dec. 29, 1865. *Sampler,* Unknown.	

NOTES.—21. Stock pile in Cleveland. 267. Stock pile in Cleveland.

LAKE ANGELINE MINE—*Hematite.*

	268.	268.	280.	*Averages.*
Phosphoric Acid	0.09	0.160		
Metallic Iron	51.40	....	50.000	50.70
Phosphorus	.038	0.070	0.104	.079
	Chemist, Taylor. 1872. *Sampler*, Taylor.	*Chemist*, Wendel. *Sampler*,	*Chemist*, Britton. Dec. 31, 1872. *Sampler*, Brooks.	

NOTES.—268. Stock pile at Cleveland. 280. Stock pile at mine.

MICHIGAMME MINE—*Magnetic Ore.*

	1.	197.	225.	225.	225.	*Averages.*
Protoxide of Iron	....	29.109				
Sesqui- or Peroxide of Iron	....	61.631				
Protoxide of Manganese	1.01	traces.				
Alumina	2.12	2.120				
Lime	.12	1.070				
Sulphur	....	0.002				
Sulphuric Acid	....	0.008				
Phosphoric Acid	.05	0.057	0.067	....	0.392	
Silicic Acid, or Silica	3.06	3.280				
Water, Total	.57	1.497				
Organic or Carbonaceous Matter	....	0.340				
Titanic Acid	....	0.032				
Copper and Carbonic Acid	....	none.				
		99.146				
Metallic Iron	....	65.767	....	....	63.01	64.388
Phosphorus	0.027	0.024	0.029	0.019	0.168	.041
Sulphur	....	0.005				
Specific Gravity	....	....	4.61			
	Chemist, Britton. Sept. 21, 1870. *Sampler*, Brooks.	*Chemist*, Ralph Crooker, Boston. *Sampler*, Ralph Crooker.	*Chemist*, Wuth. 1872. *Sampler*, Brooks.	*Chemist*, Britton. 1872. *Sampler*, Brooks.	*Chemist*, Wendel. Feb. 6, 1873. *Sampler*, Brooks.	

NOTES.—1. Drill mud from 3 holes. 197. Numerous fragments from Exploration pits. 225. Taken at mine, fragments after blasting. All were taken before mine was opened.

MACOMBER MINE—*Hematite.*

	35.	35.	87.	*Averages.*
Sesqui- or Peroxide of Iron	76.80			
Oxide of Manganese	2.06			
Alkalies (by difference)	3.47			
Sulphur	0.14			
Phosphoric Acid	0.15	0.130		
Silicic Acid, or Silica	14.64			
Insoluble Silicious Matter	....	....	14.51	
Water, Combined	....	....	2.23	
Water, Total	2.74			
	100.00			
Metallic Iron	53.76	....	56.08	54.92
Phosphorus	0.06	0.057	....	0.058
Sulphur	0.14			
Metallic Manganese	1.51			
	Chemist, Chandler. Oct. 6, 1871. *Sampler*, Brooks.	*Chemist*, Wuth. *Sampler*,	*Chemist*, Britton. Nov. 4, 1871. *Sampler*, Brooks.	

NOTES.—35. From two trains of 16 cars each, one month apart. 87. From Mine. Numerous fragments. This mine belongs to the Negaunee hematite group, and contains considerable manganese.

MAGNETIC MINE—*Magnetic Flag Ore.*

	69.	54.	232.	232.	*Averages.*
Proto-sesquioxide of Iron	78.35	78.42			
Oxide of Manganese	0.10	trace.			
Alumina	trace.	.43			
Lime	0.69	.19			
Magnesia	0.21	.17			
Sulphur	0.58	none.			
Phosphoric Acid	0.151	.13			
Insoluble Silicious Matter	19.64	19.44			
Soluble Silica	....	.41			
Water, Total	....	0.42			
Undetermined and Loss	0.279	0.39			
	100.000	100.00			
Metallic Iron	55.16	56.78	52.22	....	54.72
Phosphorus	0.066	0.057	0.087	0.071	.067
Sulphur	....	none.			
Specific Gravity	....	....	4.30		
	Chemist, Jenney. 1872. *Sampler*, Brooks.	*Chemist*, Britton. Nov. 21, 1870. *Sampler*, Brooks.	*Chemist*, Britton. 1872. *Sampler*, Brooks.	*Chemist*, Allen. Jan. 1, 1873. *Sampler*,	

NOTES.—69. From small stock pile at mine. 54. From layers of rich ore banded with rock. From outcrop. 232. Small stock pile at mine.

MENOMINEE IRON REGION—*Specular Ores and Hematites.*

	95.	98.	102.	246.	74.	254.	68.	68.
Sesqui- or Peroxide of Iron	47.27	78.30	......	......	80.63	......	81.35	
Oxide of Manganese	......	......	......	......	3.075	......	1.32	
Alumina	......	......	......	......	......	......	trace.	
Lime	......	0.53	......	......	......	......	0.41	
Magnesia	......	0.17	......	......	......	......	0.237	
Sulphur	......	......	......	......	......	......	0.14	
Phosphoric Acid	......	0.044	......	......	......	......	......	0.260
Silicic Acid, or Silica	......	19.52	......	......	......	......	12.043	
Insoluble Silicious Matter	50.22	......	......	......	15.54			
Water, Total	......	......	......	......	......	......	3.498	
		98.564			99.245			
Metallic Iron	33.09	54.81	53.742	37.720	56.44	44.720	56.944	
Phosphorus	......	0.019	......	0.053	......	0.033	......	0.113
Metallic Manganese	......	......	......	......	0.735	......	0.313	
Specific Gravity	......	......	......	3.45	......	3.83		
	Chemist, Jenney. 1872. *Sampler,* Brooks.	*Chemist,* Wuth. Sept. 19, 1871. *Sampler,* Brooks.	*Chemist,* Chandler. *Sampler,* R. Pumpelly.	*Chemist,* Britton. *Sampler,* Brooks.	*Chemist,* Jenney. 1872. *Sampler,* Brooks.	*Chemist,* Britton. *Sampler,* Brooks.	*Chemist,* Jenney. 1872. *Sampler,* Brooks.	*Chemist,* Wuth. *Sampler,*

NOTES.—95. Average of prevailing variety of lean ore, Sect. 31, T. 42, R. 29. 98. Average of five of the richest pieces found, S. 31, T. 42, R. 29. 102. Average of 10 analyses for P. S. and L. S. Ship Canal Co., Sect. 31, T. 42, R. 29. 246. Same as 95. 74. Boulders at west ¼ post, Sect. 10. T. 39, R. 29. 68. From outcrop in swamp, Sect. 13, T. 42, R. 23. 254. Slate ore south ¼ post, Sect. 30, T. 40, R. 30.

MISSOURI—IRON MOUNTAIN MINE—*Specular Ore.*

	127.	127.	127.	128.	128.	128.	*Averages.*
Sesqui- or Peroxide of Iron	93.57	....	....	95.42			
Proto-sesquioxide of Iron	0.76	....	....	0.86			
Alumina	0.08	....	....	0.06			
Lime	0.46	....	....	0.32			
Magnesia	0.23	....	....	0.21			
Sulphur	....	....	0.008	....	....	.012	
Phosphoric Acid	0.035	....	0.112	0.036	....	0.067	
Silicic Acid, or Silica	4.75	....	....	3.02			
Metallic Manganese	0.12	....	....	0.07			
		....	....				
	100.005	....	....	99.996			
Metallic Iron	66.049	....	....	67.416	....	....	66.732
Phosphorus	0.016	0.043	0.049	0.016	0.025	.029	.029
Sulphur	....	....	0.008	....	....	.012	.010
Metallic Manganese	0.12	....	....	0.07	....	....	.095
Specific Gravity	4.944	....	....	5.002			
	Chemist, Wuth. April, 1872. *Sampler,* Brooks.	*Chemist,* Allen. May, 1872. *Sampler,* Brooks.	*Chemist,* A. A. Blair. 1872. *Sampler,* Brooks.	*Chemist,* Wuth. April, 1872. *Sampler,* Brooks.	*Chemist,* Allen. *Sampler,*	*Chemist,* A. A. Blair. *Sampler,*	

NOTES.—127. "Quarry Ore." Chippings from all parts of the pit and Stock piles. 128. "Surface Ore" (Boulders). Chippings and pebbles from all the diggings and Stock piles.

NEW YORK MINE—*Specular Ore.*

	20.	20.	20.	237.	237.	238.	238.	*Averages.*
Sesqui- or Peroxide of Iron	90.00							
Oxide of Manganese	trace.							
Alumina	1.87							
Lime	1.20							
Magnesia	0.60							
Sulphur	0.03							
Phosphoric Acid	0.57	0.428						
Silicic Acid, or Silica	4.72							
Water, Total	0.98							
	99.97							
Metallic Iron	63.00	......	......	62.13	......	60.10	......	61.74
Phosphorus	0.22	0.187	0.204	.1385	0.151	0.326	0.326	.225
Sulphur	0.03							
Specific Gravity	4.64	......	......	4.88	......	4.63		
	Chemists, Chandler & Cairns. March 4, 1872. *Sampler,* Brooks.	*Chemist,* Wuth. *Sampler,*	*Chemist,* Britton. *Sampler,*	*Chemist,* Britton. September, 1872. *Sampler,* Brooks.	*Chemist,* Allen. *Sampler,*	*Chemist,* Britton. March, 1873. *Sampler,* Brooks.	*Chemist,* Allen. *Sampler,*	

NOTES.—20. Large Stock pile at Cleveland—all varieties. 237. Great South Opening—Pit No. 1. 238. Beardsley's Pit—No. 2. The two last from mine.

NEW ENGLAND MINE—*Soft Hematite.*

	87.	239.	*Averages.*
Sulphur	....	None.	
Insoluble Silicious Matter	25.66	23.30	
Water Combined	1.42		
Volatile Matter (a little organic and water)	....	2.69	
Metallic Iron	49.64	46.84	48.24
Phosphorus	....	0.08	.08
Sulphur	....	none.	
Metallic Manganese	....	0.18	
Specific Gravity	....	3.79	
	Chemist, Britton. Nov. 4, 1871. *Sampler,* Brooks.	*Chemist,* Britton. December 27, 1872. *Sampler,* Brooks.	

NOTES.—87. From mine, numerous fragments. 239. From cars and stock pile at mine. First-class specular ore was formerly mined here, but is not at present.

NEGAUNEE HEMATITES—*Manganiferous Soft Hematite.*

	243.	243.	243.	11.	11.	108.	116.	*Averages.*
Sesqui- or Peroxide of Iron	......	......	......	65.40	......	65.48		
Oxide of Manganese	......	......	......	6.71	......	1.54		
Alumina	......	......	......	1.46				
Lime	......	......	......	0.45				
Magnesia	......	......	......	0.66				
Sulphur	......	......	......	0.04				
Phosphoric Acid	......	......	......	0.16	0.171			
Silicic Acid, or Silica	......	......	......	22.67	......	29.25		
Water Combined	......	......	......	1.88				
" Uncombined	......	......	......	0.58				
				100.01				
Metallic Iron	......	35.00	......	45.78	......	45.83	50.58	44.29
Phosphorus	0.067	0.065	0.099	0.07	0.074	......	......	.074
Sulphur	......	......	......	0.04				
Metallic Manganese	0.42	......	......	4.67	......	1.03	......	2.04
Specific Gravity	3.47	......	......	3.83				
	Chemist, Jenney. 1872. *Sampler*, Brooks.	*Chemist*, Britton. 1872. *Sampler*,	*Chemist*, Allen. 1872. *Sampler*,	*Chemists*, Chandler & Cairns. Mar. 4, 1872. *Sampler*, Brooks.	*Chemist*, Wuth. 1872. *Sampler*,	*Chemist*, Chandler. June 29, 1872. *Sampler*, Brooks.	*Chemist*, Jenney. July 13, 1872. *Sampler*, Brooks.	

NOTES.—243. From exploration pits. 11. Small stock pile at Cleveland. 108. Average of three analyses of ore from exploration pits. 116. Dark brown chalky ore. All from Sects. 6, 7, and 8, T. 47, R. 26.

NEW YORK STATE ORES (ST. LAWRENCE & WAYNE CO.)—*Hematites.*

	203.	206.	205.	204.	215.	209.
Protoxide of Iron	....	....	12.49	12.72		
Sesqui- or Peroxide of Iron	75.30	77.24	56.54	57.93	63.31	
Protoxide of Manganese	0.15	....	trace.	0.07		
Alumina	1.69	0.45	0.69	4.54		
Lime	7.04	1.60	8.23	2.32	6.03	
Magnesia	0.38	0.23	2.13	0.85		
Sulphur	0.03	0.05	none.	0.07		
Phosphoric Acid	trace.	trace.	0.36	0.16	....	1.49
Silicic Acid, or Silica	10.12	....	4.28	10.97		
Insoluble Silicious Matter	....	12.93				
Water, Total	....	2.107	....	0.62		
Carbonic Acid	5.41	....	15.01	9.75		
	100.12	94.607	99.73	100.00		
Metallic Iron	52.71	54.07	49.30	50.23	44.31	41.80
Phosphorus	....	....	0.16	0.07	0.43	0.64
	Chemists, Maynard & Wendel. Mar., 1871. *Sampler*, Geo. W. Maynard.	*Chemist*, Jenney. 1872. *Sampler*, Brooks. Jan. 1871.	*Chemists*, Maynard & Wendel. *Sampler*, Geo. W. Maynard.	*Chemists*, Maynard & Wendel. *Sampler*, Geo. W. Maynard.	*Chemist*, Chandler. *Sampler*, Unknown.	*Chemist*, Taylor. Jan. 2, 1873. *Sampler*, Geo. R. Tuttle.

NOTES.—203. Sampled for John A. Griswold & Co., at mine. 204. Do. do. 205. Do. do. 206. From small stock pile at Cleveland. 215. Analysis furnished by H. B. Tuttle. 203 and 206 are from Keene Mine. 204 and 205 are from the Caledonia Mine, both owned by Rossie Iron Works. 209 and 215 are Wayne Co. ore.

NEW YORK (LAKE CHAMPLAIN REGION)—*Magnetic.*

	288.	289.	290.	291.	292.
Protoxide of Iron	26.69	25.35	23.29	8.87	19.05
Sesqui- or Peroxide of Iron	59.84	56.19	50.13	69.99	42.97
Protoxide of Manganese	.55	0.12	0.38	0.38	
Alumina	1.87	3.56	4.22	3.67	3.47
Lime	....	0.82	1.28	1.90	1.19
Magnesia	....	....	0.85	traces.	0.09
Sulphur	.20	....	....	0.24	
Phosphoric Acid	1.94	trace.	trace.	0.07	trace.
Silicic Acid, or Silica	3.45	12.34	20.02	14.60	32.94
Water, Total	....	0.47			
Carbonate of Lime	6.02				
	100.56	98.85	100.17	99.72	99.71
Metallic Iron	62.61	59.02	53.21	55.91	44.98
	Chemist, Geo. W. Maynard. *Sampler*, Geo. W. Maynard.	*Chemist*, Geo. W. Maynard. *Sampler*, Geo. W. Maynard.	*Chemist*, Geo. W. Maynard. *Sampler*, Geo. W. Maynard.	*Chemist*, Geo. W. Maynard. *Sampler*, Geo. W. Maynard.	*Chemist*, Geo. W. Maynard. *Sampler*, Geo. W. Maynard.

NOTES.—288. Wetherby, Sherman & Co., and Port Huron Iron Ore Co., No. 21. 289. New Bed; Wetherby, Sherman & Co. 290. Hammond, Crown Point. 291. Indian; Ferrona ore; Hassey, Wells & Co. 292. Fisher; Port Henry Iron Ore Co.

OHIO IRON ORES—*Black Band and Kidney.*

	293.	294.	295.	296.	297.	298.	*Averages.*
Protoxide of Iron	26.82	23.02					
Sesqui- or Peroxide of Iron	8.94	8.79	75.00	7.60	75.00	12.34	
Oxide of Manganese	1.00	1.70	1.65	1.35	1.85	1.70	
Alumina	trace.	0.70	0.60	2.60	0.60	0.50	
Lime	1.05	1.70	2.80	....	5.94	....	
Magnesia	0.97	0.88	1.48	{ carbo. 6.50 }	3.64	{ carbo. 5.33 }	
Sulphur	0.18	0.11	trace.	0.18	0.12	trace.	
Phosphoric Acid	trace.	0.492	0.773	0.863	1.26		
Silicic Acid, or Silica	11.84	26.22	17.02	8.96	8.46	11.94	
Water, Combined	....	....	....	....	2.28	.78	
Water, Total	....	....	0.25				
Volatile Matter	30.50	21.10					
Carbonic Acid	18.30	15.00					
Lime Phosphate	....	....	....	....	....	1.74	
Lime Carbonate	....	....	....	7.35	....	8.59	
Iron Carbonate	....	....	....	64.17	....	56.23	
	99.60	99.712	99.573	99.573	99.15	99.15	
Metallic Iron	27.12	24.06	52.50	36.31	52.50	35.88	
Phosphorus	....	0.216	0.34	0.379	0.554	0.797	
Specific Gravity	2.494	2.321	3.411	3.434	4.076	2.539	
	Chemist, T. G. Wormley. *Sampler*.	*Chemist*, T. G. Wormley. *Sampler*,	*Chemist*, T. G. Wormley. *Sampler*,	*Chemist*, T. G. Wormley. *Sampler*,	*Chemist*. *Sampler*.	*Chemist*. *Sampler*.	

NOTES.—293. Black Band, Mineral Ridge, Mahoning Co., O. 294. Black Band, Tuscarawas Coal and Iron Co., Tuscarawas Co., O. Raw. 295. Black Band, Tuscarawas Coal and Iron Co., Tuscarawas Co., O. Calcined. 296. "Shell" or "Kidney Ore," Tuscarawas Coal and Iron Co., Tuscarawas Co., O. Raw. 297. "Shell" or "Kidney Ore," Tuscarawas Coal and Iron Co., Tuscarawas Co., O. Calcined. 298. Nodular Ore, Washingtonville Co., Columbiana Co., O.

For further analyses of Ohio Iron Ores, consult *Geological Survey of Ohio*, 1870, pp. 47, 48, 49, 219, 223.

REPUBLIC MINE—*Specular and Magnetic.*

	233.	233.	234.	234.	Averages.
Metallic Iron	67.21	......	65.81	......	66.51
Phosphorus	0.03	0.025	0.061	0.045	.040
Specific Gravity	5.19	......	5.07	......	......
	Chemist, Britton. 1872. *Sampler,* Brooks.	*Chemist,* Allen. 1872. *Sampler,*	*Chemist,* Britton. 1872. *Sampler,* Brooks.	*Chemist,* Allen. 1872. *Sampler,*	

NOTES.—233. Specular ore. First stock pile at opening of mine. 234. Magnetic ore. First stock pile at opening of mine.

SAGINAW MINE—*Specular and Hematite.*

	281.	282.	Averages.
Metallic Iron	50.820	53.980	52.40
Phosphorus	0.184	0.080	.132
	Chemist, Britton. Jan. 9, 1873. *Sampler,* Brooks.	*Chemist,* Britton. Jan. 9, 1873. *Sampler,* Brooks.	

NOTES.—281. Small stock pile (first mined) at mine. 282. Ditto. Both samples are soft hematite. By oversight no sample of the specular ore, which is first-class, was collected.

SHENANGO MINE—*Hematite.*

	242.	242.	78.	Averages.
Sesqui- or Peroxide of Iron	....	....	82.13	
Oxide of Manganese	....	....	.15	
Alumina	....	....	2.32	
Lime	....	....	.41	
Magnesia	....	....	.08	
Phosphoric Acid	....	....	.186	
Silicic Acid, or Silica	....	....	14.46	
Water, Combined	....	....	.26	
			99.996	
Metallic Iron	55.140	....	57.49	56.315
Phosphorus	.049	0.071	0.081	.070
Specific Gravity	3.60			
	Chemist, Britton. 1872. *Sampler,* Brooks.	*Chemist,* Allen. 1872. *Sampler,*	*Chemist,* Wuth. 1872. *Samplers,* Davock, Glidden & Co.	

NOTES.—242. From small stock pile at mine. 78. "Taken from under snow, with no possible selection."—Letter from Davock, Glidden & Co.

SILAS C. SMITH MINE—*Hematite.*

	70.	70.	87.	*Averages.*
Sesqui- or Peroxide of Iron	71.70			
Oxide of Manganese	0.10			
Alkalies	2.03			
Sulphur	0.27			
Phosphoric Acid	0.09	0.127		
Silicic Acid, or Silica	23.38			
Insoluble Silicious Matter	....	....	23.79	
Water, Total	2.43	....	2.43	
	100.00			
Metallic Iron	50.19	....	49.21	49.70
Phosphorus	0.04	0.055	....	.047
Sulphur	0.27			
	Chemist, Chandler. Sept. 7, 1871. *Sampler,* Brooks.	*Chemist,* Wuth. *Sampler,*	*Chemist,* Britton. Nov. 4, 1871. *Sampler,* Brooks.	

NOTES.—70. From small stock pile at mine when first opened. 87. From mine when first opened, numerous fragments.

SPURR MOUNTAIN MINE—*Magnetic Ore.*

	2.	226.	226.	226.	97.	*Averages.*
Proto-sesquioxide of Iron	89.21	....	....	....	92.36	
Oxide of Manganese	traces.	....	....	....	0.15	
Alumina	2.67	....	....	....	1.66	
Lime	.67	....	....	....	0.73	
Magnesia	0.19	....	....	....	0.75	
Sulphur	0.35					
Phosphoric Acid	trace.	0.259	....	....	0.221	
Silicic Acid, or Silica	6.28	....	....	....	4.31	
	99.37				100.181	
Metallic Iron	64.60	....	....	59.96	66.87	63.81
Phosphorus	....	0.113	0.112	....	0.096	.104
Sulphur	0.35					
Specific Gravity	....	4.62				
	Chemist, Chandler. Nov. 1868. *Sampler,* Brooks.	*Chemist,* Wuth. 1872. *Sampler,* Brooks.	*Chemist,* Britton. 1872. *Sampler,*	*Chemist,* Wendel. Feb. 6, 1873. *Sampler,*	*Chemist,* Wuth. Sept. 14, 1872. *Samplers,* Morgan & Herne.	

NOTES.—2. Numerous fragments broken from outcrops of ore. 226. Fragments broken from outcrop 97. Numerous fragments broken from outcrop. All before mine was opened.

TAYLOR MINE—L'ANSE RANGE—*Hematite.*

	88.	81.	89.	89.	87.	*Averages.*
Sesqui- or Peroxide of Iron	82.664	....	62.25			
Oxide of Manganese	0.894	....	1.87			
Alumina	....	....	3.028			
Lime	0.312	....	0.31			
Magnesia	0.226	....	0.26			
Sulphur	0.090	....	trace.			
Phosphoric Acid	0.236	....	0.31			
Silicic Acid, or Silica	6.180					
Insoluble Silicious Matter	....	10.75	21.30	....	5.29	
Water, Combined	....	....	....	....	8.70	
" Total	9.438	9.41	8.10			
	100.040		97.428			
Metallic Iron	57.86	52.00	43.576	44.78	57.51	52.88
Phosphorus	0.102	....	0.13	0.097	....	.107
Sulphur	0.090					
Metallic Manganese	0.62	....	0.45	....	....	.53
	Chemists, Chandler & Schweitzer. *Sampler*, Brooks.	*Chemist*, Britton. 1871. *Sampler*, Brooks.	*Chemist*, Jenney. 1872. *Sampler*, Brooks.	*Chemist*, Britton. Feb. 18, 1873. *Sampler*,	*Chemist*, Britton. *Sampler*, Brooks.	

NOTES.—88. From shaft 20 feet in ore. 81. From three trenches across ore deposit. 89. From all pits, shafts and trenches showing ore. 87. From mine, numerous fragments. All before mine was opened.

WASHINGTON MINE—*Magnetic Ore.*

	39.	39.	39.	264.	264.	284.	285.	*Averages.*
Proto-sesquioxide of Iron	91.06							
Oxide of Manganese	0.23							
Alumina	0.85							
Lime	0.92							
Magnesia	0.77							
Sulphur	0.03							
Phosphoric Acid	0.25	0.406	......	0.21	0.170			
Silicic Acid, or Silica	5.13							
Water, Total	0.66							
	99.90							
Metallic Iron	65.94	......	......	67.20	......	57.280	54.800	61.305
Phosphorus	0.11	0.177	0.149	0.09	0.073	0.195	0.146	.141
Sulphur	0.03							
Metallic Manganese	0.14							
Specific Gravity	4.66							
	Chemists, Chandler & Cairns. March, 1872. *Sampler*, Brooks.	*Chemist*, Wuth. 1872. *Sampler*,	*Chemist*, Britton. 1872. *Sampler*,	*Chemist*, Taylor. 1872. *Sampler*, Taylor.	*Chemist*, Wendel. 1872. *Sampler*,	*Chemist*, Britton. Jan. 9, 1873. *Sampler*, Brooks.	*Chemist*, Britton. Jan. 9, 1873. *Sampler*, Brooks.	

NOTES.—39. Large stock pile in Cleveland. 264. Stock pile at Cleveland. 284. Shafts Nos. 1 and 4 at mine. 285. Shafts Nos. 2 and 6 at mine.

WINTHROP MINE—*Soft Hematite.*

	240.	240.	287.	*Averages.*
Sesqui- or Peroxide of Iron	....	....	84.66	
Protoxide of Manganese	....	....	1.41	
Alumina	....	....	0.13	
Lime	....	....	0.40	
Magnesia	....	....	0.007	
Sulphur	....	....	0.02	
Phosphoric Acid	....	....	0.084	
Silicic Acid, or Silica	....	....	12.70	
Insoluble Silicious Matter	24.34			
Water, Total	....	....	0.71	
Volatile Matter	0.93			
			100.121	
Metallic Iron	50.00	....	59.26	54.63
Phosphorus	0.03	0.045	0.037	.037
Sulphur	none.			
Metallic Manganese	0.53			
Specific Gravity	4.03			
	Chemist, Britton. Dec. 26, 1872. *Sampler*, Brooks.	*Chemist*, Allen. *Sampler*,	*Chemist*, Fred. H. Emmerton. Feb. 13, 1873. *Sampler*, J. T. Torrence.	

NOTES.—240. From all parts of mine. 287. Stock pile at a Chicago furnace.

WISCONSIN IRON ORES—*Iron Ridge* (*Hematite*).

	298.	*Averages.*
Pure Metallic Iron	56.44	
Oxygen with the Iron	24.91	
Protoxide of Manganese	.47	
Alumina	2.30	
Lime	2.28	
Magnesia	.99	
Sulphuric Acid	.15	
Phosphoric Acid	1.10	
Insoluble Silicious Matter	3.57	
Soluble Silica	.75	
Water and Carb. Acid	6.30	
	99.26	
Metallic Iron	56.44	
Phosphorus	.48	
Sulphur	.06	
	Chemist, J. B. Britton. *Sampler*, J. J. Hagerman.	

NOTE.—298. The ore is a fossil ore, in grains about the size and shape of flax-seed ; Dr. Topham calls it Oolitic ore. There are several old analyses showing no phosphorus, but they are not reliable.

INDEX.